THEOLOGY FOR EARTH COMMUNITY

ECOLOGY AND JUSTICE

An Orbis Series on Global Ecology

The Orbis Series *Ecology and Justice* publishes books that seek to integrate an understanding of the Earth as an interconnected life system with concerns for just and sustainable systems that benefit the entire Earth. Books in the Series concentrate on ways to:

- reexamine the human-Earth relationship in light of contemporary cosmological thought
- develop visions of common life marked by ecological integrity and social justice
- expand on the work of those who are developing such fields as eco-theology, ecojustice, environmental ethics, ecofeminism, deep ecology, social ecology, bioregionalism, and animal rights
- promote inclusive participative strategies that enhance the struggle of the Earth's voiceless poor for justice
- deepen appreciation for and expand dialogue between religious traditions on the issue of ecology
- encourage spiritual discipline, social engagement, and the reform of religion and society toward these ends.

Viewing the present moment as a time for responsible creativity, the Series seeks authors who speak to ecojustice concerns and who bring into dialogue perspectives from the Christian community, from the world's other religions, from secular and scientific circles, and from new paradigms of thought and action.

Books Published in the Series

John B. Cobb, Jr., *Sustainability: Economics, Ecology and Justice*
Charles Pinches and Jay B. McDaniel, editors, *Good News for Animals?*
Frederick Ferré, *Hellfire and Lightning Rods*
Ruben L. F. Habito, *Healing Breath: Zen Spirituality for a Wounded Earth*
Eleanor Rae, *Women, the Earth, the Divine*
Leonardo Boff, *Ecology and Liberation: A New Paradigm*
Denis Edwards, *Jesus the Wisdom of God: An Ecological Theology*
Jay B. McDaniel, *With Roots and Wings*
Sean McDonagh, *Passion for the Earth*

ECOLOGY AND JUSTICE SERIES

THEOLOGY FOR EARTH COMMUNITY

A Field Guide

Edited by
Dieter T. Hessel

ORBIS BOOKS
Maryknoll, New York 10545

The Catholic Foreign Mission Society of America (Maryknoll) recruits and trains people for overseas missionary service. Through Orbis Books, Maryknoll aims to foster the international dialogue that is essential to mission. The books published, however, reflect the opinions of their authors and are not meant to represent the official position of the society.

ORBIS/ISBN 1-57075-052-1

Printed on recycled paper

Contents

Preface   viii

Acknowledgments   ix

Contributors   xi

Introduction: Why This Field Guide?   1
DIETER T. HESSEL
Four Voices for Earth Community Theology and Ethics
    I. The Primordial Imperative   2
      THOMAS BERRY
    II. Learning to Meet the Fourth Revolution   3
      LARRY RASMUSSEN
    III. Ecology in and of Theological Study   5
      ROSEMARY RADFORD RUETHER
    IV. Reconfiguring Theological Study   7
      JAMES A. NASH

PART 1
BIBLICAL ROOTS AND MODERN INTERPRETATION   21

1   **Rethinking Traditional Approaches to Nature in the Bible**   23
    THEODORE HIEBERT

2   **Ecology and Biblical Studies**   31
    GENE MCAFEE

3   **Biblical Bases for Eco-justice Ethics**   45
    DIANE JACOBSON

4   **Jewish Theology and the Environmental Crisis**   53
    EILON SCHWARTZ

PART 2
SYSTEMATIC THEOLOGIES FOR EARTH COMMUNITY   65

5   **Reclaiming, Revisioning, Recreating in**
    Theo-Ecological Discourse   67
    SALLY NOLAND MACNICHOL

6 Ecological-Feminist Theology 77
Contributions and Challenges
HEATHER EATON

7 Postmodern "Nature," Feminism and Community 93
CATHERINE KELLER

8 Cosmology and Justice in Ecumenical Perspective 103
KOSUKE KOYAMA

PART 3
ECO-SOCIAL ETHICS 111

9 Christian Ethics and the Environmental Challenge 113
JANET PARKER AND ROBERTA RICHARDS
Appendix A: Moral Obligations to Animals 125
Appendix B: Unsustainable Population Growth 126
Appendix C: Economics and Ecology 128
Appendix D: Science and Technology 129

10 Population-Consumption Issues 132
The State of the Debate in Christian Ethics
JAMES B. MARTIN-SCHRAMM

11 The Role of Religions in Forming an Environmental Ethics 143
New Challenge for Interreligious Dialogue
MARY EVELYN TUCKER

PART 4
ENVIRONMENTAL JUSTICE 153

12 Environmental Justice 155
The Power of Making Connections
MANNING MARABLE
Afterword: Key Urban Environmental Justice Problems 159
MICHAEL GELOBTER

**13 Environmental Justice and Black Theology of
Liberating Community** 165
THOMAS L. HOYT, JR.

14 EcoJustice and Justice 176
An American Indian Perspective
GEORGE E. TINKER

PART 5
PRACTICAL DISCIPLINES 187

15 Practical Theology Focused on Eco-Justice 189
ROBERT C. N. KISPERT

16 **Where Were/Are the U.S. Churches in the Environmental Movement?**   **199**
DIETER T. HESSEL

17 **Pedagogical Issues and Teaching Models for Eco-Justice**   **208**
DANIEL T. SPENCER

18 **The Praxis of Institutional Greening**   **222**
RICHARD M. CLUGSTON
Some Critical Questions for Evaluating Theological Education in Response to the Environmental Challenge   *232*
JOHN B. COBB, JR.

PART 6
SPIRITUAL FORMATION AND LITURGICAL REFORM   **237**

19 **Christian Spirituality**   **239**
Mending the Web
NANCY G. WRIGHT

20 **Eco-Justice Liturgics**   **250**
BERYL INGRAM

Epilogue   **265**
LARRY RASMUSSEN

Bibliography   **269**

Preface

The purpose of this collaborative volume is to comprehend state-of-the-art scholarship and teaching across the fields of theological education in response to the environmental challenge. Crisp essays by seasoned teachers and emerging scholars help to bring participants in religious and environmental studies up-to-speed with the range and depth of Christian theological writing, plus some aspects of interreligious reflection on this increasingly important subject.

These essays evolved from carefully crafted papers that were prepared for and discussed at an October 1994 conference on "Theology for Earth Community." That gathering at Union and Auburn Theological Seminaries in New York was attended by 125 teachers, students of theology, and church leaders. Its overall objective was to identify leading edges of theological scholarship focused on the environmental challenge and to identify an agenda for the fields of theological education and areas of religious leadership, in order to develop appropriate teaching and effective ministry.

All of the authors of the following chapters were asked to address two questions, suggested as their organizing framework:

1. What writings and themes in this field of theology, or area of religious study and leadership, especially help to foster understanding of and engagement in the environmental challenge?

2. What new theological work and approaches to "eco-justice" teaching / leadership are most needed to engage the deepening crisis of earth community?

While some chapters answer these questions more directly than do others, this guide to theology for earth community does scout out the terrain so that many more can join the journey.

Acknowledgments

Planning for this book, including design of the conference and commissioning of papers, involved me in a close and delightful working partnership with several persons, particularly Larry Rasmussen, Reinhold Niebuhr Professor of Social Ethics, Union Theological Seminary, who chaired the conference, and advised several of the authors in developing their chapters; and with Richard Clugston, Director, Center for Respect of Life and Environment, Washington, D.C., who co-staffs with me an ongoing project called "Theological Education to Meet the Environmental Challenge" (TEMEC*). Both put long hours into conference preparation, and each helped obtain needed funding for this endeavor.

Financial support for the Conference on Theology for Earth Community came from the Trinity Eco-Justice Fund of the Trinity Grants Program, the Humane Society of the United States, the MacArthur Foundation Program on World Environment and Resources, and the Global Stewardship Initiative of The Pew Charitable Trusts. In-kind support was provided by Union and Auburn Theological Seminaries, the Center for Respect of Life and Environment, and the Environmental Justice Office of the Presbyterian Church (U.S.A.).

Laura Wilhelm, Program Administrator, Auburn Theological Seminary, and David Wellman and Janet Parker, graduate students at Union Theological Semi-

*TEMEC (Theological Education to Meet the Environmental Challenge) is an ongoing project initiated in 1992 by the directors of the Program on Ecology, Justice and Faith and the Center for Respect of Life and Environment, in collaboration with a panel of advisors and with funding from the MacArthur Foundation and The Humane Society of the United States. Its major goal is to assist religious studies departments of seminaries, schools of theology, and universities to reform course work, community life, and institutional practice, in order to better prepare religious leaders and other professionals to respond faithfully and effectively to the environmental challenge.

In addition to organizing occasional conferences and developing quality publications focused on renewing creation and seeking eco-justice, co-directors Dieter Hessel and Richard Clugston encourage schools and churches to take the lead in becoming comprehensively and deeply "green." Consultative work with schools that commit to becoming "lead institutions" for eco-justice, as well as special educational resource development on the ethics of population, consumption, and growth are added dimensions of TEMEC's work, thanks to a grant from The Pew Charitable Trusts Global Stewardship Initiative.

We also collect sample syllabi and teaching materials that are being utilized in theological schools. To join the network, or to request specific resources, such as sample syllabi or guidelines for developing sustainable institutional operations, contact: TEMEC - CRLE, 2100 L St., NW, Washington, DC 20037 (202) 778-6133.

nary, were particularly helpful in on-site conference administration. Martha Robbins, Associate Professor of Pastoral Theology at Pittsburgh Seminary, served on the planning committee and advised in preparation of particular papers. Mary Evelyn Tucker, Professor of Religion at Bucknell University and editorial advisor to the Orbis Books Ecology and Justice Series, recommended the manuscript to that publisher.

Many thanks are also due to the contributors for writing at least two drafts of their papers in response to our invitation, conference discussions, and my editorial suggestions. The result reflects a thriving ecology of good work! Most of these papers were discussed in workshops during the Conference on Theology for Earth Community. Chapters 4 and 17, however, resulted from papers delivered at other TEMEC events.

—Dieter T. Hessel

Contributors

Richard Clugston, Ph.D. (University of Minnesota, in Higher Education) is Executive Director of the Center for Respect of Life and Environment, The Humane Society of the U.S., Washington, D.C., and publisher/editor of its quarterly journal, *Earth Ethics*. He co-directs with Dieter Hessel, Theological Education to Meet the Environmental Challenge [TEMEC].

Heather Eaton teaches at University of St. Michael's College, Toronto, affiliated with the Elliot Allen Institute for Theology and Ecology. She is completing doctoral studies.

Michael Gelobter is Assistant Professor/Director, Program on Environmental Policy, School of International and Public Affairs, Columbia University, and former Assistant Commissioner, New York City Department of Environmental Protection.

Dieter T. Hessel is a social ethicist and Presbyterian minister who directs the Program on Ecology, Justice and Faith, and co-directs TEMEC. These environmentally responsive endeavors foster cross-disciplinary theological inquiry and professional development, strategic publication and institutional change. His books include *The Church's Public Role: Retrospect and Prospect*; and *After Nature's Revolt: Eco-Justice and Theology*.

Theodore Hiebert, formerly Associate Professor of Hebrew Bible at Harvard University Divinity School, Cambridge, Massachusetts, is Visiting Professor of Old Testament at McCormick Theological Seminary, Chicago, and author of *The Yahwist's Landscape: Nature and Religion in Early Israel*.

Thomas L. Hoyt, Jr., is Bishop of the Fourth Episcopal District, Christian Methodist Episcopal Church (based in Shreveport, Louisiana), and former Professor of New Testament, Hartford Seminary, Connecticut. In 1993, he keynoted the Black Church Environmental Summit and gave the Lyman Beecher Lectures on *Tradition, Particularity and Universality: Preaching in an Ecumenical Context*.

Beryl Ingram is a United Methodist clergywoman completing doctoral studies in Christian Social Ethics and Worship at Union Theological Seminary.

Diane Jacobson is Associate Professor of Old Testament and Chair of the Biblical Division, Luther [Northwestern] Seminary, St. Paul, Minnesota. She co-authored, with H. Paul Santmire, et. al., "A Theological Basis for Earthcare," *Lutheran Forum* (1993).

Catherine Keller is Associate Professor of Theology, Drew University Theological School, and author of *From a Broken Web: Separation, Sexism and Self*.

Robert C.N. Kispert is a pastoral psychotherapist at the Center for Religion and Psychotherapy of Chicago and a doctoral candidate in practical theology at the University of Chicago Divinity School.

Kosuke Koyama is John D. Rockefeller, Jr., Professor of Ecumenics and World Christianity, Union Theological Seminary, and author of *Mt. Fuji and Mt. Sinai.*

Sally Noland MacNichol is a doctoral candidate in systematic theology at Union Theological Seminary, and an editorial advisor to *Union Seminary Quarterly Review.*

Gene McAfee is a doctoral candidate in Hebrew Bible/Old Testament at Harvard Divinity School. His research interests include the biblical understanding of nature and the environment.

Manning Marable is Professor of History and Political Science and Director of the Institute for Research in African-American Studies at Columbia University.

James Martin-Schramm, Assistant Professor, Department of Religion and Philosophy, Luther College, Decorah, Iowa, is completing a doctoral program at Union Theological Seminary, with a dissertation on the subject of his essay.

Janet Parker is a doctoral candidate in social ethics at Union Theological Seminary, concentrating on feminist and ecological concerns.

Larry Rasmussen is Reinhold Niebuhr Professor of Social Ethics, Union Theological Seminary, and author of *Moral Fragments and Moral Community: A Proposal for Church in Society.*

Roberta Richards received a Ph.D. in social ethics, with a concentration in environmental ethics, from the University of Southern California. She is currently an adjunct instructor in Portland, Oregon.

Eilon Schwartz lectures at the Melton Center for Jewish Education, Hebrew University of Jerusalem, while pursuing doctoral studies, and directs the Abraham Joshua Heschel Center for Nature Studies in Israel.

Dan Spencer, who received a Ph.D. in social ethics from Union Theological Seminary, is Assistant Professor of Religion and Ethics, Drake University, Des Moines, Iowa.

George Tinker is Associate Professor of Cross-Cultural Ministries and Coordinator for Justice and Peace Studies at Iliff School of Theology. His essay was written while he was Henry B. Luce Visiting Professor at Union Theological Seminary.

Mary Evelyn Tucker is Associate Professor of Religion and East Asian Studies, Bucknell University, co-editor of *Worldviews and Ecology*, and author of *Moral and Spiritual Cultivation in Japanese Neo-Confucianism.*

Nancy G. Wright is a clergywoman of the United Church of Christ and former Environment/Communications Director at CODEL, Inc. (Coordination in Development). She is Minister of Spiritual Direction at St. Michael's Episcopal Church in New York City and co-author with Donald Kill of *Ecological Healing: A Christian Vision.*

Introduction

Why This Field Guide?

DIETER T. HESSEL

What should happen in theological education and religious studies to meet the environmental challenge? The world faces unprecedented ecological peril that intersects with many social problems. Environmental degradation on top of social injustice is already causing massive suffering among humans and otherkind. Everyone must now deal with the "wild fact"—cutting across all individual and institutional behavior—that "the scale of human activity relative to the biosphere has grown too large" (Daly and Cobb 1989, 2), while the gap between rich and poor people widens. More is going on than increasing pollution and poverty. We have entered a qualitatively different era in which humanity has greater capability to destroy civil society along with much of the rest of earth community. Now, "human history—the story of our cultural self-construction—and natural history—the story of the eco-evolutionary construction of life in the world—intersect in a manner previously unknown" (Cowdin 1994, 115). Our social institutions, technological innovations, and daily habits affect, long-term, the health of nations and of nature.

What is the significance of this mega-reality for doing theology and practicing religion? How, accordingly, should course work, pedagogy, institutional life, and community engagement be reshaped? A number of prominent theologians have spoken to these questions, delineating the what and how of learning that would be more alert to human-earth relationships. To set the stage for this volume, consider the views of Thomas Berry, Larry Rasmussen, Rosemary Radford Ruether, and James A. Nash, who spoke as a panel to the initial (1993) gathering of North American scholars concerned with "Theological Education to meet the Environmental Challenge." The gist of what they observed and proposed bears repeating, since it inspired collaborative work leading to this book.

These scholar-educators stress the need to restructure religious studies generally, and theological education in particular, to utilize "green" disciplines and a wider range of learning methods in order to renew creation and seek eco-justice—to achieve ecological integrity and social equity together. Beyond redesign of course work, they also advocate reform of theological schools to embody just and sustainable community. They conclude that learning to live justly and sustainably involves making definite shifts in world view, religious affirmation, vocational self-understanding, social ethical focus, and institutional and personal practice.

Four Voices for Earth Community Theology and Ethics

I. The Primordial Imperative
THOMAS BERRY

Thomas Berry, a Passionist Father, is a historian of cultures educated at Catholic University of America, author of The Dream of the Earth, *and co-author with Brian Swimme of* The Universe Story.

We need to focus on the deep nature and great magnitude of the environmental challenge. This is not just a crisis of Western civilization, or even of human society, but of the planet itself, because humans are disturbing Earth's chemistry and violating its biosystems. In the twentieth century, the glory of the human has become the desolation of the earth. This desolation threatens to become destiny in the terminal phase of the Cenozoic era (following the Paleozoic and Mesozoic eras).

Humans now have fantastic power to affect most of the life forms of earth. So, in some ways, this is the most significant moment of the life of the planet, with profound implications for earth's biodiversity. Humans haven't appreciated how important the other life forms are, not only within ecosystems, but for human spirit in poetry, mysticism, the arts.

To move into the Ecozoic era, educators need to:

1. Recognize how the crisis came about through the biblical, classical, and humanist world view, reinforced by intensified technological prowess.

2. Assess the failure of the university and the religious community. Neither has been teaching us what we need to know.

3. Appreciate the rise of ecological vision. It must be the background and setting of everything. Ecology is not a cause or program but the basic frame of reference. The first law of economics has to be to preserve the ecological basis of the planet. And when it comes to legal practice, we cannot settle for inter-human law; we also need inter-species law.

What are the conditions for entering into a viable future? The first and most important condition is to recognize that the universe is a communion of subjects, not a collection of objects. There are not two separate communities—human and natural—but one earth community. The second condition is to appreciate that the earth is primary; humans are derivative. Earth-health comes first. Henceforth, all human activities must be judged primarily by the extent to which they generate and foster a mutually enhancing human/earth relationship. The third condition for a viable future is to recognize that in the future nothing much will happen within and to the natural world that does not involve humans. A healthy human/earth relationship requires human subjectivity in contact with the subjectivity of the world.

Millennial thinking about human destiny has linked psychic energy with wrong views of progress. Now we need to use our wisdom differently—to interact respectfully with the continuing creative process. Living beings are interdependently bonded together. As humans, we have our own distinctive capacity for communion with the other members of the community. They deserve our attention—that we hear their voices, respond to their expressions of beauty, and interact with them creatively within the universal dynamics of existence.

We, who did not choose to live at this time, have been chosen—given a destiny to accept, protect, and foster the earth community. By utilizing us for this purpose, the earth is dealing creatively with the threat of desolation.

II. Learning to Meet the Fourth Revolution
LARRY RASMUSSEN

Larry Rasmussen is Reinhold Niebuhr Professor of Social Ethics, Union Theological Seminary, and author of Moral Fragments and Moral Community: A Proposal for Church in Society.

What is the substance of the eco-crisis that would make a difference for theological education as a whole? Why is this crisis compelling for theological educators? The shortest answer, and the one most deserving of respect, is Dan Maguire's: "If present trends continue, we will not" (Maguire 1993, 13). We face new and complex, interwoven threats from:

• Entrenched and deadly forms of injustice. A few of earth's humans enjoy unprecedented affluence and power, while hundreds of millions languish in crushing poverty, hunger and oppression.

• Violent conflicts and violations of fundamental human rights. Torture, extrajudicial killings and genocide have become features of our time.

• Rapid degradation of the environment. The processes upon which life itself depends for sustenance and health are being systematically undermined. Already many species of animals and plants are lost forever; other species are being drastically altered for human convenience.

The great danger lies in the interaction of these threats. Together they represent a global crisis. It is a crisis in the whole way of life of industrialized society, and now it is globalized in ways that affect all human cultures and nature. The dynamics are those of modernity itself; they deplete or destroy communities of culture and nature simultaneously in the most "ecumenical" ways!

Yet survival threats, especially long-term ones, don't necessarily move religious institutions to reform. Indeed they rarely do. Ringing apocalyptic bells may jangle craniums and muster attention, but fear works poorly as the motivation and energy for long, hard, creative work. So we should begin again and ask what is distinctive about the eco-crisis, and inclusive enough, to command widespread response from theological education and religious studies.

Historian of religion Ernst Troeltsch undertook his massive study, *The Social Teaching of the Christian Churches*, because he doubted that the forms of Christian social presence were viable for adequate response to the problematic presented by modernity. Thus he went in search of past church and world "logics" to see whether a usable past was there as resource for a viable present. Among his conclusions, published in 1911, was a comment that bourgeois modernity "will probably soon be an interlude between an old and a new civilization of constraint" (Troeltsch 2, 992). His good friend, Max Weber, had pondered something akin a few years earlier in *The Protestant Ethic and the Spirit of Capitalism*, when he speculated about "the iron cage" capitalist culture was building. In 1973, E. F. Schumacher, in *Small Is Beautiful*, contended that the world had never seen a quarter century like that following WW II and would likely never again. It was productivity without precedent, but it was utterly unsustainable as the global model. Even more recently, Christopher Lasch, *The True and Only Heaven: Progress and Its Critics*, and Paul Kennedy, *Preparing for the Twenty-First Century*, together with a long list of fellow travelers, have argued that a "new civilization of constraint," demanding new perspectives, institutions, and values, is hard upon us.

Yet even these prescient voices do not picture the reality in its most comprehensive dimensions. Modernity and the last five hundred years are only the latest in a series of revolutions, all of which are qualitatively different from what we now face. Tom Berry describes these epochal waves in the language of geological and cultural evolution. Rosemary Ruether, in *Gaia and God*, takes the path of grand religious narratives and world views that move with power well beyond the civilizations in which they arose, converging and diverging in ways that lead to where we now find ourselves.

I shall use the more limited language of social revolutions. According to *The 1991-92 Annual Review* of the Canadian National Round Table on the Environment and the Economy, we are now entering the human world's fourth great revolution. The first three were the agricultural, the industrial, and the information revolutions—in a story arching from neolithic village life to contemporary megapolis. All these revolutions shared one crucial characteristic, which has determined the basic contours of our present world. They all reorganized society so as to produce more effectively. The fourth great social revolution must now come to pass, for survival's sake. It is the ecological revolution and its social-economic characteristic is qualitatively different—to "reorganize society to produce without destructiveness." I add the important datum, "to produce and reproduce without destructiveness."

We have little idea of the meaning of such mandatory, nonviolent systems for our daily habits, or for our cosmologies, for inter-species ethics, for organizing a world of six, then eight, then ten, then perhaps twelve billion people, for our picture of God, and for any and all religious orientations. We don't really know what theological vision(s) hold together justice, security, and an environment sustainable for most all species. We are stymied before the question of what this social revolution means for current and alternative moral, philosophical, and theological frameworks, for our rereading of history, for virtually every prevalent way of life, for institutions, polities, policies, and laws.

We don't know how to answer well the pastoral questions the fourth human revolution raises about how to learn, decide, and act prudently in the face of uncertainty, risk, and crowded time and space parameters. What kind of life together buoys hope, clears the eyes, and draws us out of our many tribalisms when greater constraint on all sides is the common experience? What structures of daily life and devotion let grace and the mystery of life wash our grimy souls, nudge courage, enable sacrifice, and fire the imagination, just in the moment when millions squeeze diminished dreams and grasp to retain what little (or much) they have?

On a humanly saturated, environmentally fragile planet—swinging a "No Vacancy" sign while having wildly unjust distribution of resources—this coming social revolution of necessarily producing and reproducing without destructiveness is a comprehensive challenge to which theological education must respond. The challenge will move relentlessly from hermeneutics to dogma and doctrine, to worship and spirituality, to cosmology and morality, to rereading Christian history, to pastoral care. It already questions how communities of learning organize their most ordinary, everyday items of existence—like eating, meeting, working, and praying together.

No person or group bears enough gifts for a future together; all stand in need of prayer, conversion, and perseverance. I expect heightened conflict and massive public suffering in the coming decades of cruel transition and of unparalleled opportunities to learn to love our enemies, including ourselves. Hard choices are being forced upon us, and battles must be chosen with care. Yet somehow we must find those connections that lead to producing and reproducing without destructiveness, that foster sustainability as a graceful condition and not simply a more palatable term for gray survival.

The concrete purposes of theological education themselves will come into radical questioning as the overriding "mega-fact" of our time dawns upon those of us who don't already face it daily: the great struggle for humane survival in a sustainable earth community has already begun. So choose a portion to reform, and find a few colleagues. Resist all appeals to select a single vector of analysis and overlook none for the wisdom hidden there. Be humble, ecumenical, and daring. As in other ages of great discontinuity, the images of mustard seeds, of yeast, of salt, are the right ones. To say nothing of dying and rising.

III. Ecology in and of Theological Study
ROSEMARY RADFORD RUETHER

Rosemary Radford Ruether, a pioneer feminist theologian, is Professor of Theology at Garrett-Evangelical Theological Seminary in Evanston, Illinois, and author of Gaia and God: An Ecofeminist Theology of Earth Healing.

Ecology is the science of biotic communities; it identifies the processes or "laws" by which nature, unaided by humans, regenerates and sustains life. My 1992 book, *Gaia and God*, includes a discussion of guidelines, derived from ecology, for how humans must learn to live as sustaining, rather than destructive, members of biotic communities. Some of the most basic lessons of ecology are the interrelation of all things; the coevolution of plants and animals within the biosphere of life-supporting air, water, and soil; the intrinsic value of biotic diversity, which preserves versatility; the cooperative interdependency of food chains and the cycle of production, consumption, and decomposition. The reason we (affluent people) must eat lower on the food chain is to avoid distorting these relationships. Each stage of the food chain should remain roughly one-tenth the size of the one on which it depends, in order to create a sustainable relation. These laws of ecology are basic clues not only to natural resource management, but to authentic spirituality and ethics.

Cosmogenesis and natural history call us to wonder, to reverence for life, and to the vision of humanity living in community with all its sister and brother beings. Human ethics should be a more refined and conscious version of natural interdependency, mandating humans to imagine and feel the suffering of others, and to find ways in which interrelation becomes cooperative and mutually life-enhancing.

Teachers and students of religion need to: a) explore the implications of ecology for theology. Participants also need to: b) study the *ecology of theological education* itself, which has several aspects.

First, it involves *critique*—critical evaluation of the culturally dominant paradigm we have inherited. From bible and tradition, Christian theology has inherited an understanding of natural reality that often views God over creation, more than in and with the natural world, and humans as other than part of the biotic community. Classical Western cultural traditions, codified between 500 B.C.E. and 800 C.E., of which Christianity is a major expression, have sacralized relationships of domination. The bible has more promising leads, but our inherited view of God's relationship to creation, and our relationship to nature, have modeled certain patterns of (white male) domination of women, slaves, Indians, blacks, and so on. Domination of women has provided a key link, both socially and symbolically, to the domination of the earth, hence the tendency in patriarchal cultures to link women with earth, matter, and nature, while identifying males with sky, intellect, and transcendent spirit.

So we need to participate in a critical assessment of that theological heritage, and its modern cultural accompaniments, particularly the mechanistic realism of science that uses nature harshly, and the ideology of economic progress that ignores the devastating effects of growth in Gross Domestic Product (GDP) on earth community. To summarize this point, our study of religion needs to engender critique of theological traditions, scientific paradigms, and economic assumptions.

Second, we need to participate in *reconstruction* of theology, science and economics. This means relearning our history, including an exploration of suppressed elements. It also means recycling positive insights from classical traditions pertaining to the renewal of just and loving, biophilic relations. Reconstructors will also give prominent attention to the "subversive" ecological principles of holism and interdependence, which challenge patriarchal hierarchy, mechanistic science and savage (winner-take-all) capitalism. Thus everyone studying theology should learn about ecological economics—economics as if Earth mattered—that makes it possible to reconcile the struggle for social justice with the imperative of sustainable living.

Third, both the critique and construction need to occur in a *praxis-based* context. Ecologically attuned theology is not just a way of absorbing a series of new and interesting ideas; it has to be embodied in praxis. That approach to learning means paying more attention to the "field" settings of education, and it means examining the institutions of our daily lives as case studies of how to, and how not to, deal with the whole eco-community around us. The goal is to embody new understanding of, and commitment to, eco-justice in personal and institutional life.

Fourth, if we are to have theological education consistent with the ecological paradigm, we must challenge the continued splitting of theology into fields, bifurcation of science and religion, and separation of social from ecological justice. People in different fields must *collaborate*. How much longer will we split bible from theology from ethics from history? I agree with John Cobb that "disciplinolatry" is bad for teacher and student. When I came to Garrett Evangelical Theological Seminary, I was asked to accept a new professorship called the Georgia Harkness Chair in applied theology. But the problem is that often an "applied" theologian is not viewed as a "real" theologian. That kind of splitting ethics from theology, and separating "classical" doctrinal history or systematic theory from practical studies is pervasive in theological education. The new paradigm I'm talking about brings together bible, theology, ethics and history; moreover, it also interfaces with training for liturgical, educational and public leadership, pastoral care and church administration (that humble discipline).

Also to be challenged is the fragmentation of religion and science, as well as the related separation of seminary and university, which have allowed theologians to skip economics and science, while people in those disciplines have skipped religion and ethics. A profound bifurcation between examination of fact and reflection on value allows scientists and economists to go on as if they need not deal with ethics, aesthetics or value questions generally. A wholly different structure for learning is needed to weave together a culture that begins to think in ecological terms.

But meanwhile there is still much impetus to do business as usual, ignoring the deep implications of the ecological imperative. I notice that even people who have made large commitments to social justice seem to be experiencing ecological numbing. Though an environmental crisis of enormous proportions impends, they hope it will go away if they just don't think about it. Besides, they argue, "We can't take on another issue." Let me tell you, this is *not* another issue, but a matter of basic context requiring that we rethink our reality paradigm and patterns of daily praxis. Here we're getting into a question not only of knowledge, but of ways to facilitate individual and communal *conversion*, through the interrelated work of eco-justice and of spirituality, the outer and inner aspects of one process of transformation.

IV. Reconfiguring Theological Study
JAMES A. NASH

James A. Nash is Executive Director, The Churches' Center on Theology and Public Policy, Washington, D.C., editor of its journal, and author of Loving Nature: Ecological Integrity and Christian Responsibility.

The basic question before us is how do we reconfigure, even reconceive, theological education in order to respond faithfully and effectively to the eco-social crisis? Here I am concentrating on the ecological dimensions of that question, rather than on the socio-cultural ones, primarily because ecology still tends to be ignored in most ecclesiastical contexts. In so focusing, however, it is important to keep linkages in view and to avoid unrealistic expectations that the task is going to be easy. (If we have no illusions, we will have fewer disillusions.) There are formidable odds against significant success when it comes to embodying eco-justice in theological education. Yet there is a reasonable chance of success, or we wouldn't be discussing it.

1. The ecological crisis must be thought of *not* as a modest challenge to the structure of theological education, but as a radical challenge to the established order of thinking and acting theologically. It raises basic questions about the whole culture in which seminaries and colleges are embedded and to which they are accommodated. The ecological crisis is a radical challenge in three ways. First, it challenges prevailing development assumptions and particularly the utopian illusion that material economic growth is good and necessary for economic well-being. Seminaries, like the rest of higher education, rely on investments, gifts, and grants. So these institutions tend to accept the ideology of economic growth and to view environmental limits as a threat to their own economic health, in the short run.

Second, the ecological crisis is also a radical challenge to the present habits of theological and ethical thought in seminaries and colleges. It's not that there is an anti-ecological attitude, but a *non*-ecological attitude among theologians. Eco-logically attuned study in response to this crisis is going to require major rethinking and major reformulation of every traditional theological affirmation from sin to incarnation.

When it comes to critical and constructive moral reflection, the ecological crisis confronts us with a new conception of doing ethics. It demands a significant redefinition of that abominable term *moral clients*, that is, those who "count" in ethical thought. Traditionally, only present generations of human beings have counted. But now we can no longer think only in terms of immediate human relationships. We also have to evaluate human relationships with all other beings and elements in the ecosphere, and with future generations of human and otherkind.

What I am suggesting is that ecological theology and ethics is *not* simply an additional subdivision, like teaching a course on the doctrine of creation, or one in business ethics. Instead it entails an expansion of every subdivision in theology and ethics by thinking in broader terms about what God is doing in the world, and therefore, who and what constitute the "moral clients" for decision-making. In this sense, all adequate theology and ethics must henceforth be ecological.

Third, ecological concerns raise a host of new questions about appropriate concepts, discussion of which may divide the house of those who are already aware. For example, how much relevance does the concept of stewardship have for ecological responsibility? What is nature? What is creation? How are they connected, assuming these are neither synonymous nor distinct alternatives? Other questions that arise include: If the planet is God's body, what does that mean, theologically? How do we handle the conflict between ecological holism and biotic individualism (the Aldo Leopold / Albert Schweitzer dichotomy)? Can we talk legitimately about the rights of nature, or, as I prefer to say, biotic rights? At least that question is no longer being dismissed as mere foolishness. But these challenging questions will generate some major resistance, largely because of anthropocentric and dualistic modes of thought, which still dominate theological education. So be prepared for frustrations, conflicts, and failures. Paradigm changes do not come easily or cheaply.

2. Our goal with reference to eco-theological education ought to be *permeation*, not isolation or compartmentalization. In other words, we are not looking for single courses or disciplines like ecological theology or ecological ethics or eco-spirituality, though some of us would be satisfied with these as a start. The main objective is to foster a way of thinking and acting that refocuses and permeates the whole curriculum of theology across the disciplines.

Ecological sensitivity must also permeate the administration and structures of theological education, not simply curricula. Some seminaries provide bad ecological education simply by their physical character. For example, one campus with which I am familiar is a manifestation of Francis Bacon's idea of dominion as domination. Somebody in the seminary administration must live in terror that a dandelion will pop up. Everything is pruned, trimmed, and pesticided. That school, along with many others, buys into the assumption that the only good nature is artificialized. In that context I find myself appreciating every touch of wildness, including pigeon droppings on the concrete.

To take steps toward permeation, at least three questions must be pursued. First, what are the essential understandings and values that students need to confront in a variety of courses to become ecologically responsible? Second, how should theological educators themselves become reeducated to facilitate their response to the first question? Tom Berry is right in saying that seminary hardly prepared any of us for eco-theological thought. The teachers must be retooled if they are to help the students meet this challenge. Toward that end, in part, I wrote *Loving Nature: Ecological Integrity and Christian Responsibility*.

Third, what changes in style, structure, atmosphere, and community relationships are necessary for institutions of theological and religious study to become places of ecological education and participants in the quest for just and sustainable community? Our educational institutions should embody informed concern for the well-being of the diverse community of life.

Answers to these questions will become significant as we increase our understanding of and dialogue with the ecological-biological sciences (without losing interest in social movements and sciences). We cannot do ecological theology or ethics without adequate scientific understanding. Otherwise we produce a lot of romantic fluff, or just continue to reinforce hostility toward nature.

3. Finally, regarding our value framework and ethical focus, I would caution against narrow definitions of some of the terms we are using prominently, such as *eco-justice* and *sustainability*. I applaud linking social justice and ecological justice, the well-being of humans and otherkind, social equity and ecological integrity. Fulsome understandings of eco-justice, as offered by Bill Gibson and Dieter Hessel, are quite helpful. They and I have been working on this concept for more than

two decades. Most of us were influenced initially by Norman Faramelli, then of the Boston Industrial Mission, to think this way. But the problem is that eco-justice can become a slogan that is misinterpreted and subverted. And often that has happened. Functionally, for many, eco-justice has been narrowed to an anthropocentric concept that expresses concern for only the environmental dimensions of intra-human justice. To prevent misinterpretations and subversions, we need to show its deep theological roots and link the term with alternative concepts. Moreover, we should emphasize that eco-justice depends first on developing an adequate ecological ethic to interact with a social ethic—both theologically rooted.

We are running into similar problems with *sustainable development*, which has become the secular, shallow, ethical term of choice. There is an insufficiency in sustainability; that is to say, the concept of "sustainable" is rendered vague in its frequent linkage with "development." Each time it has to be defined. When J. Ronald Engel of Meadville Theological School discusses "sustainable development," I like it, because he redefines the term to mean "the kind of human activity that nourishes and perpetuates the historical fulfillment of the whole community of life on Earth." But his interpretation is rare.

The term *sustainable development* is actually showing signs of negative evolution, becoming little more than a euphemistic synonym for the continuation of economic growth, while providing environmental protection to the extent necessary to perpetuate economic maldevelopment. My preference is to avoid references to sustainable development, and to envision instead an "equitable, sustainable, and frugal" political economy. That phrase illustrates my point that we need to think ethically in terms of a combination of values that enhance basic relationships.

We also must recognize that sustainability is normatively insufficient for religiously grounded environmental ethics. If sustainability is to connote more than efficient utility, it needs to be considered in linkage with other theologically resonant norms, such as frugality (or sufficiency with redistribution) and participatory justice (or inclusive democracy). What we seek, after all, is just and sustainable community. Frugality is pertinent because of its spiritual sense regarding the distinction between necessities *vs.* luxuries in seeking the abundant life. Frugality has monastic and Reformed theological roots. It asks how much is enough and what should *not* be used now for the sake of social and ecological integrity in the future. Frugality is an earth-affirming virtue that delights in the non-consumptive joys of mind and flesh that enhance lives and communities. Frugality arises from love of God and others; it defines in part the conduct of the good neighbor. Frugality is also a precondition of distributive justice under conditions of relative scarcity. Consequently, justice for human and otherkind, present and future, connects with that virtue.

How, in theological education, do we encourage and embody equitable, sustainable, humane, and frugal ways of being? Obviously, the motive to live this way arises from important sacramental experiences with natural beauty and social sharing, experiences that often occur outside the classroom and the educational institution. So, along with better courses and community practices, we need field immersions, spiritual safaris, even forty days in the wilderness with wild beasts—to develop ecological awareness that correlates with our theological studies.

How Will Theological Education and Religious Studies Respond?

The preceding voices speak to a new situation and a very necessary transformation. They call for theological study and religious living that has the spiritual vitality and "green" sensitivity to reorient human creaturehood within the circle of Creation. With the other contributors to this volume, they expect schools of theology and departments of religion—especially those situated within democratic, technocratic, consumerist cultures—to explore comprehensive implications of the environmental challenge for course work, community life, and institutional practice. Happily, they are joined by a growing number of theological educators and religion scholars who are doing significant research and teaching with this focus.

In fact, a surprising number of scholars in several fields of theological study have written articles or books reflecting on the environmental crisis in the context of justice and faith over the last thirty years (see Engel, et al. 1995). Recently, much more quality material has appeared, providing excellent textbooks and shorter readings for courses or study groups. A growing number of theological educators are paying attention to it. Even so, a large majority of scholars, teachers, clergy, and laity are unfamiliar with this body of literature, or do not yet discern its significance.

The Occasion for This "Field Guide"

This "field guide" calls attention to excellent, "stretching" material that focuses on ecology in, and the ecology of, theological study across the fields. It enables readers: a) to discern constructive trajectories and hindering habits in theological reflection, and b) to learn from, as well as to deepen and extend, helpful work already begun. The objective of this collaborative exploration of *Theology for Earth Community* is to draw both experienced and emerging theologians into an already lively, nuanced conversation that is developing in communities of theological study and religious leadership. There is guidance here for persons teaching and studying religion, who are taking part in theological degree programs or continuing education, or leading parish or community groups concerned with maintaining ecological integrity while achieving social justice in a crowded world facing definite limits.

We think it is important to build on the work of forerunners in doing creative work both at the center and at the boundaries of religious studies, instead of inventing another separate "theology of the environment." This field guide to theology for earth community scouts out the terrain, so that many more can join the journey. Each section of the book contains overviews of relevant scholarship, identifies important work or offers fresh theological insights, and suggests how to lead others into quality engagement with this subject matter in the academy, community, or congregation.

Regrettably, most students of religion or theology, though generally more aware of an environmental crisis, are still not very alert to its cultural and religious dynamics. And as yet few are engaged with theologically articulate literature on eco-justice; only here and there do teachers invite students to dig into environmentally aware theological writing as core study material or as a basic ministerial concern.

To heighten awareness of the need being addressed, repeat this simple experiment in your seminary or religion department: Pick up a batch of texts for two or three required core courses and look in the index of each for such key words as ecology, earth, environment, nature, otherkind, animals, plants, land, water, garden, trees, sustainable community, environmental justice, ecological ministry, etc. Though "creation" is a word quite likely to be indexed in a basic theological text book, the other words just listed are still quite infrequent. To be sure, some indexers are more oblivious than authors, who occasionally give such topics honorable mention. But, the problem is pervasive; in classrooms, offices or internships of theological schools, in department of religious studies, and throughout parish education, earth community has yet to become *basic* subject-matter. It's so hard to break the habit of building or accepting outmoded forms of theology—like so much of America's suburban housing that just doesn't belong in a world of resource limits.

A quarter century after the first Earth Day, in a time of political and economic regression that threatens to further "ungreen" society, the shift of focus toward viable earth community is long overdue. Earth community must now become of central scholarly-practical interest. Given the emergence of fresh literature and teaching on this subject, there is no excuse for perpetuating environmental myopia or indifference to eco-justice.

A Focus on Eco-Justice

As already indicated, we confront a dual crisis: degradation of the natural environment and impoverishment of low-power people everywhere. The hyphenated word "eco-justice" refers to constructive human responses that concentrate on the link between ecological health and social justice. It refers to the dynamic intersection of economic and ecological well-being with the struggle for civil rights and social justice. Eco-justice occurs wherever human beings receive enough sustenance and build enough community to live harmoniously with God, to achieve equity among humans, and to appreciate the rest of creation for its own sake and not simply as useful to humanity (Hessel 1992). We should note that some users of the term "ecojustice"—often without the hyphen—have narrowed it to mean justice to nonhuman beings and eco-systems. One contributor to this volume, George Tinker, assumes the limited meaning on the grounds that public secular discourse about environmental concerns has this tendency. The ecumenical movement, however, has moved toward an integrated eco-justice ethic of stewardship and justice for otherkind and humankind together.

The faithful response to eco-*in*justice is to attend to both ecological integrity and social equity together—to seek the well-being of human with otherkind. This is a characteristic theme of the Hebrew Bible, reflected in each of the Abrahamic faiths. Sabbath sensibility and Covenant law foster deep respect for the integrity of creation as well as care for "the widow, the fatherless, the sojourner." Thus, Exodus 23, Leviticus 19 and 25, and Deuteronomy 15 exemplify the covenant obligation to respond to the poor, to give animals rest, to let the land lie fallow, and to cancel debts periodically, if not redistribute land. Theology in this context poses no either/or choice between caring for people and caring for the earth. Modern philosophy has posed that false choice. Covenant theology emphasizes that the way people treat the land and animals is as important a sign of faithfulness as the way they treat each other. "The earth is the Lord's and all that dwell therein!"

Reaffirming the Creator's deep care, however, does not clarify just what humans ought to do in and with a "good" creation. That must always be discerned contextually, in light of the way ecology and justice relate to, and qualify, each other. The biblical material never clearly answers the question: To what extent is nature "for us"; and to what extent do we exist for its good? When does the common human good have priority over the good of the commons, or vice versa? Nevertheless, modern "conservative" biblicism has made a definite decision about this: Creation exists for human beings to exploit—now more than ever; God has ordained it. In this view, "green" thought and action is threatening because it subverts supposedly theocentric but actually ultra-anthropocentric convictions.

A pertinent, integrative, theological-ethical response affirms ecocentric and anthropocentric values together. The human vocation is not to dominate nature but to respect created reality with profound appreciation for its spirited community of being. The human vocation is to worship the Creator-Deliverer, who declares that the whole creation is good, and who executes justice for the oppressed, utilizing covenant people as participants. So the human vocation also is to work with the rest of nature to meet common needs on a basis of ecological integrity combined with social equity, while doing as little harm as possible to other species and people.

Toward an Integrative and Critical Faith

Too much contemporary religious scholarship has ignored ecological reality—intersecting with social need—as basic to the context of theological reflection. This failure reinforced a misperception, popularized by Lynn T. White in 1967, that Christian scriptures and traditions in particular are useless if not downright anti-ecological, and that scholars must rely primarily on the resources of other faiths to grapple with the spiritual dimensions of environmental problems. Seeing that modern Christianity has shown "arrogance toward nature," Lynn White rightly emphasized that what we think about the human-earth relation affects what we do about it. But he wrongly implied that biblical interpretation and constructive Christian theology have little to contribute. Consequently, many environmental philosophers ignored possible dialogue with Christian ethicists and went East in search of "better" religious resources, a tendency that is finally being questioned (Oelschlaeger 1995).

The essays in this book take a more nuanced view. While religion often has an ambiguous relation to conservation, the scriptures and traditions and recent Christian experience can be rich resources for environmentally intentional theological reflection, church revitalization, and social engagement. Both an elegant complexity of environmental consciousness and a human posture of ambivalence toward nature are built into the Judeo-Christian tradition and cultures interacting with it. Part of theological study, therefore, is to draw out and to reflect on paradoxes of faith and tensions of ethics concerning a healthy future for humans with otherkind. Another part of theological study is to equip students to become constructive citizens who will help to restore and rebuild earth community.

Questions around Which the Book Is Organized

The chapters that follow are designed to answer two basic organizing questions:

1. What writings and themes in this field of theology, or area of religious leadership, are especially helpful in fostering understanding of and engagement in the environmental challenge?

2. What new theological work and approaches to eco-justice teaching and leadership are most needed to engage the deepening crisis of earth community?

The first question is openly curious about what recent theology (through 1994) delivers as reflection on and response to the environmental challenge. The overall answer is: More than any of us knew, though much of it remains undeveloped. Some rich resources are identified here; the scholarly writings cited offer helpful, though sometimes conflicting, thematic leads for "recycling" theology and ethics. We do not claim to have comprehended the whole, because some important content was inevitably overlooked. But this volume does paint a recognizable picture of work already begun.

The second question does two things: a) it sharpens the focus by concentrating on the dynamic intersection between ecological integrity and social justice, not ecological concerns abstracted from human society. Contributors to this book emphasize that all of the environmental issues attracting fresh theologizing are culturally shaped and socially freighted; conversely, cultural patterns and social policies have definite environmental consequences in a natural matrix whose reality transcends our perceptions or interpretations. In other words, this subject is broadly basic; we are *not* interested in a narrow environmentalism, but one that connects to natural sciences and social movements,[1] as well as to theological traditions and cultural patterns. We are preparing to attend to a multifaceted eco-social future that is likely to become both better and worse, in moving toward us even as we move toward it.

b) The second organizing question also emphasizes "earth community," Tom Berry's big-picture term that at the same time appreciates local places. His sacramental interpretation has helped the ecumenical community comprehend that the natural world is not mere backdrop for human society, but all being on earth is a sacred community to be respected, reconciled, restored with human cooperation. While Berry prefers to speak in naturalistic (i.e., "green" cosmocentric) terms, about the origin and destiny of earth community within an evolving universe, theocentric language is pertinent—in my view, essential. God, construed variously through imaginative metaphor, is engaged with the past, present and future of both planet and people. Thus it behooves the religious community to clarify what faith in God—as Creative Power and Lover of Being, Covenant Maker and Wise Judge, Redemptive Agent throughout Nature-History—has to do with human caring for oppressed people and a deteriorating ecological web of life, threatening manykind.

Doing Theology Oriented to Ecology and Justice

Process theologian Jay McDaniel has been thinking through some of the connections. He identifies four ways we can be rooted in and nourished by the web of life: through a sense of place, reverence for life, identification with Earth, and appreciation of our bodies (McDaniel 1992 and 1995).

1. Most of us already know what it means to have a sense of place that we enjoyed as a child, or one to which we return often as adults. Places that guide us spiritually need, of course, to be viewed in context. Bioregional philosophers such as Wendell Berry and Gary Snyder emphasize that we can expand our sense of place to include larger life communities.

2. A second source of "green grace" is to develop close relations with animals, specifically pets, as living subjects of value in their own right, as opposed to mere objects of value only to others. This way of "reverence for life" focuses not on identifiable geographical regions but rather on "individual kindred creatures." We have reverence for life when we feel kinship with the joys and sufferings of otherkind, when we treat animals humanely (insisting on no deliberate injury), and when we want for them a basic level of happiness.

3. A third source of green grace is to identify with planet Earth—a beautiful sphere cast in relief against the stars—as a whole. The planet, now seen as "alive," can become a subject of loyalty. Theologian Sallie McFague proposes that we think of the Earth as God's body. Jay McDaniel prefers to view the earth as "a community of subjects, like a forest whose 'spirit' is the sum total of the spirits of each of its living beings." The Earth of which we are a part is more than us.

4. A fourth way toward green spiritual maturation is to become aware of our own bodies as living incarnations of Earth's energies. As McDaniel says,

> Our very closest contact with the Earth comes not in our knowledge of our bioregion, or in our allegiance to the planet, or even in our sensitivity to creatures around us. It comes through simple acts of seeing and hearing, breathing and eating and walking and sleeping, but more than that in immediate awareness of the body as subject of trust and as source of wisdom [carrying] the accumulated wisdom of millions, indeed billions, of years of cosmic, geological, and biological evolution. To be rooted in our bodies is to recognize them to be finite spiritual guides.

These four dimensions of a healthy, ecological spirituality are available to everyone, of course, whether or not he or she believes in God. What, then, does God have to do with it? A spirituality and theology of eco-justice repositions the human project in the web of life, certainly. But it does more; it also does theology in the strict sense, reshaping our images of God in relation to earth and all being.

Thus, I would suggest that McDaniel's four dimensions of green grace connect with four images of God, prominent in process theology: Holy Presence, Great Becoming, Sacred Whole, Incarnate Spirit.

God as Holy Presence is the Great Mysterious throughout the planet, manifest particularly in, and on the horizon of, sacred places. God as Great Becoming is dynamic power responsive to a changing cosmos and world, evolving with the universe as lure for freedom and Sharer of joy and suffering. "The Great Becoming is thus Lover of individual beings and God of oppressed human and otherkind. To be sensitive to the Great Becoming is to be identified with 'the least of these'" (McDaniel 1994). God as Sacred Whole is "more" than the universe, but not "external" to it. Rather the universe has interiority; earth's differentiated beings are animated by God, who gives vital unity to all of this valued variety. "Similarly plants, animals and people are parts of, but not reducible to, God. While we humans might neglect the intrinsic value of penguins and people, the Sacred Whole recognizes and delights in the value of both. What makes the Sacred Whole 'God' is that, like Christ on the cross, it receives each being into its own heart with 'a tender care that nothing be lost'" (McDaniel 1994). God as Incarnate Spirit inspires the universe. The Spirit enlivens and enlightens the creation, which bodies God forth. In Sallie McFague's terms, the universe is to God as our own bodies are to us. "Just as what happens in and to our bodies happens in and to us, so what happens in and to the universe—the full range of joy and suffering—happens in and to God" (McDaniel 1994).

Theology thus refocused illumines the spiritual significance of the web of life even as it introduces multiple ways in which life's Creator and Redeemer can be perceived. Such ecologically alert theology utilizes images that are potentially more appropriate and satisfactory than merely continuing to picture God as potentate. God's sovereign love is not supposed to be confused with divine dictatorship, but this still tends to happen in popular interpretations of the biblical God as King. As Holmes Rolston III observed upon completing a critical survey of science and religion,

> In the Bible there is too much of the Oriental Sultan remaining from the contexts in which monotheism was first engendered and not enough of the Divine Author who creates for us meaningful roles in a historical narrative. Nevertheless, the better biblical picture is of a persuasive God who wrestles with a wandering people, who coaxes them to a land of promise, and who sends a Son, not to bring down fire from heaven, but to set loose the appeal of sacrificial love in the midst of a world of scattered aims and confused responsibilities (Rolston 1987, 318-19).

That quotation, coming from a leading environmental philosopher who also knows Reformed theology, is an important reminder that Christian thought must become conversant with contemporary ecology and cosmology, and ponder how the insights of natural science intersect with faith stories of social struggle for justice and community. Christian theology especially should pay more attention to natural (general) sources of revelation to accompany its reflection on biblical (special) sources of revelation, since both nature and history have cruciform character—the cross being a pivotal sign. In Rolston's words,

> Life is suffering, but life is suffering through to something higher. . . . Earth is a providing ground. Some providential power—can it be merely a naturalistic one?—guarantees that the story continues across all its actors. In this perspective, regenerative suffering makes history. . . . One believes that life will be provided for through suffering, and bettered by it (Rolston 1987, 289-93).

To undergird spirited earth ethics, it is necessary to explore contemporary interacting foundational stories of ultimate meaning. Thus, theology to meet the environmental challenge should dialectically relate, *not* choose between, a naturalistic "process God" within the biocosmological story of Earth on one hand, *or* a historical "biblical God" acting to redeem people on the other. Such a false choice must be avoided, because God is present in both nature and history, working for shalom. *Theology for Earth Community* is not trying to substitute evolution for God, or to discern ultimate value in nature instead of valuing human culture too. Theology seeking eco-justice will also speak of God's relationship to human society within nature and emphasize the full-orbed justice ethic featured in the biblical covenant story. Today we need to reread and act upon that covenant story with more of a view from outdoors, namely, within nature, to accompany the view from below and the view from abroad. The outdoors view emphasizes that all of earth community matters, and has intrinsic value, to the One who continues to create, sustain and redeem the whole.

Covenantal awareness in the Hebrew and Christian traditions emphasizes "faithfulness to the God who displays and wills righteous love authoritatively but noncoercively. In the eco-justice crisis, restoring creation both human and nonhuman—for ecological wholeness and socioeconomic justice—becomes the content of faithfulness" (Gibson 1994). To foster appreciative participation in this common human vocation, "Do we need to find some honest combination of covenantal theology with a sacramental theology that emphasizes the spiritual dimension of natural reality and exults in the continuity, connectedness, and interdependence of the human and nonhuman? Does the emphasis on faithfulness to God need the emphasis on unity of the whole in order to care for the whole?" (Gibson 1994).

A 1990 Presbyterian "Call to Restore Creation" proposes that

> restoring creation is God's own work in our time; . . . the Creator-Redeemer calls faithful people to (join) in keeping and healing the creation, human and nonhuman. . . . Response to God's call requires a new faithfulness, for which guidance may be found in norms that illuminate the contemporary meaning of God's steadfast love for the world. Earth-keeping today means insisting on *sustainability*—the ongoing capacity of natural and social sys-

tems to thrive together—which requires human beings to practice wise, humble, responsible stewardship after the model of servanthood that we have in Jesus. Justice today requires *participation*, the inclusion of all members of the human family in obtaining and enjoying the Creator's gifts for sustenance. Justice also means achieving sufficiency, a standard upholding the claim of all to have enough—to be met through equitable sharing and organized efforts to achieve that end. *Community* in our time requires the nurture of solidarity, leading to steadfastness in standing with companions, victims, and allies, and to the realization of the church's potential as a community of support for adventurous faithfulness.

The above illustrations of pertinent God-talk highlight the need for more varied metaphors in theology, coupled with earthier ethical discourse, to meet the environmental challenge. Recycled and enriched affirmations about the God of life, Spirit of being, Actor for eco-justice in the world, should enable people to recover spirited stories, to discover earth as context for self-understanding, and to act for just and sustainable community.

Such green theocentric discourse—illustrated above in the modes of process theology and Reformed covenant thought—affirms God's immanent presence and power as well as transcendent being and purpose. It utilizes terminology that connects with contemporary scientific cosmology and ecology, and that deepens engagement in the struggle for social justice so characteristic of Hebraic spirituality. An adequate theocentric ethic, weaving these threads together, offers a religiously grounded moral framework for human participation in nature and culture that would neither exploit the natural nor subordinate the human species. Humans with this orientation share a common vocation: to show reverential respect for diverse being while exercising wise responsibility that "fits" God's providential ordering and meets earth's eco-social need.

Getting Started—Developing Depth

Learning better how to fit into Creation in its wholeness and mystery is architectonic of everything else we humans aspire to achieve. Toward that end, we should become earthier doers of theology and ethics, building on the available scholarship discussed in this field guide. The following essays—authored by seasoned teachers and emerging scholars—delve into themes of, and point to a new agenda for, the fields of biblical studies, systematic theology, social ethics, practical disciplines, spiritual formation–liturgical reform, and community action.

We underscore the need to recast each field of theological study and seminary community life accordingly. If that is the first point of an agenda for theological education, our second point is that a praxis of sustainability and justice is reciprocally related to adequate intellectual reflection, informing and being informed by it. Third, a seminary or religions department should resist becoming a mere enclave of religious knowledge that is indifferent to public life; instead it needs to join with community groups, voluntary organizations and other institutions to move in the direction of just and sustainable community. Fourth, it is important for theological schools to venture into carefully designed interdisciplinary study encompassing "green" science as well as some social science, so that religious leaders may become effective educators and competent participants in the eco-justice movement.

This Book's Promise and Limits

These essays offer a rather comprehensive orientation to the existing state of the art in theologies for earth community. They point the way to enriched theological study with this focus. Pondering the range and specific aspects of these chapters, several things are evident.

1. This field guide shows how environment touches everything a theological school or religion department might study, *and various methods of learning*! There is need for creative teaching and concentrated course work within a comprehensive approach to this basic subject. But attempts to cover environmental dimensions of theology by offering an elective course or two miss the point. Theology for earth community must permeate the curriculum, pedagogy and institutional practice of theological education communities, to enable all learners (including teachers, administrators, and trustees) to think and act faithfully in ways that are more fitting.

2. The volume goes into more detail on some aspects of theology for earth community than on others. For example, the following chapters give more attention to developments in eco-feminist theology than to the literature on science and religion. And as for practical dimensions of education to meet the environmental challenge, several chapters explore learning through liturgy and praxis, but this collection does not go on to specify models of congregational life or community action for eco-justice. These matters are illumined in recent educational resources produced by several ecumenical and denominational agencies,[2] which give at least some ecclesial visibility to a ministry of environmental responsibility.

3. Our field coverage is incomplete; inevitably, some items are still missing from this guide. For example, no essay in this volume explores "green" study of religious history. That is particularly regrettable since very few members of the church history guild have explored a "green" history of Christianity, beyond environmentally alert reviews of the thought of great theologians. To compensate somewhat for this lack, and to whet reader appetites for more, chapter 16 of this volume presents my own assessment of recent ecumenical church participation in the environmental movement. Examination of the churches' environmental teachings (in connection with their social teachings), and of church behavior seeking to embody those teachings, is a new agenda for religious historians. It should open up a conversation with secular environmental historians regarding the destructive trajectory of Modernity—accompanied in the last half-millennium, and especially through the modern missionary movement, by an increasingly anthropocentric Christianity, which has only belatedly begun to grapple with the requirements of full-orbed justice.

4. This field guide does not include a plan for cross-disciplinary study in secular disciplines that also grapple with the environmental challenge. Studies of

religion, ethics and environment through cross-disciplinary discussion among scholars in theological fields and cognate secular disciplines offer complementary possibilities that are exciting to contemplate. Through the ecumenical Program on Ecology, Justice and Faith,[3] it is my privilege to relate to a network of theologians and ethicists who value structured cross-disciplinary learning among scholars, professionals and leaders of non-governmental organizations. That topic, however, is beyond the scope of this particular book. The larger goal is to bring both specialists and generalists in theological and religious studies, environmental studies, and social and policy sciences out of disciplinary isolation into more fruitful public dialogue for the common good and the good of the commons—making each scholarly sector more comfortable with mutual inquiry and contributory praxis. But that will not proceed effectively until each sphere of study (here, theological education across its various fields) takes seriously as core subject matter the needs of earth community.

The time is opportune, perhaps even a *kairos*, for a focused examination of vital work to be done. Theology has much to contribute to philosophical and ethical frameworks that embrace the goals of ecological wholeness and social justice together. The question to you the reader is this: What will happen in your study, teaching or community leadership to meet this challenge?

Notes

1. Environmentalism has several branches, and thanks to grass-roots social movements that seek equity as well as ecology, is becoming more inclusive of gender, class and race. See Nash 1989; Shabecoff 1993; Gottlieb 1993; Schwab 1994. Only the first of these authors, however, explores the religious aspects of this century-old story.

2. The National Religious Partnership for the Environment, headquartered at the Cathedral of St. John the Divine, 1047 Amsterdam Ave., New York, NY 10025 [1-800-435-9466] has coordinated the dissemination of resource packets for congregations in four associations: the National Council of Churches, the National Conference of Catholic Bishops, an Evangelical Alliance, and the American Jewish Committee / Union of American Hebrew Congregations. A particularly adaptable model of congregation-based eco-justice ministry is presented in the NCC packet, *God's Earth Our Home*, edited by Shantilal Bhagat of the Church of the Brethren. Many denominations also offer their own education and action resources.

3. The concept of the Program on Ecology, Justice and Faith (PEJF) developed in conversations with J. Ronald Engel of Meadville / Lombard Theological School while I was a Visiting Professor at McCormick Theological Seminary in Chicago. This ecumenical program, supported by several foundations, fosters professional development, strategic publication and timely study of eco-justice theology and ethics in theological schools and university religion departments.

PART 1

BIBLICAL ROOTS
AND MODERN INTERPRETATION

The land you are crossing over to occupy is a land of hills and valleys,
watered by rain from the sky, a land that the Lord your God looks after. The
eyes of the Lord your God are always on it, from the beginning of the year
to the end of the year.
—Deuteronomy 11:11-12

Biblical quotes like that challenge Lynn T. White's assertion, over a quarter century ago, that Judeo-Christian thought just shows "arrogance toward nature." In the modern period, a lot of biblical interpretation has. But the following essays also assume that scripture, tradition, and recent Christian experience can be rich resources for environmentally intentional theological education and church life.

The narrative, poetic, and injunctive "conversion literature" gathered up in the Bible has to do with earth as well as people. Old and New Testament scholars are uncovering and examining surprising riches embedded there. The effect, however, is to offer more than one "take" on the human vocation in creation, conveyed in many images and stories designed to form communal sensibilities. An elegant complexity of environmental consciousness and an ambivalent human posture toward nature are both built into the Bible and cultures interacting with it. So, patient study is necessary to discern how a biblical text works—what it meant then, what the church did with it, and how we read it now that we are more eco-alert.

Taken as a set, the chapters of Part I invite us to think differently about the human-nature relationship in light of biblical roots and the problems of modern interpretation. First, Ted Hiebert exposes several questionable controlling ideas that originated in nineteenth-century philosophical idealism and then drove twentieth-century biblical scholarship. He questions especially the tendency—among both Christian and Jewish scholars—to dichotomize redemption and creation, or history and nature. Eilon Schwartz, in his chapter on Jewish theology, offers a similar critique.

After identifying some basic false assumptions that have permeated recent biblical exegesis and exposition, Hiebert takes another look at the story of the Garden of Eden written by the Yahwist, or J, for whom "arable land is the primary datum . . . ; land is the very realm of redemption . . . What emerges from this literature of ancient agriculturalists is a strong sense of attachment and interrelatedness to the natural environment." Humans are intended to be people of the land. One might extrapolate: we are earth creatures who should value particular places, and treat every land as promised.

That major new theme of biblical interpretation needs to be accompanied by others, as Diane Jacobson suggests, in identifying several biblical starting points for eco-justice ethics. Besides Genesis 2, these include Genesis 1 and Psalm 8, the Sabbath and Jubilee tradition, the Noah story of God's covenant with earth, the Wisdom tradition epitomized in Proverbs 8, and the promise conveyed throughout both testaments to undergird hope and responsibility. Throughout the biblical narrative, there is a vision of what the future could be as a society of all being within God's reign.

Gene McAfee's state-of-the-art essay, "Ecology and Biblical Studies," provides an excellent overview of significant scholarly writing over the last two decades. McAfee concludes that sophisticated exegesis of the Bible is an inescapable task, arguably the first task, in meeting the environmental crisis. He also recommends that participants in biblical studies focus on the continuing dynamic relationship between natural processes and the human journey, explore the physical environment of those who wrote the texts, and attend not only to the goodness of creation but also to the tragic and redemptive significance of suffering in natural and cultural history. Finally, he urges biblical interpreters to move toward post-anthropocentric portrayal of humanity's role in the commonwealth of creation.

1

Rethinking Traditional Approaches to Nature in the Bible

THEODORE HIEBERT

In order to consider the contributions our scriptural traditions might make to the construction of a theology for earth community, the task we face is a much bigger one than we might at first suppose. It will not be sufficient in this case simply to redirect the results of past scholarship on the Bible in order to bring them to bear upon a new issue. Nor will it be satisfactory to apply these results to the interpretation of underused or forgotten texts, which are now recognized as important for addressing this topic. On the contrary, the very results of past scholarship and the methodologies that lie behind them, which together have provided the ground rules for describing nature in biblical religion, are going to have to be rethought.

This is so because most past scholarship on the place of the natural world in biblical thought has been driven by several controlling ideas, ideas which are not as reliable, upon careful scrutiny, as they have generally been considered. The first and foremost of these ideas is the conception that biblical religion is concerned about history, not about nature. According to this view, ancient religious thought could be reasonably characterized in terms of a rather sharp dichotomy between redemption and creation, between the realm of human culture and history on the one side and the world of nonhuman nature on the other. Whereas Israel's neighbors associated God with nature, Israel saw God and God's activity in historical experience. By consequence, the world of nature was pushed into the background in biblical faith, where it was not only marginalized but to some extent also vilified because of its association with the ancient paganism Israel had rejected.

Many major scholars could be cited to illustrate this point of view. Just a few influential figures will have to suffice here. In an essay with the revealing title "The Theological Problem of the Old Testament Doctrine of Creation," Gerhard von Rad argued that Israelite faith was primarily concerned with redemption and that within it the creation performed, as he put it, "only an ancillary function . . . It [was] but a magnificent foil for the message of salvation" (von Rad 1966b, 138-39). G. Ernest Wright was of like mind. He thought Israel possessed a unique historical consciousness, which he considered "the one, primary irreducible datum of biblical theology." For Wright, the facts of history were "the facts of God," and nature itself was reduced to "a handmaiden, a servant of history" (Wright 1952, 38, 45). Nahum Sarna, in his recent interpretation of Genesis for the JPS Torah Commentary series, expresses similar sentiments. "The theme of creation," he writes, "important as it is, serves merely as an introduction to the book's central motif: God's role in history . . . The God of Genesis is the wholly self-sufficient One, absolutely independent of nature, the supreme, unchangeable Sovereign of the world, who is providentially involved in human affairs. He is, therefore, Lord of History" (Sarna 1989, xiv). James Barr has described this orientation as one of our great modern orthodoxies. "Historians in the future will look back on the mid-twentieth century and call it the revelation-in-history period," he writes. "No single principle is more powerful in the handling of the Bible today than the belief that history is the channel of divine revelation" (Barr 1963, 193-94).

The characterization of biblical religion as a religion of history and not of nature has been associated with another key idea that has also heavily influenced biblical scholarship on this topic, the idea that Israel's first and formative environment was the desert. According to this view, the ancient Near Eastern landscape could be reasonably characterized in terms of a rather sharp dichotomy between the desert and the town, and its cultures could be related to one or the other of these environments, with the nomadic shepherds on one side and the sedentary farmers on the other. Israel, according to this view, was born in the desert, and preserved this perspective in its culture and thought even after settling down and adopting the life style of Canaanite farmers. It was a perspective, so the argument goes, arising out of nomadic movement not out of rootedness in the land, a perspective that connected the deity with people not with places, a perspective that, in a word, gave birth to a religion of people and their movements, that is, of history not of nature.

This connection between the desert and history in biblical religion was put into classical form by Albrecht Alt, who, in a series of articles in the 1920s and 1930s, argued for the origins of Israel's distinctive historical consciousness and its unique body of law in its primal desert experience (Alt 1968a and 1968b). This same connection was popularized by H. and H. A. Frankfort for a whole generation of students of antiquity in *Before Philosophy: The Intellectual Adventure of Ancient Man*. According to the Frankforts, we may best "understand the originality and coherence of [ancient Israel's] speculations if we relate them to their experience in the desert . . . In the stark solitude of the desert, where nothing changes, nothing moves (except man at his own free will), where features of the landscape are only pointers, land marks without significance in themselves— there we may expect the image of God to transcend concrete phenomenon altogether [and to claim] a metaphysical significance for history and for man's actions" (Frankfort and Frankfort 1949, 246-47). A whole literature tracing a "desert ideal" through biblical thought has particularly stressed this idea in biblical scholarship (See Budde 1895; Flight 1923; Nystrom 1946; Seale 1979; Schneidau 1976; for a critique, see Talmon 1966).

Together, these two concepts, the desert and history, have provided the intellectual framework in terms of which the world of nature and the human place within it have been handled by biblical scholars. They have produced an image of Israel as a desert society that developed out of its nomadic existence a historical consciousness new in the history of religions, on account of which the natural world was in the end marginalized, devalued, and stripped of its sacred significance. I do not think that Lynn White knew anything about this scholarly history when he wrote his now famous ecological critique of biblical religion. But it is not hard to see the rather close parallels between the conventions of biblical scholarship and White's characterization of biblical religion as dualistic, that is, sharply separating nature and humanity from one another, and anthropocentric, that is valuing the human above all else (White 1967). The problem with White's critique of the Bible was not so much that it lacked good exegetical method—which it did—but that it so closely mirrored the results of the best biblical scholarship on nature, a scholarship which, as I wish to argue here, needs some serious rethinking.

There are at least two reasons for reevaluating the methods and results of past biblical scholarship on nature. The first of these is their dependence on nineteenth-century modes of thought. The conception of Israel's desert origins and of its austere historical consciousness both rest heavily on theoretical models of ancient environments and of the evolution of human thought which, while popular in the late nineteenth and early twentieth centuries, when modern historical scholarship came into its own, would not necessarily be accepted as adequate for the study of antiquity today. The marginalization of nature in biblical interpretation based on these models has had more to do with the world of the interpreter than with the world of the Bible.

Dubious Philosophical and Anthropological Models

The conception that Israelite religion was historical rather than natural is, for its part, indebted in many respects to German idealistic philosophy, exemplified preeminently in the writings of G.W.F. Hegel. As an idealist, Hegel divided the world into two metaphysically distinct orders, mind and matter, the spiritual and the material, and he believed that the world's religions had evolved from religions of nature, which identified spirit directly with matter or nature, to religions of spiritual individuality, which distinguished spirit absolutely from matter or nature. While the religions of the ancient Near East exemplified for Hegel the stage of nature religions, Israel's religion exemplified the next stage of human thought. It represented a religion of spiritual individuality, a religion of humanity and freedom in which, as Hegel put it, nature was "undeified . . . entirely negated, in subjection, transitory" (Hegel 1962, 2:128, 189, 194).

The connection between Hegelian idealism and scholarly constructs attributing to Israel a distinctively pro-history, anti-nature religion is not hard to see. While there is some debate about the extent to which the great Julius Wellhausen was influenced by Hegelian thought, his contrast between natural and historical religions and his belief that Israelite religion evolved into a religion of history that signified an absolute "negation of nature" reflect obvious Hegelian categories (Wellhausen 1957, 102-4, 437-38). G. Ernest Wright, a prominent spokesman for Israel's historical religion, to whom I have already referred, quotes Hegel prominently in defense of his view that Israel broke decisively from the nature religions of antiquity" (Wright 1952, 42). As does Mircea Eliade, the renowned comparativist, who divided sharply between natural—that is primordial, cyclic, archetypal—and historical views of reality, and who saw in Israelite religion the first decisive rejection of the former and adoption of the latter. He believed he saw "a parallel between Hegel's philosophy of history and the theology of history of the Hebrew Prophets," in that both value the invisible event of history as a manifestation of the will of God over against "the viewpoint of traditional societies dominated by the eternal repetition of archetypes" (Eliade 1954, 148).

Among a group of recent theologians, including Wright, this pro-history, anti-nature depiction of biblical religion has also been associated with another agenda, the concern for human dignity and social justice. In this context, religions of nature, involved with nature's unchanging cycles, are equated with the status quo, hierarchical structures, and entrenched political power. By contrast, the historical consciousness of biblical religion is related to human freedom and social change (Wright 1952, 15-29). Such a dichotomy can be seen in the biblical interpretation of liberation theologians, one of whom, J. Severino Croatto, uses it explicitly in his interpretation of the Exodus. "Mythic persons are not free . . . they are subject to the cosmos," he writes. In biblical religion, by contrast, "history displaces the cosmic. God is visualized in human events more than in the phenomena of the physical world . . . The relationship between God and humans is no longer cosmic, but rather dialogical, within a historicity in which human beings are responsible for a destiny . . . Thus we understand that human beings created in the image of God are free" (Croatto 1981, 34-35). Thus a philosophical dichotomy, going back ultimately to idealistic categories, has been harnessed to provide biblical support for theologies of anthropocentric liberation and justice.

The idea of Israel's desert origins, to which the notion of its historical consciousness has often been linked, is also grounded in late nineteenth- and early twentieth-century constructs, in this case the tripartite theory of cultural development common in early anthropology. According to this theory, human societies evolved naturally and in unilinear fashion from hunters and gatherers, to nomadic herders, to sedentary farmers (Khazanov 1983, 1-14, 85-118). Thus, when one wanted to locate the origin of new populations in the ancient Near East, whether of the Semitic peoples in Mesopotamia or of the Israelites in Canaan, one looked to the desert as a great reservoir of nomadic peoples on the way to sedentary life. In the case of biblical scholarship, such theories have fit nicely with the common practice of locating the beginning of Israel's history proper in the Exodus and wilderness events rather than in the generation of Abraham or Noah or even Adam where the biblical historians located it.

This early anthropology, which provided such a useful model for reconstructing Israel's nomadic beginnings in the desert, has been largely abandoned, both because of the artificial dichotomy it drew between pastoralism and cultivation and because of its belief in the natural evolution from one to the other. It is now believed that pastoralism originated in, and was for the most part a subdivision of, sedentary agricultural societies (see BarYosef and Khazanov 1992, 1-6). Even for the small minority, for which it may have become a more specialized pursuit, pastoralism was always closely integrated into and dependent upon sedentary agricultural communities (Marx 1992, 255-60). Thus, to the best of our knowledge, the kind of autonomous desert nomadism reconstructed for biblical Israel by scholars like Alt and the Frankforts and regarded as the source of Israel's unique historical religion simply did not exist in biblical times. Whatever the environment that provided the context for Israel's encounter with nature, we will have to give up the image of the "stark solitude of the desert" as the formative setting for biblical religion and as the source of its beliefs about the natural world and the human position within it.

The case against nineteenth-century philosophy as a foundation for biblical scholarship on nature is not dissimilar from the case against its anthropology. The Hegelian idealism, which has influenced the characterization of biblical religion as historical rather than natural, also posits a sharp dichotomy, in this case between matter and spirit, and it also thinks in evolutionary terms, seeing in human history the development from religions of nature to religions of the spirit. Neither the matter-spirit dualism nor the evolutionary view of human thought in such Western philosophical idealism can anymore be taken, without serious qualification, as the starting point for analyzing the intellectual traditions of the ancient Near East. Bertil Albrektson, in *History and the Gods*, has shown some time ago the fallacy of traditional claims for the uniqueness of Israel's historical consciousness and for the evolution of this consciousness from the nonhistorical religions of its neighbors (Albrektson 1967). Much rethinking still remains to be done on the other side of this equation, that is, the role nature plays in ancient religious thought, both that of Israel and of its neighbors, a kind of rethinking which does not assume idealistic categories in its analysis of biblical texts.

Revisiting the Garden of Eden

Traditional biblical scholarship on nature and on the human relationship to it must be reconceived, not only because it has been founded so heavily on nineteenth-century anthropological and philosophical models inappropriate for the study of antiquity, but also because it cannot, in the end, make proper sense of the biblical text itself. To illustrate this and to provide a few suggestions about what a more adequate approach to the biblical view of nature might involve, I would like to take another look at one of the Bible's creation narratives, the story of the Garden of Eden.

The creation stories at the beginning of the Bible have received by far the most attention in discussions of environmental values, not only because they describe the natural world in such detail but also because they are founding narratives, narratives explaining and legitimating the realities of the world as the author knew them. In the story of the Garden of Eden, the second account of beginnings attributed to the Yahwist or J, human life is conceived entirely in terms of agriculture. When J wants, in the story's opening clauses, to describe pre-creation nothingness by negating life as he knew it, he claims that "there was no human to cultivate the soil" (Gen 2:5). J describes the first assignment God gives to the first human after creation as the cultivation and care of the garden (2:15). And the expulsion from the garden at the end of the narrative, as far as J is concerned, does not affect this archetypal agricultural vocation. It just makes it harder. God sends the couple out of Eden to cultivate the same soil out of which the first human was made (Gen 3:23).

Much has been made, particularly in recent years on account of our new ecological sensibilities, of the fact that in this story the first human, *'adam*, is made from the earth, *'adama*, and that this relationship is captured in a play on words, *'adam* from *'adama*. Various English translations have been proposed to capture this linguistic and philosophical connection, such as "earthling" from "earth," or "human" from "humus." But when one recognizes that throughout the epic, the J writer consistently uses the term *'adama* for arable soil in particular, one realizes that there is an even more precise claim about human life being made here. It is the claim that humanity's archetypal agricultural vocation is implanted within humans by the very stuff out of which they are made, the arable soil itself. Humans, made from farmland, are destined to farm it in life and to return to it in death (Gen 3:19, 23).

Pastoralism, when it appears in the narrative of this first human generation, is not a specialized pursuit which alone defines human culture. It is rather one activity within a multipurpose household where cultivation and herding are combined. Of the first couple's two sons, the older, Cain, is primarily involved in cultivation, as was his father, and the younger, Abel, as is customary, takes care of the family's flocks. This is a picture of the mixed agricultural economy which has typified highland Mediterranean farming down through the ages and which was the backbone of the economy of biblical Israel. It was in terms of this agrarian landscape, not the desert, that the J writer described the creation of the human race and the place assigned to it in the order of things. And with some modifications for their social positions and political agendas, one could attribute to most biblical writers this same agricultural environment as the context within which their views of nature are shaped and expressed.

Mediterranean Farmer Values

Whatever values about nature and humanity were held by writers of the Hebrew Scriptures, and whatever we might wish to make of these values in constructing a theology for earth community, we must recognize their origin within the struggles for survival of ancient Mediterranean farmers. Let me, in conclusion, mention several of these values that we might wish to give further thought. One of them is the belief that human well-being is closely tied to—in fact, practically defined by—productive, fertile land. For J, to whose creation narrative we have already referred, arable land is the primary datum in his theology of divine blessing and curse. In J's dark age before the flood, the divine curse which punishes human immorality diminishes the land's productivity until the curse is lifted after the flood in the days of the righteous Noah. God's blessing on Israel's obedient ancestors, especially Abraham, consists primarily of the gift of the arable land of the biblical hill country.[1] Furthermore, the religious rituals of Israel's ancestors are related above all to the productivity of its land. J's cultic calendar in

Exodus 34 is based on Israel's three great harvest festivals, and the primary cultic act of devotion is the presentation to God of the first fruits of the land and the flock.

Such is not the picture of a culture for which the bond with the phenomenal world has been severed, as the Frankforts put it. Nor is it the picture of a religion in which nature is "a magnificent foil for the message of salvation," as von Rad expressed it. Land is the very realm of redemption, its produce the very stuff out of which it is made. As a means of describing the intricate connection between people and land in such an agricultural context, the disembodied and dualistic concepts of nature and history, in terms of which we have become so accustomed to think, are simply inadequate and misleading.

What does emerge from this literature of ancient agriculturalists is a strong sense of attachment and interrelatedness to the natural environment. Such a sense is, of course, natural in a subsistence economy in which the outcome of each growing season can mean life or death. But it is not so natural in a highly special- ized modern culture in which our dependence on the environment has been largely obscured by our technology. Nor is it so natural in our Western idealistic theo- logical tradition, which has taught us to divide the spiritual from the material. Yet it is a sense we will have to recover in some new way, as our best instincts, our best scientists, and our best theologians all tell us, if we are to survive this crisis. Gordon Kaufman has described the new sense of interrelatedness we seek as a "biohistorical" view of life, the World Council of Churches refers to it as "The Integrity of Creation," Thomas Berry has called for a new creation story to cap- ture "the integrity and harmony of the total cosmic order," and there have been many other suggestions for a new kind of holistic thinking and speaking (Kaufman 1993, 109; Thomas Berry 1988, 129-33). We will have to recover this sense of interrelatedness in terms of the modern scientific, social, and intellectual world which is our reality. But we must neither overlook nor fail to reconnect our theo- logical reflection with the roots of such a perspective in our scriptural traditions.

Let me push this one step further. The biblical sense of interrelatedness be- tween humans and the earth springs ultimately from the attachment of ancient subsistence farmers to their productive soil. Now I can hardly think of two ways of life more drastically different from one another than that of the primitive little farmer in the Bible and that of our own urban, industrial society. And this should caution us against any naive appropriation of biblical images of interrelatedness which do not also take account of modern realities.

But there is one thing that has not changed between then and now: our primary dependence on the soil. We are just as bound to agriculture as were our biblical ancestors. There is no such thing, as Tim Weiskel reminds us, as a "post-agricul- tural society" (Weiskel 1992a). But since only 4 percent of us are left on the farm, our society doesn't think in these terms. And the result, as Wendell Berry has put it, is the "unsettling of America," the destruction of our rural infrastructure, and our increasing reliance on large agribusiness industries which practice an unsustainable brand of agriculture that cannot last (Wendell Berry 1977). Our productive soil, without which we will not endure, is in serious peril, and we as a society must be somehow reminded of our dependence on it in order to respond to the threat to it. In this regard, I can think of no more powerful and necessary image than the creation of human life in J's creation story, which claims that we are all, whether we like it or not, farmers. Made out of arable soil, our destinies are forever and irrevocably tied to its productive health.

One other theme that emerges from the perspective of pre-industrial farmers and that deserves our attention is a profound sense of human limit. In this regard, I must say, however, that the Hebrew Scriptures provide us with some rather different images, nowhere better typified than in the two creation stories, the Yahwist's we have been discussing and the Priestly version in Genesis 1. It is the Priestly dominion theology of Genesis 1, by which humans alone are made in the divine image and given authority over the rest of creation, that has really captured the imagination of modern environmentalists interested in the Bible—critics and defenders alike. The main debate has been whether the Priestly Writer thought of this powerful human being as a ruthless despot or a benevolent steward.

But there is another view of the human position in the natural world in J's creation narrative that has gone undernoticed but that has significant implications for a theology for earth community.[2] For J, humans at creation are in no respect elevated above the rest of creation. They are made out of the same dirt out of which God makes the animals and in which he plants the garden. They have the same physical breath that gives life to the animal world as a whole. And when assigned their role in the world, they are told not to rule the animals or to subdue the earth, but to cultivate it. The Hebrew word J employs for cultivate, as you may be well aware, is the verb 'abad, which means literally "to serve." Here is an image of the human being as a plain member of creation engaged in its "service," so to speak, an image John Muir once recognized as a persuasive picture of our true position in the natural ecosystem (quoted in McKibben 1994, 40). Such an image is the very one Job had to be reminded of in God's great speech from the whirlwind. It is one we will also have to be reminded of if we are to recognize our true limits as a species and practice the restraint necessary to live in a sustainable relationship with the rest of creation as a genuine earth community.[3]

Notes

1. Walter Brueggemann (1977) emphasizes the importance of land in biblical theology when he claims that "land is a central, if not the central theme of biblical faith" (p. 3). Yet Brueggemann preserves, in certain respects, the traditional historical reading of biblical religion: "Israel's faith is essentially a journeying in and out of land, and its faith can be organized around these focuses . . . Israel is a landless people when we meet it earliest and most often in biblical faith . . . Israel is embodied in Abraham, Isaac, and Jacob in the earliest presentations as sojourners on the way to a land whose name it does not know" (pp. 6, 14).

2. J. Baird Callicott (1989, 1991) is one of the few who has recognized the ecological significance of J's perspective.

3. This critique of traditional scholarly approaches to the role of nature in biblical thought is presented in more detail, together with a comprehensive analysis of the orientation toward nature in the Yahwist's epic, in my forthcoming volume *The Yahwist's Landscape: Nature and Religion in Early Israel.*

2

Ecology and Biblical Studies

GENE McAFEE

The Study of Nature in Biblical Scholarship

Nature and the environment are receiving steadily increasing attention in biblical scholarship, but in general they remain marginal concerns. The subjects "Human ecology—biblical teaching" and "Nature—biblical teaching," for example, together retrieve only thirteen items (some of which are duplicate titles) from Harvard library's union catalog. Similar results are obtained for such subjects as "Agriculture in the Bible" (six items), "Agriculture—Palestine-history" (eight items), and "Palestine—rural conditions" (two items). To the extent that they comprise a concern of biblical scholarship at all, nature, the environment, and ecology are generally subsumed under the rubric "Creation—biblical teaching" (122 items). Similar results would be obtained in any major library catalog, and an examination of the standard bibliographies and indexes for biblical studies (e.g., *Elenchus Bibliographicus, Internationale Zeitschriftanschau für Bibelwissenschaft und Grenzgebiete, Old/New Testament Abstracts, Religion Index One, JSOT Booklist*) reveals a similar distribution of scholarly attention.

What is perhaps more significant than raw numbers, however, is that most of the works written on the subject of nature and the environment in biblical studies were written within the last two decades, especially since 1990. The ecological concept of the natural world, as distinct from the theological concept of creation, is clearly only an emerging subject in biblical studies and, in the words of one biblical scholar, "we have a lot of catching up to do" (Fretheim 1987, 16).

Reasons for the Delay: Historicism in Biblical Scholarship

Although the contemporary discussion of nature, the environment, ecology, and the environmental crisis was triggered in biblical scholarship largely by Lynn White's 1967 article in *Science*, concern about the possibility of a bias in Hebrew Bible scholarship toward historicism (that is, an excessive concern for Israel's alleged unique historical consciousness against a background of nature religions [found, e.g., in Wright 1950, 16-29], with a concomitant neglect of the study of the natural environment in which the historical texts were written) had already been expressed by some scholars. James Barr, for example, questioned the appropriateness of the "revelation-through-history" orientation of much of Old Testament scholarship in this century, arguing that a considerable body of Israel's religious literature—wisdom literature and psalms in particular—cannot be forced into that paradigm without doing considerable violence to the texts, and even those texts which form the stock of the revelation-through-history corpus (such as the Exodus story) require more than simply the bare historical events for their religious significance (Barr 1963, 196-97).

Barr's reservations concerned a broad scholarly consensus that accorded to biblical Israel a unique historical consciousness, one which understood acts of history to be the medium through which revelation of God was transmitted to human beings. This awareness of the "God who acts" (the title of one of the most important works in this field by one of its leading practitioners) was assumed to be in sharp contrast to the worldviews of Israel's polytheistic neighbors in Mesopotamia, Canaan, and Egypt, where a mythopoeic view of reality held sway, and in which nature played the primary revelatory role. Bertil Albrektson, among others, has questioned this sharp dichotomy between nature and history, and has presented many examples of Sumerian, Akkadian, and Hittite writings in which deities normally associated with natural elements are invoked to bring about military, political, and social upheavals (see the examples in Albrektson 1967, 17-22). It is clear from Albrektson's study that Israel was not unique in understanding the divine as acting in history (Albrektson 1967, 12-22). This familiar scholarly paradigm, then, which has contributed significantly to the neglect of the study of nature in the Hebrew Bible, is no longer tenable (cf. Westermann 1971a; Schillebeeckx 1980).

Another important early warning against historicism in biblical studies, issued by the eminent Old Testament scholar Gerhard von Rad in 1964 (ET 1966), was largely eclipsed by White's more sweeping and widely circulated generalization that the Hebrew and Christian traditions, with roots in the Genesis creation account, were responsible to a great degree for the human exploitation and destruction of the environment (White 1967, 1206-7). Only one aspect of White's essay demands careful attention here: his assertion (p. 1205) that the source of Christian teaching on the relationship between people and their environment is the "striking story of creation" Christianity inherited from Judaism and which is found in the biblical book of Genesis.

New Studies of the Creation Accounts

According to White's version of the creation account, a loving and all-powerful God created by gradual stages light and darkness, the heavenly bodies, the earth and all its plants, animals, birds, and fishes, ending with the creation of Adam and, as an afterthought (to spare Adam loneliness), Eve. The human being named all the animals, "thus establishing his dominance over them." God planned all this, according to White, "explicitly for man's benefit and rule: no item in the physical creation had any purpose save to serve man's purposes. And, although man's body is made of clay, he is not simply part of nature: he is made in God's image" (White 1967, 1205).

This is the extent of White's exegesis of the "Christian dogma of creation" (White 1967, 1206) as found in Genesis. The significance of White's article for discussions of the Bible and the environmental crisis lies less in his biblical exegesis than in the fact that he established the terms of the debate on the role of the Bible and religion in the ecological crisis for biblical scholars as well as for scientists, philosophers, ethicists, and theologians. Those terms may be organized into three broad areas, each concerned with an issue that has occupied the attention and efforts of biblical scholars in the ecological discussion. Two of those issues— the role of human beings in creation and the status of nonhuman creation—were key components of White's essay; the third, the nature and scope of redemption, is a concern that has emerged in biblical studies independently of White's influence. These three areas—the role of human beings in creation, the status of the nonhuman creation, and the nature and scope of redemption—comprise the bulk of scholarship on nature in the Bible and the bulk of this essay. Representative works from each of these areas will be discussed briefly to provide an overview of the discussion.

The Role of Human Beings in Creation

The influence of White's essay among biblical scholars can be seen in James Barr's essay "Man and Nature: The Ecological Controversy and the Old Testament" (Barr 1974). Barr's essay is important as a bellwether for the ensuing discussion of biblical attitudes toward nature and the environment; he was one of the first and most important biblical scholars to follow the channel cut by White, and many others followed.

Barr proposed to look anew at Genesis and the Old Testament as a whole, to consider whether the connections which had been established by White and others between the Bible and exploitative science or technology were the result of fair interpretation of its interests and tendencies (Barr 1974, 58-59). Barr presents a detailed exegesis of the problematic passages in Genesis, focusing on two aspects of the creation account: the statement that humans are created in the image of God and the commandment that they are to have dominion over the earth. Although at pains to argue what being created in the image of God does *not* mean (i.e., that humans act as God's representatives on earth), Barr is less able to suggest what it *does* mean, and shifts attention away from speculation about what being created in the image of God means to the consequential nature of the statement: since man is in the image of God, let him have dominion, etc. (Barr 1974, 61).

Barr spends considerably more effort in his exegesis of the subject of human dominion, focusing his attention, like most exegetes of the creation accounts, on the Hebrew terms *rādâ* ("have dominion") and *kābaš* ("subdue"). Barr criticized the current exegetical fashion of interpreting these verbs as "strong" words suggesting domination, control, or the brute use of force (as, for example, by von

Rad, in his commentary on Genesis (von Rad 1973, 60). Such an understanding, Barr argued, runs against the context of Genesis, which portrays a paradisiacal scene at the beginning of time like that envisioned by such later writers as the prophet Isaiah (in, e.g., ch. 11) for the end of time (Barr 1974, 63-65).

Barr's approach to the question of nature in the Hebrew Bible is typical of the work of most biblical scholars until very recently in three respects: (1) he focuses most of his attention on the creation accounts in Genesis (and on Genesis 1 in particular as the creation account); (2) he attempts to define what human creation "in the image of God" means vis-à-vis creatures not so created; and (3) he attempts to reinterpret the meaning of the Hebrew verbs *rādâ* and *kābaš* in nonviolent terms.

Another scholar who has written extensively on the question of nature in the Hebrew Bible is Bernhard Anderson (Anderson 1955; 1975; 1984a; 1986; 1987; 1992). As an examination of the titles of his works indicates, Anderson's approach to the question of nature in the Hebrew Bible has been under the rubric of creation (e.g., "Creation and Ecology," in *Creation in The Old Testament*, 1984; "Cosmic Dimensions of the Genesis Creation Account," 1986; *Creation versus Chaos: The Reinterpretation of Mythical Symbolism in the Bible*, 1987). In this approach, Anderson is representative of the majority of biblical scholars, who come to the ecological question of nature through the theological category of creation (see the statistics from the library catalog searching above). The most important implication of this fact is that it has tended to force biblical scholars to mine the creation accounts in Genesis repeatedly for their data on nature, resulting in less emphasis on nature as an ongoing fact of life for all the writers of the Bible.

Early in the discussion of ecology and the Bible, Anderson attempted to broaden the literary context in which creation was discussed. In his 1975 essay, "Human Dominion Over Nature," Anderson argued that the language applied to humans in the creation account in Genesis 1—that they are created in the "image of God" and are to have "dominion" over the earth and are to "subdue" it—is royal language and should be read in the context of other royal language describing human beings, most significantly, Psalm 8 ("and with glory and honor you have crowned him, you have caused him to rule over the works of your hands"). Doing so, Anderson argued, would reveal that the priestly writer of the Psalm had begun to "democratize" the royal theology Mesopotamian and Egyptian cultures had applied to their monarchs, and referred it, in the Hebrew context, to every person (Anderson 1975, 39).

Anderson spends considerable time discussing what it means for humans to be created in the "image of God" (pp. 34-44), and considerably less time on the Hebrew verbs meaning "to have dominion" and "to subdue" (p. 44; contrast Barr 1974). He concludes, however, that although the verbs may be used in contexts with violent meanings (e.g., Joel 3:13, Jer 34:15), such is not the context in which they appear in Genesis, and, thus, "Man's special status, as the image of God, is a call to responsibility, not only in relation to fellow men but in relation to nature" (pp. 44-45). Humans are not to exercise dominion wantonly, but wisely and benevolently as representatives of the divine (p. 45).

Anderson reiterated this central point—that "the Judeo-Christian heritage stresses human dominion over the earth" (1975, 44)—in subsequent essays (e.g., 1984a; 1992), always arguing that the context in which the authority of dominion is granted precludes exploitation, and, properly understood, means responsible stewardship (see, e.g., 1984a, 163; 1992, 4).

Anderson's approach, like Barr's, continues the debate along the fundamental lines originally established by Lynn White: the roots of the present ecological crisis are traceable, ultimately, to the announcement in the account of creation in Genesis 1 that the divinely ordained role of humans in creation is that mastery. For the greater part of the history of the discussion since, interpreters of Genesis have sided either with White and his camp, viewing the mandate in Genesis as giving rise to environmental "despots," or with Barr, Anderson, and the majority of biblical scholars, who see in the biblical mandate a call not to domination but to responsible stewardship (cf. the summaries in Callicott 1991, 108; Whitney 1993, 159-60; for an example of a New Testament scholar's attempt to engage in the same type of rehabilitation of maligned texts, see Bahr 1991 on the language of ownership in the gospel of John; for a thorough analysis of the steward symbol see Hall 1990).

In more recent scholarship, two approaches have been taken to broaden the context of the discussion of nature in the Hebrew Bible beyond the impasse created by an exclusive focus on proof-texting the opening verses of Genesis: (1) a source-critical approach, which recognizes that the story of creation in the Hebrew Bible is a composite account from more than one source; and (2) a traditio-historical approach, which recognizes that creation motifs recur throughout the entire span of the Hebrew Bible and are not confined to the opening verses of Genesis.

J. Baird Callicott, although not a professional biblical scholar, has made important contributions to this discussion. In particular, Callicott criticized White for not recognizing, with the overwhelming majority of biblical scholars, the existence of two separate creation accounts in Genesis, one written by the sixth-century B.C.E. Priestly source (Gn 1:1—2:4a), the other by the tenth/ninth-century B.C.E. Yahwistic source (Gn 2:4b-25). Had White paid more careful attention to the question of sources he might have noticed that the portrayal of the role of human beings is quite different in the two accounts (Callicott 1991, 113-16). Whereas in the Priestly version of creation humans are given a clear divine mandate to be the masters of the nonhuman creation, in the Yahwistic version, humans are placed in creation to care for it—humans are citizens of creation, not its masters, or, in Callicott's terms, creation was not created for us, but we for it (p. 124; cf. Cobb 1970; Cobb and Daly 1989, chap. 20; Gustafson 1983; Meeks 1985).

Callicott's understanding of the participatory role of humans in creation, according to his reading of the Yahwistic creation account, leads him to propose a third alternative to the usual two of despotic or stewardian in the debate on the role of humans in creation. That alternative he calls the "citizenship reading" of Genesis (Callicott 1991, 108). This reading, inspired by John Muir's attack on the anthropocentric reading of Genesis current in his day (less than a decade after the publication of Darwin's *Origin of Species* [1859]), asserts that humans are intended to be neither nature's tyrannical masters nor benign, managerial stewards. Rather, God created us, in the words of Aldo Leopold, to be "plain members and citizens" of nature (Callicott 1991, 108; the Leopold quote is from his *Sand County Almanac* [New York: Oxford University Press, 1949], p. 204; cf. Callicott 1991, 113 n. 20). Callicott's approach, unconventional as its point of departure is by the standards of biblical scholarship, represents one attempt to advance the discussion of the role of the human in creation by penetrating to the earliest layer of the biblical tradition. The forthcoming work by Theodore Hiebert on the Yahwist's social landscape represents another more detailed and comprehensive exploration of the Yahwist's perspective.

The second approach to the problem of the role of human beings in creation is that taken by scholars who have attempted to broaden the context of the biblical understanding of nature to include more than simply the account(s) of creation. These scholars have emphasized that the creation theology found in such passages as Psalms 8 and 104, Deutero-Isaiah (chs. 40-55), and the book of Job was evocative and durative, not designed to offer precise details (cf. Anderson 1984a, 153)

One scholar working in this area is Terence E. Fretheim, who has explored Israel's creation theology especially outside the book of Genesis (Fretheim 1987; 1991a; 1991b; 1992). Recognizing the symbiotic relationship of the ethical order and the cosmic order held by most ancient societies, Fretheim explores the correspondences in vocabulary and images between the plagues and the Passover/sea crossing in Exodus to show how the biblical writer linked the ecological disasters of the plagues with the historical and political event of the deliverance from Egypt (1991a, 387-92). In constructing such a unified worldview of the natural and the historical, the writer of the Exodus story presents a central tenet of biblical thinking: moral actions have natural consequences, and nature, therefore, was not the inert object of God's activity in the creation accounts in Genesis, but was an integral component in Israel's ongoing historical existence with God (Fretheim 1991a, 395-96; cf. Westermann 1971b; 1978; Kay 1989).

The Status of Creation before God

Concerning nature, as concerning everything else, the perspective of both the Hebrew Bible and the New Testament is radically theocentric: "The earth is the Lord's, and the fullness thereof; the world, and they that dwell therein" (Ps 104:1). Although the Hebrew Bible is persistently concerned with human affairs, that reality is depicted from the perspective of the divine. The Hebrew Bible in this sense is not anthropocentric in its perspective, as many charge (see below). It is also not bio- or ecocentric[1]; none of these aspects of reality is autonomous or independent of the divine aspect. This, more than a disinclination toward speculation on the part of a so-called Hebrew mentality, is the likely reason there are no words for "nature" or "creation" (or many other abstract and semi-autonomous words in our vocabulary) in the Hebrew Bible. Nature, as an autonomous reality apart from the divine, is simply not the perspective of the writers of the Hebrew

Bible (cf. Gregorios 1987, 86). "The earth" (*ha-'ares*), the closest equivalent in biblical Hebrew for our terms "nature," "creation," and "environment," is a term which denotes a created entity.[2] The Genesis creation account is placed first in the biblical canon not because of its chronological priority, but because of its theological formulation of the relation of the divine to the mundane: every aspect of existence is the result of divine will and activity. This applies as much to the historical, social realm as to the natural, physical realm; reality is a seamless whole created by God. This is the theocentric monism of the Hebrew Bible (Hiebert, forthcoming, ch. 5; cf. the discussion of this "unified field" view of nature in the context of nascent monotheism in Frymer-Kensky 1992, 83-99, esp. p. 98). This view of a totally interrelated reality provides the basis for several important observations on the status of (nonhuman) creation.

The first principle derived from the fundamental understanding of the natural world as God's creation is an intimate link among the natural, supernatural, and the historical realms. The single reality which comprises both the sphere of divine activity and natural/historical existence is expressed clearly in the Hebrew Bible in the theophany, the direct self-disclosure of the divine presence and will (Hiebert 1992, 505). The intimate connection Israel perceived between the natural physical environment and the historical interaction between Israel and God is evident in the fact that the overwhelming majority of theophanies in the Hebrew Bible involve natural phenomena, such as mountains, trees, rocks, springs, clouds, wind, smoke, thunder, lightning, hail, and rain (for specific examples see Hiebert 1992, 505-10). This coalescence of divine self-disclosure with natural phenomena, combined with Israel's distinctive prohibition against iconic representations of the deity, suggests a much closer self-identification between the God of Israel and the natural world (as opposed to the world of human history) than scholars have heretofore recognized (e.g., Wright 1950; 1952; cf. Hiebert 1992, 510).

Secondly, divine creation of the world presumes divine ownership of the same: "For every wild animal of the forest is mine, the cattle on a thousand hills. I know all the birds of the air, and all that moves in the field is mine . . . for the world and all that is in it is mine" (Ps 50:10-12; cf. Lv 25:23). Divine ownership of the entire earth, including the sociopolitical reality of the land of Israel, belongs to God, and human entitlement to the earth's resources extends only to the right of usufruct. This understanding of the relationship of divine ownership, human usufruct, and natural resources is clearly evident in deuteronomistic theology, where the land Israel possesses is granted on condition of Israel's obedience to the Mosaic covenant; Israel's disobedience results in expulsion from the land and the return of the land to its original owner, God (cf. Deut 4:25-26; 6:10-15; 7:12-16; 8:6-20, etc.; see further Miller 1979; Brueggemann 1977, esp. pp. 45-70).

Thirdly, as theologian Francis Schaeffer has noted, a fundamental point of the Genesis creation account has been neglected historically in Christian biblical interpretation. Because everything in the natural world was created by God, each thing, including (but not limited to) human beings, has an independent status before God, and each thing has intrinsic worth, not because of itself, but because of its origin (Schaeffer 1970, 47). In distinction to God, who is uncreated, human beings share with every other creature the status of having been created and, as far as that ontological status is concerned, human beings are equal with every other creature (pp. 53-54). Schaeffer finds this fundamental independence of nature before God to be reiterated in the Noahic covenant (Gn 9:8-17), which God established not with humans but with "all flesh which is upon the earth" (v. 17; pp. 60-61).

Although Schaeffer agrees (p. 70) that human beings have dominion over the rest of creation, his insistence that nature's intrinsic value derives from its status of having been created by God is a significant step toward the "democracy of all God's creatures" which most biblical scholars have been reluctant to recognize (cf. Anderson 1975, 32 and further below). This unwillingness rests on retaining the Priestly writer's "dominion mandate" as an integral part of the creation account. It has remained for other exegetes to move beyond this canonical reading of Genesis in order to recover the rich tradition which has been overshadowed by priestly redaction.

One of the most important areas to which scholars have looked for evidence of Israel's understanding of nature is its wisdom literature (e.g., Proverbs, Job, Qoheleth; Crenshaw 1993, 801). Scholars have long recognized that the natural phenomena of creation play a significant role in wisdom literature, providing a "call of the world order" Yahweh may use, along with priests and prophets, to inform human perception of the good life (von Rad 1972, 162-63; Crenshaw 1993, 803). H. H. Schmid (1984) has argued that in wisdom literature the foundation of history is the cosmos, and that the point of moral and intellectual orientation is not history but creation (cf. also Harrelson on the common ancient Near Eastern background of this perspective, 1969, 5-6). This theme is explored perhaps most thoroughly in the book of Job. Langdon Gilkey has noted that the close and mysterious link between suffering and death on the one hand, and redemption and new life on the other, found in Job and clearly observable in the life of nature, expresses a profound religious awareness extending from the earliest religious impulses to the contemporary theologies of Tillich and Moltmann (Gilkey 1992, 168; cf. the contrast between Hermisson 1984, 132, on wisdom's struggle in the form of theodicy, with Fretheim 1984, on the suffering of God; cf. also Gilkey 1974; Moltmann 1979 and 1985; McDaniel 1989). Similarly, Carol Newsom has shown how Job's perception of justice, defined in the social terms of patriarchal village life, is radically assaulted (and perhaps changed) by the "moral sense of nature" presented in God's speeches focusing on nature in Job chs. 38-41 (Newsom 1994, esp. pp. 17-18; cf. Hermisson 1984, 121, 128-30). In these works, the intrinsic value of the nonhuman creation before God, wholly apart from human needs, desires, or even comprehension, finds biblical support and affirmation (cf. Gordis 1985).

The Nature and Scope of Redemption

The concept of redemption plays a significant role in both the Old and the New Testaments, and the natural world, in one way or another, comprises an essential component of redemption for all biblical writers. The understanding of redemption, however, like the understanding of any concept, changes throughout the biblical writings, transformations which are beyond the scope of this essay. Redemption nonetheless provides a convenient context in which to explore the New Testament's understanding of nature; the nature and scope of redemption, therefore, forms the third major area of research on nature and biblical writings.

The exploration of nature in the New Testament has been hindered, however, by two problems. The first is textual: the traditional identification of the ecological concept of nature with the theological category of creation. The result of this identification has been that investigation of nature is largely confined to the creation texts of Genesis; there is virtually no scholarly perception of creation as a prominent concern of New Testament writings.

The second problem is sociological and theological. The sociological reality underlying many of the New Testament documents was the urban society of the coastal regions of the Mediterranean (e.g., Rome, Corinth, Ephesus, Thessalonica), rather than the rural village society of ancient Israel, and this exerted a strong influence on the ideas that became the major concerns of the first Christian writers. Those concerns were, by and large, not concerns of foundation but of redemption. In the New Testament writings, the land of Israel has become a "land-symbol," a reflection of one of two broad reactions to the loss of control of the land by the Jews first in the Babylonian exile (587-539 B.C.E.) and then in subsequent foreign occupations of the land by Persian, Greek, and Roman powers through the next several centuries.[3]

More important than the sociological background of the writers of the New Testament, however, was their theological orientation. Rosemary Ruether has argued that both the classical Neoplatonism and the apocalyptic Judaism to which Christianity was heir presupposed a thoroughgoing estrangement from nature. While Christianity did not originate this synthesis, "it appears to correspond to a stage of development of human consciousness that coincided with ripening classical civilization" (Ruether 1972, 121-22). Jonathan Z. Smith has referred to this development in the Mediterranean world of the Hellenistic period as a kind of "cosmic paranoia," in which the sense of human belonging in the cosmos was replaced by a sense of deep threat and alienation, and the goal of existence was not to find one's place in the phenomenal cosmos, but to escape from it. In this radical transformation of the perception of self in relation to the world, the hero (e.g., Gilgamesh) became the savior (e.g., Jesus) (Smith 1970, 466-67). This profound alienation between the natural and the spiritual, the earthly and the heavenly is what H. Paul Santmire has called "the spiritual motif" of New Testament writings: the motif of ascent from this physical world of earth to a spiritual world in heaven. This is the dominant motif in such New Testament writings as the gospel of John and the book of Hebrews (Santmire 1985b, 210-15). Such is the traditional scholarly view of the New Testament's understanding of redemption.

Both of these traditional scholarly understandings of the dominant concerns of the New Testament—that nature is confined to creation texts in the Hebrew Bible, and that redemption is the deliverance of humans from a fallen world—are undergoing reevaluation by scholars sensitive to the ecological dimensions of the documents. Although creation texts remain the principal locus for the theology of nature, scholars are increasingly recognizing that creation theology appears throughout the biblical texts and functions in the Bible not merely to recall events from the past but to maintain and affirm the natural and historical order of the present (Hermisson 1984, 122, 125-28), and that the biblical understanding of creation as the foundation of righteousness and salvation implies a much broader understanding of creation than modern scholars have been prepared to recognize (Schmid 1984). This broader understanding of creation involves, among other things, a new understanding of redemption, an area which has recently formed an important scholarly bridge between the Hebrew Bible and the New Testament.

Using Isaiah 35 as an illustration, Frank Moore Cross has attempted to recover "the wholeness and unity of human and natural history" that stamp the language of the Hebrew Bible, a comprehensiveness in which the natural world is an actor that both "engages in and is transformed by the epic events" of biblical redemption (Cross 1989, 94f.). This active involvement of nature in the epic drama of salvation—nature's fleeing the divine wrath, transfigured by the divine glory, redeemed insofar as humans are redeemed, damned insofar as they are damned—compels Cross to speak of the "redemption of nature" (pp. 95-96).

Romans 8 and 1 Corinthians 15 form the epicenter of the idea of cosmic salvation—the redemption of nature as well as humans—in the New Testament (Cross 1989, 101; Santmire 1985b, 200-2; Beker 1980; Goetz 1987). The starting point for the New Testament's theology of nature is not Jesus's celebrated (and often romanticized) concern for the birds of the air and the lilies of the field (Mt 6:26-30), but the apocalypticism which runs throughout the New Testament and has redemption at its core. Jesus's apocalypticism, for example, according to H. Paul Santmire, was not Gnosticism's earth-denying dualism, but, in continuity with the Hebrew Bible, was earth transformation in cosmic dimensions: the redeemer God is also the creator God (Santmire 1985b, 200-2).

Likewise, Gordon Zerbe argues that the most comprehensive conception in the New Testament for God's redemptive activity—the kingdom of God—is an ecological concept because (1) the New Testament's vision for salvation includes the restorative re-creation of the entire universe—both human and nonhuman integrally—to its intended ecological balance; and (2) this vision of holistic redemption motivates Christian ethics—priorities for Christian action in the world—including stewardship of the natural world (Zerbe 1992, 16). New Testament salvation, expressed as the establishment of the kingdom of God, entails most fundamentally—and in continuity with the prophetic hope of the Old Testament—"the restoration of the entire universe to its original state. That is, it is a renewal of creation" (Zerbe 1992, 17).

Zerbe takes pains to insist that the numerous New Testament texts which refer to the "passing away" of heaven and earth should not be used as justification for escapism from ecological responsibility (1992, 23) or for the neglect or abuse of the present earth, any more than the parallel New Testament belief in the resurrection body justifies abuse of our present bodies (1992, 20; cf. Cross' comments on resurrection, 1989, 101). God's interest in creation is evident in the announcement that those who destroy the earth will themselves be destroyed (Rev 11:18, 19:2), and whether the old cosmos is restored or replaced, redeemed humanity is always on a redeemed earth. Earth, here and hereafter, is humanity's only proper habitat. "The final hope of Christians is not heaven," Zerbe concludes, "but participation in God's restoration of all things" (1992, 20-21).

The Contribution of Biblical Scholarship to Theological Education

Many people have concluded that the Bible is part (perhaps the greatest part) of the problem of the West's ecological dilemma, and they find little reason to continue searching the scriptures of an ancient people for solutions to problems that are ours and not theirs (cf. Thomas Berry's designation of the biblical text as "dysfunctional" and the wholesale abandonment of the Bible by ecofeminists, e.g., Gray 1984 and 1985; Adams 1993). There is a certain cogency to this position. As Bernhard Anderson notes, some of the problems we are facing, such as overpopulation, potential exhaustion of natural resources, and the exploration of outer space, were not even anticipated in biblical times (Anderson 1984a, 154).

Nonetheless, the Bible remains, in Martin E. Marty's phrase, "America's iconic book" (Marty 1982) and it cannot easily be ignored in public debate of moral issues in the United States. When then-senator Al Gore discussed the necessity of attending to the spiritual dimensions of environmentalism in his *Earth in the Balance*, he framed his discussion along the lines of the despotism/stewardship debate launched by Lynn White based on the creation account in Genesis (Gore 1992, 238-65). It is clear from Gore's use of the Bible, exceptionally sensitive though it is coming from a public official, that a great deal of the work of many of the scholars cited in this paper remains outside the cultural understanding of a biblical theology of nature. To illustrate the importance of the Bible in the church's deliberations on the environmental crisis, the environmental statement of the Presbyterian Eco-Justice Task Force, *Keeping and Healing the Creation*, takes as its point of departure the biblical mandate for environmental responsibility, focusing on the biblical themes of the intertwining of human and natural history (Hos 2:18; 4:1-3), the suffering of creation (Rom 8:22; cf. the discussion of the scope of redemption above), and the creation of humans as earth-keepers (Genesis 2; cf. the discussion of the role of human beings in creation above) (pp. 1-4). Throughout this document, biblical statements concerning aspects of creation, agricultural practices, the distribution of resources, and the nature of the human condition provide the touchstones around which the arguments for eco-justice are constructed (cf. e.g., pp. 6,8,9,45,46,47,51). The Presbyterian document is typical of the way biblical conceptions of the interaction of humans and nature form the basis of reflection and education in most religious bodies.

The most important contribution biblical scholarship has to make to theological education and religious studies in the area of the environment is to bring greater methodological sophistication to the exegetical component of theological and ethical reflection. As long as the primary religions of the West form the core of theological education and a part of the religious studies curriculum, and as long as the Bible remains the foundational document of those religions, exegesis of the Bible will be an inescapable task, arguably the first task, and the work of biblical scholars will remain the point of departure for theological and ethical reflection on the environment for the foreseeable future.

Areas for Future Exploration

A number of issues have been raised in this review of the biblical scholarship on nature and the environment that point to future research and reflection.

First, the environmental crisis, as Bernhard Anderson noted a decade ago (1984b, 152), is interdisciplinary, and an adequate response will require the inter-disciplinary work of scholars from the natural and social sciences, the arts, and the humanities. In the field of biblical studies in particular, much closer and greater attention must be directed to the relationship between the actual physical envi-ronment of the writers of biblical texts and the ideologies reflected in those texts. If genuine interpretation, Gadamer's "fusion of horizons," is to occur between modern believers caught in a deepening ecological crisis and ancient writers with no consciousness of ecological limits or abuse, biblical scholars will have to in-corporate into their interpretations of texts more of the findings of scientists attempting to reconstruct the actual physical environments in which the texts' authors worked. Only in this way can the natural world of biblical writers, the common basis of all human life, be distinguished from the historical, cultural, and religious ideologies of texts' authors. The works of Zohary (1982), Hareuveni (1974; 1980; 1984), Borowski (1987), and Hopkins (1985; 1987) are examples of such efforts; the works of Stager (1985; 1988) and Hiebert (forthcoming) repre-sent attempts to integrate physical scientific findings into an understanding of specific biblical texts.

Second, biblical scholars must continue to exercise a critical self-conscious-ness regarding the relationship between nature and history, including the relationship between a theology of nature and natural theology, which needs to be reconsidered (cf. Kaufman 1972; McFague 1993). In particular, the degree to which the Bible is concerned exclusively with human/historical affairs and re-gards nature merely as a background against which those events transpire remains an ongoing debate. While a natural setting may be assumed throughout the bibli-cal material (Zerbe 1992, 17), it may not have been an object of sufficient reflection by biblical writers to provide us with any clear and workable guidelines for our present situation. To put the question another way, whereas classical natural the-ology used nature to tell us something about God, a contemporary biblical theology of nature seeks to find in the Bible what God has to tell us about nature.

Third, although the growing ecological awareness of biblical scholars is to be applauded, there is a danger of oversimplifying the goodness of creation and the evils of cultural existence. Nature is most assuredly fertile, beautiful, creative, nurturing, and sustaining; but such blessings are bought at the price of struggle, pain, suffering, destruction, wastefulness, cruelty, and death. Nature participates in redemption (cf. the discussion above) not because of sin, but because of suffer-ing and pain, present as certainly in the world of nature as in the world of culture. In the words of Holmes Rolston, "Struggle is the dark side of creation" (1992, 157). The works on Job discussed above (especially Gilkey) are a beginning in the exploration of this "dark side of creation," but much work needs to be done, especially in relating the suffering at the center of the historical Christian drama with natural suffering.

Another potentially fruitful area of research in this context is the relation between the deuteronomistic theology of reward and punishment (e.g., Deut 28:23; cf. Weinfeld 1972, 307-19) and the biblical critique of the cause-and-effect relationship of sin and natural evils (e.g., John 9). In an age when ecological prophets are warning of imminent disaster due to our profoundly disturbed relationship with our environment, the Bible offers a reminder of the ambiguous nature of malfeasance and misfortune (contra Kay 1989, and, to a lesser extent, Fretheim 1991).

Finally, the notion of human particularity—"exceptionalism" in Timothy Weiskel's terminology (Weiskel 1990, 6), "speciesism" in ecological parlance— remains a fundamental axiom of the anthropology of the West, and a major obstacle to a more holistic understanding of the place of humans in creation. Although considerable effort has been exerted by biblical scholars to expand the concept of nature beyond the confines of the accounts of creation, the assertion in Genesis of human creation in the image of God has contributed to the largely unconscious and deeply held belief that humans are exempt from the natural processes that determine reality for all earthly creatures. Timothy Weiskel in particular has urged a reshaping of fundamental religious and scientific beliefs that will relocate the human species alongside other citizens in the commonwealth of creation, a creation we did not create and do not control (Weiskel 1993; see also Weiskel 1990; 1992a; 1992b; 1992c). It is very much an open question whether a theology based on a fundamentally anthropocentric scripture can bring us to the awareness that we live on earth "on the planet's terms and not on our terms" (Berry and Clarke 1991, 45; for a recent discussion of anthropocentrism that basically reiterates the stewardship model discussed earlier, see Huber 1991).

The pertinent question is not whether our perspective on environmental questions will be anthropocentric if, by "anthropocentric" we mean "from the perspective of a human being." The answer to that question is patently yes, because humans have no choice except to approach all questions from that perspective. The real issue confronting us with our admittedly anthropocentric scriptures is: what kind of anthropocentrism will we embrace? Will we embrace an anthropocentrism in which human beings are the locus of meaning and authority, or the theocentric monism in which meaning and authority derive from the perspective of reality as a seamless whole with God and God's creation (including humans) at its center?

Notes

1. That the Bible is not bio- or ecocentric poses problems for its wholesale appropriation by environmentalists. The theocentrism of both testaments subsumes all other categories of analysis, including ecocentric environmentalism. If "-centric" means one's center, one's point of reference, the Bible is both unambiguous and stubbornly insistent on positing the divine in this role. The relationship of living and non-living creatures to their environment is not, finally, the ultimate center of meaning and value for the Bible, as it is for a bio- or

ecocentric environmental ethic. See the discussion of anthropocentrism which concludes this essay.

2. The hapax legomenon *běrîâ* (Nu 16:30), from the verbal root meaning "to create," denotes a preternatural, unparalleled event and not mundane reality.

3. These reactions may be roughly summarized as follows. On the one hand, the restoration under Ezra and Nehemiah and the rebuilding of the Jerusalem Temple were regarded by many as the fulfillment of the promises to the fathers; the people of Israel were dwelling in the land of Israel, and the focus of concern shifted to the conditions under which such residence took place. This was the dominant concern of both the nationalist movements (such as the Maccabean and Zealot revolts) and the more assimilationist Pharisaism, which eventually came to shape Judaism definitively (Davies 1974, 93-99).

On the other hand, it must be remembered that the majority of exiles did not return from Babylon, but remained settled where they were as part of a growing Jewish diaspora. For these Jews, as well as for a number who actually returned to Israel—only to find their hopes for the restoration of a purified covenantal people increasingly frustrated (not least by the destruction of the second commonwealth in 70 C.E.)—the actual physical land became spiritualized into a symbol of a transcendent reality not yet fully present. Such was the reaction of such sectarian movements as the Qumran covenanters and the early Christians (Davies 1974, 98-104). For the Christians in particular, the destruction of the Jerusalem mother church (and, with it, Petrine Christianity) meant that Palestinian Christianity became almost totally dissociated from the land and seemingly lost its moorings in that regard altogether (Sanders 1984, 10; cf. the fuller discussion in Davies 1974, 336-75).

3

Biblical Bases for Eco-justice Ethics

DIANE JACOBSON

I see six different starting points with reference to a "biblical basis" for eco-justice ethics. The six are not entirely consistent; rather they draw out some of the paradoxes and tensions of scripture itself with its delicious gift for inescapable dialectic. I begin, simply because people so often do begin, with Genesis 1 and 2, which offer not just one basis for an eco-justice ethic, but actually at least three.

First, Genesis 1 leads to an ethic which is centered on the divine judgment that the world is good. I take this not so much as a moral judgment, but rather part aesthetic and part almost technical—the world works well and is beautiful. Genesis 1 tells us right from the beginning that we are merely one part of a vast and wonderful, intricately complex yet harmonious creation, the whole of which God the Creator pronounces to be "very good." The earth is the Lord's, we are told in Psalm 24, and the fullness thereof; the whole world is under God's watchful eye and under God's control to use for good or for ill. In true scriptural fashion, humans are introduced into this world by a Hebrew pun, a play on words—God created 'adam, the human, out of the dust of the 'adamah, the earth or ground. We are, from the beginning, inseparable from the very stuff of creation, only one in a long list of God's creatures. At least two other places in scripture pick up this emphasis on the goodness of creation and the notion that humanity is only one part of creation: Psalm 104 and the answer of God from the whirlwind in the book of Job (also Psalm 65). In God's answer in Job, God cares for the chaotic sea, the desert, and the grass in the wilderness where no human ever ventures. God cares for the wild beasts who are the ostensible enemies of humanity, for the mountain goats and wild ox and ass, for the horse, and even for ravens, ostriches, and vultures—all unclean beasts whom Israel is otherwise taught to detest. In emphasizing the care for the unclean, God in Job is taking on the regnant worldview of the status quo, much like Copernicus or Galileo.

God cares even for the chaos monsters—Behemoth and Leviathan (the original chaos theory!). And in this expansive, no-holds-barred caring, God invites Job to see all of creation as part of God's family whom God births, cares for, sustains, disciplines, and admires. This part of our tradition invites us to see ourselves as intimately connected with all creation, as brothers and sisters with the whole of creation—all God's children, with the world as home. All creatures and all creation are therefore our neighbors, which the Law [Torah] enjoins us to care for. It is sadly a part of the tradition we often neglect although it is well articulated within the mystic tradition, or the American Indian tradition, or by such as St. Francis in his hymn to the sun.

Second, Genesis 1, and its partner text, Psalm 8, also lead to what might be called a dominion ethic. For while we are told, on the one hand, that we are only one part of a vast creation, on the other hand, we are also told that humanity has a particular place and role to play in creation. You know the passage well.

> Then God said, "Let us make humankind in our image, according to our likeness; and let them have dominion over the fish of the sea, and over the birds of the air, and over the cattle, and over all the wild animals of the earth, and over every creeping thing that creeps upon the earth." So God created humankind in his image, in the image of God he created him; male and female he created them. And God blessed them, and God said to them, "Be fruitful and multiply, and fill the earth and subdue it; and have dominion over the fish of the sea and over the birds of the air and over every living thing that moves upon the earth" (Gn 1:26-28).

This language is, at the same time, exciting and extremely dangerous. The exciting part comes when one compares the picture of humanity found here to the picture found in other creation stories of the Ancient Near East. In Babylon, in the *Enuma Elish*, humanity is created to be slaves to the gods so that the gods might rest. The only human given any status was the king called either the *Son of God* or the *Image of God*. But in Genesis, all humans, male and female, rich and poor, slave and free, were created as royal images of God. There is a democratization of kingship whereby we are declared to be royalty rather than slaves, sharing divine work and divine rest. This is a remarkable picture of divine graciousness and favor which calls us to know our own worth in God's eyes.

The dangerous part comes next, with the blessing and the commission to fill the earth and subdue it. The all-too-common reading of this divine proclamation goes something like this: "God has given us dominion over all the earth, therefore I can do anything with it that I please. I can trample the earth under my feet and use up all its resources" (what some have called the James Watt approach to ecology). Such sentiments, as we all know, have contributed heavily to ecological disaster. We are presently living with the results and threats of such an understanding.

Perhaps the dominion image is thus too dangerous, and we should abandon it altogether. Perhaps, but I'd like to suggest another possibility. If we accept the proclamation of Genesis 1 and Psalm 8, we believe that we are God's royal representatives charged with the oversight of the divine kingdom, the earth. If we say we are God's royalty, if we partake of God's royalty, then we must know something of the nature of God's reign, because, in fact, the way God rules has a particular flavor and shape.

If we read scripture closely and think about kingship as God defines it, we find that God's ruling is always marked by justice and righteousness, by service and sacrifice. In God's kingdom, the mighty are thrown down from their thrones, and the meek are lifted up (Hannah's song, Mary's magnificat).

Look at Psalm 97:1-2:

> The Lord reigns; let the earth rejoice;
> let the many coastlands be glad.
> Clouds and thick darkness are round about him
> Righteousness and justice are the foundation of his throne.

Or Psalm 99:4

> Mighty king, lover of justice, you have established equity;
> you have executed justice and righteousness in Jacob.

Or Psalm 89 or on and on.

God's way of ruling is marked by justice. More than this, God's kingdom is marked by ironic servitude. The king's job description in Israel is precisely to serve the kingdom in justice and righteousness (see Ps 72). Not rule over, but rule for and rule in behalf of. This is seen clearly in the suffering servant passages in Isaiah. And, let's go one step further. For Christians, the kingdom of God, in which we are privileged to be royal viceroys, is mirrored most closely and most particularly in the person of Christ the king, hanging on a cross. If we are to know our role in this operation, we must look to Jesus as both the model and goal of royal humanity. Christ is our king, and he wears a crown of thorns.

As Christians, we work not just forward from Genesis 1, but also backward from Christ to our role in creation. Because of our understanding of what God has done in Christ, because of our understanding of who we are in relationship to God in the light of what God has done in Christ, our reading and understanding of Genesis 1 and its companion Psalm 8 is—or at least ought to be—transformed. We read both passages as proclamations of what God has done. We proclaim that God has made the heavens and the earth. We proclaim that God has made this creation in such a way that we humans have a dramatically important part to play in creation. We are God's royal viceroys, royal representatives, crowned with glory and honor. We are given dominion over the earth, and the beasts, and the fish, and the birds. But the shape of this dominion is startling. This dominion is marked by justice and concern, by care and by radical service, even unto death.

In melding the notions of dominion and service, I am also showing strong connections between the implications for an eco-justice ethic found in Genesis 1 and those found in Genesis 2. In Genesis 2, humanity, in the person of 'Adam, is given the task of serving (often translated "tilling") and keeping God's garden. I find it fascinating that in tilling the soil in this image, we are actually serving the earth, thus imagining the earth to be a garden, a garden to be cared for and served like the very temple of the LORD (a job description for humanity that is, as my colleague Fred Gaiser points out, passed on to the next generation. Cain is a "tiller of the ground" in Genesis 4:2).

Thus I am suggesting that Genesis 1, with its dominion ethic, is redeemable—if dominion is viewed through the cross. Moreover, by accepting care for creation as our royal task, we are also acknowledging not only what should be but also what is. Here I come to a problem. Many would say, with good cause, that even as redefined, notions of dominion are dangerous in so far as they remain anthropocentric.

What happened to Psalm 104 and Job? Their message is continually of great importance to contain our hubris and limit our anthropocentricism. Yet, to maintain the biblical dialectic, we acknowledge that humans do have tremendous power in creation. We do, in very real ways, have dominion. We are aware of our capability to affect creation. What good does it do to deny real power. Denied power is abused power! The question then becomes not should we have power, but rather what will we do with the power we have? The usefulness of the dominion image is something, perhaps, to wrestle with together.

Third, Genesis 1 provides the foundation for a biblically grounded eco-justice ethics that has its roots in the Sabbath tradition, which Exodus also emphasizes, and Leviticus expands into the Jubilee tradition. In many ways, the whole of Genesis 1 is aimed toward the Sabbath rest. The pattern of six days of work and one day of rest is crucial to the structure and aim of creation. As I mentioned earlier, in the Babylonian creation epic, humans were created to be slaves of the gods so that the god might rest. But in Genesis, divine rest becomes the occasion for instituting the Sabbath so that all humanity, indeed all creation, might rest. Listen to how this is articulated in the Ten Commandments:

> Remember the sabbath day, to keep it holy. Six days you shall labor, and do all your work; but the seventh day is a sabbath to the LORD your God; in it you shall not do any work, you, or your son, or your daughter, your male or female slave, or your livestock, or the alien resident who is within your gates; for in six days the LORD made heaven and earth, the sea, and all that is in them, but rested the seventh day; therefore the LORD blessed the sabbath day and hallowed it (Ex 20-8-11).

The issues of social justice are here intimately connected to the issues of creation. All people—slave and free, Israelite and alien—as well as all animals are to partake in the created pattern of Sabbath rest. That is, work does not consume everyone's life, and even animals get to rest, a sign of their value. Such rest from labor is part of the fabric of harmonious creation. In Leviticus 25, this notion of Sabbath rest is expanded further to Sabbath year and into the proclamation of Jubilee, which brings into its purview the care and rest of the land.

Leviticus 25 is a chapter of reorienting, of coming home, of renewal, reordering, and liberation. The Law, the Torah, has basically to do with keeping the world an ordered place, with reflecting God's intended order for the world. And God's intended order for the world is expressed here precisely in terms of economics, wealth, family, and land. The chapter proclaims or expects us:

1) to have the opportunity to live within our own extended families and basic communities (thus freeing slaves);

2) to have all that we need to live a full life, but not more than that;

3) to live in harmony with the earth, with the land, and with all the creatures on the land and in the waters;

4) to live knowing that life is a gift from the Creator, whom we can trust to care for us and to whom we owe thanksgiving and devotion. (Lv 26:34— The Land rejoices at its own Sabbath rest.)

5) These themes are carried forward in the Jubilee as proclaimed by the boy Jesus in the Temple (Lk 2).

The possibilities of rooting a biblical ethic for eco-justice in this portion of scripture are numerous indeed.

With my fourth starting place for eco-justice ethics, I finally move away from Genesis 1 and 2. But I won't move very far afield, yet. An ecological ethic can begin in the covenant tradition as we find it expressed through the covenant with God, Noah, and the earth in Genesis 8. Here God intimately links the promise to humanity with the promise to all creation. Not only are Noah and his family saved from the flood, but so also is every species of animal, creeping thing, bird, and everything that moves upon the earth. More than this, the very covenant with Noah is expansive:

> "I will never again, says the Lord, curse the ground because of humankind, for the inclination of the human heart is evil from youth; neither will I ever again destroy every living creature as I have done. As long as the earth endures, seedtime and harvest, cold and heat, summer and winter, day and night, shall not cease" (Gn 8:21-22).

Similar sentiments are expressed in the eschatological covenants found in Hosea 2 and Jeremiah 31. The movements of the earth and sun, the day and night, the seasons, are linked both with God's promise and with God's covenantal demands for human justice. Basing a biblical eco-justice ethic in the covenant thus has the advantage of also affording us an opportunity to examine the prophetic witness concerning what happens to the earth and all its creatures when we humans fail to keep the covenant. We are shown again and again in scripture that the world responds to the choices we make and to the actions we take. Our scriptural ancestors understood well that when we are out of joint with nature or with each other, when we fail to live up to our calling and responsibilities to serve God and one another, when we fail to live justly and to love mercy and to walk humbly with our God, then nature responds as a creation out of sync with its creatures. Scientifically, we might speak in terms of every action having a reaction. Scripture addresses us more poetically.

When, in Deuteronomy, Israel makes a covenant with God, heaven and earth are called upon as witnesses to that covenant (Dt 4:26; 30:19; 31:28). Israel understood that the very earth would react if Israel betrayed her covenantal

responsibilities. So also in later years Israel understood Jeremiah's pronounce-
ment that Israel's rebellion leads ultimately to an earth which is once again waste
and void. The passage is chilling:

> I looked on the earth, and lo, it was waste and void;
>   and to the heavens, and they had no light.
> I looked on the mountains, and lo, they were quaking,
>   and all the hills moved to and fro.
> I looked, and lo, there was no human at all,
>   and all the birds of the air had fled.
> I looked, and lo, the fruitful land was a desert,
>   and all its cities were laid in ruins
>   before the Lord, before his fierce anger (Jer 4:23-26).

I feel that as we near the twenty-first century, we have come once again to understand the truth that stands behind the poetic diatribe of Jeremiah. We know, as we
look at the world around us, that our actions, ofttimes through greed and self-
indulgence, sometimes through ignorance or mere inevitability, *do* have a profound
effect upon the earth. In any case, we once again realize that we humans are
capable of deep destruction.

I want just briefly to speak of two other scriptural traditions which offer us a
starting place for an eco-justice ethic. One is found in the wisdom tradition of
scripture, particularly in the proverbs, most particularly in the figure of Woman
Wisdom found in Proverbs 8.

- One can define wisdom as being a movement in ancient Israel, indeed in
  the entire Ancient Near East, which deals on the one hand with everyday
  life and how to get along in it—how to cope—and, on the other, with speculation about how the world works and why.
- One can perhaps best explain wisdom as being a certain attitude toward the
  world or a certain quest. The attitude is that the world makes sense. The
  quest is twofold: to discover the sense of the world, and to order one's life
  in compliance with this sense.
- Wisdom is that part of the biblical tradition which does not start with revelation and tradition; rather wisdom starts with observation of the world and
  with the conviction that truth can be learned, attained by such observation.
- For our purposes, one of the most significant facts about the wisdom tradition is that wisdom is rooted in the notion that God created the world, and,
  for this reason, the world has some sense, some order to it.

One of the basic beliefs of the sages is that observations about the world are
not random or haphazard; rather, some logic underlies these observations, a logic
which is discoverable if one is clever enough to figure it out. If something happens one way once, it should happen that way again, and if it doesn't, there should
be some reason for it. In fact, because the world is ordered, reason itself is possible. We might observe that this line of reasoning is the original scientific thinking.

We might indeed call the wisdom literature of the Hebrew scriptures the original science so long as we are careful to note that it is also poetry, art. A conviction runs through this original science that the most accurate observations are artistic, subtle, and thus more true to life. They are also moral. And this is a crucial point. Science and art and ethics are married. An observation cannot be true if it is not also just and good.

Note that, at this basic level, science and the Bible are not in conflict. Scripture invites us, in fact, instructs us to use reason and the power of observation. But note also that this biblical science brings with it a critique of modern science. It says two important things: 1) We can't know everything; humans have limits; and 2) facts and values cannot be split, cannot be separated one from the other. Ethics is a crucial part of truth. Think about the implications of this for eco-justice ethics.

As we converse with the world and use our modern technologies and sciences, they become true *only* when they are also good and beautiful. Such thinking leads very naturally into such ethical principles as sustainability and sufficiency and weds those principles to proper and the only true scientific observations.

But the links between wisdom and creation do not stop here. In Proverbs 8, Woman Wisdom, who was present at creation and is intimately linked with the continuing order of creation, calls to humanity and invites us to live our lives, both individually and societally, in accordance with the cosmic harmony and divine intention of creation. That is, in Proverbs we are invited to live wisely and to align ourselves with the very wisdom with which God created the world in order that it might go well with us and with the world.

The final aspect of scripture I want to offer as a biblical basis for eco-justice is that promise and hope which is given to us throughout the biblical witness. The human role in and with the natural world is, for Christians (and people of the other Abrahamic faiths), always understood in the context of salvation, promise, and hope. I claim that the promise is already present in the beginning of creation. Psalm 24 and many other psalms proclaim that the Lord is our Creator, not any old god. And because the Lord, the God of Israel, the God incarnate in Christ Jesus, is the Creator, therefore the created world reflects God's character rooted in justice and mercy.

Take a look at Psalm 33:

> For the word of the LORD is upright;
> and all his work is done in faithfulness.
> He loves righteousness and justice;
> the earth is full of the steadfast love of the LORD.
> By the word of the LORD the heavens were made,
> and all their host by the breath of his mouth (vv. 4-6).

Further, because our God is an incarnational God, who came in human form and uses the bread and the wine and water, our very humanity carries in it the promise of God. Incarnation is a sign that God works in and through God's creatures. To be open to the promise is to be willing to be used as God's instruments of promise by living up to our tasks and becoming bearers of God's grace to the world.

Finally, we have also seen that not only is promise inherent in the creation, so also creation is present in the promise. The world is included in the promise as with Noah, and the world stands as a sign of the promise as in the covenant in Jeremiah 31. I would go one step further. The promise in Christ is for the whole creation. Listen to what Paul says:

> The creation waits with eager longing for the revealing of the children of God; for the creation was subjected to futility, not of its own will but by the will of the one who subjected it, in hope that the creation itself will be set free from its bondage to decay and will obtain the freedom of the glory of the children of God.
>
> We know that the whole creation has been groaning in travail until now; and not only the creation, but we ourselves, who have the first fruits of the Spirit, groan inwardly while we wait for adoption, the redemption of our bodies. For in hope we were saved (Rom 8:19-24).

Humanity, together with all creation, stands under the promise of redemption in Christ. *This promise is not a promise which absolves us of responsibility; rather, this promise undergirds the very hope which makes responsible living possible.* We become, in the words of Zechariah, "prisoners of hope," rather than prisoners of despair.

All of the ideas I've alluded to are firmly rooted in the biblical tradition. Each is a potentially important starting place for a theologically motivated ethic of ecological integrity linked with social justice. Each offers a different perspective to engage our imaginations for the task ahead, and all can help us in our churches and communities as we consider our stance toward the environmental challenge and the bases for action together that would serve eco-justice. To sum up:

1. All creation is good, and all creatures and all parts of creation are children of God (Gn 1:12, 18, 21, 25, 31; Gn 2:7; Ps 104; Jb 38-41).
2. We are all created in the image of God, and our job is dominion over all of creation (Gn 1:26-30; Ps 8).
   a. God's way of ruling (Ps 97:1-2; Ps 99:4; Ps 89).
   b. Dominion as service (Deutero-Isaiah; gospels; Genesis 2).
3. All humanity and all creation are invited to partake in the Divine Sabbath and the Jubilee (Gn 1-2; Ex 20:8-10; Lv 25).
4. God has made a covenant with humanity and with all creation (Gn 8; Hos 2; Jer 31; Dt 4:26; 30:19; 31:28; Jer 4:23-26).
5. Wisdom invites us to live our lives in accordance with the divine plan and intention for creation (Prv 8).
6. Our role in and with the natural world is understood in the context of salvation, promise, and hope (Ps 24, 33; Rom 8; Zech 9:11-12).

4

Jewish Theology
and the Environmental Crisis

EILON SCHWARTZ

There has been noticeably little response from within the Jewish community to the environmental crisis. Although organizationally there have been some preliminary attempts to place it on the agenda of Jewish community life—notably by Shamrei Adama: Keepers of the Earth and Shalom Center, both in Philadelphia, and Hadassah—by and large it has remained a peripheral issue to what are perceived to be the more pressing concerns of the community. The Jewish academic community is no different in this regard. Theologians and philosophers have mostly ignored the environmental challenge. Such a lack of response is, in itself, indicative of certain tendencies within the Jewish community. Addressing environmental issues, or any other issues of applied ethics beyond the immediate community, might seem frivolous at a time when studies show the very survival of the Jewish community seems to be in jeopardy (see Commission on Jewish Education 1991). The environmental movement has been viewed as particularly problematic in that nature has sometimes been linked with paganism, and thus a theological taboo.

Among present trends in Jewish theology, especially in the "liberal" denominations, has been a renewed interest in "God-talk," that is, readdressing the individual religious experience and the idea of personal and communal revelation. Such a trend makes sense at a time of restating the meaning of Jewish survival and searching to reconnect with the basic meanings of Jewish existence. It also makes sense at a time when post-modernism has refocused our attention on the very legitimacy of textual interpretation, which is the manner in which revelation has been traditionally understood in Judaism. God-talk can lead to discussion of the theological implications of the environmental crisis, as well, by motivating a renewed understanding of God as Creator and nature as Creation. Such a discussion can, in fact, be an important tool in addressing the community's fear of losing Jews to assimilation, as it bridges the often perceived gap between the tradition and the issues which most affect people's lives. It has, however, appeared as only a minor theme in many of these works (see Borowitz 1991; Green 1992; Plaskow 1990).

53

An important exception to such a relatively sparse picture has been the initiative of the Coalition on the Environment in Jewish Life. This coalition, which coordinates activities about the environment among all four major Jewish denominations in the United States, recently held a conference whose professed aim was to place the environment on the Jewish agenda. The reaction among participating theologians and philosophers was encouraging. Whether such interest and concern will be translated into serious writings is yet to be determined.

Perspectives on the Environment

Much of what has been written about Judaism and the environment can be largely viewed as a response to Lynn White's attack on the Judeo-Christian ethic whose biblical injunction to "fill the earth and master it" was seen to be the theological and ethical source for an anthropocentric and ultimately exploitative relationship to the natural world (White 1967; Cohen 1990). Articles came to defend the tradition, often by presenting Judaism's environmental credentials in the growing cultural debate (see Swetlitz 1990; Artson 1991). Although these articles presented a variety of claims as to the Jewish perspective on the environment, they can all be understood in the context of exploring the Jewish relationship with paganism, which I contend still informs much of the Jewish discussion around nature.

Judaism is a reaction to paganism which is linked to nature. So goes the conventional wisdom. This relatively unexamined tenet of Jewish thought maintains that Judaism came about as a radical distancing of the Holy from immanence within the world (see Kaufman 1960, 1-148). In this account, idolatry is defined theologically as viewing God as being contained within the material world, whereas Judaism came to assert the transcendental, wholly-other nature of the Holy. Paganism, both in its biblical and Hellenistic manifestations, conventionally is understood as believing God to be contained within nature. Jewish monotheism distanced the Holy from paganism and its concept of nature.

Such a presentation of the Jewish relationship to nature by way of its polemic against pagan idolatry suggests an antagonism to nature, and an acute theological affinity between paganism and nature. Indeed, the modern environmental movement is filled with writings which have picked up on such a reading, calling for a rejection of monotheistic approaches to the world and a rebirth of paganism.[1] This reassertion of pagan theologies, customs, and language understands paganism as a worldview which sees nature as Holy. Eastern religions are often included in the list of religions of nature, as well, with the many significant theological and cultural differences between the various historical cultures glossed over.[2] These are juxtaposed with an archetypal monotheism which sees God as transcendent of nature, apart from her. The operative conclusions are clear: paganism, seeing nature as sacred, respects the natural world; monotheism, desanctifying nature, abuses it. The rebirth of paganism is a call for the assertion of the natural over the supernatural, Mother Earth over Father King, holistic nature over the hierarchical dichotomy of heaven and earth.

Aharon Lichtenstein, an Israeli Orthodox theologian, in his writing about Judaism's approach to nature, accepts this typology, as well. While not reaching the operative conclusion that Judaism abuses nature while paganism respects it, he certainly accepts the theological distinction of monotheism seeing God apart from nature, and more important, the linking of paganism with present environmentalism. Much of the environmental movement, viewing nature as Holy, Lichtenstein indeed holds to be idolatrous. And while there might be some practical commonality in action conceivable for a time between the two in order to respond to the practical manifestations of the environmental crisis, the theological (and what may be assumed, moral) gulf between them is no different than that between Judaism and Greek-Roman paganism (Lichtenstein 1971).

Everett Gendler, a Reconstructionist theologian, can be seen as representing the other end of the continuum of modern Jewish responses to the "pagan" critique by the environmental movement. Gendler holds that there is a latent nature tradition within Judaism, a tradition suppressed due to the ancient polemic with paganism, exile from the land of Israel, and subsequent historical forces. Gendler sees this tradition expressing itself in the nature motifs of Jewish festivals, in female rituals surrounding the blessing of the new moon, and in the reassertion of connection to nature in the Zionist movement. Judaism has spiritually suffered due to its exile from the natural world; it is time to reassert the role of nature in our understanding of the human spirit (Gendler 1971).

Gendler is, in effect, asserting a place for an immanental religious tradition within Judaism. Both he and Lichtenstein accept the idea that a relationship with the natural world has tremendous implications for the life of the spirit: Lichtenstein holds Jewish religious life to be transcendental and apart from the natural world, while Gendler believes Jewish religious life has always had a place for a complementary models[3] of spirituality contained within the relationship of the Jew to the natural world.

A Historical Debate

Lamm, an Orthodox theologian, elaborates on the content of our continuum by presenting a range of authentic Jewish relationships to nature whose poles he defines by the Hasidic/Mitnagdim controversy (Lamm 1972a). Hasidut, while "utterly different" from pagan thought, nevertheless also had manifestations which affirmed the holiness of nature. Such views, most pronounced in Beshtian Hasidism, the original strand of Hasidism espoused by the Baal Shem Tov (Besht), but present throughout the Kabbalistic tradition, held that the spirit of the Creator is immanent in the Creation, and thus God can be approached through the natural world. While this is different from saying that God *is* the natural world—which would be a pantheistic/paganistic approach—it does suggest eliminating the hierarchical differences between sacred and profane and recognizing the theological possibility of the sacred in the profane. From here it is a short distance to antinomian beliefs and behavior, seeing Holiness in the most profane of actions. Nevertheless, Hasidut remained safely within the Halachic structure, perhaps partially because of realizing the dangerous antinomian tendencies inherent in such belief.

The Mitnagdic school of the Vilna Gaon, also rooted in the Kabbalist tradition, believed that Hasidut had indeed begun to cross outside of the normative Halachic framework, following the implications of their belief system. The Mitnagdim re-emphasized the transcendence of God from the point of view of the human being, and separated holiness from the world, "allowing for the exploitation of nature by science and technology" (Lamm 1972a, 177). Halacha, on this side of the pole, acts to prevent ecological abuse in a philosophical system which otherwise legitimates it. In short, the Hasidic tradition came dangerously close to turning the world into the sacred, the Mitnagdim dangerously close to removing Divine presence from the world.

For Lamm, there is a dynamic tension between the two approaches: created in God's image, the human being is both part of the natural world but also transcends it. Living with the paradox of the two approaches, without compromising either, is what it means to be human. Extrapolating from such a view, paganism and its environmental supporters err on the side of the natural in the human, modern Western culture on the side of the transcendent. Judaism has traditionally offered a plurality of approaches, some flirting dangerously close to the extremes, but with safeguards to ensure remaining within acceptable boundaries. Gendler, using Lamm's terminology, represents the Hasidic tradition; Lichtenstein, the Mitnagdic tradition.

Lamm never addresses the question of where Judaism's modern variations stand on his continuum, perhaps suggesting that such a creative tension continues to exist between various modern Jewish approaches. Schorsch, a Conservative theologian presently chancellor of the movement's theological seminary, contends that, in response to intellectual currents in the larger cultural setting, modern Judaism was pushed beyond Lamm's Mitnagdic pole:

> We must dare to reexamine our longstanding preference for history over nature. The celebration of "historical monotheism" is a legacy of nineteenth-century Christian-Jewish polemics, a fierce attempt by Jewish thinkers to distance Judaism from the world of paganism. But the disclaimer has its downside by casting Judaism into an adversarial relationship with the natural world. Nature is faulted for the primitiveness and decadence of pagan religion, and the modern Jew is saddled with a reading of his tradition that is one-dimensional. Judaism has been made to dull our sensitivity to the awe inspiring power of nature. Preoccupied with the ghosts of paganism, it appears indifferent and unresponsive to the supreme challenge of our age: man's degradation of the environment. Our planet is under siege and we as Jews are transfixed in silence (Schorsch 1991).

For Schorsch, modern Jewish historians projected a distance between Judaism and the pagan world, a distance which is overstated because of their historiographical biases. This modern version of a "one-dimensional" Judaism is a distortion of the reality of pre-modern Jewish thought and life.

Time's Arrows, Time's Cycles

The Jewish polemic against paganism was not only a theological one; as Schorsch implies, it was primarily a moral one. The theological conflict had deep moral implications. Nature worship was seen not simply as a theological/philosophical mistake, but a worldview with deep immoral consequences. The pagan and monotheism debate is a debate about morality. And Schorsch's corrective of not blaming nature for pagan excesses notwithstanding, it seems essential to explore what the moral conflict was while we are renegotiating our relationship with the natural world.

Mircea Eliade offers a helpful distinction between historical religion's and nature religion's different notions of time (Eliade 1959). Eliade maintains that religions focusing on history have a linear view of time, those focusing on nature, a cyclical view—what Stephen Jay Gould calls time's arrows and cycles (Gould 1988). Eliade holds that Judaism was responsible for contributing a linear sense of history to the world, that is, a progressive sense of history (Eliade 1959, 104). While offering a possibility of change to history, in fact while creating the very possibility for history, when not counterbalanced with the repetition of time, such a perspective can lead to history without a sense of purpose. So Eliade sees our modern period (Eliade 1959, 151). Linear history, with its beginning and end, needs to be understood in terms of cyclical history, with its transcendent and repeating truths. Or in Jewish terms, the march forward of Egypt to Sinai to Zion must be understood in terms of our continual return to Egypt, Sinai, and Zion in each generation. Time has both its arrows and cycles.

While Eliade believes that the modern period lives in the moral danger of losing sight of the purpose of history through losing a sense of time's cycles, the moral critique works in the other direction, as well. An overemphasis on time's cycles can lead to a history without change. Time is understood cyclically in terms of the sun rising and setting and seasons revolving, making change seem illusory. Time stands still. A sense of history demands that human beings break out of the cycle, and accept responsibility for a history that can move forward, and backward. Time's cycle is connected with what is; time's arrows with what can be. Focusing on a religion of nature, one focuses on the cyclical nature of time. A religion of history offers the moral responsibility that is the meaning of its arrows. While Eliade holds that arrows without cycles leads to a history without meaning, an emphasis on arrows has often been understood to mean an emphasis on human responsibility.

Schwartzchild (1984) understands the pagan-Jewish debate as exactly one of differing views of nature coupled with different views of morality. Nature represents what is. Morality is born in the question of what ought to be. Judaism is profoundly at odds with the natural world, a world which functions according to certain laws to which history is then subjected. Judaism sees the human being as transcending those laws, with the power to impose a moral order on an otherwise amoral reality. Through human reason, that which makes the human "in the image of God," moral thought can impose its order on the natural disorder, completing the process of creation. In Midrash Tanhuma, Parshat Tizroah, there is, for example, the exchange between the Roman General Turnisrufus and Rabbi Akiva. When asked whether God's creation or human creation is superior, Akiva anticipates the challenge to the Jewish practice of circumcision, and argues for the superiority of human action, in that they complete the unfinished work of creation. Thus even the human body, perfect in Greek-Roman aesthetic perception, is born imperfect, so that the Jew through mitzvot can participate in the act of creation. Schwartzchild recognizes that the tradition is not monolithic in this regard. The "heretical, quasi-pantheistic tendency" found expression in medieval Kabbalah, Hasidut, and modern Zionism (see Tschernichovsky 1968, 97-98, 36-41, 41-52). However, such a stream remained tangential, contrary to the traditional Jewish perspective on nature.

Wyschogrod, an Orthodox theologian, follows Schwartzchild's argument (1992, 6-7). The heart of the pagan-Jewish controversy is the moral question of whether what is, should be. And Wyschogrod, like Schwartzchild, sees the modern environmental movement as resurrecting the pagan notion of morality being equated with the world as it is. While there are certainly many environmentalists who understand the need for change in anthropocentric terms—the need to protect our health and the earth's resources for future generations—"deep" environmentalists subscribe to what Wyschogrod calls "the higher ecology," an environmentalism which attempts to shift our culture from an anthropocentric to a geo/biocentric worldview.

Wyschogrod contends that Adolf Hitler and the Nazi movement were deeply influenced by such a perspective (see Pois 1986). Borrowing heavily from Nietzsche, Hitler believed that nature teaches us the basic laws of morality: that the strong kill the weak and through such a process, nature moves forward. Wyschogrod writes:

> Evolutionary morality is the right of the stronger to destroy the weaker. Nature wants the weak to perish. The weak contribute to the march of evolution by perishing; and when they refuse to perish, then the weaker have triumphed over the stronger (Wyschogrod 1992, 7).

Judaism (and Christianity)[4] interferes with the natural order by letting the weak survive. A morality which changes the natural order prevents nature from taking its rightful course. Such a perspective on morality Wyschogrod sees shared by Plato, as well. In his ideal state, modeled after an organism, there is no place for protection of the weak. Imperfectly born infants are to be disposed of.

Of course, attempting to understand morality as an outgrowth of the natural order does not necessarily demand understanding morality as "survival of the fittest." Nature's lessons were interpreted in radically different ways by its social Darwinist interpreters (see La Vergata 1985, 958-62; Young 1985). But, regardless of the particular interpretation of nature's morality, there is a categorical difference between a morality based on the natural order, however that natural order is understood, and a morality based on values whose source is outside of materialist understandings of the world. And in the confrontation between the morality of the world as it is and the world as it should be, both Wyschogrod and Schwartzchild understand Judaism as the flagship of a morality which imposes itself on the natural order.

Yet, in spite of his antagonism for such a higher ecology, Wyschogrod accepts that the moral philosophy of Judaism, which demanded the desacralization of nature, has contributed to the destruction of nature. Returning to a religion of nature is profoundly dangerous, yet, given that, a reconsideration of the human interconnection with the natural is demanded by the ecological crisis.

The response to such a morality of nature need not be a denial of the place of the natural within Jewish worldviews. Ehrenfeld and Bentley (1986), for example, while understanding Judaism as having a strong anthropocentric component, maintain that the great chain of being does not place man at the pinnacle, but rather God. The human place in the God-given scheme of things is caring for God's creation, the role of steward. It is the secularization of the world, the removal of God from the hierarchy and placing the human being at its pinnacle, which results in what Ehrenfeld calls "the arrogance of humanism" (1981). The stewardship argument is heard often in the environmental ethic debate, changing the perspective from anthropocentric to theocentric (Wendell Berry 1981, 267-81). Negotiating the middle ground between an anthropocentric and biocentric view of the world, through the manifold possibilities of theocentric perspectives strikes me as fertile ground for continued contemplation.

It should be clear from the survey undertaken that the dialogue within the Jewish community about the environment is only beginning. Two books are presently being assembled which contain in them a number of fine articles on theological perspectives in Jewish environmental ethics, articles which will hopefully further the dialogue within the tradition on theological perspectives on the environmental crisis (Waskow and Elon 1995; Bernstein, forthcoming). What follows is a number of topics I believe need to be addressed—some already suggested in the works previously surveyed, others not yet discussed—in order that the Jewish discussion about nature and the environment can be explored in its complexity.

An Agenda

A. Before addressing the particulars of a Jewish approach, or more appropriately, Jewish approaches, to nature and the environmental crisis, it is first necessary to establish the framework in which such a discussion can take place. Just how does one determine what constitutes an authentically Jewish approach to the environment? Judaism, as a text-centered religion, turns to its texts in order to interpret its meanings and relevance. But how is one to know whether one's interpretation is a correct one?

Too often, as has been noted, interpretations of Jewish attitudes digress into apologetics, in which contemporary attitudes of the larger culture shape the way the past is understood. When rationalism was the cultural paradigm, Judaism was understood as a rationalist religion. Now that environmentalism is gaining cultural clout, Judaism is interpreted as "green." Any discussion about Jewish ethics is predicated on the ability to present an interpretive theory of texts which is defendable. In other words, a precondition to any discussion of Jewish ethics, Jewish environmental ethics included, is a defense of the epistemology used to interpret texts. Without establishing the possibility of legitimate interpretation, there can be no serious exegetical process.

While addressing textual interpretation, the possibility of translating traditional culture into modern contexts needs to be explicitly addressed. Successful "translation" from one culture into another, establishing the relevance of traditional culture without sacrificing its authenticity, is a precondition to a meaningful discussion of Jewish attitudes toward nature and the environment.

B. The central theological challenge which emerges from the nascent discussion about Judaism and nature previously surveyed has been to describe the intricate link between human beings and the rest of nature, and its implications for a spiritual understanding of the human condition. From what has been written so far, Jewish attitudes are described as being distributed between two poles. The first, perhaps the dominant, pole holds that the human being is unique in the creation and is its very purpose. This has been the pole often latched onto and criticized by the detractors of the Judeo-Christian ethic. The second pole views all of nature, humans included, as God's creation, and thus containing sparks of the Divine. The first maintains a strong body/soul dichotomy, in which the human being is seen as unique in the creation by virtue of his or her distinctive intelligence/rationality/soul. Such characteristics have made the human being "a little lower than the angels." The second maintains a far less dramatic dichotomy, either suggesting that all of nature contains some degree of spirit as well as material existence, or that such a distinction doesn't really exist. The first holds that morality exists apart from the material. The second suggests that morality is rooted in the natural order of things.

Jewish thinkers have pointed out the danger of seeing nature as holy, but the environmental crisis is testimony to the dangers of a desacralized material world. Abandoning the poles, and exploring the meaning of a material world given spiritual significance without reducing the spiritual world to a natural determinism is a prime challenge for Jewish theologians interested in addressing the environmental crisis (Boyarin 1993). As environmental ethics continues to flirt with a natural determinism similar to the one Wyschogrod describes, the middle ground becomes an area of exploration important not only for Jewish thought, but for the environmental movement, as well.[5] Because of the acute Jewish sensitivity to the link between questions of morality and nature religion, it is the place where Jewish thought could have the most meaningful contribution to environmental ethics.

C. The Darwinian revolution challenged certain traditional notions of human uniqueness in the creation. Interestingly, such a challenge has never been properly recognized by Jewish theology. Unlike Christianity, which is still filled with debate on how to digest Darwin, Judaism basically accepted a sort of de facto truce with science in general and evolution in particular, accepting the Humean distinction between is and ought as the divide between science and religion.

Science however, has traveled quite a distance since the Rationalist days and its positivist inheritors. Historians of science have effectively undermined the myth of an objective science, and it is time for Jewish theologians to readdress its relationship with the new science. The discussion around Judaism and the environmental crisis needs to take place in conjunction with another discussion about Judaism and science. The conventional understanding of Darwin has been essentially a materialist one, offering an alternative description of creation to the popularized religious one.[6] The time has come to reemerge from the imagined safety of divisions of territory between is and ought, which degenerated all too easily into true and false, and readdress our understandings of the world as both religiously and scientifically sophisticated thinkers. The outcome could be quite rewarding.

D. As has been mentioned, ecofeminism has reexamined pagan imagery appreciatively for its environmental significance. The feminist movement in Jewish theology should pay closer attention to the implications of its critique of mainstream Jewish culture for an understanding of an alternative relationship with the natural world. While a Jewish feminism need not of necessity converge with ecofeminism, the fact that others have linked the two demands at least an informed consideration of the link. Feminist readings of the tradition could very well contribute the most substantial discourse to the renewed discussion on paganism, nature, and Judaism, challenging both conventional readings of the tradition, and contemporary neopagan feminist beliefs.

E. The connection of Jews to Zion has been the major metaphor in Jewish understandings of the relationship of culture to place. Zionism has offered the possibility of readdressing the spiritual dimension of the idea of home and the connection to a particular landscape. It is interesting to mention again that some of the language used to describe this renewed relationship was purposely pagan. Such a connection has had a political dimension, as well, as the land of Israel has fostered a relationship with many different cultures. Both Zionist and Arab history, as well as contemporary cultural attitudes, offer fertile ground for exploring diverse models of connection to place, and their often differing political consequences.

Paradoxically, the return of the Jewish people to its homeland and the return to a concrete relationship with a particular place has created a dilemma for diaspora Jews. As the environmental movement has brought recognition to the importance of place for spiritual richness, and as Zionism has renewed the Jewish connection to place, Jews of the diaspora are caught in a dual loyalty between their metaphoric connection to their promised land and their very real connection to the landscapes of their homes. Whether a connection to Zion is at the expense of a spirituality of place, or whether a spirituality of place is at the expense of a connection with Israel is an important issue which emerges from environmental perspectives.

Three Spheres of Discourse

Franz Rosenzweig claimed that there are three spheres of Jewish theological discourse which interact with one another: creation, revelation, and redemption. Michael Rosenak, a philosopher of Jewish education in Israel, has argued that theologies which emphasize creation focus on the miraculous nature of the world, our sense of "radical amazement" in confronting its awesomeness, the ultimate goodness of the world which is often hidden from our imperfect senses, and our consequent respect for God's creation. A theology of revelation, on the other hand, emphasizing the dialogue between God and human being, rooted for the

Jewish people in the experience of Sinai and manifested in the Halakhah, demands learning God's ways through God's words. The unfathomable gap between God and human being is inexplicably bridged through the gift of Torah. Revelation allows the potentially suffering soul to transcend the vanity of existence and to realize meaning in an otherwise meaningless world (Rosenak 1992). Much of the modern period has focused on a theology of redemption—of the three theological emphases the most secularized and therefore the most congenial to the modern cultural paradigm.

The environmental movement is, among its other agenda, a call for the reassertion of the Rosenzweigian category of creation in theological discussion. A theological response to the environmental crisis means readdressing creation theology. Indeed, those Jewish theologians who have addressed the environmental crisis have done so often from within the framework of creation theology (for example, see Green 1992). But, while it is necessary to articulate a creation theology in response to the environmental crisis, it is no less important to articulate a theology which is aware of the dynamic between the three theological poles of Jewish existence. While articulating a theology of creation, care must be taken to affirm the importance of the other two poles within the larger theological discourse. Only then will Jewish perspectives toward the environmental crisis be articulated so as to transcend apologetics, and to make the creative dynamics of Jewish theology relevant to the most profound crisis of our time.

Notes

1. Lynn White sees paganism as the alter–ego to the Judeo–Christian theologically sanctioned exploitation of nature (White 1967, 1205); some ecofeminists have called for a renewal of pagan customs of May Day, celebrations of the moon, witchcraft (see, for example, Starhawk 1990); one of the more radical biological theories of our day holds that the earth is a living organism, and has named her Gaia, the name of the Greek earth goddess (see Lovelock 1990).

2. Note that both monotheism *and* paganism have been stereotyped for the purpose of the polemic. The pagan debate with early Christianity, for example, argues that Christianity is flawed for being a religion of the material body, and that paganism is purely of the spirit. This is obviously a very different paganism than that stereotyped above.

3. The idea of complementary models, mutually exclusive models which describe parts of the same reality, was originally presented by Niels Bohr. For a discussion of Bohr's theory and its implications for religious thought, see Ian Barbour, *Myths, Models and Paradigms: A Comparative Study in Science and Religion* (San Francisco, Harper & Row, 1974), pp. 71-92.

4. Wyschogrod and Schwartzchild differ in their evaluation of Christianity's position on morality and nature. Wyschogrod sees Christianity as a partner in the Jewish polemic against a nature morality. Schwartzchild believes that Christianity is to be found on the pagan end of the moral divide.

5. Parts of the deep ecology movement, notably the Earth First! movement, have expressed what Schwartzchild's and Wyschogrod's interpretation would suggest:

Some Earth First!ers, who are supposedly motivated by deep ecological ideals, proposed Draconian birth control measures, spoke approvingly of AIDS as a self-protective reaction of Gaia against an over-populating humanity, used social

Darwinist metaphors, and displayed apparent racist attitudes. Earth First! co-founder Dave Foreman even stated that humans "are a cancer on nature."

Some advocates of deep ecology have grown alarmed at this social Darwinism in the guise of natural determinism which has emerged in part of the deep ecology movement. Michael Zimmerman, for example, quoted in the above passage, explores the link between Heidegger, his Nazi sympathies, and such tendencies in deep ecology. Heidegger has been portrayed as a forerunner of deep ecology. Zimmerman, by acknowledging the philosophical link between Heidegger and National Socialism, confronts the need to disassociate deep ecology from those philosophical assumptions of Heidegger's thought which lead to sympathy for Nazism (see Zimmerman 1993, 205).

6. Historians of science are rereading Darwin, however, and some are showing that such a materialist reading of Darwin's own understanding of the implications of his work are premature. For an especially suggestive reading of Darwin, which explores the spiritual dimension of his understanding of nature without compromising a materialist reading, see Beer 1985, 543-86.

PART 2

Systematic Theologies
for Earth Community

If humans behave somewhat like hermit crabs by using ideational shells that are both protective and perspective-shaping, then human well-being depends upon avoiding useless shells, and crawling into or stepping out of appropriate shells of belief.

When Jesus looked out over the fields of Galilee, he recalled how "the earth produces of itself" (Mk. 4:28, Greek "spontaneously"). That was an echo of Genesis, in which "a prolific Earth generates teeming life, urged by God. The Spirit of God broods, animating the Earth, and it gives birth. As we would now say, Earth speciates."

This interpretive quotation from Holmes Rolston III, a theologically trained environmental philosopher, reminds us that biology and theology both focus on a fecund earth, and that seemingly "archaic" accounts in the gospels and in the Genesis saga teach a reverence for life more basic than utilitarian logic. Thus, Noah is not told to save just those species that are of "aesthetic, ecological, educational, historical, recreational and scientific value" to people, as in the Endangered Species Act, but to save them all! The point is not simply to conserve global stock. "The Noah story teaches sensitivity to forms of life and the biological and theological forces producing them. What is required is not mere human prudence but principled responsibility to the biospheric Earth—to God."

Systematic theologians here and there are getting the point, and want to correct for the late-modern preoccupation with celebrating "progress" while confessing the "word of God" in merely anthropocentric terms. Otherkind are also included in the near and distant "neighbors" whom God loves and expects us to treat justly.

Ecologically aware theologizing about creation challenges modern atomistic individualism and consumerism that have been so environmentally destructive. It no longer projects a self-contained God, humanity over nature, and a mechanistic attitude toward other being. Instead, ecotheological discourse sees God to be inherently related to—indwelling—the world, breathing spirit into creatures, loving all being.

Part 2 begins with a brief overview by Sallie Noland MacNichol, of key books that systematically illumine ecotheology. They meet a pressing need to do first things over, to reexamine, recycle, and reconstruct various doctrines of Christian faith. MacNichol also discusses several theological dilemmas, such as how to overcome Christianity's habit of splitting time and space, resulting in the nature/ history dichotomy, and how to understand God as both part of and distinct from earth history.

Chapters by Heather Eaton and Catherine Keller explore the recent development of, and current issues in, ecofeminist theologies which unite concerns for ecology and feminism in "a weave of analysis and envisioning." Eaton discusses ecological-feminist theology under six headings: cultural analysis, systematic theological reinterpretation, scriptural motifs, liberationist theology and ethics, multifaith and multidisciplinary perspectives, and spirituality. A crucial criterion she applies to the ecofeminist theological corpus is whether a particular approach can move participants into the work of resistance, revisioning, and reconstruction.

Catherine Keller ponders the consequences of postmodern pluralism, particularly poststructuralist feminist theory, which is so preoccupied with non-essentialist socially constructed worlds that it ignores the ecological base of reality, practically "making earth disappear." She decries "the political indifference of postmodern texts concerning nonhuman beings, . . . systematic silence [or] hostile boredom toward all things non-human."

To challenge oppressive naturalism without walking away from environmental concerns, Keller proposes an alternative, globally aware, theologically articulate appreciation of our natural embeddedness. The final part of her chapter discusses community, commons, common sense, and communion as four basic dimensions of ecofeminist relationism.

The last chapter in this section, by Kosuke Koyama, suggests an environmentally alert agenda to pursue in studying ecumenical (or *oikos*), theology where "God-talk" and "cosmos-talk" meet at "life-talk." The key word in this chapter is *periphery*. "Jesus Christ established his centrality by going to the periphery," a term here given three meanings—biocosmological, ethical, and theological. Since the biosphere is the primary locus of human salvation, periphery theology integrates ecological preservation and social justice, both of which require our "staying in" a blessed relation with the land and the people. Koyama also proposes that "ecological universality is a new critical element that deepens our traditional understanding of the universality of the Christian Gospel."

5

Reclaiming, Revisioning, Recreating in Theo-Ecological Discourse

SALLY NOLAND MacNICHOL

Systematic theology in the nineties wrestles with how to name and respond to bewildering complexities and massive suffering from a wide variety of particular standpoints. Now less concerned with denominational differences, systematic theology these days is born out of broader Christian movements—conservative, orthodox, liberal, and liberation. Gabriel Fackre divides what appears to be a healthy increase in systematic theologies into ecumenical, evangelical and experiential categories (Fackre 1993). However, regardless of classification, which rarely does justice to the multiplicity and complexity of theological perspectives, it is the new breadth of theological voices which has engendered a new depth and vitality in theological thinking. Enriched by the plurality and ambiguity operative within much contemporary Christian thought, and bolstered by the determination to put an end to Christian chauvinism, a number of systematic theologians also explore ways to open meaningful dialogue with other religions. Thus the tensions and challenges, from within and without, move today's systematic theologians to ask how theology can "enable a christian view of the world through lenses of difference, fragmentariness and oppression" while also concerning itself with "the values of solidarity, openness and liberation (Chopp and Fackre 1994, 4).

In the larger arena of theological activity, the direct response to the environmental crisis appears limited, still on the back burner of much current theological discourse and Christian consciousness. However, if the task of systematic theology is indeed the "continual refashioning of Christian teachings in relation to the needs of Christian praxis" (Chopp and Fackre 1994, 3), then the vigor and creativity of a number of these responses have much to contribute to the task of theology as well as to the enriching of theological imagination in general.

Inasmuch as the environmental crisis is "no less than a crisis in human beings themselves" (Moltmann 1985b, 1), it is possible to understand some of the directions and reformulations projected by theologians and theologies of ecology, nature, and creation as part of a larger shift in theology. This shift involves the retrieval, reconstruction, and recreation of various doctrines meant to contribute to reshaping the Christian response to the urgent need for transformation demanded by the rapidly changing nature of our world.

Like all theology, eco-theologies seek to persuade. When we "convert our minds to the earth" (Ruether 1983b, esp. ch. 3), deeply ingrained patterns of theological thought are challenged. Recent works like Jürgen Moltmann's *God in Creation*, Sallie McFague's *Body of God*, Rosemary Radford Ruether's *Gaia and God*, Douglas John Hall's *The Steward*, James Nash's *Loving Nature*, and several important collections of essays like *After Nature's Revolt*, edited by Dieter Hessel, *EcoFeminism and the Sacred*, edited by Carol Adams, and *Liberating Life: Contemporary Approaches to Ecological Theology*, edited by Charles Birch, William Eakin, and Jay B. McDaniel, rejuvenate and refresh musty doctrines and, if seriously attended to, will open theological conversations to new vistas of exploration and praxis.

Theologians addressing the issue enter the conversation at different doctrinal points—creation, the cross, pneumatology, or eschatology—and from a variety of theological perspectives. While there are distinct tensions among these theologians, all are seeking to make sense of the Christian understandings of the relationship among nature, human beings, and God and, in this endeavor, encourage Christians to develop what John Cobb calls "wholistic habits of thought" (Cobb 1992, 25-27) that will empower the struggle for justice, peace, and the integrity of creation (see Niles 1992a and 1992b).

Starting with Lynn White's "The Historical Roots of our Ecologic Crisis" (1967), a significant, if small number of theologians have struggled in various ways with the charge that Christianity is essentially anti nature, and ecologically bankrupt. The fact that many people concerned with environmental issues have turned to other religious traditions and spiritualities to find the intellectual and spiritual resources on which to build new and transformative ecological consciousness and practices has compelled Christian theologians to ask if Christianity has anything to offer the struggle to heal and liberate creation. Theologian Catherine Keller asks:

> Can there be a greening of Christian theology? If so, a new kind of theological self-understanding, one with a method expressive of its content must develop. We need a theological practice of recycling. It will issue from a kind of ecology of discourse. Discerning the toxins at work in Christianity and its cultures allows us, or rather requires us, to break down the elements of Christian hope, to cleanse them where possible of their own patriarchal poisons and late modern capitalist deteriorations. An ecology of discourse requires the recycling of the elements of what we are—as persons grown in a culture replete with Christian influences, however disconnected these influences may be from their healthier contexts and communities of origin. Those of us somehow called or situated to recycle the Christian theological heritage must understand this work and have it understood as a needful and radical contribution to our relevant subcultures, not as some Sunday school nostalgia (Keller 1993, 43).

To Begin Recycling

A good place to start the work of recycling is H. Paul Santmire's historical study, *The Travail of Nature: The Ambiguous Ecological Promise of Christian Theology* (Santmire 1985b; see also 1976, 460-64; and 1970). Here Santmire explores both the problems and promise of the theologies of nature that are actually present in the biblical-classical tradition. Closely scrutinizing the work of Irenaeus, Origen, Augustine, Aquinas, Bonaventure, Dante, St. Francis, Luther, Calvin, Barth, Teilhard de Chardin, and the Bible, Santmire counters both those theologians and critics who assume the tradition has little, if anything, to offer, and those who are overly eager to redeem the tradition. He identifies two theological motifs—the spiritual and the ecological—that, while distinguishable from one another, are intricately intertwined and represent a fundamental tension in Christian faith, especially when we begin to talk about nature.

What Santmire calls the spiritual motif focuses on the relationship between God and the soul, or God and the "elect" and is predicated "on a vision of the human spirit rising above nature in order to ascend to a supramundane communion with God and thenceforth to obey the will of God in the midst of the ambiguities of mundane history" (Santmire 1985b, 9). Within the parameters of this motif, nature is understood as mere backdrop, more or less visible, to the divine-human drama of redemption. Man is front and center. (Woman's location is more complicated.)

The ecological motif proves far more promising as a starting point from which to construct a new theology of nature and is predicated on "a vision of the human spirit's rootedness in the worlds of nature, and on the desire of self-consciously embodied selves to celebrate God's presence in, with, and under the whole biophysical order as the context in which the life of obedience to God is to be pursued."[1] Along with Rosemary Ruether, Matthew Fox, James Nash, and others, Santmire points to the desert Fathers, the Celtic saints, St. Francis, Hildegarde of Bingen and Julian of Norwich, and Eastern Orthodox theology as solid evidence of the power of the ecological motif within Christian tradition and as rich resources for further development (see Joranson and Butigan 1984).

Almost all attempts at ecological theologies and theologies of nature generally rest on and build from the ecological motif which directs theological imagination toward interrelatedness, diversity, inclusivity, embodiment, and wholeness. Most theologians and ethicists find putting the primary and sole blame for the ecological crisis on Christianity far too simple an explanation. Yet most attempt to find the places where Christian doctrine has led us so drastically astray—the otherness and self-transcendence of God, the anthropocentrism of the doctrine of humanity, the hierarchical order of creation, the overemphasis on time and human history, as well as the prominence of eschatological visions which exclude nature.

A significant part of the response centers on the reclamation and revisioning of the Bible. In *Loving Nature: Ecological Integrity and Christian Responsibility*, ethicist James Nash, speaking out of the liberal tradition of reform and pragmatism, counters White's arguments by defending the biblical tradition and arguing that it already contains everything it needs to construct an ecological ethic of responsibility. The development of a genuinely ecological theology, he contends, requires nothing new or radical, but "reinterpretations, extensions, and revisions" of Christianity's main theological themes, particularly the Christian tradition of love and justice (Nash 1991, 94). Starting with the fundamental presupposition that ecological problems are moral problems, Nash's method turns on extending ethical and theological concepts pertaining to humanity and human social relations to the entire creation, that is, the "global biosphere" (Spencer 1994, 58). Thus, for example to love one's neighbor is to love other human beings and otherkind and the earth. Like most ecologically directed theologies, sin in *Loving Nature* is understood as the degradation of the earth, and final redemption includes all creation. Nash calls Christians to love nature (but not at the expense of human beings), act politically, and argues that the church has a moral obligation to participate in the struggle for ecological justice and liberation.

In response to heavy criticism leveled at Christian anthropocentrism, attempts made to reinterpret, reimage, and reconstruct understandings of humanity's relationship to nature often center on the fresh explorations of the biblical image of stewardship. In *The Steward: A Biblical Image Come to Age*, Canadian theologian Douglas John Hall argues that the steward is one of the most "provocative and accessible concepts" that Christians and non-Christians have to work with as we go about the business of reinventing ourselves and our responsibilities in the face of ecologic disaster (Hall 1982, 9). Directing his arguments primarily to the North American Protestant mainline churches, Hall affirms the biblical notion of humanity's vocation as God's covenant partner whose role as God's representative is contingent on proper obedience to God and not an occasion to act as Lord and master. Here Hall adds a christological dimension and grounds his theology of stewardship in the gospel of the cross.

An Ecological Model of God

Since Christians believe that human beings are made in the image of God, who we think God is has profound consequences for Christian anthropology. In *The Body of God* Sallie McFague argues vehemently against the triumphalist images of God that pervade Christian tradition, noting that while they may have made sense in the past, they are now totally inappropriate, if not harmful. A monarchical God who rules from a distance, controlling the world through domination and benevolence, supports anthropocentrism and androcentrism as well as promoting both human passivity and social models of domination and submission. Furthermore, this model focuses exclusively on divine-human relations leaving the rest of creation as all but invisible.

McFague offers an ecological model of God that is both "organic and agential" (McFague 1993, 139-41), drawing on a new "picture" of the world provided by contemporary scientific theories emerging from cosmology, astrophysics, and biology. This new picture or creation story, as she calls it, sobers our anthropocentrism. Yet it diminishes neither humanity nor God. "Human beings are decentered as the point and goal of creation and recentered as partners in its continuing creation. God has been decentered as king of human beings and recentered as the source, power and goal of the fifteen-billion-year history of the universe" (McFague 1993b, 94). McFague asks us to think of the universe as God's body, the visible sacrament of the invisible God. For McFague, this way of thinking about the divine makes more sense in terms of postmodern science and focuses understanding of divine action "on empowerment, not direction" (McFague 1993, 148).

In this cosmocentric view God empowers us to take responsibility for our place in creation as neither superior nor inferior to the plants and animals and stars who are in fact our brothers, sisters, and cousins. Sin resides in our denying the reality of interdependence through greed and exploitation.

The profound immanence of God in McFague's model is a central and persistent issue in almost all theo-ecological discourse. The thought of process theologians and their precursor Alfred N. Whitehead is characterized by its panentheism—the idea that everything is in some way manifesting God, that the divine is in some way present in everything. In much the same way that McFague understands God as the Empowering One, process theologians, such as John Cobb, envision God as one who persuades and influences rather than compels. Many ecologically oriented theologians build on process theology's understanding that the processes of creation and redemption are the seamless web of God's unceasing activity (see Cobb, Loomer, Bonifazi in Joranson and Butigan 1984).

The work of Matthew Fox, a thoroughgoing panentheist himself, concentrates on the development of a "creation spirituality" by unearthing and recovering the creation-centered theologies of neglected theologians and mystics, and lifting up motifs found in feminist, liberation, and Eastern theologies (Fox 1988 and 1983). Consonant with a number of other ecological theologians, Fox starts from the idea that human beings are co-creators and the cosmos a divine work of art. Fox contends that theology that has dominated Western Christianity since Augustine, what he calls "fall/redemption" theology, is dualistic, patriarchal, anti-nature, and contrary to the human creativity and responsibility needed for justice-making. Creation and salvation cannot be separated, and redemption includes the entire creation. While some find Fox's enthusiastic affirmation of human creativity refreshing and empowering, others point to the need for a more developed doctrine of sin.

The trinitarian and messianic creation theology of Jürgen Moltmann likewise emphasizes God's immanence and lifts up notions of radical interdependence, participation, and interpenetration. Moltmann's cosmological theocentrism sees the sabbath, not human beings, as the crown of creation. Like McFague, Moltmann wants to understand humanity within the context of evolutionary history. Although human beings are the stewards of creation and as *imago dei* represent God's glory, they do so only as "creatures in the fellowship of creation (Moltmann 1985b, 86). *Imago dei* is also the *imago mundi*.

Ecofeminist thought plays out the themes of interdependence, immanence, the sacrality of nature, and the ethics of care for the creation in widely diverse ways. Yet common to all ecofeminist theologians is the argument that the connections between the oppression of women and the rest of nature must be recognized and analyzed if either is to be understood adequately (see Diamond and Orenstein 1990; Plant 1989; Adams 1993; for a critique, see Biehl 1991). Some ecofeminist theology and theory, though not all of it, expands this connection between the destruction of the biotic community and the oppression of women to include all structures of domination that engender destructive relations, not only between men and women, but between ruling and subjugated groups, between races and classes, and so on.

Feminist theologian Rosemary Ruether, in particular, has developed this view in a number of different works (Ruether 1992; 1983b; 1981, 57-70). *Gaia and God*, while highly critical of Christianity and the streams of thought and myths of creation and destruction that have fed it (Babylonian, Hebrew, Greek and Gnostic), claims that the reexamination of the traditions of covenant and sacrament are keys to healing the earth. Her reading of the Hebraic and Christian covenantal tradition draws out the reality of kingdom building as inclusive of justice and right relation not only between peoples but between people and the earth. Ruether contends that nature cannot be separated from history, that it is only "fallen" by virtue of the fact that it is "marred and distorted by human misdevelopment" (Ruether 1983b, 91) and "suffers along with humanity in the ups and downs of relationship with God" (ibid., 78).

Like aspects of Fox, Teilhard de Chardin, process theologians, McFague, and other ecofeminists, Ruether attempts to illuminate and expand submerged aspects of the sacramental tradition (which she understands as being complementary to the covenantal). In search of a more holistic Christian vision of creation, Ruether wants to resurrect the once lively tradition of the cosmic Christ as both Creator and Redeemer. Ruether is critical of the ecofeminist tendency to romanticize and mythologize matriarchal neolithic cultures, and her critique, unlike a number of ecofeminist theorists, is grounded in history and global realities. Ruether maintains that no one culture or religion can provide all the answers and understands "Christianity's syncretistic ability to synthesize diverse elements . . . as a strength to be built on to provide the creativity needed to address today's eco-spiritual crisis" (Spencer 1994, 163).

Most theologians mentioned above seek to find ways in which theology can authentically be in dialogue with contemporary scientific knowledge. Protestant theologians Wolfhart Pannenberg and Langdon Gilkey have engaged in extensive conversation between theology and science. Pannenberg's 1993 collection of previously published essays on theology and science, *Towards a Theology of Nature: Essays on Science and Faith* (1993), challenges both theology and science to reach for new levels of interchange with and accountability to one another. If we understand the world we live in as "a creature of a creating God" and theology as a "field-encompassing field" which incorporates the scientific domain, then a more adequate theology of nature will be possible. Gilkey's *Nature, Reality, and the Sacred: The Nexus of Science and Religion* critiques scientific knowledge and religious (particularly "primal" religions) apprehensions of nature and argues that neither by itself can move us to the deeper understanding of nature now mandatory if we are to confront the ecological crisis intelligently (Gilkey 1993; see also Rolston 1987, chs. 7-8).

Key Theological Dilemmas

1. One of the more interesting theological dilemmas tackled in theo-ecological discourse is Christianity's split between time and space, which plays out the nature/history dichotomy. McFague suggests three reasons why space should become the "primary" category for thinking about ourselves and other life-forms (McFague 1993, 99-102). In the past several hundred years, we have forgotten that space is a common need of all life-forms *and* that all life-forms must share one common space—the planet. Remembering this and taking it seriously, McFague claims, will have a leveling and democraticizing effect. Second, this spatial perspective illuminates the relationship between ecology and justice—the need of *all* bodies to have the space they need. Third, our near obsession with time and history has cut us off from a deep sense of place, from wholeheartedly embracing the earth as our beloved home. Since Augustine, a significant portion of Christian theology has understood human beings as sojourners or resident aliens, fostering the sense that the earth is a kind of a weigh station for bodies with souls on the way to the heavenly afterlife.

Moltmann investigates the space/time problematic as well in *God in Creation*. Although his discussion is more abstract, metaphysical, and less praxis-oriented than McFague's, he covers some important historical, philosophical, theological, and biblical ground in his exploration, and he arrives at a similar understanding of God's radically engaged relationship with the world. "God and the world are related to one another through the relationship of their mutual indwelling and participation" (Moltmann 1985b, 14).

The holistic worldviews that inform the work of Native American theologian George Tinker; Asian theologians Kwok Pui-lan, C. S. Song, Kim Jong Bock, Preman Niles, and Chung Hyun Kyung; and African theologians John S. Pobee and Mercy Amba Oduyoye are particularly important for Western Christian ecological conversations seeking to rebalance and reimagine conceptions of immanence and transcendence, time and space, nature and history, God and creation. Furthermore, because social, economic, and political issues cannot be separated from issues of geography, land, and survival in the context of oppressed people, the work of indigenous and third-world theologians often unearths the connection between justice and ecology in ways that those of us who struggle rather comfortably in the "belly of the beast" failed to notice.

Tinker (similar to McFague) argues that consciousness shaped by space promotes egalitarianism, while the emphasis on time and history promotes hierarchies of domination and subordination. The profound respect for the earth central to the Native American worldview and spirituality gives birth to the principle of reciprocity, where people honor and give back what nature gives to them.

2. How do we handle the precarious tension between the view of nature as something in its own right, with its own intrinsic value apart from humanity, and the view of nature as that which we are an inextricable part of and dependent on? The first view can be dangerous if it promotes alienation from nature with attendant attitudes of fear, denial, and domination, which many of us are already heir

to. The second view, if not carefully conceptualized in terms of mutuality, participation, and diversity (values quite foreign to Western culture) points to yet other
dangers, primarily the all-pervasive instrumentality of the science and technologies that provide the ways and means for exploitative economic dynamics and
structures that presently shape everyday realities. What is needed is balance (a
word seldom used in Christian discourse), respect for the integrity of the myriad
forms of life that make up the species, radical inquiry into the reality and nature
of our interdependence, and a new vision of our place in the web of life as responsible and responsive earth creatures.

Santmire promotes a triangular mode of thought that corresponds to the
trinitarian structure of divine life. The line drawn between God and nature must
be drawn as visibly as the line between God and humanity (Santmire 1992). We
can only fully grasp the integrity of nature if we understand that God has God's
own history with nature just as God has God's own history with us. Santmire does
not see these realities as separate but as clearly distinct *and* interdependent.

3. Theologians who center their theology around the contemporary scientific
picture of creation comprehend human nature as evolving quite recently out of
the natural world. In this conception, God's history with nature and God's history
with us are not quite so delineated and in some models approach a thoroughgoing
symbiosis. Various analogies of God's divine action inform the theo-ecological
discussion and give the relationship between the transcendent and the immanent
new dimensions and meaning. Grace Jantzen attempts to solve the mystery of
radical transcendence and immanence by understanding God as totally embodied
in the world (Jantzen 1984), while for John Polkinghorne this model dangerously
promotes the idea of God's tyranny over the world, or total capitulation to it
(Polkinghorne 1989). The process relational panentheism of Jay McDaniel argues that the world is somewhat independent from God in the same way that our
bodies are somewhat independent of our psyches (McDaniel 1989).

Exploring the theology of the cross as the theology of eco-justice, Larry
Rasmussen lifts up what both Luther and Bonhoeffer affirmed: that the finite
bears the infinite—*finitum capax infiniti*. Rasmussen writes about earth-bound
panentheistic theology:

> The meaning of *finitum capax infiniti* is simple enough: God is pegged to
> the earth. So if you would experience God, you must love the earth. The
> infinite and transcendent are always dimensions of what is intensely at hand.
> Don't look up for God, look around. The finite is all there is, because all
> that is is there (Rasmussen 1992, 42).

Rasmussen asks that we "return to our senses" by overcoming the apathy which
is the "denial of the senses and of our inherent connectedness to all things." Compassion is the antidote: in human suffering-with (compassion) and standing-with
(solidarity) all creation as Jesus did on the cross. The "practical necessity" of this
ethic of the cross lies in the fact that we cannot begin to transform the massive
suffering of creation unless we are willing to enter in and undergo the "unhealed
but not unhealable" nature of our present reality. Rasmussen reminds us that power

is only power when it resides, "where community and creation are most obviously ruptured and ruined," and is only the kind of power that can heal when it is "instinctively drawn to the flawed places of existence, there to call forth from the desperate and needy themselves extraordinary yet common powers that they did not know they had" (Rasmussen 1992, 49).

Indeed, it is the question of empowerment that underlies much of the theo-ecological conversation and which, it could be argued, needs to be made more explicit in terms of just exactly what a Christian praxis of eco-justice will mean and require. There is no question that ecological thinking shaped by cosmic and spirit theologies suggested (in different ways) by McFague, Moltmann, Fox, Tinker, and Ruether gives birth to notions of radical interdependence, immanence, and diversity and promote more holistic ways of thinking that are necessary prerequisites for the possibility of establishing embodied relationships, practices, and policies of justice and love. However, given the way the world is presently structured—politically, economically, and socially—there are dangers still inherent in the cosmic, universal, and spiritual worldview. History shows us that universalizing has often meant colonizing, and a focus on the spirit has often sacrificed the body and the material earth that is our home. Ecological theologies not grounded in particular, everyday life and not profoundly critical of the "politics of domination" (Hooks 1989, 175) that shape reality will prove stillborn at best, or obstacles to social and ecological transformation at worst.

4. Nevertheless, in theo-ecological discourse, one feels the call to experience and participate in the mystery of God's Spirit—elusive, dynamic, and transformative—in bold new ways. For it is the Spirit, as scripture attests to, who is the author of creation and new creation, and it is not only nature but the Holy Spirit, as Catholic theologian Elizabeth Johnson points out, that Christian theology has neglected and forgotten. Christians who have lost a sense of the Spirit, "God's personal engagement with the world in its history of love and disaster" (Johnson 1993, 131), "the breath which knits together all creation" (McFague 1993, 145) have lost their way, treading paths, consciously and unconsciously, that defile and destroy the earth. Wherever and whenever Christianity's fear, loathing, and suspicion of nature, of flesh, of women is evident, so is fear, loathing, and suspicion of the Spirit.

Ecological theologies have just begun to recycle the Christian wisdom that knows creation and all its creatures as the gift of the Holy Spirit, "Lord and Giver of Life." Let us pray in words from the New Zealand/Maori Anglican liturgy (quoted in McFague 1993, 158) for the "greening" of theology and the Christian praxis of eco-justice as it continues:

> Eternal Spirit,
> Earth Maker, Pain Bearer, Life Giver
> Source of all that is and that shall be,
> Father and Mother of us all,
> Loving God, in whom is heaven:
> The hallowing of your name echo through the universe!
> The way of your justice be followed by all the peoples
> of the earth!

Your heavenly will be done by all created things!
Your commonwealth of peace and freedom sustain our hope
and come on earth.
          With the bread we need for today, feed us.
In the hurts we absorb from one another, forgive us.
In times of temptation and test, strengthen us.
From trials too great to endure, spare us.
From the grip of all that is evil, free us.
For you reign in the glory of the power that is love,
now and for ever.

                                             Amen.

Note

1. In pursuing this motif, Santmire builds on the thought of Joseph Sittler, *Essays on Nature and Grace* (1972). He insists that the understanding of the world-as-nature gives rise to a more spacious doctrine of grace. Sittler argues for the reinvigoration of the cosmic Christology of Colossians and Ephesians, as well as retrieving the Trinitarian theologizing of Irenaeus and the Eastern Orthodox tradition. For the Eastern Orthodox perspective, cf. Paulos Mar Gregorios, *The Human Presence* (1978).

6

Ecological-Feminist Theology

Contributions and Challenges

HEATHER EATON

Overview of Current Trends

Ecological-feminism, or ecofeminism, is an international movement, global in concern and multi-disciplinary in approach. Ecological feminism comprises analysis, critique, and vision, and is the study of and the resistance to the associated exploitation and subjugation of women and the earth. It includes academic research and discourse, critiques and vision—spawning books, articles, conferences, retreats, liturgies, art, dance, and political organizations. There are publications covering ecofeminist philosophy, spirituality and theology, science, psychology, sociology, economics, agriculture, animal rights, socio-political analysis, and political activism.

Current work is progressing in two directions. First, examining the roots of the ecological crisis and misogyny, and their entwined linkages, is central to *ecofeminist theory*. The ideological foundations and presuppositions of Eurowestern cultures continue to be exposed in search of the historical and theoretical constructs of "women and nature," and the ensuing oppressions. Ecofeminist theory also envisions alternative philosophical and social conceptual frameworks based on benign relations among humans and with the earth, rather than on mutually supporting systems of domination. The second direction of ecofeminist work is global analysis of *agency*—namely, gathering data and insight on the who, what, why, where, and the how of the global socio-ecological crises. These interlocked crises involve issues of access to power and decision-making. Concerns about action or praxis to grapple with the international economic system, trade patterns, militarism, maldevelopment, and consumerism, within contexts of growing social instability, ecological ruin, environmental refugees, and the desperate life conditions of women, preoccupy this work. A polemic has existed between the path of ecofeminist theory and this orientation to analysis for praxis, although it is subsiding.

77

Ecofeminist theologians work primarily in the (Judeo-Christian) theoretical arena, revealing the theological, cosmological, and ideological frameworks of the religious legacy. They focus on doctrine, scripture, tradition, and history, in both critique and vision.

The uniting of ecology and feminism grants that one concern may take precedence. Often the theoretical work considers ecology as decisive, and thereby appears to be more responsive to the earth as context. The political analysis seems to regard ecological problems only when related to social crises or women's issues, hence remains anthropocentric. Yet this latter group exerts a strong influence on environmental concerns in the global political arena. These perspectives tend to emerge from the North and South, respectively. Both can be effectual.

Critical Research in Ecofeminist Theology

The multi-disciplinary and many-layered work of ecofeminism is very much a weave of analysis and envisioning in search of a viable future. Ecofeminism and theology/religion have explicitly intersected for two decades, initiated by Rosemary Radford Ruether's *New Woman, New Earth*, in 1974. Here, ecofeminist theological writing will be discussed under six headings: theoretical and historical analysis of culture; systematic theological reinterpretation; scriptural motifs; liberation theology and ethics; multi-faith and multi-disciplinary perspectives; and spirituality. Comments and questions will be presented within each area. Keep in mind that these categories can be artificial and the contributors do not belong to any one alone. The essay concludes with a discussion of several contributions that arise from the interaction between ecofeminism and theology/religion as well as some reflections on the challenges still ahead.

Theoretical and Historical Analysis of Culture

The initial link between ecofeminism and theology was within the critical analyses of the Eurowestern cultural history and heritage, which implicated the Hebrew and Christian traditions in fostering the dual oppressions of women and "nature." Philosophical and theological ideals and presuppositions were studied to discover the determining roots of misogyny and the domination of the earth (see Ruether 1974, 1983b, 1992; Gray 1984; Griffin 1978). Such work has been foundational to further ecofeminist study. Ecofeminist thought has mushroomed within feminist inquiry, pursuing the critique of Eurowestern culture within the disciplines of philosophy, science, and religion (see. e.g., Warren 1994; Merchant 1982).

I suggest that a useful distinction can be made between a critical analysis (theory) of religion and culture from an ecofeminist perspective—and ecofeminist theology. The former draws from research outside theology (primarily from ecofeminist philosophy and social critical theories), and is increasingly moving into interdisciplinary feminist discourses. Ecofeminist theology usually limits its categories and discussion to those of the theological disciplines, and is often an internal conversation.

Ruether's *Gaia and God* is the most comprehensive work she has proposed from an ecofeminist perspective. It is a combination of a historical-critical theory of religion and an ecofeminist reinterpretation of theology. In *Gaia and God* Ruether traces the Western cultural heritage of Christianity to its roots within the ancient Near Eastern, Hebrew, and Greek worldviews, and relates significant concepts of creation, sin, and healing to the current socio-ecological crises. The book is ample in scope, presenting general ideas with specific examples, and offering a loose reevaluation of the tradition. Using the concepts and praxis of covenant, sacrament, and spirituality and politics, Ruether presents a renewed vision of the religious tradition within contemporary culture. Clearly her interest lies in beneficially reshaping some general parameters of Western Christianity and its relation to culture, through the lens of ecofeminism.

Cosmological Concerns

Since ecological problems have emerged primarily from Western cultural ideologies and actions, shaped by Christianity, recent work in ecofeminist cultural analysis and theology has probed the underlying cosmology. Cosmology provides what Ruether calls a "combined scientific, social-ethical and theological-spiritual worldview" (Ruether 1992, 32). The interest in cosmology lies in the fact that the hegemonic interpretation of the Western creation story suggests a basic alienation from the earth. The tradition has excluded earth history from salvation history, and in some interpretations has sanctioned ecological ruin. Christian cosmology has focused on the human, and primarily the male. The joining of ecofeminism and cosmology challenges the *andro* and *anthropo*centrism, of Western religious *and* secular stories of meaning and values. Contemporary study of the universe reframes this dysfunctional cosmology; a renewed cosmocentric worldview could assist in overcoming "humancentrism," and help to guide Western culture through the ecological crisis.

Ecofeminists working in cosmology examine the historical shifts from perceiving the universe as organistic and living to mechanistic and dead, and the dangerous liaison between religion and science in promoting the oppression of women and the domination of the earth (Merchant 1982). The feminist critique of science, the new physics, and a return to cosmology are all primary areas of research and reflection. Both Rosemary Radford Ruether and Sallie McFague examine the Hebrew and Christian creation stories related to this field of cosmology, and the ensuing influence on the ecological crisis (McFague 1993). Both attempt to reshape theology from a cosmological vantage point.

Ruether proposes an ecofeminist theocosmology using the new science and an organistic (Gaian) view of the universe, based on three premises: "the transience of selves, the living interdependence of all things, and the value of the personal in communion" (Ruether 1992, 251). McFague contextualizes her work within a cosmological framework, seeking a common creation story—*from which to respond* to the ecological crisis. McFague, a feminist, seeks to join theology to ecology through metaphoric theology via the image of the world as the body of God. There are strengths and weaknesses to this methodology and the metaphor. What is of interest here is that cosmology is one basis of her theological position.

Others using an ecofeminist lens, such as Elizabeth Johnson and Charlotte Ward, also dabble in cosmological questions (Johnson 1993b; Ward 1990, 18-

21). Denise Peeters, along with Ruether, proposes that the Gaia theory (somewhat analogous to a cosmological perspective) is the best paradigm for Christian thinking as well as for ecological healing. Peeters sees the current Christian paradigm as being completely outdated. She maintains that Christian theology must be based on a new ecological ethic and a rediscovery of the Spirit, "the mystery of power-within and power-with Gaia, which is shown in the capacity to produce and sustain life" (Peeters 1993, 117). Johnson, Ward, and Peeters recognize the need for a Christian ecofeminist cosmology, without themselves engaging in any systematic reinterpretation.

Ecofeminist cosmology challenges the constitutive context of theology, and not only its androcentrism. For example, if the universe is considered the primary revelatory experience, as Thomas Berry posits (1988), then humanity, with our complex and rich cultural heritages, is derivative. This alters the basic categories of understanding our theological traditions, and ultimately our role in the universe. It calls forth a new religious sensitivity and meaning to the universe which may or may not be present within existing traditions. Prevailing religious traditions continue to hinder suitable responses to the ecological crisis.

The work in cosmology and ecofeminism must delve further into the connection between cosmology and the ecological crisis, without losing the ecofeminist critique. Greater clarity is required as to what questions are being addressed. Are we seeking to preserve, albeit in reinterpreted forms, the Christian heritage? Or are we evaluating responses according to what will assist in meeting the socioecological crises? How can a religious sensitivity to the earth nourish resistance to the destruction of life? Can it transform postmodern Western culture? What happens to our religious traditions?

Systematic Theological Reinterpretation

Ecofeminist *theology* is an appropriate term for those discussing the basic context of theology; an analysis of theological method; and the Christian doctrines of God, Trinity, Christ, as well as considering creation, revelation, anthropology, eschatology, notions of sin, salvation, redemption, role of scripture, and authority. Such ecofeminist theology usually involves the examination and reinterpretation of the classical or hegemonic tradition. Most of the discourse in ecofeminist theology occurs in articles that are in dialogue with *aspects* of the tradition. Elizabeth Johnson summarizes the basic idea.

> I am persuaded by the truth of the ecofeminist insight that analysis of the ecological crisis does not get to the heart of the matter until it sees the connection between the exploitation of the earth and the sexist definitions and treatment of women . . . and these distortions influence the Christian experience (Johnson 1993b, 10).

Systematic Reconstructions

A systematic ecofeminist reconstruction of the Western Christian tradition is an immense task. Anne Primavesi (1991) and Sallie McFague have attempted a methodical renovation—both taking the ecological crisis as central, and Primavesi explicitly from an ecofeminist position. Primavesi proposes replacing the traditional Christocentric hierarchical paradigm with an ecological paradigm, in light of the Gaia hypothesis. Such a perspective would be inclusive of women, as of all life. This shifts the terrain, and the question becomes, What do these Christian notions mean within an *ecological* paradigm? Through a reinterpretation of Genesis, Primavesi considers notions of sin, evil, redemption and salvation, doctrines of the Trinity, and the role of the Spirit in earth/human history. She offers a comprehensive survey of the tradition, suggesting alternative meanings for Christianity in an ecological age. Primavesi tackles the tradition and seeks reinterpretation of the totality, rather than Ruether's method of an apparent selective use of tradition in her critical analysis of culture and religion.

It is suggested here that Primavesi's ecological paradigm, while altering hegemonic Christian notions, does not sufficiently examine the roots of the relationship between the religious heritage and the socio-ecological crises. This may be due to the fact that Primavesi comprehends theological language as metaphor and imagery, respecting their power yet accepting the contextual limitations of Christian imagery. Thus the work of theology is to "gather and diffuse" metaphors, and allow their "identity and difference to shock us into wonder and delight, into new ways of relating to, thinking of and speaking about God" (Primavesi 1991, 177). The work of theology is fluid by nature.

McFague, from another perspective altogether, begins "an ecological theology" with the theological position that "the world is our meeting place with God . . . it is wondrous, awesomely, divinely mysterious" (McFague 1993, vii). Yet this very world is being rampantly destroyed. Her reinterpretative work is directed to *theology*, but with the goal of stemming ecological devastation. As mentioned above, McFague introduces the significance of cosmology to both theology and attitudes toward the natural world. With this in mind, she develops a theology of nature. She then moves among various assumptions of creation, anthropology, Christology, and eschatology, extending to each a metaphoric theology of the world as God's body. The strength of this contribution is that, as metaphoric theology, such an image can be empowering. The weakness is that this metaphor, like all others, is limited. It can conjure up detrimental images, such as the heinous allusions surrounding women's bodies in patriarchal cultures. Related to Christology, McFague proposes a cosmic Christ who, in addition to the historical Jesus and the paradigm of liberation, is co-extensive with God's body *and* the direction of nature (McFague 1993, 179-91). Although McFague's theological insights are based in a metaphoric theology, the Christology she offers can still be interpreted as the hegemonic imperialistic Christianity . . . on a cosmic scale. To recommend a universal Christology, even within the parameters of metaphor, seems at odds with the many feminists who are trying to relativize the Christ of faith.

Doctrinal Reinterpretations

Many ecofeminists locate the theoretical origins of the crisis in the distortions and hierarchical dualism of Western culture and Christianity. Elizabeth Johnson's theological response is to shift the focus from a monarchical, patriarchal idea of God (which has blinded us to the sacredness of the earth and excluded women and the earth from the sphere of the sacred), to a creator Spirit, Lifegiver, who is intimately related to the earth. Most ecofeminists, including Johnson, are leery of the stewardship model for the following reasons. It keeps the hierarchial dualism in place and misses the fundamental reality of human dependence on the earth. The theology behind environmental stewardship seems incompatible with an ecofeminist perspective because it claims a divine-human relationship which preserves a human-earth division, thus maintaining hierarchy. Stewardship theology signifies a shift within the present system more than a vision of a new and different order, Ruether observed a decade ago (Ruether 1985, 206). Nor is stewardship a feminist ethic expressive of "different, non-hierarchical, and destabilizing metaphors" (see Beavis 1991, 75-82).

Johnson moves her Spirit theology through notions of the "Goodness of God" in a Trinitarian image, which sees the Spirit as signifying the presence of the living God, arriving in every moment, creating, renewing, and refreshing the earth. She seems to drift from doctrine to scripture, creative imagery, and spirituality. In one paragraph alone Johnson refers to Psalm 104, the Nicene Creed, Pentecost, Luke's gospel, and resurrection—all interpreted as congruous signs of the Creator Spirit! (Johnson 1993b, 43). Her theological/spiritual methodology is perplexing, from a systematic perspective. Also, while Johnson maintains that ecocide is the most prevalent moral and religious challenge (ibid., 9), it is startling that ecofeminism and the ecological crisis are virtually absent in her recent work *She Who Is* (1993).

The implications of ecofeminism for Christian anthropology are also being explored. Mary Ann Hinsdale (1990) seeks insights within the tradition that correspond to an ecofeminist perspective on the interrelated doctrines of creation, the human person, and grace. The reality of the interdependence of life, from which we derive categories of relationship, as well as a recovery of biblical notions of Jubilee and Sophia, counter the embedded tenets of anthropocentrism and hierarchical order found within aspects of the doctrine of creation. A creation-centered tradition is favored over the familiar doctrines of fall/redemption; nature understood as coming into fullness rather than in need of redemption (Hinsdale 1991, 156-64). With respect to sin and grace, her ecofeminism situates sin within the interlocking oppressions of race, class, gender, and domination of the earth. The basic question for Hinsdale is, Where does ecofeminism get us with respect to Christian anthropology?

Eschatology has also been studied through an ecofeminist lens. Catherine Keller, for example, offers reflections on the connections between the "wasting of the world" and historical notions of eschatology. She associates the doctrines of eschatology and creation, as both became distorted together. Keller reorients eschatology to mean that our eschatological task is to renew "this Earth, this sky, this water," and to make a home for ourselves here. We do not need a new heaven and Earth (Keller 1990, 249-63; see also Keller 1993, 30-49). Further, she believes that the Christian consciousness is one of a prophetic minority, called to work for a renewal of creation, done in the Spirit of the creation.

Keller's work is an interesting contribution due to her awareness that both the ecological crisis and the feminist analysis are profound challenges to the very core of theological method and substance. For Keller, realistic (eschatological) hope lies in a consciousness that "apocalypse is unacceptable, that causes are analyzable, and that people can make a difference" (Keller 1993, 47). This is kin to a liberationist stance, whereby theology is oriented to the salvation of *this* world, drawing on socio-political and ecological analysis to inform a theology which is focused on praxis.

Theological Method

Others are researching *models* of theology, prior to or in conjunction with discussing the tradition. For example, Primavesi suggests that to empower theology is to change the basic hierarchical model and draw from constructive, contextual, feminist, and relational models that could counter the objectivist and hierarchical thinking to which theology is accustomed (Primavesi 1994, 186-97). Thus an ecofeminist theology would be radically different from the hegemonic tradition in its method, context, content, and focus.

Finally, several contributions to ecofeminist theology exist in the forms of short reflections on numerous subjects, such as sacraments and eucharist; divine transcendence; the role of scripture; Trinitarian theology; and Christology (see Dyson 1990, 2-31). From a methodological standpoint, these suggestions tend to add ecology and feminism to existing theological positions, not unlike rearranging the furniture to add new pieces.

Divergence exists among ecofeminist responses to the relationship between women and the natural world. Carolyn Merchant suggests no fewer than five kinds of ecofeminism: liberal, cultural, social, socialist, women in the Third World (Merchant 1992). Ruether would add radical ecofeminism (Ruether 1993, 13,14). Unfortunately Merchant and some others locate any spirituality/theological interest within cultural ecofeminism, and usually linked to an essentialist position. This has led to a confused and confusing barrage of critiques against ecofeminism and the spiritual/theological dimensions. Such criticisms, especially when directed to essentialism, can be considered relevant to a small proportion of the ecofeminist discourse, but not to the discourse as a whole.

Differences exist within the spectrum of ecofeminism, analogous to the various feminisms. Equally, the divergences between the environmental and the ecology movements are also present within the scope of the ecofeminist discourse. For example, with respect to ecological stress, some see the necessity to respond only to the specific "environmental" situation, while others suggests that a profound cultural analysis and revisioning is required to alter basic values, beliefs, and actions, and deal with primary causes. Given the breadth of possibilities, ecofeminist theologians must know the discourses in both feminism and ecology.

I contend that in theology, ecofeminist efforts of reinterpretation without addressing fundamental presuppositions or theological methodology are inadequate given the magnitude of the crisis and the urgent need for an authentic and transformative tradition. Feminist theology has revealed the hazards in hidden assumptions of religious traditions, and the immense social power of religion.

Ecofeminist theology is immersed in critique and analysis (deconstruction), and has only recently moved into the business of building. While the systematic deconstruction of the foundations of the tradition is common, reconstruction is typically offered with respect to particulars. Few deal with the aforementioned radical discontinuity that both the ecological *and* feminist evaluations *together* pose to theology, although this is changing as the theological exchange grows. To take eschatology seriously, for example, in light of the ecological crisis, leads one to reevaluate completely previous understandings of this doctrine and its relation to other doctrines. Keller offers a radical reinterpretation of eschatology. However, the vast challenge to theological presuppositions is left untouched.

This is hardly a facile task, and perhaps is more readily accomplished by tackling aspects. An attempt to reconstruct theology from an ecofeminist-cosmocentric worldview proved precarious and enigmatic to Elizabeth Green (1993). She found that tradition does not move with ease into an ecofeminist perspective. In an evaluation of this process, Green concluded that combining ecofeminism with theology suggests a fascinating and disturbing transmutation of theology.

I deduce that several events are occurring simultaneously in ecofeminist theology. While specific contributions are being made, for example, in expanding metaphors or imagining alternative models of the Trinity, the reshaping of theology as a discipline remains the substantive (and more difficult) work. To some extent this tension mirrors the feminist ambivalence with the Christian tradition—among those modifying the existing system, those continuing the analytic (deconstruction) work, and those creating new traditions. These divisions also permeate the global feminist discourse. Since deconstructionism is its own discipline, the conversation is further troubled. Yet some ecofeminist theologians, myself included, are less interested in reinterpreting particular doctrines that seem relevant for ecology or feminism. We are engaged in rethinking the basis and perspective of "doing theology" in the West.

Scriptural Motifs

A modest amount of ecofeminist theology has been done in relation to scripture. Three examples will indicate different approaches found within an ecofeminist use and application of scripture.

While much of scripture-based ecotheology has seized upon Genesis, and in particular the countless deliberations on dominion (steward, manager, gardener, co-creator), ecofeminists remain dubious of both this scriptural methodology and the reinterpretations, because it appears to be a revised rather than revolutionized Christianity. Primavesi combines a Spirit theology with a fresh look at Genesis, and as noted earlier, suggests that the Spirit in Genesis has been overlooked. Her return to the Spirit is insightful and theologically rooted, and is a radical challenge to the hegemonic tradition. It is viewed by some as imperative if Christianity is to be relevant and empowering in an ecological-feminist age (Primavesi 1991 195-263).

A second example is from the work of Carol Robb, who finds that the biblical Judeo-Christian covenant tradition has much to offer an ecological age. Membership in the covenantal community is extended to all species. The natural world becomes included in the history of salvation. Within this renegotiated covenant, right relations will be maintained—as a framework for justice. The extended covenant is built on a theology which maintains that we are "the new humanity participating with God/ess as co-creators of the universe" (Robb and Casebolt 1991a, 18-21). Finally, such a new covenant is the theoretical base for "environmental" ethics.

The strengths of the covenant symbol are manifold. It moves from a strictly theoretical and theological discourse to developing a base for public policy, with a view to contest systemic injustice and generate ethics. The limitation I see is that the covenant tradition has not, thus far, precluded misogyny, so how can it prevent ecological destruction? It is a feminist query to ponder just how far the work of resisting distortions, or the rearranging, even drastically, of various interpretations of internal symbols of theology, can go.

A third and final example of the use of biblical motifs is an interesting combination of feminist perspectives on science and the use of biblical Wisdom literature as a basis for an ecological theology of creation. Anne Clifford (1992, 65-90), like Robb, suggests a creation-covenant partnership of humans with nonhumans, because it emphasizes the solidarity of both in relation to God. The Divine Sophia, often at the heart of creativity in biblical Wisdom texts, provides a corrective to the dualistic and dominating conceptions of the relationship between the divine and creation. Clifford stresses that new root metaphors are necessary to make the divine order intelligible. To really listen to Sophia "immanent within nature as God's creation, means we will discover ourselves within rather than apart from our complex global ecosystem" (ibid., 65-90). Clifford perceives this process as analogous to genetic researcher Barbara McClintock's unique emphasis that scientists must develop a "feeling for the organism."

In a similar vein, Primavesi (1993) suggests that Wisdom writings are a "science of doxology," a direct appeal to the human mind to penetrate the order of the cosmos, and to know and love it. Wisdom invites contemplation of the earth. For Primavesi, Rachel Carson is an excellent example of such wisdom—the bringing together of knowledge (scientific training) and a profound sense of wonder and respect (ibid., 2).

These theologians suggest that an appropriate Christian response to the ecological crisis is to stretch, reinterpret, and/or correct existing metaphors so that they actively function as mediators in religion, science, and politics. But other ecofeminists would say that the mediation itself can remain part of the problem. As creatures of the earth we have direct experience of life. Our most basic connections with the earth go far deeper than any cultural mediation. What is the role of our religious traditions when we consider the earth as the fundamental context of life? Are religions necessary arbitrators between humanity and the earth? These are questions to be pursued!

Liberation Theology and Ethics

An emerging area of ecofeminist theology can be considered kindred to liberation theologies. The global ecofeminist discourse has concerned itself with systemic patterns of domination, addressing primarily the global economic system; militarism; bio-, reproductive, and agro-technologies; and the development agenda. This ecofeminist arena combines theoretical analysis and political activism, led primarily by women of the South. This work has similarities to social ecology, although with a feminist emphasis based in praxis. In my opinion, it is the cutting edge of ecofeminism (see Mies and Shiva 1993; Seager 1993; Mellor 1992).

An ecofeminist theology oriented not only to critique of the ideological origins of the socio-ecological crisis, but to moral agency, moves theology into the political realm, similar to Latin American and earlier feminist liberation theologies. Such an ecofeminist liberation theology is only beginning to be developed, although one can draw from the works of Dorothy Soellë (1990), for example. The methodology of Latin American liberation theology is useful, though as Brazilian ecofeminist theologian Ivone Gebara indicates, it is neither feminist nor ecological; nor has it changed the patriarchal anthropology and cosmology upon which Christianity is based (quoted in Ress 1993, 9-11). She advocates a paradigm shift to a holistic or critical ecofeminism, a panentheism rooted in cosmology, coming out of a global critique of modernity. The result is that many cherished notions of a pure and personal God, biblical revelation, resurrection, and salvation are significantly altered and unequivocally relativized. An ecofeminist liberation theology would focus on cultural transformation rather than greening Christianity, although these are connected.

Within this liberationist perspective, links are forged between social justice and ecological well-being. For example, several ecofeminists have addressed the ethics of human/animal relations, challenging cultural and economic practices involving animals (see Adams 1994 and 1990; Gaard 1993). Further, Val Plumewood (1993) proposes a critical ecological feminism that offers philosophical frameworks intended to support liberation movements, although her thought grapples with Western philosophical tradition and does not yet engage the global ecofeminist discourse.

Ecofeminist theology often takes its cues from ecofeminist *theory*, in which ideological issues are prevalent, while steering away from the global ecofeminist discourse. The fact that the "women and environment" discourse and "ecofeminism" are considered by some to be separate does not assist the debate or the responding to the issues.[1] An ecofeminist liberation theology would need to be cognizant of these realms of discourse, and of their issues. Such an ecofeminist liberation theology, with the necessary and sophisticated global analyses, could have the potential for a transformed and viable future for ecology, feminism, and theology.

Liberation Ecofeminist Ethics

Lois K. Daly observes that ecofeminist ethics are thoroughly contextual and radically communal in practice as well as in theory. "Ecofeminist reflection arose out of the particular experiences of specific groups of women who struggled against the interconnections between their own situation and the environmental degradation taking place around them. These include the women at Love Canal, at the Women's Pentagon action, at the women's encampments, in the anti-nuclear movement, in the animal rights movement, in the feminist spirituality movement, and in the Chipko movement in India" (Daly 1994, 286). Daly affirms Karen Warren's observation that relationships are "central to our understanding of who we are. . . . [What matters is] *how* a moral agent is in relationship to another . . . not simply *that* a moral agent is a moral agent or is bound by rights, duties, virtue, or utility to act in a certain way" (Warren 1990, 142-43). This way of acting and thinking emphasizes communal values of care, love, friendship, and trust; it reasserts the worthiness of other beings in the world; and emphasizes that social location affects how nature is seen and experienced. "Eco-feminism is not about denying the differences among human beings or those between human beings and the natural world. It is about building community and envisioning new ways of living on the planet" (Daly 1994, 289-90; see also Haney 1989).

Liberation Theology: Voices from the South

Recent work in feminist theology is directed to collaboration and sustained dialogue between women of the North and South (e.g., King 1987; Eck and Jain 1987). Feminist theology from the South is beginning to enter Northern feminist curriculum and consciousness (King 1994), and is well-represented in anthologies on ecotheology from the North and South (see Birch, et al. 1990; Hallman 1994; see also Boff 1995 for a comprehensive work on Latin American liberation theology and ecology). Northern theologians, such as Ruether and Primavesi, are deliberately working and writing from an awareness of the analyses from the South. Ruether has been instrumental in fostering gatherings with ecofeminist theologians in the South. Primavesi, looking back on the Earth Summit, addresses militarism, showing how social and ecological justice and peace are inextricably linked (Primavesi 1993, 20-26). She supports the argument that "secular" ecofeminists have presented, that "injustices to women, the poor, indigenous peoples and children are linked to the degradation of the environment and to the effects of economic militarism" (ibid., 26). Primavesi notes that it is through global feminism that a rapport is created among women, not because of or in spite of color, race, class, "but because we care passionately about what happens to women and wish to break the silence and to change the social and economic structures which keep them especially powerless and at risk from environmental degradation" (ibid., 20).

Women of the South are increasingly speaking in their own voices, and articles in ecofeminist theology are appearing in many parts of the world. The journal *Con-Spirando: Revista Latinoamericana de Ecofeminismo, Espiritualidad Y Teologia* has been publishing from Chile, in Spanish, for several years, extending its influence from the South to the North. The journal publishes several times a year and includes articles by women from around the world on a variety of themes connecting ecofeminism to theology and spirituality.[2]

In a recent publication from the World Council of Churches several articles appeared on ecofeminist theology. Chung Hyun Kyung examines how an ecofeminist spirituality would blend with earth-based images from Asia and Africa, focusing particular attention on the cosmological aspects of the "cosmos as God's womb (Hyun 1994, 175-78). Aruna Gnanadason (1994), from an Indian perspective, notes that the work for justice must now include the earth. As she

states, "Creation is not a secondary issue." Further, an ecofeminist vision challenges both the global economic policy and the development agenda. It is interesting
to note that Gnanadason draws from the "dynamic feminine principle *shaki*" to
argue that acts against creation break the spiritual bond between women and the
natural world. It will be important to follow responses as this perspective enters the
global ecofeminist discourse. Finally, in a recent volume edited by Elisabeth Schüssler
Fiorenza, Gebara furthers her reworking of Latin American liberation theology by
offering a fresh understanding of scripture, from a Latin American ecofeminist view,
in light of relation, resurrection and transcendence (Gebara 1993).

As a global ecofeminist theology develops, using the research coming from
the global feminist and ecofeminist discourse, as well as that from the liberation
theologies and ecotheology, this work should become the critical edge of, not
only ecofeminist theology, but of contemporary theology.

Multi-faith and Multi-disciplinary Work

In response to the ecological crisis, there have been several multi-faith initiatives that have occurred by way of conferences, books, and articles. Reflection on
the integrity of earth, on how religions influence cultural practices toward the
natural world, and on the global/local nature of many communities, is shifting the
multi-faith dialogue into a more comprehensive realm. Basic assumptions about
the truth of religious traditions are being shaped in this new global/ecological
context.

But to date, writing on this subject is not voluminous. While there have been
several multi-faith publications on ecology (e.g., *Cross Currents* 1994; Rockefeller
and Elder 1992; Tucker and Grim 1993), there was only one article on ecofeminism
within these collections (Spretnak 1993, 181-89). Carol Adams did edit a volume
entitled *Ecofeminism and the Sacred*, which is a notable contribution to the discourse between ecofeminism and religion. She collected twenty articles covering
a range of subjects including revisioning religion in a multi-faith context,
ecofeminist theory and religions, and the practices of and actions from ecofeminist
spiritualities (Adams 1993). Included is an article by Shamara Shantu Riley on
Afrocentric Ecowomanism (1993, 191-204).

It is significant that the ecological crisis is generating profound levels of analysis,
and effecting a thorough re-thinking of religions and their cultural roles. Research
has suggested that many of the attitudes towards the natural world have been
shaped by the traditional religious worldviews, as well as indicating that resources
exist within these traditions which could encourage benevolent human-earth relations. Further, this new multi-faith perspective on ecology and religion is
challenging each tradition to revisit its presuppositions, and accepting the particular strengths and lacunae. Ecofeminist thought and theology are finding their
way into these discourses, conveying other levels of erudite analyses, and bringing an attention to the particular as well as to the cosmological.

Multi-disciplinary

Two of the earliest multi-disciplinary anthologies on ecofeminism were *Healing the Wounds: The Promise of Ecofeminism* (Plant 1989) and *Reweaving the*

World: The Emergence of Ecofeminism (Diamond and Orenstein 1990), both containing articles on spirituality and/or theology. These volumes combine theory and praxis, spirituality and politics, South and North perspectives, critique and vision. These contributions are invaluable and indicative of the immense cultural shifts that are occurring.

Increasingly, there are multi-disciplinary publications on ecology that consider spirituality within the relevant themes. It is unusual for religious perspectives to be included on subjects not explicitly religious, and this has suited all disciplines which maintain state-church divisions. However, the ecological crisis prods disciplines to collaborate and learn from each other.

A recent publication in ecology, using critical theory, has included sections covering aspects of ecofeminism and spiritual ecology, as well as postmodern science, ecojustice, and social ecology. Edited by Carolyn Merchant, this masterful collection of theoretical work predominantly uses analyses from the North (Merchant 1994). Multi-disciplinary work is also emerging from the "women and environment" research in the South. These are superb publications on the intricate and complex web of forces which are causing the socio-ecological crises, especially from the South where the effects continue to be the most acute. What is of interest is not only that this material indicates the context for any relevant theological reflection, but that occasionally an ecofeminist theologian is cited! (Braidotti, et al. 1994, 70-72, 161-68; Harcourt 1994, 170).

The multi- and interdisciplinary work is expanding, and there exists a genuine openness to working from multi-faith perspectives and collaborating with other fields of study. This is a constructive approach to the socio-ecological crises, and a place for the ecofeminist critique to shape the exchanges.

Spirituality

Ecofeminist spiritualities are a bounteous aspect of ecofeminism and theology/religion, a practical response to the ecofeminist critique of theological and liturgical deficiencies of the tradition. As noted above, it is often through spirituality that religion enters the interdisciplinary ecofeminist discourse. The earliest ecofeminist anthologies included a section on spirituality (Plant 1989; Diamond and Orenstein 1990). Charlene Spretnak has encouraged creative envisaging of ecofeminist spiritualities throughout her work (Spretnak 1986, 1991, 1993). Ecofeminist spiritualities transcend theological and religious boundaries, and proliferate in images such as Gaia, Mother Earth, Sophia, Christ(a), Spirit, God/ess, Divine Matrix, and Cosmic Egg. A critique of these spiritualities would be difficult, as they exist outside of any one tradition and are not linked to any particular theological school of thought. While some theologians work from one tradition, others draw symbols from Wiccan, Jewish, Christian, Gaian, and indigenous peoples. Some combine traditions in a confusing manner. For example, Susan Smith writes of Mother Earth as the Absorber, Redeemer, Lifegiver, Sacrament, and the first Christ (Smith 1992, 259-66).

Women are engaged in creative exploration of the fresh images which are emerging from the cultural context of the ecological crisis and the feminist movement. It is a trustworthy sign that these spiritualities do not fit into any theological box. Equally, it is premature to judge these invigorating movements, as through them spirituality is enlivened in Western culture. Post-and current Christians are finding themselves within the myriad of ecofeminist expressions, but with little systematic theological analysis. I am not sure this work is currently possible, as ecofeminism represents a "new" insight, and needs to be explored openly before it is theologically scrutinized.

However, these same spiritualities are the greatest inhibitors of ecofeminist theology/religion entering the global ecofeminist discourse. Due to their fluid nature, and conceivably unsophisticated theoretical bases, these spiritualities are dismissed in academic ecofeminist discourses as being apolitical, naively essentialist, and irrelevant to cultural transformation (see critiques in Seager 1993; Mellor 1992; Biehl 1991). As noted, there are ardent internal arguments among Western ecofeminists about this, but as Seager suggests, "these internal arguments among feminists are perhaps a tempest in a North American teapot—not particularly interesting or relevant to outsiders or non-Western feminists" (Seager 1993, 251). Yet in virtually all recent "women and environment" publications from the South, spirituality is aligned with essentialism, apolitical concerns, personal transformation, and Goddess worship—and then dismissed (see Harcourt 1994; Braidotti, et al. 1994). If the state of life on earth were not so precarious, perhaps we could merely wait for such bickering to subside. Meanwhile, "scorned, trivialized or ignored by many in the academy, the strength of ecofeminism is in the streets . . . inspired by earth-based spirituality" (Seager 1993, 251). Western culture is in crisis, and all manifestations of its dominant ideology are being dismantled, theoretically at least. Theologically informed ecofeminism, including the spiritualities, is an emerging response—still able to grow.

These six areas of ecofeminist theology have been presented to acknowledge the diverse approaches when ecology, feminism, and theology are united. Many areas overlap, such as cultural critique and spirituality, theology and scripture, and ethics and theology. Several questions arise, and responses vary from rearranging the existing system, to foundational deconstruction of the pillars of Western culture. Each is attempting to honor the genius and sacredness of life, and all are part of the ecofeminist theological endeavor.

Contributions and Challenges

Ecofeminism is a movement in search of discipline. Its critique appears in systematic reflections and popularized versions, art forms, liturgies, in marches and protests, political resistance, United Nations gatherings and backyard barbecues (vegetarian of course). Significant contributions are inevitable with this plethora of expressions.

In theology, as previously indicated, women are beginning both specific and systematic research into developing an ecofeminist theology, or an ecofeminist perspective on theology. Some work, such as the religion and cultural critique, succeeds within an interdisciplinary milieu, enriching all conversation partners. Of greater significance is that this work then brings theology into the public domain, similar to the liberation theologies in the way it elicits response and reaction. Such a contribution persists amid significant conflict and is subject to the changing world order, the neo-conservative backlash, and the attempts to solidify Western imperialism. Ecofeminist theology is many things, not the least of which is a voice for a healthier future.

However, to acknowledge the socio-ecological crises, to green Christianity, and to discuss endlessly the paradigm shift needed, neither confront the crises, nor challenge the power structures. As Beverly Harrison states, misogyny's real force arises only when women's concrete power is manifested (1985, 5). This is equally true when one confronts the ecological crisis with authentic power and knowledge that the global agenda must and will change. The triple critiques of liberationist ecofeminism—ecological, feminist, and global political/social analysis—are forcing theology out of the ivory tower and the protected parish into the harsh streets of concrete reality and its transformation. Only the liberationist stream of ecofeminism, from both the South and North, yet to be fully developed, has the ability to move theology into this realm. The World Bank does not care whether Wisdom/Sophia was present in Genesis, or that the Christian eschatological doctrines are distorted. But it will care if Christians, inspired and empowered by their faith (with a new understanding of Wisdom and eschatology), resist the efforts of the World Bank and the International Monetary Fund in order to prevent ecological ruin! It has suited both theology and the culture that religion remain an internal, personal, and private affair. Thus, to evaluate what of the ecofeminist theology corpus especially contributes to understanding and addressing ecological concerns, one measure is whether the approach can move the effort into the work of resistance, vision, and reconstruction.

A further observation is that while the ecofeminist critique pushes into the culture, it is within small circles—well-educated, often white women in North America. Ecofeminist theologians are surely thus. Class is a more difficult indicator as the middle class shrinks. Globally, women engaged in ecofeminist works are of many races, with the spokeswomen being well-educated but often advocating for poorer women in grass-roots movements. Again, who is this ecofeminist theology, which has come predominantly from North America, trying to reach?

Another complication is the conflict between social justice and ecological sustainability. Many peoples are only beginning to feel the rights of their human subjectivity, desiring to move out of abject poverty, while ecological devastation becomes the new elite agenda. This is a terribly difficult and complex reality. As numbers of environmental refugees surpass political refugees, and as daily survival is threatened, ecological preservation is not the top priority. Yet to destroy biodiversity; to eradicate rainforests; and to pollute the water, air, and soil, is to render conditions for life having any semblance of health impossible. It is when deliberations enter this realm of socio-ecological crises that the magnitude of the global predicament becomes stark. How will ecofeminist theology respond to this turbulent and suffering reality? How can we speak of survival of earth in front of massive human suffering? Yet again we encounter the insidious human-centeredness of the world. Then population enters the conversation, and women are aware of the direction of current policy—according to the familiar race, class, and gender lines. In fact this is happening already. How can social justice and ecological health—not just sustainability, advocacy for the oppressed and reenchantment of the world for the sake of life's abundance and magnificence be addressed together? Currently this is a great tension, at all levels, and from many agenda.

Finally, the depth and magnitude of the ecological crisis remain, affecting all levels of health, and the outcome is unpredictable. Conferences abound on atmospheric conditions, species extinction (thirty thousand annually), top soil loss (fifty billion tons annually), and ozone depletion. For North Americans, water is becoming a critical issue. The aquifers are shrinking and becoming toxic. In most Northern water systems, levels of estrogen-like compounds from organic chlorides are so high that many inhabitants of the water-ways are unable to reproduce because their reproductive organs have mutated. And on it goes, with global consequences.

Given this context, how can we measure the contributions of ecofeminist theology? If it does not correspond in some way to the genuine reality, then perhaps it has little liberative potential. If it does, then its deep spiritual energy and firm commitment to the genius and sacredness of life will be a powerful force to change the world, respect the earth, and honor the holy.

Notes

1. In many works on "women and environment" there is an ecofeminist section, aligning it with the white, middle-class essentialist, Goddess, and motherhood positions, and then refuting its validity in terms of the global (racial, class, cultural, political) issues (e.g., see Braidotti, et al. 1994, 161-68). While some Southern feminists have distanced themselves from "ecofeminism," the division is neither useful nor accurate to the breadth of the ecofeminist discourse. Some voices are attempting to reconcile ecofeminism, "women and environment," and socialism (see D'Souza 1989, 29-39; and Mies and Shiva 1993).

2. Address: *Con-Spirando* Castilla 371-11, Correo Nuñoa, Santiago, Chile.

7

Postmodern "Nature," Feminism and Community

CATHERINE KELLER

I

I dreamed that I am ascending a mountain in some sort of vehicle. Gradually the trees thin out, making a few buildings visible. This disappoints me. Then suddenly a whole city springs into view. It clings vertiginously to the side of an immense cliff, suspended Dr. Seuss-like over the abyss. While the technology to have accomplished this seems impossibly futuristic, in fact the whole facade already shows signs of decrepitude. The fact and the idea of this city horrifies me. I imagine what it was like to build it. I go into it with others, feeling my fear of heights with every step. Some people live there, but it seems depressed and underpopulated. I ask about its origins: I am told it was built with the forced labor of Indians; they have better balance, though of course some plunged to their death. I have an appointment in a doctor's office here, where a good friend meets me to help the doctor give me the diagnosis of cancer—"70 percent," meaning advanced, I take it.

It was not difficult to personalize the dream: as an academic I know myself to dwell too far up, "in the head," and to suffer from the carcinogenic overproduction of my class. But the dream offers itself also as a parable. Our culture in its vertiginous and gruesome perch at the top of the world, built at the expense of the colonized, the "better balanced" earth-people. It displays itself as hyper-modern and yet is already aging, vacuous, depressed. The self-diagnosis made available within this space seems appropriate.

Precisely as a result of our inappropriately high culture, we live dissociated from our material base. As a result we experience "nature" as something alien and external, beginning with the bodies we look down on and purport to "have." Our ecological reality normally mediates itself to us through a veil of externality, in the psychic atmosphere of something always less important than truly human affairs: at best aesthetically enjoyable, usually humid, chilly, mosquito-ridden and inconvenient. When its importance asserts itself, it threatens with disaster and shadows us with death. The rhetorical device of the dream means to suggest that our relation to the environment doesn't just leak into our consciousness. Rather, it contextualizes our most intimate self-relation. I do not therefore mean to suggest that it is a merely or mainly interior reality, either—it is precisely the binary production of subjective interiority over against material exteriority that needs to be questioned, as it animates the very privileging of culture over nature with which we are struggling.

Let me suggest that this otherness, this sub-subaltern, this difference, constituted of the materially nonhuman, cultivated by a mix of premodern Christian, modern Protestant and secular aspirations, is currently being reconstituted within postmodern theory. The gravitational pull of a certain highly influential postmodern anti-naturalism is especially dangerous, I argue in what follows, for feminist theologians and religious leaders operating from a Protestant base; dangerous, that is, if ecofeminist thought remains of value in the articulation of the differences which *matter*. In the meantime, the "city on the hill" shivers and rusts over the abyss.

II

Contrary to academic rumor, the discourse of "difference" is not a donation of French theory. Difference burst into U.S. feminist theory in theology through the interventions of Africanamerican women thematizing their difference from white feminism (Lorde 1984). Difference—the otherness to be honored—had tended to be assimilated into the illusory unity of sisterhood until the ineradicable differential of race, with class breathing down its neck, clarified itself. Ecofeminism, already liberated from the zone of single-issue politics by its very nature, soon began to attend to the parallels and crossings between the politics of the environment, gender and race. Ecowomanism has begun to find its voice. It is arguably because of our race dilemmas that feminist theory became vulnerable to poststructuralist theory. In its self-critical feminist forms, its postmodern pluralism helps to write our subjectivity through the radical intersections of multiple force fields of otherness. Thus Teresa de Lauretis writes:

> What is emerging in feminist writings is . . . the concept of a multiple, shifting, and often self-contradictory identity, a subject that is not divided in, but rather at odds with, language; an identity made up of heterogenous and heteronomous representation of gender, race, and class, and often indeed across languages and cultures; an identity that one decides to reclaim from a history of multiple assimilations, and that one insists on as a strategy (de Lauretis 1986, 9).

De Lauretis, refusing to identify human identity with language, leaves open a window for the nonhuman. Indeed she represents a happily impure voice among female poststructuralists. But let me at the same time claim that feminist poststructuralist theory in general, far from lending any support to ecofeminism as such, in fact threatens to undermine any possible terms of effective environmental awareness. I will offer two examples of how this happens.

First, poststructuralism can be defined as one great anti-naturalist project. Actually the "nature" it deconstructs is not the nature we wish to rescue. It seeks to dislodge essentialist understandings of nature as a set of fixed laws governing a universe of substances in an order which not coincidentally turns out to posit the dominance of males over females, whites over people of color, humans over animals, and so on. Poststructuralist feminism, especially as queer theory, cogently dismantles any residual notion of a given gender, of a natural femininity, of a fixed set of heterosexual or homosexual characteristics.

In order to liberate gender from its "natural" heterosexuality, Judith Butler liberates it from any nature at all. "Denaturing gender" becomes homologous to emancipation from heterosexism. The body is not to be understood as an abiding natural ground but always as a "cultural sign." Butler considers even Foucault's inscribable body as in some regrettable sense already *there*, preceding its cultural construction. Ultimately "the body is not a 'being' but a variable boundary" (Butler 1990, 139). The baby seems to have dissolved into the bathwater, the better to drain it; rather than deconstructing dominant paradigms of naturalism, it becomes impossible to speak of anything like a nature which preexists human significatory practices, let alone any such body. Body loses its material thickness, its animal animation, along with its static heritage of substance. I mean here to signal a minor alarm.

Other feminist philosophers have already been pushing for more nuance than this sort of anti-naturalism allows. Carol Bigwood explicitly engages Butler on this issue: "If we reduce the body as a whole to a purely cultural phenomenon and gender to a free-floating artifice, then we perpetuate the deep modern alienation of our human being from nature" (Bigwood 1993, 44). Or as Teresa de Lauretis has written, "Merely to say that sexual difference is 'cultural' allows no greater understanding of female subjectivity and of women's actual and real differences, than to believe it to be 'natural'" (de Lauretis 1986, 12). One might add that until it responds constructively to such critique, deconstructive feminism perpetuates the paradigmatic western triumph of "culture" over "nature." Given that it is a cultural construction of "nature" which is rightly deemed repressive, it is odd to then uncritically prefer "culture" as the corrective term.

But my concerns would be moot were it not for the political indifference of postmodern texts concerning nonhuman beings. Poststructuralists and most of the feminisms and theologies adapting its "discourse" maintain an urbane and systematic silence, a kind of hostile boredom, toward all things nonhuman. In other words, the criticism of "nature" does not, as in the case of "culture," re-create its object: the anti-naturalism becomes a cancerous critique, an auto-destructive process.

I would suggest that the oppressive naturalism inherited both from classical and modern scientific metaphysics is better dislodged by an alternative "nature"— or "earth," or "creatureliness," or animate materiality. It is not that we *are* unnatural—that denaturing our genders performs the needed act of honesty. Perhaps rather we are best conceived as a species to be radically and substantially natural beings, exhaustively social like all animals, and especially creative of intra-species difference in our inter-species differences. Then we needn't understand ourselves as such pure productions of culture, but rather as bodies retaining some power precisely as animal bodies to resist the cultures which interpret us. Specifically our carnal lot, if acknowledged, allows us to provide a material base of support in the struggle of specific body-friendly cultures with other body-dominative cultures.

Body is then neither a blackboard on which one writes nor a mere boundary, but the home base we never leave; a psychosomatic site of the intersections of conflicting cultures; our living place with a will of its own, however rent and sickened by abuse, addiction and alienation from itself and therefore its material support systems throughout the earth.

Second, I am concerned with the way in which the anti-naturalism teams up with postmodern anti-globalism. Julia Kristeva (from whom I have learned much of value) in a recent interview formulaically responded as follows in response to a question by Alice Jardine about the apocalyptic trends of certain global issues such as economics, population and ecology: "In my present state of mind, I think that all global problematics are archaic; that one should not formulate global problematics because that is part of a totalitarian and totalizing conception of history" (Kristeva 1990, 84). This now familiar rejection of global accounts—the "suspicion of meta-narratives" which defines postmodern theory—originates in a healthy attempt to shut down the universal subject of the Enlightenment, with its global energy for colonization. She continues: "Where are things actually happening? In specific regions in our intimate lives, or in different fragmentations of knowledge through very specific research." Hence only very precise psychoanalytic or anthropological and linguistic knowledge remains acceptably nontotalitarian.

We must learn to ask at this point just whose interests are protected by avoiding "global problematics?" My suspicion is that it is not at all those of the global victims of that universal colonizing done by Europe. Indigenous and two-thirds world peoples, as well as ethnic minorities within, ask quite the contrary: that we attend carefully to the reality of our global interdependence and its costs for the southern nations. They themselves work at once globally and locally and ask us for the analog. As long as we perform our "very specific research" while sipping coffee and wearing garments sewn in Sri Lanka, we are willy-nilly enacting "global problematics." What locality does Kristeva suggest? "One must ask different specialists." In other words, leave it to the experts. But the experts, for example in economics, already leave ethical concern to ethicists, ecology to ecologists, issues of justice for poor women to feminists, and so on. If the local means after all academic specialization, we are neatly returned to the very paradigm which has served the modern Euroamerican project of global domination so well.

For Kristeva it all comes back to the individual. She looks forward to the shrinkage of all ethical struggles to "smaller and smaller groups, and from there will move closer to the individual. At that moment it may be the individual discourses which will acquire greater importance" (Kristeva 1990, 85). In other words, ethics is to be liberated from global concern or communal discourse; nostalgia for the disengaged, rootless individual of modernity could hardly be more honestly admitted.

Because poststructuralism does not directly engage issues of planetary integrity, let alone ecological ethics, I have seen fit to point to certain tendencies which not only account for that absence but aggressively mitigate against an earth ethics. As my evocation of de Lauretis suggests, however, I am not interested in demonizing or even in standing outside of postmodern discourse, but in extending a critique which has already developed in relation to feminism itself. Certainly it is difficult to produce ecological, feminist or theological discourses, let alone ecofeminist theology, without engaging in "quasi meta-narratives" (Nicholson 1990).

At stake however is the character of "the local" which post-structuralism proposes as a replacement for "the global" and its imperialist meta-narratives. The site of "local knowledges" helpfully invites us to give renewed attention to the dense networks of interpretation and power through which life circulates up close, in contradistinction to emphasizing self-serving over-generalizations which abstract from the local. Yet Harvey's warning, that in the postmodern priority of place lurks an evasion of the global economics which fuels postmodernism itself, could just as well be applied to the evasion of the ecological:

> Postmodernism has us accepting the reifications and partitionings . . . all the fetishisms of locality, place or social grouping, while denying that kind of metatheory which can grasp the political-economic processes . . . that are becoming ever more universalizing in their depth, intensity, reach and power over daily life (Harvey 1989, 117).

Abstracting the local from its economic and ecological situation in the global order implicates one in a version of Whitehead's "fallacy of simple location" (1925). If instead we understand particular places, like particular bodies, as sites of sites, as complex social regions embedded in networks which one can only arbitrarily isolate, we will find ourselves better situated to accept responsibility for the ecopolitics of our own privilege. I am suggesting that the postmodern propensity for deconstruction, when it reduces body to cultural production and locality to the discursive individual, stimulates the cancer by which human culture, excited and agitated by its own artificial appetites, devours its host—the earth.

III

The poststructuralist disappearance of the earth poses a threat to the development of an ecological theology only if it reinforces tendencies of our own. I suspect it is tempting for us—especially as women and Protestants—to join in the chorus of anti-naturalisms. Let me suggest four levels of the feminist anti-naturalist temptation.

(1) Our desire to free ourselves from the bonds of that feminine, heterosexual "nature" which kept us in bondage to the demands of patriarchal culture roots in

DeBeauvoir's *Second Sex*, which identifies freedom as transcendence of the "immanence" associated with the drag of nature, procreation and body. To flag ourselves as bodies tends to re-objectify us, whether in service of a misguided romanticism or a Paglian reaction.

(2) For academic women a considerable degree of cultural power has now become available within elite cultural spaces. Therefore ecological concerns, fleshy, dirty, and dumb as they are—involving all those animals, vegetables and minerals who cannot speak our language—would resist the terms of the emerging poststructuralist hegemony and therefore are best left to "specialists."

(3) Perhaps most important, because women have so much pain, abuse, repression, shame, loneliness, self-loathing, and disappointment locked into our animal flesh, opening it up threatens private apocalypse. Yet if opening up our embodiment to self-scrutiny offers the only honest path to ecological consciousness, repressing bodiliness in general tragically colludes with global apocalypse.

(4) For Christian women, no matter how critical we may be of patriarchal theology, healing from our cultural conditioning to supernature—to a salvific interiority or a disembodied transcendence —cannot be achieved by mere political choice. Moreover, as Protestants, our latent anti-Catholicism (kept timely by the present pope's performance) works to reinforce anti-naturalism. Remember Luther's polemics against every form of medieval cosmology for giving any inherent value to fallen nature. Jesus' incarnation tends to function still as the exception which proves the rule of anti-nature.

IV

Let me quote concisely a couple of exemplars of the Protestant background as it comes into North American colonialist relief:

William Bradford, the first Puritan historian, recalls the first landing at Provincetown years later with a vividness that marks a formative cultural impression: "What could they see but a hideous and desolate wilderness, full of wild beasts and wild men" (quoted in Turner 1983/92, 208). References to the "howling waste" proliferate in Puritan texts. The apocalyptic hope for the "city on the hill" inverts readily in our history to apocalyptic dualism and doom. Far from the Paradise of the first southern conquests, this landscape is from the outset inscribed as demonic.

When in 1692 witchcraft broke out in Salem, embodied in the dark incantation of two West Indian women slaves, the apocalyptic sensibility turns hysterical: "The New-Englanders," wrote Cotton Mather,

> a People of God settled in those which were once the *Devil's* Territories; and it may easily be supposed that the *Devil* was exceedingly disturbed, when he perceived such a People here accomplishing the Promise of old made unto our Blessed Jesus, *That he should have that Utmost parts of the Earth for his Possession* (quoted in Turner 1983/92, 227).

Note the chain of associations: the devil's territories as the wilderness of wild beasts and natives—the devil always designated with horns and tails and goat hooves, in other words, as Pan, a Pre-christian nature spirit—linked with women as especially vulnerable to witchcraft—and particularly women of color; these nature-native-female-dark forces are diagnosed as in a state of hysterical resistance to the triumph of Jesus, for which read the absolute colonizing and capitalizing of the earth: in other words, the apocalyptic triumph, again.

These examples suggest that it is unlikely that we can readily release ourselves from these habits not just of thought but of self-construction; it is unlikely that we who benefit from the ongoing colonization of the earth and its autochthonous peoples will soon outgrow the accompanying externalization and commodification of nature. And as women with a dim memory of being demonized, if not merely objectified, as the natural, our inheritance consists not only of the practices of (self-) demonizing and (self-) distancing but at the same time of self-defense against our impure association with nature.

These habits of distantiation from the animal-material cosmos, of abstractions of ourselves as spiritual beings, or as rational minds or as creators of culture, mainstream or subversive, run deep. Indeed they have already always constituted who we are; we embody the distance. We somatize our abstraction: women as well as men, if perhaps for complementary reasons along the continuum of white European dominativity. That dominativity has come into its own apocalypse. Its endtime may be a cosmic cataclysm of global self-destruction stretched over a few decades, or a painful but still possible time of self-disclosure. Probably both will be going on for the rest of our lives. Eco-apocalypse inscribes our present with the revelation of the doom inevitable for a civilization which does not repent.

V

I have been writing toward a counter-apocalypse (Keller, forthcoming), and suggest that countering apocalypse while honoring its wounded rage requires the recuperation of a certain sense of community. Affirming community as the sociality of solidarity requires acknowledging both the anthropocentrism and the chauvinisms to which the idea of community has been prone. It means, however, resisting the poststructuralist call to abandon the ideal of community as irredeemably homogenizing—that is, as committed to overcoming difference (cf. Young 1990, 227ff.).

In conclusion, let me highlight four commingling dimensions of *ecofeminist relationalism*. These spill out of the construction of counterapocalyptic sensibility to "theology for earth community," and are meant as criteria for discussion:

1. The ideal of *community* is an inherently utopian and revolutionary model steeped in the history of western millennialist apocalypse. It has been thus prone to apocalyptic homogenizations of the in-group; at the same time it has provided the progressive energies of the west, encoding in its history the aspirations to especially economic and eventually ethnic and gender egalitarianism. But it now requires biocentric transformation. We are at a point in history when economic

forces have so grouped themselves as to propose the final disempowerment of communities. The Uruguay Round of GATT greatly accelerates the already rapid mobility of goods and capital across the planet. As Michael Shuman, in a paper called "GATTzilla *vs.* Communities," puts it: "It thwarts local economic development, blocks local efforts to conserve natural resources, and undermines local self-determination." GATT insidiously "strips communities of powers they could use to protect themselves against the adverse effects of the globalized economy" (Shuman 1994, 5). Resistance to the Uruguay Round must come from communities. Probably there is no stopping its installation as law. But there will still be ample opportunity to organize for a "community friendly GATT." Herman Daly, the progressive economist who strangely survived for the past six years at the World Bank, prophesied as he departed that "ten years from now the buzzwords will be 'renationalization of capital' and 'community rooting of capital'" (cited in Meadows 1994, 4).

We all know how GATT threatens the environment. But what does this economic sense of community have to do with women? Everything. As the statement from the Women's Caucus working on the draft for the U.N. Social Summit reported, "We ask for a commitment to socially-responsible economic reform programs, not structural adjustment programmes socially-oriented . . . these programmes must be designed in consultation with those who are affected by them and must be accountable. We applaud commitment number 5 to achieve full equality between women and men, but must weave gender analysis throughout the commitments." The proposed concept is that of "an enabling environment that will permit the full and creative participation of all peoples." For Marta Benevides, the Salvadoran who presented the statement—and who functions simultaneously as a local and a global activist—"enabling environment" is resonant with the right to a healthy ecology and means of livelihood independent of free trade. This is consonant with the idea of "sustainable livelihoods" proposed as a means of redefining the global social crisis by the people-centered development forum.

2. The *commons*—the word sounds archaic, but has a powerful political valency today as environmentalists call for a new approach to resource-management. Enclosure, which replaced the ancient practice of the commons, redefines community. Especially women,

> who in a vernacular setting were generally accorded respect as women, who had their own spheres of influence both within the household and outside, have seen their domain encroached upon. In many pre-colonial African societies, for example, tasks such as taking goods to market and trading, clearing fields, preparing land for planting, weeding and harvesting were divided between the genders. . . . Much of the land to which women had access as the commons has been enclosed, capitalized, and thus absorbed by men, stripping women of what independence they had. But today, examples multiply of women reclaiming the concept of the commons (Ecologist 1993).

The Indian tree-hugging Chipco movement is famous. Kenya: the *mwethywa*; Philippines: the Metro Manila Council of Women Balikatan Movement.

As Vandana Shiva writes, "The intellectual heritage for ecological survival lies with those who are experts in survival. They have the knowledge and experience to extricate us from the ecological cul-de-sac that the western masculine mind has manoeuvred us into. And while Third World women have privileged access to survival expertise, their knowledge is inclusive, not exclusive" (Shiva 1988, 224).

3. Such a sense of the commons requires a new *common sense*: an ecological, economic, social, feminist sensibility. But this greening of common sense will require more than rational appeals to what ought to be but is not common sense about the viability of the earth, its species and even our own. Environmentalism remains even among progressives faintly alienated discourse, drifting on the edge of most of our vital concerns, subject to all the resistance which guilt provokes. The practical, material survival sensibilities it requires may only be motivated by an accompanying sense of wonder—a piece of our work as religious leaders that we dare not neglect. Might it help if we could appeal to human selves as soulful bodies, as animals animated by an anima mundi, a world soul—the concept Plato reports in the *Timaeus*, in which he recognizes the world as a "wonderful animal"?

I return here to New England for a sense of what this might mean. Thoreau, driven on to a third quest in the Maine mountains, guided by a Penobscot, seems finally, right before his death, to have found what he had been seeking. He feels possessed by it, but unafraid:

What is this Titan that has possession of me? Talk of mysteries!—Think of our life in nature,—daily to be shown matter, to come in contact with it,—rocks, trees, wind on our cheeks! the *solid* earth! the *actual* world! the *common sense! Contact! Contact! Who* are we? *where* are we? (Thoreau 1873, cited in Turner 1983/92, 208).

What would it be like to imagine our common sense as animal access to actuality—given how shriveled, deformed, and numbed is our human species-solidarity, let alone our sense of community with all the other creatures who co-constitute us in our economies of eco-space? Can such ecstatic contact find resonance within the urban spaces of overstimulated alienation? Is this pneumatological possession what it takes to reverse the frenzy of late capitalist possession: the possession that encloses rather than discloses? What if our survival now depends upon a critical mass of us making "contact"? Experiencing *matter* as *privilege*?

4. Such common sense will for most of us not break through in a mountaintop ecstasy. Indeed it would feed our abstract individualism to seek it today on Thoreau's terms. But surely we will be discerning new rituals of *communion*, fresh materializations of spirit. The common sense of sustainable livelihoods and empowering environments requires communal practice. And it is for me more than a professional prerogative to suggest that only spiritual practice sustains the

needed ecosocial practices. Many of us are finding refuge in the third person of the trinity, developing a pneumatology of earth-spirit.

The spirit, which according to the Book of Wisdom "knits all things together," that newly defamed Sophia, offers a cosmic metaphor: "There is in her a spirit that is intelligent, holy, unique, manifold, subtle, mobile, clear, unpolluted, distinct, invulnerable, loving the good, keen, irresistible, beneficent, humane, steadfast, sure, free from anxiety, all-powerful, overseeing all, and pervading all spirits that are intelligent, pure and altogether subtle" (Wisdom 7:25). Communion with this cosmic spirit of wisdom in ourselves, the wisdom of our bodies, the wisdom of all life as it breaks subtly and multiplies into community, leads us to commune with multiple spirits—thus I presume with the subtle spirits of the earth, the water, the air, the spirits of place and of ancestors. That the elemental spirits of the nonhuman creation counted as "intelligent, pure and altogether subtle" from the vantage point of the apocryphal Jewish author, I do not wish at this moment to argue for historically; I am reading out the desire for a contemporary panentheism of the earth.

Such pneumatology may paradoxically insist on embodiment—precisely by soliciting the indomitable sentience, the unfathomable diversity, the spirited purposefulness of all that "bodies forth" in the earth. Without this sense of the bodied community of animate beings, of spirited sentiences, do we not continue to externalize "nature"? To homogenize it as the dumb Other, as all that is not-us, that lacks the differences which lend life character? If we do not learn to hear the spirits of place—certain Native American, especially female, voices have pronounced clearly—environmentalists despite good intentions may be wasting their time. Of course I'm not sure we can; and when we try to, we tend to join the New Age market in ripping off Native American spirituality. Thus we deny our own white difference and the grim responsibilities it carries. For us the spiritual work, the dream work, may not be romantic and refreshing much of the time. It may confront us with our disease rather than reassure us of a cure.

Still, no matter what, Proverbs—which at least in some contested sense is our own—suggests we commune with *Hochma*: "She is a tree of life to those who lay hold of her." Gazing abyssward, I'd sooner grasp a living tree than a pillar of the city on the hill.

8

Cosmology and Justice
in Ecumenical Perspective

KOSUKE KOYAMA

This essay responds to the following two questions: 1. What in your work/ field contributes constructively to exploring the global problematic of social and environmental degradation? 2. What in your work/field of theology still needs to be undertaken to pursue this?

I

The Contribution of Ecumenism

My chair at Union Theological Seminary is called Ecumenics and World Christianity. Ecumenism is an antithesis to imperialism. It originates in Christian repentance. Both words, "ecumenics" and "ecology," derive from the Greek word *oikos*, "house, homely environment." Thus they signify the idea of our taking good-housekeeping—earth community seriously.

When considering what ecumenical study/movement has contributed constructively to understanding "the global problematic of social and environmental degradation," I discern that it has given humankind the vision of the unity of humanity. The vision is sacred, and it is historical in character. It has a far-reaching horizon and complex inner dynamics. The ecumenical message is that there is only one history for humanity. There are *not* two histories; theological and nontheological, sacred and secular, or saved and damned.

The story of the ecumenical movement in this century began with the theological quest for human unity in the raging storm of World War I. Soon after that war, the demonic power of Hitler's Third Reich engulfed humanity. The traumatic World War II was immediately followed by nearly half a century of a devastating global Cold War. By steadily upholding its vision of the unity of humanity grounded in theological conviction, the ecumenical movement constructively addressed issues of degradation.

The theological conviction of One Humanity is the core message expressed in numerous ecumenical conferences between the International Missionary Conference in Edinburgh (1910) and the Seventh Assembly of the World Council of Churches in Canberra (1991). In 1924, J. H. Oldham introduced the problem of racism into the ecumenical discussion with his book *Christianity and the Race Problem*. Stockholm (1925) dealt with social and economic issues. Jerusalem (1928) addressed the problematic of secularism. Berlin (1974) tackled the issue of "Sexism in the '70s." The theme of Chinengmai (1977) was "Dialogue with People of Living Faiths and Ideologies." Lima (1982) focused on the renewal of human community through the grace of "Baptism, Eucharist and Ministry." Seoul (1990) addressed "Justice, Peace and the Integrity of Creation."

The ecumenical movement and its member churches began to address the environmental challenge in the mid-1970s, following the first UN Conference on Environment and Development at Stockholm (1972). The fifth Assembly of the World Council of Churches in Nairobi (1975) emphasized the need to establish "just, sustainable, and participatory society." In his address, Australian biologist Charles Birch explained

> A prior requirement of any global society is that it be so organized that human life and other living creatures on which human life depends can be sustained indefinitely within the limits of the earth. A second requirement is that it be sustained at a quality that makes possible fulfillment of human life for all people. A society so organized to achieve both these ends we can call a sustainable global society in contrast to the present unsustainable global society. If the life of the world is to be sustained and renewed, . . . it will have to be with a new sort of science and technology governed by a new sort of economics and politics.

A follow-up WCC conference on "Faith, Science and the Future" (MIT, 1979) pursued the subject in more detail (for preparatory conference reading, see Abrecht 1978). But it was another ten years before the WCC began to address an ethic for the liberation of life demanding respect for animals and preservation of species for their own sake, not just their benefit to humankind (see Birch et al. 1990, app.).

Meanwhile, the *aggiornamento* of Roman Catholic theology and mission begun at Vatican Council II (1962-65)—an event for all humanity—resulted in key documents: *Dogmatic Constitution on the Church* (1964), *Decree on Ecumenism* (1964), *Declaration on the Relation of the Church to Non-Christian Religions* (1965), *Pastoral Constitution on the Church in the Modern World* (1965). These also proclaim the Christian vision of human unity. But official Roman Catholic teaching about environmental stewardship did not develop until fifteen years later when, during a trip to the Americas (Puebla and Des Moines, 1979), Pope John Paul II emphasized land ethics. Belatedly in 1990 he issued a *Message on the Ecological Crisis: A Common Responsibility*, which notes:

> We cannot interfere in one area of the ecosystem without paying due attention both to the consequences of such interference in other areas and to the

well-being of future generations. . . . The earth is ultimately a common heritage, the fruits of which are for the benefit of all. . . . It is manifestly unjust that a privileged few should continue to accumulate excess goods, squandering available resources, while masses of people are living in conditions of misery at the very lowest level of subsistence.[1]

Then, on Pentecost 1992, at Baixada Fluminense, Brazil, parallel to the UNCED Earth Summit, a gathering of Protestant, Roman Catholic, Orthodox and Anglican leaders issued a *Letter to the Churches* that underscores the urgency of making

strong and permanent spiritual, moral and material commitments to the emergence of new models of society, based in deepest gratitude to God for the gift of life and in respect for the whole of God's creation. . . . Our churches themselves must be places where we learn anew what it means that God's covenant extends to all creatures. . . . We need to mourn and repent for our massive neglect, injustice and destruction. We have offended God, 'maker of heaven and earth,' and we have blasphemed life and one another. We have come to our senses only very late, and do not do so even yet. . . . We plead for forgiveness and pray for a profound change of heart, a radical turning from the way of death to God and the way of life.
　　The Spirit is the giver and sustainer of life. All that fosters life, such as justice, solidarity, and love, and all that defends life, such as the evangelical commitment to stand with the poor, the struggle against racism and casteism, and the pledge to reduce armaments and violence, concretely signifies living according to the Spirit. This is more than a political act for the Christian; it is spiritual practice. . . . Where we must always begin is with veneration and respect for all creatures, especially for human beings, beginning with those most in need. The Spirit teaches us to go first to those places where community and creation are most obviously languishing, those melancholy places where the cry of the people and the cry of the earth are intermingled. [There] we meet Jesus, who goes before, in solidarity and healing (for full text see Granberg-Michaelson 1992, 70-73).

One way to bring into focus important ecumenical words and actions affirming earth community is to listen to these words from Martin Luther King, Jr.'s *Letter from a Birmingham Jail* (1963). "Injustice anywhere is a threat to justice everywhere. We are caught in an inescapable network of mutuality, tied in a single garment of destiny." *A single garment of destiny!* The passion and commitment expressed in these ecological-ethical-theological words uttered by the Baptist minister who was martyred in 1968 point to the burning focus of the ecumenical faith in this century.
　　Through the ecumenical study/movement, Christian faith has been presented as a faith rooted in historical repentance. Wherever people have grasped this faith they have gained the freedom to get involved in the issues of social and interfaith justice. And they have deepened their criticism of idolatry, including self-idola-

try. But the tares have grown with the wheat. Idolatry has become a global system in this century, increasing the need for a true religion for humanity.

In 1935, the ecumenical study/movement heard Reinhold Niebuhr say, "There is no deeper pathos in the spiritual life of man than the cruelty of righteous people. If any one idea dominates the teachings of Jesus, it is his opposition to the self-righteousness of the righteous" (*An Interpretation of Christian Ethics*). No authentic engagement in ecological and social justice is possible apart from the knowledge of the damage that "the self-righteousness of the righteous" causes to human community.

True religion is rooted in true repentance. Theological knowledge of one humanity, fundamental to the idea of ecological and social justice, brings us to a moment of repentance. This is what makes the ecumenical study/movement a sign of being true religion. The unity of humanity is upheld and defended by the blood of twentieth-century martyrs (Martin Luther King, Jr., Steve Biko, Oscar Romero, Dietrich Bonhoeffer, and many others).

Salvation from the Periphery

It is significant that the summary words of the ecumenical study/ movement come from a member of the oppressed minority in the United States. The ecumenical movement regained its authenticity as its witness was uttered from the rejected periphery. The saving mystery of the periphery has confronted the ecumenical movement. The message of one humanity has come from the periphery; *the locus of true religion is periphery.*

The church and theology in the manner of the imperial Constantine arrangement have crumbled for a theological reason: imperial Christianity does not conform to the form (morphe) of Jesus Christ, who has gone to the utter periphery. The ecumenical study/movement is again in transit from the *theologia gloriae* (center theology) to the *theologia crucis* (periphery theology).

Ecumenism must remember that the center person, Jesus Christ, established his centrality by going to the periphery (Mk. 2:16). As soon as a periphery becomes a center (a point of prestige and power), Jesus Christ, the head of the church and of its ecumenical movement, moves again to the authentic periphery. One who remains homeless ever (Lk. 9:58, 1 Cor. 4:11) inspires us to repentance and engagement.

A temptation to romanticize the periphery must be rejected. The periphery is the place of ignominy—without any honor or prestige whatsoever.

In the context of the present discussion, there are three meanings of the word "periphery": ecological, ethical and theological. The *ecological* periphery represents a macro and micro web. Even the most peripheral frog has its place in the vast cosmic ecological totality.

The *ethical* periphery is where people are murdered, oppressed, uprooted and hungry because of the violence of ecological and social injustice. The *theological* periphery comes from an utterly peripherized Christ. He who is the head of the church goes outside the church, ignoring the weighty definition "extra ecclesiam non salus est." The periphery calls humanity to become one human community (Jn. 12:32, Jer. 7:5-7) for the sake of a single planet with diverse peoples.

II

Agenda 1. From Periphery to Center

In light of the periphery theology, how shall we respond to the clash between good housekeeping ("shalom"—social and environmental wholesomeness) and bad housekeeping ("un-shalom"—social and environmental degradation) throughout the inhabited world (*oikumene*)? In this ecumenical vista, I see three vital intersections:

a. *Cosmology and Theology.* Theology intersects with the primordial life-giving and life-sustaining biocosmological reality. Cosmology is biocosmology. The cosmos, being a primary life-giving reality, has its own civilization of incredible duration. If civilization involves cultivation of life, then "God-talk" and "cosmos-talk" meet at "life-talk."

b. *Culture and Justice.* Theology intersects with human culture in the form of struggles to overcome maldistributions of power. The *oikumene* is a cultured space in which power is always maldistributed, due to human concupiscence. Thus a cultured space is inherently violent and potentially just, at the same time.

c. *Interfaith Perspective.* Theology intersects with the messages of salvation proclaimed by the great religious traditions. There is no such thing as a chemically pure faith in isolation. Every faith inevitably has cultural overlays and interfaith dimension. This is always a situation of crisis (danger and opportunity).

The progression, in these points, is from (a) *cosmos* as a dynamic process that exhibits primordial grace, to (b) *cultures* within time and space shaped by humans who often misuse power, to (c) the symbols and words of great *religions* that invite us to examine the present un-shalom in the light of time and space "beyond tragedy." In ecumenical theological perspective, I can envision *cosmos* (universe and planet) as an *oikos* (home), and the *oikos* becoming an *ecclesia* (church).

This vision moves from periphery to center. This is opposite the traditional direction which goes from center to periphery. The reversal of direction poses a critical challenge to traditional religious and theological thoughts, whose spiritual and intellectual orientation has been "from center to periphery." The centripetal methodology (from cosmos to *ecclesia*) reveals things hidden from the centrifugal methodology (from *ecclesia* to cosmos). Three observations follow to illustrate this assertion:

a. One affirms in theology that "God created the heavens and the earth." In contrast, one recognizes in biocosmology a "theological" passion which says, "The heavens and the earth created God (gods)." The second position must not be rejected outright, especially not in the Christian West, which gives cognizance to the first position for only two hours on Sunday morning, and during the rest of the week lives according to the second position. This culture suffers from schizophrenia ridden with latent guilt, excepting for a Joseph Campbell, who proposes a cosmological gospel according to "the power of myths." One half of humanity is aware of the first position. The other half accepts the second position without argument. A search for the meaning of the first position necessarily involves an understanding of the second position, and vice versa. The ecumenical study/movement must correctly understand Baal (the religious culture of space distribution) in order to understand Yahweh (the religious culture of time distribution), and vice versa.

b. Is there any positive theological value in the biocosmological idea that "the heavens and the earth created God (gods)"? In what ways do this and the other position contribute, positively or negatively, to the idea of one humanity? The oppressors at the center of socio-economic power distort both theological and biocosmological positions. The people at the periphery perceive that the power-wielding class twists theological and biocosmological positions alike. Wall Street (investment capital) frequently controls or overrides both.

c. One must carefully examine whether the biocosmological position is really more detrimental to the maintenance and nurture of eco-social justice in earth community than the traditional theological position. Isn't it possible that Christian theological culture is more, or at least as, violent and unjust as the biocosmological culture? "We were taking the black young men who had been crippled by our society and sending them eight thousand miles away to guarantee liberties in Southeast Asia which they had not found in southwest Georgia and East Harlem (King 1967).

Agenda 2. The Impossibility of "Exiting Earth"

In 1968, the human race first saw a color picture of planet earth photographed from outer space. It was a moment of intuition deeper than rational discourse. The earth-ball traversing in the infinite ocean of the universe impressed the human soul with the conviction that the earth itself is none other than the life-sustaining "Noah's Ark." This immediate and intuitive observation has cosmo-theological—that is, both cosmic and theological—meaning. None of us can live naturally outside the planet's biosphere. There is only one history, natural and human, no matter how complex and confusing it may be. The sacred is webbed with the profane, and vice versa, in one history (Mt. 13:29). That there is only one human history means the following:

a. The biosphere is the primary location of human salvation. Outside the biosphere there is not salvation. Universal access to oxygen (through clean air) must be a fundamental topic of justice. There is less oxygen in Harlem than at Park Avenue, because of environmental injustice reinforced by racism. Periphery theology is keenly aware of the integration of life and justice; it recognizes that "you shall not kill" is understood differently by those living on the periphery than by the people of the center. Justice for one humanity must be defined from the periphery perspective.

b. The biocosmological world view instructs us to build justice by "staying in," not by "getting out." The biblical "exit from Egypt" is possible; but "exit from earth" (exiting oxygen) is impossible. The impossibility of exiting earth challenges the various religious and theological doctrines that present the ultimate salvation as "getting out" of a troubled situation (e.g., the Hindu-Buddhist doctrine of Nirvana, the Christian "rapture theology," etc.). The paradigm of biosphere authenticates the ethical direction of "staying in" when we are challenged by injustice. The favored form of salvation for the center people is "getting out," leaving the trouble behind. The periphery orientation is far more committed to healing the wounds by "staying in."

True religion must be harmonious with the paradigm of the biosphere. When the cosmo-*oikos* itself becomes *ecclesia* (a congregation of people who are called-out), what we now think of as *ecclesia* disappears.

c. If there is only one history, there will be a need to redefine the divide within one humanity, central to most religious messages, between the saved (those in the ark—"sheep") and the condemned (those drowning outside the ark—"goats"). This redefinition must come from those who are rejected and peripherized. If one carelessly identifies the "sheep zone" with the Christian West, and the "goat zone" with the non-Christian nations, then one must be immediately advised that concern for social justice—the sign of true religion—is more present in the "goat zone" than in the "sheep zone." The *ecclesia* is to do justice. When justice becomes complete in our world, the realm of God is with us and the *ecclesia* disappears.

d. One must "stay in" a happy and blessed relationship with the land and with the people. "The land will vomit you out for defiling it" (Lev. 18:28). "When an alien resides with you in your land, you shall not oppress the alien" (Lev. 19:33). This imperative is authentically ecumenical. It points to the basis for the shalom of one humanity.

e. The thought that there is only one history challenges an accepted Christian theology of "universality." According to periphery theology, the universal saving efficacy of the gospel must be presented in the context of "Go and do likewise" (conducive of social and environmental wholesomeness [Lk. 10:37]), rather than in the context of "God, I thank you that I am not like other people" (conducive of social and environmental degradation [Lk. 18:11]). The first universality is truly ecumenical, since it is rooted in repentance. The second goes against the vision of the unity of humanity. It is false religion.

Agenda 3. Periphery Theology and Interfaith Perspective

Christian theology cannot function meaningfully without being in dialogue with the world of religious symbols of other spiritual traditions. How do other traditions address themselves to the issue of the human spirit and the natural environment?

Ecological universality is a new critical element that deepens our traditional understanding of the universality of the Christian gospel. Would ecological universality bring Christian theology and religious study together? Seminary and university courses on "religions" should provide a deeper level of discussion on the nature of humanity's diverse religious life by understanding the place of nature in all religious traditions.

The interfaith perspective is different from a common-denominator religious perspective. The former entertains tensions and even contradictions, while the latter searches for balance and becomes "settled." The former demands an existential study of religious traditions; the latter can be built upon the basis of schematic observation. Ecumenical study must recognize that the common-denominator religious perspective cannot have a cutting edge that contributes to the unity of humanity.

Hence, there is no such thing as a universally valid interfaith perspective. It must always be created contextually, in response to cultural dynamics and local needs or challenges. An interfaith perspective must be different now than it was during the Reformation, and interfaith perspective in Bombay must be different from that in New York City. It is so because the cultures of Bombay and New York, and distributions of power in each locale, are distinct.

Interfaith perspective becomes an empty concept unless it is spoken by a person of commitment who says, "Here I stand." In the periphery theology, "here" is the periphery where Christ is crucified. No one could be less imperialistic or more open than one who is crucified. The Christian ecumenical perspective knows where it stands, and because of this knowledge, is radically and critically open to other religious traditions.

Summary

In all three topics emphasized above—Periphery to Center, Impossibility of Exiting Earth, Periphery Theology and Interfaith Perspective—the guiding principle is the theological value of being at the periphery. The periphery is the place of *satyagraha* power, which is *not* imperialistic. In our ecumenical theology for earth community, how do we make this guiding principle more concrete and meaningful?

Note

1. Irish missionary Sean McDonagh critiques the social teachings of the Roman Catholic Church for lacking environmental urgency and calls for the church's conversion to a pastoral ministry of sustainability (1994, 103-10). Protestant ecological thought also has blind spots, some of which are discussed in Fowler 1995, 159-79.

PART 3

Eco-Social Ethics

What does Christian environmental ethics look like? The chapters in this section show that it has more than one shape, even as it shares certain characteristics: showing confessional resonance, expressing comprehensive social concern, and demonstrating public significance.

The state-of-the-art paper by Janet Parker and Roberta Richards explores the nuanced development and multiple aspects of Christian eco-social ethics. They discuss published contributions to four types of approaches—confessional/ecumenical, liberationist, process theology, and official church teachings—that are on the leading edge of environmentally and theologically alert ethical reflection. Each approach, in a distinctive way, chooses to be for nature and people within one interrelated community. This shared ethical orientation—concerned to do eco-justice—widens the ethical horizon and fosters moral agency at individual, institutional, and societal levels.

Parker and Richards call for more dialogue between ethicists and scientists, better integration of ecology in all areas of Christian ethics and daily practice, clearer focus on the "interstructured nature of human injustice and environmental degradation . . . [and] finally, a priority must be placed on transforming the way the 'rich' live." The appendices are an important feature of chapter 9; they "flag" important writings on moral obligations to animals, economics and ecology, science and technology, response to unsustainable population growth.

The latter subject of ethical reflection is linked with unsustainable production-consumption patterns in a separate essay by James Martin-Schramm. His chapter provides a useful overview of key Christian thinkers on population ethics, and then asks whether or when ecological jeopardy requires the imposition of limits on reproductive freedom to protect security and subsistence rights. A guideline might be this: Before coercion is implemented to limit population growth, it should be used in relation to overconsumption. The church ecumenical must push for systemic change accompanied by distributive justice to challenge the culture of acquisitiveness and to serve equity.

Martin-Schramm illumines the constructive role of religious ethics generally and Christian ethics particularly in addressing issues of reproductive health, family planning, and abortion; reproductive rights and respect for other cultures; migration and immigration issues; U.S. population growth and its heavy impact through resource-use. He encourages integrative ethical reflection on achieving sustainable consumption-population levels.

A May 1992 gathering in Washington, D.C., of religious leaders, scientists, and public officials called upon government "to change national policy so that [it] will begin to ease, not continue to increase, the burdens on our biosphere and their effect upon the planet's people." Participants affirmed the need to achieve "social justice and the preservation of the environment," and noted that "we do not have to agree on how the natural world was made to be willing to work together to preserve it." The common search for an adequate social ethic to meet the environmental challenge is a special opportunity for interreligious dialogue and cooperation.

As Mary Evelyn Tucker's chapter indicates, a study of religious resources for environmentalism will employ multiple methods, which should result in livelier theologies and ethics, informed and transformed by the dialogue. She suggests how to undertake this work.

9

Christian Ethics and the Environmental Challenge

JANET PARKER AND ROBERTA RICHARDS

Overview of the Field

A commitment to justice and other ethical principles lies at the heart of Christian life and spirituality. But until recently, the scope of that commitment has been truncated; Christian ethics has concentrated almost exclusively on human moral obligations to other humans, to their communities, and to God. A study of the annual meetings of the Society of Christian Ethics revealed that between 1959 and 1983 the primary topics raised in papers and panel discussions were foundational issues; the oppression of blacks, women, and other disadvantaged peoples; moral problems raised by war; politics, law and human rights; economics, technology and vocational ethics; and a few miscellaneous topics including comparative religious ethics, ethics and liturgy, sexual ethics, and ethics and education (Long 1985). Ecology received scant attention from Christian ethicists of this period; like other Christians, they tended to view the extra-human elements of nature as mere backdrop for the central drama of history: (human) redemption.

In the last couple of decades, and especially the last few years, Christian ethicists have joined their secular counterparts in reexamining human obligations to plants, animals, and ecosystems in light of growing ecological devastation. Although the writings on ecology by Christian ethicists are diverse, two themes have been dominant: that a theocentric ethic requires loving care of all of creation; and that the Christian commitment to justice is incomplete without a concomitant concern for ecology. The growing involvement of Christian ethicists in environmental issues is reflected in the Society of Christian Ethics, which now includes an interest group on "Environment and Ethics," and which has published a number of articles on ecological themes in its annuals. In an address to the Pacific Section of the Society of Christian Ethics in 1990, President Larry Rasmussen stated that ecological concerns would be the top issue facing Christians during this decade.

Leading-edge Scholarship on the Environmental Challenge

The recent interest in ecologically informed ethics has resulted in an increasing number of books and articles on the subject. Happily, there are now too many theologians and ethicists writing on ecological issues to include them all in this state-of-the-art survey. In order to cover the leading-edge scholarship emerging in this area, this section will identify four basic approaches characteristic of the work being done by Christian ethicists. While these approaches enable us to grasp the contours of current ecological ethics, it must be remembered that they are types. No one fits into any of these approaches perfectly, and some exhibit aspects of more than one approach. Moreover, these four approaches do not exhaust all the possibilities for classifying Christian ecological ethics. Rather, they represent important and identifiable standpoints for theologians and ethicists currently addressing the ecological crisis. The approaches are confessional/ecumenical, liberationist, process theology, and official church teachings.

Confessional/Ecumenical Scholarship

Many scholars incorporating ecological concerns into their work operate self-consciously out of a particular confessional tradition, which they mine for theological and ethical resources, and to which they pose the challenge of the global ecological crisis. Their starting point is their tradition, rather than a particular theological school (i.e., process theology), or a particular method (i.e., liberationist). Yet while they identify themselves as rooted in a confessional tradition, they also exhibit a marked ecumenical commitment and outlook in their work. Many of the Protestants who fall into this category are closely connected to the World Council of Churches and other ecumenical agencies. Further, many of these scholars move beyond religious ecumenism into interdisciplinary endeavors involving the natural and social sciences, politics, and economics. While entering into dialogue with the wider world, however, confessional/ecumenical scholars usually address Christians and Christian churches as their target audience. Theirs is an ethics emerging from and directed to the church, as well as the academy. In contrast with official church teachings, however, these scholars speak for themselves; their work does not represent the official policy or position of their tradition.

One prevalent position Protestant ethicists and theologians take with regard to the ecological crisis emphasizes eco-justice (e.g., see Hessel 1992). The contributors to Hessel's book represent a variety of Protestant denominations, but all develop the relationship between eco-justice and theology. In the introduction to the book, Hessel defines eco-justice as "constructive human responses that concentrate on the link between ecological health and human justice" (ibid., 9). He adds that "the common goal of such careful efforts to engage the world crisis of ecology and justice is to restore earth community" (ibid.).

Two prominent ethicists who represent the eco-justice position are Larry Rasmussen and James Nash. Drawing on his Lutheran heritage, Rasmussen explores how a theology of the cross might inform an eco-justice ethic in his essay,

"Returning To Our Senses: The Theology of the Cross as a Theology for Eco-Justice" (Rasmussen 1992). In numerous other articles and in his recently published book, *Moral Fragments and Moral Community,* Rasmussen articulates a communitarian eco-justice ethic which integrates commitment to Christian community, passion for social and ecological justice, and a sacramentalist vision of the cosmos (Rasmussen 1993 and 1992b, 83-87).

James Nash, a Methodist, is the executive director of The Churches' Center for Theology and Public Policy. Nash enriches the eco-justice position with his persuasive argument for "biotic rights" (Nash 1993, 137-62) in the 1993 *Annual of the Society of Christian Ethics*. In *Loving Nature,* Nash incorporates his interest in biotic rights into his larger project of reinterpreting traditional Christian doctrines in ecologically sound ways and offering substantive policy directions for ecological integrity (Nash 1991).

Another common position centers on the stewardship of God's creation. The most prominent representative of the stewardship position is undoubtedly Douglas John Hall. His ground-breaking work, *The Steward: A Biblical Symbol Come of Age,* is probably the most widely known articulation of the stewardship ethic to date (Hall 1982/90). The book was originally written at the request of the Commission on Stewardship of the National Council of Churches, and in its revised form incorporates material from the WCC's "Justice, Peace and the Integrity of Creation" process. Hall argues that stewardship is the "rightful role" for which humans have been created, and that the ancient metaphor of the steward is a "vital contemporary symbol" which has "come of age" (ibid., 95, 11). Positioning the role of the steward between the two extremes of domination and abandonment of nature, Hall asserts:

Against the concept of human sovereignty that modern industrial *hubris* taught us to covet for our species, the symbol of the steward challenges human beings to assume the posture of those who serve. And contrary to the retreat from the world into which we have been seduced by our failure at mastering it, stewardship challenges us to serve responsibly and as those committed to creation (ibid., 95).

Hall expands his concept of stewardship as servanthood in *Imaging God: Dominion As Stewardship* (Hall 1986), in which he makes a valiant attempt to ameliorate the much-maligned biblical concept of "dominion." He argues that, christologically interpreted, "dominion . . . can only mean stewardship, and stewardship ultimately interpreted as love: sacrificial, self-giving love *(agape)*" (ibid., 186). Whether or not one eschews the use of the term "dominion," the stewardship position is rapidly gaining ground as the most common Christian approach to the ecological crisis, at least among the churches. Other representatives of the stewardship position include Loren Wilkinson, and Nancy Wright and Donald Kill (Wilkinson 1980; Wright and Kill 1993).

In surveying the leading edge Catholic scholarship on ecological issues, one is puzzled to discover that Catholic responses to the ecological crisis are not, for the most part, coming from moral theologians. The Catholic scholars who are addressing ecological concerns tend to work out of other disciplines. Two of the most important Catholic scholars working in this area are Thomas Berry and Rosemary Radford Ruether, neither of whom is trained as a moral theologian. Perhaps the reason for this lacuna in Catholic moral theology can be found in the moral norm Catholic theology has settled upon: the dignity of the human person. This norm has resulted in stellar work from Catholic moral theologians on human rights and liberation theology. Unfortunately it is also a deeply anthropocentric norm, which may account for the lack of attention to ecological issues.

The Catholic contribution to ecological theology and ethics has been greatest in the areas of cosmology and creation spirituality. Drawing upon their deeply sacramentalist tradition, Catholic scholars remind us that an adequate cosmology is a fundamental building block for any viable ecological ethic. The most famous Catholic scholar to offer an ecological cosmology is undoubtedly Thomas Berry. While all may not subscribe to it, few Christians concerned with ecological issues have not heard of Berry's "common creation story." Christians from all denominations and religious traditions are reading *The Universe Story* and incorporating its poetic and scientific insights into their ecological praxis (Swimme and Berry 1992). The vision of cosmogenesis and homogenesis (the story of cultural evolution) found in these pages has the potential to transform the way Christians understand ourselves and the universe, our home.

Rosemary Radford Ruether's contribution has been in the areas of historical theology and ecofeminism, where she has been both prolific and brilliant. She is one of the premier ecofeminist theologians of our time, crossing the boundaries between the confessional/ecumenical and liberationist approaches. Her *Gaia and God* has greatly advanced the sophistication and visibility of ecofeminist theology (Ruether 1992). While trained as a historical theologian, Ruether effectively functions as a moral theologian as well; in *Gaia and God* she integrates incisive ethical analysis into her ecofeminist critique of Western Christian history and tradition. In a sense, Ruether's work represents the fruitful integration of the Catholic concern for cosmology and spirituality with the Protestant emphasis on eco-justice. She writes:

> A healed relation to each other and to the earth then calls for a new consciousness, a new symbolic culture and spirituality. . . . Needless to say, spirituality or new consciousness will not transform deeply materialized relations of domination by themselves. We must be wary of new forms of privatized intrapsychic activity, divorced from social systems of power. Rather, we must see the work of eco-justice and the work of spirituality as interrelated, the inner and outer aspects of one process of conversion and transformation (ibid., 4).

To conclude this survey of Catholic scholarship on the environment, mention must be made of a book published by Orbis Books in late 1994. *Embracing Earth: Catholic Approaches to Ecology* is an anthology with articles by John Carroll, Richard Rohr, William McNamara, Paula Gonzalez, and others. This volume makes a significant contribution to the growing Catholic corpus of ecological theology, with essays covering such diverse topics as Catholic population policy, technology, eucharistic theology, and "ecological resources in the Benedictine Rule" (LaChance and Carroll 1994; see also Cowdin 1994). The diversity of subjects treated presages the increasing involvement of Catholic scholars from a variety of disciplines, including moral theology, in ecological concerns.

Liberationist Scholarship

Theologians and ethicists working out of the confessional/ecumenical approach may be very concerned with justice, as we have seen. What distinguishes scholars with a liberationist approach is not their concern with justice, per se, but the radical nature of their critique of Christian traditions and the method which they bring to their work. Leonardo Boff, while asserting that liberation theology maintains continuity with Christian tradition, writes: "With respect to the limits and incompleteness of the systems of the past . . . liberation theology maintains a stance of *criticism*" (Boff and Boff 1987, 36). The liberationist approach is perhaps most clearly identified by the unique and relatively new method which it has developed. As Gutiérrez writes, "The theology of liberation offers us not so much a new theme for reflection as a *new way* to do theology" (Gutiérrez 1973/88, 12). This "new way" introduces the radical step of putting praxis, or liberating action, before theology. Theological and ethical reflection is always the "second step."[1] Thus concrete historical realities, not confessional traditions, are the entry point for a liberationist approach.

Liberationist theology and ethics are practiced today by a wide variety of communities and groups. In its earlier stages, liberationist theology focused primarily on the liberation of a particular community, such as women, African-Americans, the poor of Latin America. In the past decade or so, liberationist theologies have begun to recognize and articulate the connections between their struggles for liberation and the struggles of others. They have begun to form alliances with one another and to join in solidarity with other groups to pursue liberation and justice for all peoples. Formerly, however, the focus was always on *human* liberation and *human* justice.[2] The environmentalist movement, until recently largely populated by white males, was viewed with suspicion as a distraction from human social justice issues. Within the past five to ten years, however, the ecocidal assault of human beings on the life systems of the planet has become impossible to ignore. In particular, liberationist theologians/ ethicists have been mobilized by the realization that the communities they represent—the poor, women, people of color, indigenous people—are disproportionately affected by ecological devastation. In response, liberationists are increasingly incorporating ecological concerns into their work. Today, a sophisticated and mature liberationist perspective recognizes that domination of oppressed peoples and domination of the earth are interstructured and interdependent realities.

Three types of liberationist theology/ethics currently engaging ecological issues are ecofeminism/ecowomanism, Latin American liberation theology, and Native American theology. An entire state-of-the-art paper is being dedicated to ecofeminism, so the treatment here will accordingly be brief. An anthology entitled *Ecofeminism and the Sacred* provides an excellent introduction to religious ecofeminism (Adams 1993). In her introduction, Carol Adams explains:

> Ecofeminism identifies the twin dominations of women and the rest of nature. To the issues of sexism, racism, classism and heterosexism that concern feminists, ecofeminists add naturism—the oppression of the rest of nature. Ecofeminism argues that the connections between the oppression of women and the rest of nature must be recognized to understand adequately both oppressions (ibid., 1).

Earlier (primarily white) ecofeminism emphasized the patriarchal identification of women with nature but failed to pay much attention to other forms of oppression. Now, however, many ecofeminists focus not on gender, but on the common "logic of domination" that constructs and connects all human oppression and the exploitation of nature (ibid., 2). Beverly Harrison was one of the first feminist ethicists to make this shift in focus. Her essay, "The Politics of Energy Policy," remains an excellent example of an ecofeminist scholarship that places power analysis at the center of ethical inquiry and reflection (Harrison and Robb 1985). More recent works of exceptional quality and importance by ecofeminist theologians include *The Body of God* by Sallie McFague (1993); *Gaia and God* by Rosemary Radford Ruether (1992); and *From Apocalypse to Genesis* by Anne Primavesi (1991). A particularly exciting development is the emergence of ecowomanism in the last few years. Two of the articles in Adams's anthology are written by ecowomanists: Delores Williams (1993) and Shamara Shantu Riley (1993). Ecowomanists emphasize the often unrecognized connections between the despoilment of nature and the exploitation of black women's bodies. They are further concerned with the "environmental racism" that sentences their communities to live in areas with much higher toxic waste and pollution.

It is safe to say that an ecological Latin American liberation theology is still in its infancy. The Western paradigm of the historical transformation of society has dominated Latin American liberation theology. Time and human history, rather than space and the cosmos, have been the primary categories of Western thought (Tinker 1990, 145-48). This paradigm is beginning to shift, however, as Latin American liberation theologians are starting to incorporate the voices and insights of women, indigenous peoples, and people of African descent. As they listen to these marginalized voices within their culture, some theologians are beginning to overcome the nature/history split. Biologist and theologian Ingemar Hedstrom was one of the first Latin Americans to address the ecological crisis. He has written several books in Spanish and has at least one article published in English (1990). Hedstrom argues that the preferential option for the poor must be recast as a preferential option *for life*. Avoiding the temptation to choose either *anthropocentrism* or *ecocentrism*, Hedstrom calls for a balance between meeting human needs and respecting environmental limits (ibid., 120-21).

Leonardo Boff has been working on ecological issues for the last several years. His new book, *Ecology and Liberation*, now available in English from Orbis Books, is the first *book* published in English that addresses the ecological crisis from a Latin American liberationist perspective (Boff 1995). Ivone Gebara brings a feminist, ecological critique to Latin American liberation theology and calls for a new vision of transcendence as *relation* among all that exists. Resurrection is redefined as the "transcendence of situations in which death, murder, injustice, or destruction of a people, a group, or a person has been present" (Gebara 1993, 182). Gebara emphasizes the "collective ethical character of resurrection in the sense of a continual challenge to respect life, to act for the sake of life" (ibid., 183). Gebara's new vision of transcendence promises to bring rich eco-ethical dimensions to old theological and biblical concepts.

When indigenous cultures are held up as valuable models for an ecological relationship to the earth, non-Christian native cultures with their traditional religions intact are usually envisioned. Unfortunately, this conception of indigenous cultures is distorted. Christian missionaries have made inroads into all but the most isolated indigenous areas, and many tribal people have converted to Christianity. This is particularly true in North America, although Native American religious traditions continue to survive and are being revived. Any appeal to indigenous peoples that fails to acknowledge this "missionary conquest" (see Tinker 1993) misrepresents their lives, ignoring both the violence Western Christianity has perpetrated upon their cultures and the gifts Native Christianity has to offer Christian theology and ethics.

George Tinker, a Native American theologian, speaks out of the lived experience of Native American Christians who are struggling to integrate ancient tribal spirituality with Christian liturgy and theology. In his article, "The Integrity of Creation: Restoring Trinitarian Balance," Tinker argues that an adequate theology of creation is the basis for any progress toward justice and peace (Tinker 1989, 527). The Indian understanding of creation as sacred embraces all of life, from the smallest life form to international relations. It informs the *life* of the Indian community, thus it is the foundation of their ethics (ibid., 532). The key ethical stance the Native American takes toward creation is one of respect. Respect for the sacredness of all creation and recognition of the need for balance and reciprocity characterize Native American dealings with the non-human world. Tinker asks haunting questions: "What reciprocal act restores the earth as the rain forests are cleared? As we take from the earth to build bombs or create new luxuries, what do we return to the earth?" (ibid., 534). Tinker offers an ecological ethic which establishes respect for creation as the starting-point, and argues that justice and peace (for all our human and non-human relatives) will flow naturally as a result (cf. Tinker 1990, 145-48; 1992b, 322).

Process Theologians

Process theology, with its understanding of God and the universe as an interconnected, ongoing process, provides a natural foundation for an ecological ethic. Process theologians are among the earliest and most forceful Christian advocates of sweeping ecological reform. Theologians in the tradition of Alfred North Whitehead and Charles Hartshorne maintain that all creatures are of value for their own sakes as subjects of experience, as well as being of value to God, who participates in their joys and pains. Unlike those who perceive God as dictating and controlling events, process theologians understand that reality is a process of creative evolution, and thus the future is truly open. John Cobb, one of the foremost contemporary process theologians, explains that "God calls us to life, but God does not close the door to death, if that is what we choose" (Cobb 1982, 27). Process theologians call on humans to exercise our creative freedom to promote the flourishing of life in all of its richness and diversity.

While process theology has on occasion been chided for its obscurity, process thinkers have used their philosophical roots to develop a compelling ethics of life, with powerful normative implications. In *The Liberation of Life* theologian John Cobb and biologist Charles Birch call for the liberation of the very *concept* of life from the "bondage" which results from interpreting life through the lens of the reductive mechanistic model (Birch and Cobb 1981/90, 2). They contend that life should be viewed through an ecological model, which perceives all of the interconnected forms of life—from the simplest entities through to God—as subjects of experience. All subjects of experience are of intrinsic value, Cobb and Birch maintain, and this value increases in proportion to the richness of experience. God, known here as Life, is the lure which encourages the striving for richer experience, and thus higher value.

The ecological model of life supports a non-anthropocentric ethic which aims at the enhancement of total rich experience. This ethic gives special consideration to complex creatures with advanced nervous systems, and thus continues to recognize the unique status of human beings, while simultaneously valuing all of the interdependent parts of ecosystems for their intrinsic and instrumental value. The best strategy for increasing total rich experience, Cobb and Birch maintain, "is one in which a large human population learns to live comfortably yet frugally and thereby relaxing pressure on the biosphere as a whole." Small-scale farming and technology should be used to create a society which is "just and sustainable" rather than "affluent and profligate." "Every step that could lead either to making room for more people or for more animals, especially wild animals, without lowering the quality of life, would be a victory" (ibid., 173).

The process view of the cosmos has informed ethical reflection on a number of topics important to Christians. In *For the Common Good,* Cobb teams up with economist Herman Daly to write a stunning challenge to the economic dogma that human well-being can be measured by increasing GNP (Cobb and Daly 1989, see app. C). In *Of God and Pelicans* Jay McDaniel unites insights from process theology with feminism and Buddhism to develop a "life-centered" ethic and spirituality which inspires goodwill toward all living creatures (McDaniel 1989). In *Technology, Environment, and Human Values* and *Ethics in an Age of Technology,* Ian Barbour includes the process theology understanding of value in his analysis of technology (Barbour 1980, app. D; also see Barbour 1993).

Official Church Teachings on Ecology

The moral obligations of human beings to the embattled elements of nature have been examined by almost every Western Christian denomination and international church organization. Churches began producing statements on ecological problems in the mid-1970s as confidence in technology began to wane and evidence of the "limits-to growth" mounted.[3] The majority of official church statements on ecology appeal to the doctrine of creation, in spite of the conventional wisdom which holds that social and ethical positions grounded in creation theology tend to be excessively conservative (see Ellingson 1993, 41-48, 201-18; Sheldon 1972).

The World Council of Churches (WCC) set the tone for many of the subsequent church writings on ecology with its adoption in 1979 of the threefold goal of "justice, participation, and sustainability." This goal was reformulated as "justice, peace, and the integrity of creation" in 1983. The central point of WCC writings on ecology is made forcefully and repeatedly: "Justice is truly indivisible, not only as a matter of theological conviction but in practice" (WCC Canberra Assembly 1991, 3:2 no.5). Justice and peace for human beings cannot survive while nature is being exploited, and ecosystem integrity cannot be secured while poverty and injustice prevail.

The seventh WCC Assembly, held in Canberra in 1991, had as its theme "Come Holy Spirit: Renew the Whole Creation." Using a creation theology based on biblical warrants and a relational view of the human person, the Assembly calls for a new ethic of economy and ecology.

> Our vision is of those with enough material goods beginning to live with less while replacing their idolatry of consumerism with a new spirituality. . . . We envision a world in which the needs of all creation are integrated with the workings of governments and international business, where importing and exporting do not spell hunger and environmental degradation for the poor. In such a world bio-regions are more important than national boundaries. . . . The goal of technology will be to work with nature and its mysteries and not to master it (no. 17).

The WCC calls for churches to acknowledge that vulnerable humans and other living creatures are being endangered by practices which "belong to life-styles and power structures which have received theological support and sanction" (no. 13). Accordingly, the churches must redirect their priorities and policies through a renewed commitment to justice, peace, and the integrity of creation.

Official Catholic responses to the ecological crisis have taken two primary forms. The U.S. Catholic Bishops expressed their concern for the environment in a recent pastoral letter entitled "Renewing the Earth: An Invitation to Reflection and Action on Environment in Light of Catholic Social Teaching." The letter emphasizes human ecological responsibility arising out of respect for the Creator and the creation.

> By preserving natural environments, by protecting endangered species, by laboring to make human environments compatible with local ecology, by employing appropriate technology, and by carefully evaluating technological innovations as we adopt them, we exhibit respect for creation and reverence for the Creator (USCC 1991, 7).

The encyclicals and proclamations of Pope John Paul II constitute the second source for official Catholic teaching on the environment. These documents incorporate ecological concerns into his vision of "authentic human development" through justice and solidarity. In contrast to most mainline Protestant ecological theologies, which have largely repudiated the language of domination, John Paul II maintains that human beings are called to subdue and have dominion over nature; "Man is made to be in the visible universe an image and likeness of God himself, and he is placed in it in order to subdue the earth" (John Paul II 1981, opening greeting). But the dominion granted to human beings is not absolute. In accordance with divine law, humans must share the earth's bounty equitably, even when this requires sacrificing property rights, and must respect the created order of the cosmos. When "man" violates the natural order, "nature rebels against him and no longer recognizes him as its 'master,' for he has tarnished the divine image in himself" (John Paul II 1987, no. 30).

In *Sollicitudo rei socialis,* John Paul II lists three considerations for why development must include "respect for the beings which constitute the natural world." The first consideration maintains that one cannot use "the different categories of beings, whether living or inanimate," in any way which one wishes, but rather must "take into account *the nature of each being* and of its *mutual connection* in an ordered system." The second and "perhaps more urgent" consideration concerns the recognition that treating nonrenewable resources as if they were inexhaustible "seriously endangers their availability not only for the present generation but above all for generations to come." The third consideration concerns the pollution which accompanies industrialization, "with serious consequences for the health of the population." Development must respect the laws which govern the natural world, which are not only biological but moral as well, and which "cannot be violated with impunity" (ibid., no. 340).

Evaluation and Constructive Agenda

Although the number of ethicists and theologians who are addressing the ecological crisis is growing, theological education and the field of Christian ethics still tend to treat ecological issues as a marginal concern at best. The leading-edge scholarship covered in the previous section challenges theological studies and the field of ethics to wake up to the moral and religious dimensions of the eco-crisis. Each of the four approaches to ecological ethics pushes the field to expand its understanding and analysis of the new global problematique. All of the approaches emphasize the interconnections between degradation of the natural environment and the impoverishment and exploitation of human beings. Ethicists and church documents stress that *justice* as a moral category must be extended to embrace otherkind as well as humankind. The concept of eco-justice provides an excellent framework for articulating the linkages between domination of the earth and human oppression.

From the confessional/ecumenical approach, particularly among eco-justice advocates, comes the call to attend to creation/nature as *context* for theological/

ethical study. Rather than adding the ecological crisis to the laundry list of imperative *issues* to be addressed, concern for the environment should be foundational to all other work. An understanding of the earth as our home and the necessary setting for all ethical endeavors would ensure that attention to ecological factors accompany ethical analysis of any kind. Such an understanding is unfortunately *not* widespread in the ethical field at this time.

All of the approaches push contemporary ethics to widen the moral horizon to include human responsibilities to otherkind and the earth. Process theology stresses the development of a non-anthropocentric ethic that values non-human creatures as subjects of experience and thus intrinsically valuable. Some eco-justice ethicists advocate recognition and protection of "biotic rights," while stewardship ethicists emphasize human responsibility to care for God's creation. Liberationists are extending the category of the "poor" or "oppressed" to include nonhuman beings, while church teachings are instructing Christians to respect the inherent worth of all God's creatures. Whatever the particular approach, human moral responsibility is being extended to include non-human beings. The process of transforming the anthropocentric ethics of recent history into an ethic inclusive of all life has begun.

Christian traditions are being mined for their ecological potential by scholars from all of the major confessional traditions, and official church teachings on the ecological crisis are beginning to reflect these efforts. Ethicists are reinterpreting Christian doctrines and ethical teachings from an ecological perspective, rejecting interpretations that legitimate exploitation in favor of those that promote respect for creation. The radicality of these reinterpretations of the Christian faith vary widely. Some scholars, such as James Nash, retain the basic content of classical theo-ethical affirmations, while finding ways to stretch these affirmations to include ecological justice. Others, such as Rosemary Radford Ruether, critique many traditional doctrines and call for a complete reassessment of Christian theology and ethics. Liberationist scholars whose communities have been victimized by dominant forms of Christianity approach Christian traditions with a hermeneutics of suspicion, and often bring a deeper critique than other scholars. Both the efforts to recover ecological resources from Christianity and to critique the church for ecological irresponsibility contribute greatly to the field of ethics and theological education.

While the work covered in the previous section has greatly increased the quality of ethical reflection on ecological issues, new work is needed to respond adequately to all the dimensions of the global crisis. A constructive agenda for the field of ethics may be envisioned which includes the following elements (not arranged in order of priority).

More dialogue needs to take place between Christian ethicists and the complex of scientists, scholars, and activists working on the ecological crisis. While some interdisciplinary dialogue is occurring, the nature of the crisis requires that the expertise of other disciplines inform Christian ethical analysis and proposals. People actively involved in ecological issues, including non-Christians, should be encouraged to sharpen the critique of Christian complicity in environmental degradation and exploitation. Greater interfaith dialogue would also enhance Christian ecological ethics, as all faith traditions must learn to work together to bring their spiritual resources to bear on the global environmental crisis.

Second, much more progress needs to be made in *integrating ecology into all areas of Christian ethics*. The ecological crisis must not be treated as an independent issue; further recognition of the interconnected web of life and of the current ecological problematique must be the *context* of all ethical reflection.

Further, all ecological ethics, not just liberationist ethics, need to address the *environmental racism, sexism, and classism* which accompany ecological degradation everywhere. The majority of people in the world who suffer directly from environmental causes are non-white, female, and/or poor. The unequal and unjust exposure of these groups of people to environmental hazards demands much greater attention by Christian ethicists than it currently receives. Attention to ecological issues must always consider the interstructured nature of human injustice and environmental degradation. North American ethicists must be challenged to direct their attention not only to the situation of the third-world poor, but also to the people on our own doorstep: the communities of the poor and people of color in North America who suffer from greater exposure to environmental hazards.

A dimension of the eco-justice crisis which has received very little attention thus far is the *relationship between heterosexism and the ecological crisis*. As some scholars are beginning to point out, the ecofeminist analysis of the relationship among sexism, racism, and the ecological crisis needs to be extended to include *compulsory heterosexism* as a contributing factor (see Clark 1993; Spencer 1994). These scholars argue that the treatment of gay and lesbian people as *expendable* mirrors the dominant culture's relationship to the natural world. Further, the fear of embodiment and sensuality that fuels homophobia contributes directly to the modern quest to master and control nature. The interconnections between heterosexism and other forms of human and ecological injustice require much more exploration and analysis.

A fifth element should be the *integration of Christian ecological ethics into the practice of Christian life.* "Disciplinolatry" and intellectual elitism need to be overcome so that scholarly Christian ethical reflection is accessible and useful to the Christian layperson. Ethical reflection on the eco-crisis needs to be translated into ethical *action* both in the ecclesial and public spheres. Seminaries and other theological institutions could offer lay education programs on ecological ethics, and ethicists could be encouraged to share their work with local congregations.

Finally, a priority must be placed on *transforming the way the "rich" live.* Christian ethicists need to offer a much greater challenge to the materialist, consumerist culture of North America and Europe. Sustainable development must start at home. The contribution of the overconsumption of the rich to the eco-crisis must receive at least as much attention as unsustainable development and overpopulation by the poor. The spiritual resources of the Christian tradition, including its ethical teachings, must be focused on generating more sustainable ways of life among North Americans and Europeans, as well as third-world elites. A key aspect of the change needed is a transformation of the *values* of North

Americans and Europeans. Without a transformation of values, changes in living habits will be extremely difficult to procure.

Appendix A: Moral Obligations to Animals

While there is widespread agreement that Christians are called to be loving caretakers of creation as a whole, our obligations to individual animals are far less clear. In an anthology entitled *Animals and Christianity,* Andrew Linzey and Tom Regan show that "Christian faith is a house divided against itself" concerning the moral status of animals. Drawing from a range of voices including the Bible, Aquinas, Calvin, Barth, and contemporary theologians, Linzey and Regan explore divergent positions within the Christian tradition concerning human duties to animals, theodicy issues arising out of animal pain, and the possibility of animal redemption (Linzey and Regan 1990, xi-xiv). What concerns Linzey, Regan, and other Christians committed to the well-being of sentient creatures most, however, is not the *diversity* of views presented by those Christians who address animal welfare, but the overwhelming *indifference* by most of the faithful toward animal suffering.

Andrew Linzey was one of the first to defend the rights of nonhuman animals on Christian grounds (Linzey 1976). In *Christianity and the Rights of Animals* (1987), Linzey makes the case that the Christian faith offers the most compelling foundation for a rights-based theory of human obligations to animals. The moral status of animals is not based solely on their sentience, but on their value to their creator, God. Linzey explains that the claim that animals are "possessors of rights" means:

(i)   that God as Creator has rights in God's creation;

(ii) that Spirit-filled, breathing creatures, composed of flesh and blood, are subjects of inherent value to God; and

(iii) that these animals can make an objective moral claim which is nothing less than God's claim upon us (Linzey 1987, 69; see also Linzey 1994).

In short, the rights of animals are "theos-rights." Theos-rights extend at least to all warm-blooded living creatures, as these creatures are part of God's covenant and participate in redemption. In respect of their theos-rights, Linzey calls for the liberation of warm-blooded animals from wanton injury, from institutionalized suffering through intensive farming, painful experimentation and fur-trapping, and from oppressive control.

A quite different type of defense of animal rights arises out of Christian feminism. In her provocative text *The Sexual Politics of Meat* (1990) Carol Adams shows the fundamental connection between the subjugation of women and the consumption of nonhuman animals. The patriarchal practices of objectification and domination reduce both women and animals to "meat"; the eating of flesh is the very essence of male virility. Vegetarianism, in contrast, "acts as a sign of autonomous female being and signals a rejection of male control and violence" (Adams 1990, 16). To reject the violence of patriarchy, Adams shows, we must repudiate the violence on our dinner tables. "Eat Rice Have Faith in Women," she counsels, evoking an image from a poem by Fran Winant. "Our dietary choices reflect and reinforce our cosmology, our politics" (ibid., 190).

If nonhuman animals possess rights which set moral limitations on our relationships with them, as Linzey, Adams, and other theologians, philosophers and activists claim, then many of the daily activities of Christians must be altered. Practices such as meat-eating, vivisection, hunting, and use of animals for entertainment have now been shown to be morally problematic. Accordingly, Christian ethicists face the task of reexamining the morality of uses of nonhuman animals which have long been sanctioned unreflectively.

Appendix B: Unsustainable Population Growth

Human population grew to a billion in the early 1800s, after hundreds of thousands of years of human evolution, then doubled by 1930 and doubled again to four billion by 1975. Currently the world's population is expanding by some two hundred fifty thousand humans *per day,* and will reach six billion by the turn of the century. If, hypothetically, all of these human beings lived simply and shared equitably, even a population of six billion could perhaps live sustainably. But in fact, the population growth of this century has been characterized by extreme inequities. Most of the growth has occurred in poor nations which lack the means to provide for their new citizens sustainably, while affluent nations consume and discard a disproportionate share of the world's resources. The results of unsustainable population growth and consumption are well known: squalid cities teeming with human misery, famine, extinction of thousands of life forms, dwindling resources, and burgeoning garbage heaps.

But while the miseries resulting from unsustainable population growth are widely recognized and almost universally denounced, the methods and practices involved in achieving ecologically sound growth rates are fraught with ethical dilemmas. Control of fertility may require coercive government intrusion into the sacrosanct realm of the family, and may unjustly limit the freedom of society's least powerful. The most direct means of controlling fertility—sexual education, contraception, abortion—raise fierce moral controversy. Any adequate analysis of overpopulation focuses attention on overconsumption by the affluent, an extremely unpopular topic. Accordingly, many ethicists, religious and secular alike, steer clear of this treacherous topic. Fortunately, there are a few exceptions; this section will present some of the writings by Christian ethicists on fertility control, while Appendix C will address the need for economic reforms which promote justice and sustainability.

Through a detailed study of history, economics, and the Bible, Susan Power Bratton clears away some of the roadblocks preventing Christians (specifically

Protestant Christians) from supporting population control. In *Six Billion and More: Human Population Regulation and Christian Ethics* (1992), she shows that the blessing "Be fruitful and multiply" was given to other species as well; thus, population growth which imperils the rest of the natural world does not have God's blessing. With careful biblical and historical study, she challenges the assumption that Christian faith requires a commitment to large families. She shows that Christians can support population growth effectively without endorsing abortion and coercion. Most important, she demonstrates that the biblical ideals of justice lie at the heart of population reduction. "A Christian method of population regulation that is ethically acceptable must not only encourage loving sexual behavior, it must share resources fairly" (Bratton 1992, 94).

In a chapter of *Issues in Sexual and Medical Ethics,* Roman Catholic ethicist Charles Curran expresses regret at the slowness of the magisterium to acknowledge and address the multifaceted population crises. This hesitation probably stems from Catholicism's official objection to contraception, a position Curran challenges: "The official teaching of the hierarchical magisterium of the Roman Catholic Church condemns artificial contraception, but dissent from such official teaching is, in my judgment, both justifiable and widespread in Roman Catholicism" (Curran 1978, 189). Curran warns against simplifying the population crisis into a need to control the fertility of citizens of poor nations; he proposes holistic solutions which address the social and economic roots of population growth, as well as the correlative problem of over-consumption in rich nations.

Protestant theologian James Gustafson takes up the question of population and nutrition in volume 2 of *Ethics from a Theocentric Perspective.* A theocentric ethic is one which makes God, not humans, the measure of all things; it places moral questions "in the context of large wholes," as God is concerned not only with individual humans but also with the entire ecosphere (Gustafson 1984, 11). From a theocentric perspective, the ethics of population control cannot be simply a matter of the autonomy of individuals, but must recognize the critical significance of personal and policy choices for other existing persons, for future generations of human beings, and for the life of the world" (ibid., 249). The Roman Catholic opposition to population control measures using artificial contraception is extremely problematic, as it disregards the effects of overpopulation on the human species and the rest of the planet. "Indeed, with the distinctive emphasis on the common good that is a feature of this book, the use of contraceptives has an authority that is little short of an imperative" (ibid., 246). In a world where hunger is so prevalent, Gustafson contends, a theocentric ethic may require "self-denial, if not self-sacrifice," for the interests of the whole (ibid., 241).

The 1994 International Conference on Population and Development refocused public attention on this divisive topic for the immediate future, and Christian ethicists have much to contribute to this vital debate. They must ensure that the profound justice issues raised by population control efforts receive due consideration, and that these efforts address not only fertility (90 percent of population growth is occurring in developing countries), but also consumption (the average American consumes twenty-three times the goods and services of the average citizen of poor countries) (Balzar 1994, A5). In addition, Christian ethicists can lead the self-examination of the churches concerning their roles in fostering or hindering the quest for sustainable human population.

Appendix C: Economics and Ecology

Environmental degradation is caused by the failure to live sustainably. Those economic systems which foster pockets of intractable poverty are not sustainable, because the poor are forced to exploit the land to subsist. Nor are economic systems based on excessive consumption sustainable, because they deplete resources and produce more waste than can be absorbed. Clearly, economic reform is a fundamental component of ecological restoration.

Perhaps the most significant recent analysis of economics from a Christian perspective is *For the Common Good* by theologian John Cobb and World Bank economist Herman Daly. In an analysis which is both detailed and sweeping, Cobb and Daly recommend that political economies change from a focus on *chremanistics*—"the manipulation of property and wealth so as to maximize short-term monetary exchange value to the owner"—to *oikonomia*—"the management of the household over the long run" (Cobb and Daly 1989, 138). Prevailing economic dogma, based on abstractions and reductions, has conflated human well-being with increasing GNP. It is based on a reductive view of the human person as *homo economicus*, whose essence is "unlimited wants." But relationships—to other individuals, to community, to the land—are at least as important as possession of commodities, and these relationships are often destroyed by growth-oriented economies which alienate individuals from their human and natural communities.

Instead of a global economy dominated by the cruel practices of free trade, Cobb and Daly advocate a decentralized "community of communities." Community-oriented economics requires viewing humans as more than consumers and the land as more than "matter and rent." It measures economic welfare on the basis of education, health, and environmental quality, rather than GNP. Cobb and Daly propose concrete reforms of our current growth-oriented political economies: preventing free trade from demolishing community standards; limiting population growth; increasing wilderness and placing caps on resource extraction; restoring small-scale, community-based agriculture; instituting worker control and wide-scale tax reforms, and so forth. The "geocentric" vision of a community of communities Cobb and Daly uphold is grounded in Christian theism and in the biblical prophetic tradition which teaches concern for the suffering of individual creatures while placing final loyalty on the whole.

Cobb continues his discussion of economic reform in *Sustainability: Economics, Ecology, and Justice,* a short, accessible compilation of oral addresses. This text offers an attractive vision of an economy based on decentralized, relatively self-sufficient communities. Instead of increasingly unlivable cities surrounded by energy-guzzling suburbs, Cobb champions Paolo Soleri's arcologies as perhaps "the most livable form of urban society ever devised" (Cobb 1992b, 38). Rural communities could revive if the government abandoned its ill-fated support of capital and energy intensive forms of agriculture in favor of the labor-intensive, ecologically sound model of the family farm. Instead of pursuing the goal of universal affluence, "the world unity we want is a community of diverse and self-reliant peoples, not a standardized pool of labor working for subsistence together with globally homogenized consumerism" (ibid., 51). By uniting the goals of ecology and justice, Cobb shows that Christians can achieve a type of society consistent with biblical mandates.

Environmental conservation and stewardship are important elements in Philip Wogaman's analysis of economic policy in *Economics and Ethics: A Christian Inquiry*. Wogaman uses six theological concepts to evaluate economic policies: 1) physical existence as God's creation; 2) the priority of grace over works; 3) physical well-being and social relationships; 4) vocation; 5) stewardship; and 6) original sin. His theological analysis leads him to support five economic priorities: 1) production adequate to meet the needs of the community; 2) equality and security; 3) employment and educational opportunities; 4) conservation; and 5) a vision of a new world order. The political economy Wogaman envisions, one which protects the environment so that society can continue to function, is based on mutual love rather than mutual self-interest. To achieve this society, more economic choices should be controlled by political processes (Wogaman 1986).

Christians have long worked for economic reform in pursuit of the goal of human justice. With the recognition that justice and ecological health are inextricably connected goods, the impetus to achieve economic reform has doubled. Christian ethicists clearly have ample grounds for challenging the destructive, spiritually vacuous mores of the consumer culture; what is needed is the courage and honesty to expose the true costs of the comforts and luxuries most of us take for granted.

Appendix D: Science and Technology

The interface between science and religion is described by Holmes Rolston as a "no-man's land," but one "where we increasingly must live" (Rolston 1987, vi). This is especially true for Christian ethicists, who cannot hope to address topics such as nuclear waste and ozone depletion effectively unless equipped with scientific knowledge. Of equal importance, the power of science and technology is far too extensive to allow it to operate in a moral vacuum. But the relationship between science and religion is so strained that many scientists and theologians resolutely avoid interaction. Fortunately, a growing body of literature paves the way for the constructive relationship between religion and science which the ecological health of our planet demands.

The scholar who has done the most to illuminate the relationship between the realms of religion and values and science and technology is undoubtedly Ian Barbour. His decades-long analysis of human and environmental values in an era of technological complexity culminates in the prestigious Gifford Lectures of 1989-1991, published in two volumes. In *Religion in an Age of Science* Barbour asks, "How can the search for meaning and purpose in life be fulfilled in the kind of world disclosed by science?" (Barbour 1990, xiii). He provides a comprehensive examination of the place of religious belief in an era when logical positivism and scientific materialism have lost their credibility. This exploration continues into the realm of the normative in *Ethics in an Age of Technology*. Barbour analyzes significant technological problems in light of social values such as justice, participatory freedom, and economic development, and environmental principles such as resource sustainability and respect for all forms of life. He calls for citizen participation in democratic control of technology as well as international action to address global environmental threats, and he explores appropriate technologies and alternative views of the good life. "The challenge for our generation is to redirect technology toward realizing human and environmental values on planet earth" (Barbour 1993, xix).

After critiquing various types of relationship between theology and the sciences in volume 1 of *Ethics from a Theocentric Perspective,* James Gustafson presents his own view: the "substantial content" of our ideas about God should not be "incongruous" with compelling data and principles established in the relevant fields of the sciences (Gustafson 1981, 257). Gustafson presents evidence from the contemporary sciences which shows that there is an "order and ordering" to natural processes, and that humans are both fully a part of and radically dependent upon these processes. Scientific data also indicate that the account of creation in Genesis is not factually true, which throws into question the cherished conclusion drawn from this cosmology: that human beings are the center of value. Gustafson believes that the assumption that God's attention is focused solely on our species is hard to reconcile with the billions of years of development of the universe and the multifaceted complexity of the evolution of life on this planet. "Both the time- and the space-spans indicate . . . that if there was divine 'foreknowledge' of human life, there was no particular merit in bringing it into being through such an inefficient and lengthy process" (ibid., 267). In light of this and other evidence from the sciences, Gustafson concludes that Christian anthropocentrism, which has long disregarded the moral worth of the extra-human elements of nature, is no longer tenable.

The challenges of decision-making in our technologically complex era are portrayed by Roger Shinn in *Forced Options: Social Decisions for the Twenty-First Century.* Shinn analyzes the ecological and social justice issues raised in some of society's "big problems": energy, food, water, population, genetics, and nuclear war. Our options in addressing these and other crises are "forced" in the sense that to ignore an issue is itself a decision, and often a fateful one; further, our alternatives are limited and our knowledge is incomplete. The method Shinn recommends for addressing the big issues is one which integrates scientific evidence with a firm commitment to values; we must be able to judge when to be open to new information and when to hold firm to religious and ethical principles. Wise decision-making must unite human and ecological needs in an increasingly interdependent world, as "ethical responsibility includes care of the earth as well as human advantage" (Shinn 1982, 229).

A more lyrical work, which transcends the divide between science and the humanities, is *The Universe Story* by cosmologist Brian Swimme and cultural historian Thomas Berry. Swimme and Berry unite history and anthropology with leading-edge knowledge from the contemporary sciences to construct a comprehensive story, rich with meaning and mythological language, about the emergence of our universe. Human beings should celebrate the story of the cosmos with music, poetry, and religious ritual as we fulfill our fundamental role on this planet, "enabling the Earth and the universe entire to reflect on and to celebrate themselves, and the deep mysteries they bear within them, in a special mode of conscious self-awareness" (Swimme and Berry 1992, 1).

At present the unfolding story of humanity and the universe is at a transition point: the extraordinary influence of human beings on virtually all of the life cycles on this planet may be bringing the Cenozoic era to a close, and we are entering a new period which Swimme and Berry optimistically designate the Ecozoic era. The presence of humans on the earth in the Ecozoic period will be "mutually enhancing" as we come to realize that human beings and the earth are part of the same story. The primary concern of religion in this era must be "to preserve the natural world as the primary revelation of the divine" (ibid., 243), and we must develop an economy, education, ethics, and governance which are inter-species.

Science and technology clearly shoulder much of the blame for the current ecological crisis; mechanistic physics reduced the universe to "matter in motion," and technology provided the means for exploiting this devalued "matter." But it is just as clear that Christian ethicists must incorporate science and technology into the quest for concrete solutions to the moral crises which occur in a degraded environment. What is needed, in the words of David Ray Griffin, is the "reenchantment of science" (Griffin 1988) so that science will reflect the vitality of the universe and facilitate the quest for meaning. Christian ethicists can foster the reenchantment of science by furthering the relationship between scientific and moral knowledge.

Notes

1. Liberationist theologians/ethicists are suspicious of firm distinctions between theology and ethics. Theology must be immediately and clearly connected to ethics for it to have any validity for a liberationist. Neat separations between theological reflection and ethical analysis cannot often be made in their work. Thus, when the term "theology" is referred to under this approach, it includes ethics as well.

2. White feminists began earlier than most other liberationist groups to address ecological concerns, perhaps because they were in less of an "emergency" state than people of color and the poor.

3. The creation of church documents on ecology became more common after the 1974 World Council of Churches conference on Science and Technology for Human Development in Bucharest and the 1975 WCC Assembly in Nairobi.

10

Population-Consumption Issues

The State of the Debate in Christian Ethics

JAMES B. MARTIN-SCHRAMM

This chapter examines substantive writing on population and consumption is-sues primarily in the field of Christian ethics. Moral concern for the relationship of these issues has been substantially rejuvenated by recent studies examining the amount of ecological degradation attributable to the affluent few and the numer-ous poor. While all studies show that the vast majority of ecological degradation to date has been produced by the over-consumptive lifestyles and environmen-tally harmful technologies of the wealthiest citizens of the planet, a growing level of concern is being raised about the increasing level of degradation posed by the many citizens who are poor.

To examine the nexus of debate around population and consumption issues, this essay is divided into three sections. The first section provides a brief sum-mary of important demographic figures and trends shaping the rate of human reproduction and the quality of life on the planet. The second section offers a description of the key issues and main figures in debates about population and consumption issues primarily in the field of Christian ethics. The third section outlines several issues or items that need further moral and theological reflection.

The Current Demographic Situation

According to the most recent (median variant demographic) projections by the United Nations, the world's 1994 population of approximately 5.7 billion people is expected to nearly double to 10 billion by 2050, before, it is to be hoped, stabilizing at approximately 11.6 billion by the year 2150. Of this growth, 97 percent will take place in the impoverished countries of the developing world, and 83 percent of that growth will occur in cities. At current growth rates, the world will add over 93 million people to the planet in 1994 and up to 100 million people per year through this decade. Put in perspective, this is equivalent to adding a population larger than the size of Mexico each year and, by the year 2001, adding a population equivalent to the current size of China (see Sadik 1993).

This global demographic situation is a paradox. Statistically, the situation has never looked better; yet in terms of the lives of actual human beings, things have never been worse. Through international family planning and development efforts, the annual rate of global population growth has decreased from 2.06 percent in 1965-70 to 1.73 percent in 1985-90 (World Resources Institute 1991, 253). In addition, the total fertility rate (TFR) in less-developed countries has declined from 6.0 children per woman in 1960 to 3.6 today, bringing the TFR more than halfway toward the goal of a replacement rate of 2.1 children (Sadik 1993b, 2). Unfortunately, because the age structure of many developing nations has been substantially altered, this diminished rate of population growth still produces unprecedented growth in human numbers. In addition, the significant gains that have been made in economic growth and food supply since 1950 have been diminished by a world population that has doubled during this same period, with the current rate of population growth now outstripping the rate of global grain production (Mathews 1991, 25; see also, World Resources Institute 1991, 86). The sad fact is that, while the *statistical proportions* of per capita income, food supply, access to health services, potable water, and so on, have all improved, the *actual number* of people who are poor, hungry, sick, and without drinkable water has never been higher. In 1990, the World Bank estimated that more than 1.1 billion of the world's population live in conditions of absolute poverty (The World Bank 1990, 28). Other studies place that number at nearly 2 billion people (Leonard, et al. 1989, 9-10).

Faced with the likelihood that global population will nearly double during the lifetime of most people alive today, experts project that a fivefold to tenfold increase in global economic activity will be necessary to meet the needs and aspirations of ten billion people. While this appears to be an impossible task, economists emphasize that such growth has already taken place and similar growth can be accomplished by continuing annual economic growth rates of 3.2 to 4.7 percent (see MacNeill, et al. 1991, 5; World Commission on Environment and Development 1987, 15). The problem, however, is that the explosion of economic growth in the twentieth century has created enormous environmental degradation. Ecologists emphasize that the planet will not permit another fivefold to tenfold expansion of the global economy, and some argue that—barring some significant changes in the destructive lifestyles of the affluent—humans may have already surpassed the planet's carrying capacity (Daily and Ehrlich 1992, 761-71).

A widely noted study by a group of ecologists at Stanford University provides a poignant summary of the present global ecological situation. The study concluded that human beings, directly and indirectly, currently use approximately 40 percent of the net primary product of terrestrial photosynthesis (NPP). In less technical terms, this means that one species, *homo sapiens*, consumes 40 percent of the various forms of life that are nourished by the sun on land. Even more alarming was the study's warning that, at current levels of consumption, the expected doubling of global population levels would mean that humanity's consumption of terrestrial NPP would also double to 80 percent and, with additional population growth, would soon reach 100 percent (Vitousek, et al. 1986, 368-73).[1]

The ominous conclusion of the study is that the multiplication of human life is crowding out all other forms of life on the planet. Perhaps the most dramatic and direct evidence of this phenomenon is the loss of biodiversity through an alarming rate of global species extinction. Land degradation, deforestation, and global warming also exemplify the threat humanity poses to all forms of life on the planet. While it is unfair and inaccurate to place the blame for these ecological problems solely on population growth, it is clear that high rates of growth have exacerbated these conditions and will play a critical role in the future. It is important to stress, however, that humanity's ecological impact is determined not only by our numbers but also by our levels of consumption and the types of technology we use in our production of goods. While some problems are significantly influenced by population growth, other problems are due primarily to inefficient production and irresponsible levels of consumption.

It is also important to emphasize, however, that the multiplication of human life will have a significant impact on human societies. With almost all population growth projected to take place in the nations of the developing world, the linkages among population growth, poverty, and environmental degradation will become more devastating.[2] Migration pressures will increase as the poor leave rural areas seeking a better life in urban communities and wealthier nations. In addition, ecological refugees will join the estimated 17 million people who are displaced outside their countries and the 23 million people who are displaced within their countries (Sadik 1993, iii). Unfortunately, almost all nations of the world are closing their doors to migrants and refugees, and in many cases are deporting those that do live within their borders. Without the historical safety valve of migration, several scholars and national security analysts are emphasizing the potential for military conflict and civic unrest between and within nations that will experience rapid population growth. As renewable resources become degraded and depleted, and as population growth places increasing demands on these supplies, significant conflicts will likely arise. Other analysts focus on how population growth will likely lead to a decline in U.S. power and Western democratic ideals. They emphasize that by the year 2025 the United States will be the only industrial democracy among the five largest nations, and Japan will be the only other industrial democracy among the twenty largest countries. This has led some to recommend various pro-natalist policies to shore up declining birth rates (Wattenberg 1987). Others argue that it will be vital for the U.S. to advance Western democratic ideals in societies where they will increasingly be perceived as alien (Eberstadt 1991, 115-31; Huntington 1993, 22-49).

Key Figures and Main Issues

In international forums, this projection of an unprecedented increase in global population has stimulated much concern and occasionally rancorous debate. At the heart of this discord is the view of many in the South that the nations of the North focus too much on the ecological dangers posed by population growth and not enough on the dangers posed by their own over-consumption. Those from the South have correctly emphasized that the ecological impact of human societies is measured not only in terms of the rates of reproduction but also in terms of the patterns of consumption and the means of production. For this reason, it is becoming increasingly apparent that all discussions of population growth must also include moral reflection on consumption issues.

The *relationship* of population and consumption issues has not been substantially emphasized in the field of Christian ethics during the last two decades. Christian moral reflection on population issues during this time was often shaped in response to the challenges posed by world hunger (Shinn 1982) and the controversial proposals for "triage" or "lifeboat ethics" which were proposed as responses (Wogaman 1973; Vaux 1989). Moral reflection on consumption issues during this time ranged from a focus on discipleship and simpler lifestyles in some mainline denominations and evangelical communities to a relatively rigorous critique of capitalism in the U.S. Roman Catholic Bishops' pastoral letter, *Economic Justice for All* (NCCB 1986). The most substantial integrated reflection on population and consumption issues has been generated by those exploring the "limits to growth" debate (Stivers 1984 and 1976; Birch and Rasmussen 1978) and the notion of "sustainable development" or a "sustainable society" (Engel and Engel 1988; Cobb and Daly 1989). In comparison, however, to the amount of moral reflection that has been devoted over the last twenty years to liberation concerns, peace issues, and bio-medical ethics, it is fair to say that the quantity of reflection on population and consumption issues has been minimal even though the quality of that reflection has been quite high. In the remainder of this section I will identify the main figures in current discussions of population issues and indicate how they are making connections with consumption issues.

The area of population policy has gone through some significant changes over the last twenty years.[3] Since the failure of ill-conceived and invasive policies in the 1960s, a narrow focus on population control and contraceptive technologies has been largely rejected in favor of placing population programs within the broader context of development policies, and to a far lesser extent, women's reproductive rights and health. While most nations and non-governmental organizations now accept this broader approach, there still remains a substantial gap between rhetoric and action on these fronts. As numbers continue to grow, it is likely that proponents of population control will rejuvenate their appeals for specific measures that go beyond voluntary family planning. For example, while China's population policy is criticized by some for its coercive aspects, it is hailed by many as a model of effective population control.

In the past, ethicists have evaluated population policies that contain various types of incentives, disincentives, and forms of coercion by considering their impact on four primary human values of freedom, justice, general welfare, and security or survival. While responsible moral evaluation of specific population polices involves reflection on all four of these primary values, ethicists have arranged these values in different orders of priority. For example, some have made the values of general welfare and security/survival subordinate to the more fundamental values of freedom and justice. Ethicists like Ronald Green and Daniel

Callahan have argued that efforts to maximize freedom and equality are more effective means of securing the common good than coercive means that violate human dignity (Green 1976; Callahan 1976). Callahan warns that "the end— even security-survival—does not justify the means when the means violate human dignity and logically contradict the end" (Callahan 1976, 34-35). Others have taken the opposite approach and have emphasized that without a fundamental measure of general welfare and security it is impossible to experience the values of freedom and justice. Ethicists like Michael Bayles and James Gustafson have argued that it may be necessary and justifiable to limit certain individual rights and regulate human fertility out of a concern for the common good of present and future generations (Bayles 1980; Gustafson 1984b). Bayles writes: "Inequality and lack of freedom are acceptable if without them people would lack welfare or security" (Bayles 1980, 35).

This difference in the ordering of primary moral values is reflected in more recent moral reflection on population issues as well. Following Green and Callahan, Rosemary Radford Ruether has argued that it is vital to ground population issues in a broader context of social and economic justice. Arguing that population growth is rooted in poverty and injustice, Ruether insists that one essential dimension to this task is the need to narrow the gap between the rich and the poor (Ruether 1973, 172). Linking population and consumption issues, Ruether argues that the "high consumption of the wealthy" and the "low consumption of the many" are not separate but interdependent realities caused by global economic systems which benefit the affluent few and harm the numerous poor (Ruether 1992, 89). Ruether also insists, however, that another essential dimension of population policies must be the goal to improve the status of women and to empower them in terms of moral agency. Ruether is convinced that population policies which do not place a priority on improving the status of women and their moral agency will be abusive to women and also will not "work" (Ruether 1991, 6-7). Ruether acknowledges that "humanity has no real alternative to population control," but she argues that the best way to avoid a doubling in the world's population is by addressing the twin challenges of poverty and patriarchy (Ruether 1992, 263-64).

Another important figure in more recent discussions of population and consumption issues is John B. Cobb, Jr. On the consumption side, Cobb has worked hard to offer conceptual foundations and workable policies for a more just, peaceful, and sustainable world (Cobb and Daly 1989; Cobb 1992b). One of the unique contributions Cobb has made recently is his bold, albeit quite biblical claim that the Western industrial nations *worship* endless economic growth (Cobb 1992c, 6-9). When viewed through the prism of civil religion it is easier to understand why consumption issues are so volatile and difficult to address. Consumption issues apparently involve not only our habits of consumption but also our rites of faith. Cobb's most important contribution, however, has been his attempt with Herman Daly in *For the Common Good* to sketch the outlines of an alternative form of development that would be just, participatory, and—above all—sustainable ecologically. Daly and Cobb caution against overly optimistic and simplistic appeals to the fruits of development and emphasize that sustainable development will require revolutionary changes in current patterns of human production, consumption, and reproduction.

Cobb's contributions to population issues have varied quite significantly, however, according to his chosen dialogue partners. For example, in *The Liberation of Life*, which he co-authored with Charles Birch, Cobb and Birch articulate the moral foundations for a population policy which bears a striking resemblance to the consensus emerging in the international community today. In league with Ruether, Birch and Cobb recommend that population growth must be seen in the larger context of the process of development and that the real key to lower fertility rates rests with improvement in the lives of women. Birch and Cobb write:

> If there were a serious commitment to justice for women, the problem of population stability would largely take care of itself. . . . Justice and sustainability coincide. There can be no sustainable world unless population stability is achieved. There can be no justice for the 53 percent of the world's population that is female until women have greater control over their own bodies, better education, and better opportunities for employment. These social changes together lead to reduced birth-rates. No other approach to reducing population growth is either just or sustainable (1990, 315).

It might have been best if Cobb had stopped with this view, but he did not. In 1989, Herman Daly and John Cobb offered a controversial proposal for population stabilization in less developed countries in the chapter they devoted to population policy in *For the Common Good* (1989, 236-51). In this chapter, Daly and Cobb consider the governmental implementation of "transferable birth quota plans," which would issue birth rights certificates to parents to sell or use as they deem fit on an open market. With the goal of a replacement rate of 2.1 children, governments would distribute to each couple twenty-one child unit certificates, ten of which would be required for each birth. Couples would then be free to use or sell these certificates on an open market. One of the major flaws with their proposal, however, is that on an unequal economic playing field the poor would be faced with the terrible option of having to sell their fundamental right to bear children in order to purchase basic necessities like food, clothing, and shelter. Daly and Cobb acknowledge that one of the weaknesses of this plan is its inability to assure "just distribution" of births, and they do not think that current demographic circumstances are serious enough to warrant the use of the plan now, but they do believe that the plan should be held in reserve "should present demographic trends reverse themselves" (ibid., 251). Echoing the views of Bayles and Gustafson, Daly and Cobb conclude by stressing "that we do not rule out elements of restriction of individual preference by the community as a whole in the interests of the well-being of all" (ibid.).

Like Cobb, James Nash has offered similar realistic sentiments in his work. In *Loving Nature*, Nash consistently links his treatment of population and consumption issues, referring to both as manifestations of "anthropocentric imperialism"

(Nash 1991, 211). While Nash addresses over-consumption by calling for a more just distribution of resources and the importance of the virtues of frugality and sustainability, his discussion of population growth often takes on a bit of a Malthusian tone. Nash writes:

> To paraphrase a famous manifesto, a specter is haunting the globe—the specter of population progression, which will require a holy alliance of nations to exorcise (ibid., 50).

To his credit, Nash argues that contraception must serve as the centerpiece of a morally adequate policy aimed at curbing population growth (ibid., 49). This would include the fundamental right to information and education about birth control as well as access to various means (Nash 1992, 54). In addition, Nash also emphasizes that a morally adequate population policy will need to be part of a broader goal of increasing socioeconomic justice and sustainable development. But Nash's concerns about *effectively* lowering the rate of population growth also lead him to propose criteria for evaluating population polices that seek to do more than just inform and enable voluntary family planning. At the forefront for Nash is the criterion of equality. That is to say, "The prosperous should not recommend any population policy for the poor that they are not willing to follow themselves" (Nash 1991, 48). In addition, Nash has recently suggested that "enforcement procedures ranging from bans to incentives" must be "effective, just, and sufficient" (Nash 1992, 55). Unfortunately, Nash does not elaborate further on definitions, or on what conditions would satisfy these criteria, or on the process that should be used when evaluating their status. Clearly, however, Nash is open to more coercive means than the base-line of voluntary family planning.

Nash's willingness to consider more coercive means of regulating human fertility flows out of his rights-based approach to a Christian environmental ethic. Cutting against the increasing international emphasis on reproductive rights and the United Nations Declaration of Universal Human Rights, Nash argues that humans do *not* have the right to reproduce, although they may have the right not to be *forced* to reproduce (Nash 1991, 49). In his discussion of the relationship of human rights to human environmental rights, Nash argues that "security and subsistence rights always impose limits on other citizen's freedoms of action" (ibid., 50). Thus, Nash is able to support the limitation of human reproductive freedoms on the grounds of ecological security and couches such action in terms of ecological justice.

Susan Power Bratton is another important figure in current discussions of population issues. Trained as a biologist, Bratton has published widely in the field of environmental ethics and has produced an important book-length treatment of population issues entitled *Six Billion and More: Human Population Regulation and Christian Ethics* (Bratton 1992). Rooted in and writing for a predominantly evangelical audience, Bratton sets out to identify the Christian values and principles that should shape a distinctively Christian population ethic. In the first half of her book, Bratton examines the historical roots of the global demographic situation, biblical and theological perspectives on human reproduction, and the historical response of Western European Christians to the challenges posed by population growth in Europe. The second half of the book explores the social and ecological challenges posed by population growth, the issue of over-consumption in developed nations and rapid population growth in less developed nations, and the foundations for a Christian population ethic.

While Bratton emphasizes that high per capita consumption rates are the primary "population" issue for industrial democracies, she also stresses that distributive justice must be central to any Christian response to accelerated population growth in developing nations. In her penultimate chapter, "Population Regulation and Justice," Bratton advocates a variety of social reforms including reduction in infant mortality, widespread literacy, easy availability of contraception, relative equality for women, and improved access to health care and education. Bratton emphasizes in the conclusion to this chapter that the best way to avoid coercion in the future is to employ these reforms now.

Bratton's final chapter, however, does address the problems posed by coercion and abortion in population management. Here Bratton offers helpful moral reflection on various positive and negative incentives for family planning, and she also considers the justifiable grounds for any forms of coercion. Within this context, Bratton abandons her prior emphasis on the dignity and value of women and opposes abortion out of a concern for the rights and personhood of the fetus (ibid., 216-17). In response to the view that the unjust treatment of women makes abortion justifiable, Bratton suggests that a "better solution is to provide adequate medical care, contraceptive access, and nutrition"—as though abortion advocates were not already demanding these things, and more (ibid., 190). Bratton does a good job of demonstrating to her conservative Christian audience that opposition to abortion should not lead Christians to oppose various measures to improve sex education and family planning programs. Bratton emphasizes that blocking funding for reproductive health care solely on the grounds of abortion "is merely trading one source of mortality for another, which is unacceptable and unnecessary" (ibid., 197).

Unfortunately, though they have much in common, the Vatican has not grasped the logic of Bratton's views. In the various preparatory meetings for the United Nations' International Conference on Population and Development in Cairo, the Vatican opposed terms like "reproductive rights," "reproductive health," and "safe motherhood" on the grounds that these terms implied an approval of abortion. In reaction to the views of the Vatican, debate in Roman Catholic circles on population issues splits along at least two lines. Some, like Frances Kissling and Daniel Maguire, see the Vatican's views as essentially misogynistic and hopelessly patriarchal (Maguire 1993b, 12-15; Kissling 1994, 320-29). Others like Charles Curran and Sean McDonagh, challenge the Vatican's opposition to artificial means of contraception and question how "pro-life" these policies are when they contribute to higher rates of infant mortality, poverty, and environmental degradation (Curran 1985, 229-45; McDonagh 1990, 64-65; see also Howard 1993). Finally, Maura Ann Ryan has recently tried to frame moral reflection on population policy within the broader context of Roman Catholic social teaching (Ryan 1994, 330-40).

In my own work, I have sided primarily with Ruether and her dual emphasis on social and economic justice as well as the importance of improving the lives of women. I share her confidence that development policies redesigned to serve the needs of the poor and social reforms designed to improve the status of women will "work" and represent the best chance to achieve global population stabilization. I also agree with Cobb, however, that simplistic approaches to development have not worked and will remain "unworkable" until the failed paradigm of development as economic growth is replaced with a new paradigm of sustainable development. Until it becomes clear, however, that this alternative approach has been tried and has failed, I will remain reluctant to abide much discussion of various forms of coercion in population programs, although I do believe there is a place for carefully monitored incentive packages.

In my current research, I am examining the challenges that high rates of consumption in the North and population growth in the South pose to several approaches to environmental ethics emerging within the Christian tradition. Whereas most moral reflection on population policies has been organized around their impact on the values of freedom, justice, general welfare, and security, I have been exploring the utility of five ecojustice norms (sustainability, sufficiency, participation, solidarity, and equity) for shaping a moral response to population and consumption issues. The hallmark of an ecojustice approach is the attempt to hold together the twin imperatives of social justice and ecological integrity. Breaking down the traditional barriers between social and environmental ethics, an ecojustice approach attempts to discern and adjudicate various responsibilities owed to the poor, to future generations, to sentient life, to organic life, to endangered species, and ecosystems as a whole (Martin-Schramm, forthcoming).

Areas Requiring Further Moral and Theological Reflection

With this brief review of major figures and key issues in current conversations about population and consumption issues, I would like to outline briefly three areas that I think are worthy of further moral and theological reflection.

The first involves the need for more *theological* reflection about the foundations for Christian moral deliberation on population and consumption issues. The discussion of these issues has been characterized by fairly rich moral deliberation but rather poor theological reflection. Susan Power Bratton has probably given the most substantial attention to this task with her focus on biblical views of reproduction. She emphasizes that while the Old Testament reflects a pro-natalist bias, the New Testament is more neutral in terms of such a bias with its emphasis on salvation by grace through faith. More work is needed here, however. In the context of unprecedented human population growth and global ecological jeopardy, what are we to make of texts like "be fruitful and multiply, and fill the earth and subdue it" (Gen. 1:28) or God's promise to make Abraham's descendants "as numerous as the stars of heaven and as the sand that is on the seashore" (Gen. 22:17-18)? Theologically, how might the themes of creation and covenant provide a theological foundation for Christian moral reflection on population and consumption issues? Theologically, how do we address the destructive anthropocentrism that has precipitated the present crisis while at the same time acknowledging and empowering the vital human task of moral responsibility?

A second area involves the need for increased *moral* reflection on measures which go beyond voluntary family planning. Behind the scenes, and off the record, there are some ethicists who doubt the long-term efficacy of the current international emphasis on development and improving the welfare, status, and agency of women. To some extent they believe Garrett Hardin's maxim that "if the proposal (for population control) might work, it isn't acceptable; if it is acceptable it won't work" (Hardin 1989, 11). Undoubtedly, soon some of these ethicists or other policy-makers will argue for the use of various incentives, disincentives, and possibly even some forms of coercion to stem population growth for the sake of the common good. Research and reflection in this area and on these types of measures should be done now so that it does not have to be done hastily. We should look for leadership in this area from feminist ethicists and from grass-roots communities of women. Because the consequences of human reproduction almost always fall on the shoulders of women, it is precisely women who should design, implement, and evaluate various population policies and programs. Related to this question of coercive methods are the various ethical issues which reproductive health care providers face in the field. For example: What resources should be used to develop and encourage male *vs.* female forms of contraception? Where does abortion fit in family planning and reproductive health-care services? How do providers respect the social values of the culture while also honoring their own commitments to rights of privacy, confidentiality, etc.?

Finally, a third area that needs increased attention is *U.S. population policy* in general. Remarkably, despite the fact that the U.S. has been a major player in the ICPD process and has actively sought to shape the recently approved World Plan of Action on Population, the United States does not have an official, national population policy of its own. Such a policy might address the current lack of universal access to family planning methods, the dangerous attempts to link implantation of certain contraceptive technologies with the receipt of welfare assistance, and the enormously volatile topic of legal and illegal immigration. All of these issues require sophisticated moral reflection and analysis.

In closing, I would also like to identify briefly three ways that population and consumption issues should be addressed in the fields of theological education and religious studies.

The first is the emphasis that, for citizens of wealthier, industrialized nations, it is more appropriate for us to begin our reflection on these issues by focusing on the impact of our own consumption than on the dangers posed by population growth in poorer, less industrialized nations. Sallie McFague makes this point very well:

> The population versus high life-style issue divides the developing from the developed nations, with each claiming *the* ecological issue is the *other's* excess. Both are critical problems, but since this essay is directed to middle-class Westerners, the focus will be on *our* excess, the highest energy-use life-style the world has ever known. If we refuse to moderate this life-style, we participate in systemic injustice, demanding an excessive piece of the pie. Unless and until we drastically modify our life-style, we are not in a position to preach population control to others (McFague 1993, 4-5).

A second issue that needs to be addressed in discussion of population and consumption issues is the helpfulness but also the limitations of the I=PAT formula made famous by Paul Ehrlich and John Holdern (Ehrlich and Ehrlich 1990, 273 n19). Put simply, the formula demonstrates that the ecological impact of human beings is determined by the product of population size, per capita rate of consumption, and per capita rate of pollution produced by technology. The problem is that the formula does not easily distinguish between legitimate and illegitimate forms of consumption, nor does it isolate the ecological degradation perpetrated as a result of militaristic and nondemocratic policies (see Hynes 1993).

Finally, an appropriate topic for theological educators and scholars in religious studies is comparative study of world religions in terms of their views on population and consumption issues. A volume entitled *Population, Consumption and the Environment* (Coward 1995) should be a helpful resource in this regard.

In closing, what we know for certain is that the entire world's population is going to nearly double during the lives of most people alive today, with almost all of that growth occurring in the less developed world. This means the exponential growth of suffering and misery among people who are already hungry, ill, and poverty-stricken. Moreover, at current levels of consumption and economic maldistribution, it is clear that this growth poses grave ecological consequences. The consensus among policy-makers and demographers is that decisions made during this decade will significantly determine the rate and consequences of population growth in the future. Clearly, religious and theological ethicists must step forward to bring rigorous moral and theological reflection to the issues posed by population and consumption growth. This essay has been an attempt to summarize the work to date and outline some of the challenges ahead.

Notes

1. If aquatic (ocean) NPP sources are included, human consumption totals 25 percent of global NPP. *Direct* human consumption of terrestrial (land) NPP only amounts to 3-4 percent of the total. An additional 37 percent of terrestrial NPP, however, is consumed *indirectly* through parts of plants we do not eat, through plants that are used as feed for livestock which we do eat, and by clearing forests to plant land for crops. For further discussion of this study see Meadows 1992, 1-4; Goodland 1992, 7-9; Ramphal 1992, 231; Harrison 1992, 62-63; Cobb and Daly 1989, 143-44.

2. It is important to stress that population growth is only one of several factors that fuel migration. Other factors include urbanization, rising material expectations, unjust distributions of wealth and power, and political oppression.

3. For historical perspectives, see Peter J. Donaldson, *Nature Against Us: The United States and the World Population Crisis* (Chapel Hill: University of North Carolina Press, 1990) and Stanley P. Johnson, *World Population and the United Nations* (New York: Cambridge University Press, 1987). For an excellent feminist perspective, see Betsy Hartmann, *Reproductive Rights and Wrongs: The Global Politics of Population Control and Contraceptive Choice* (New York: Harper & Row, 1987).

11

The Role of Religions in Forming an Environmental Ethics

New Challenge for Interreligious Dialogue

MARY EVELYN TUCKER

The anthropologist Loren Eiseley offers haunting vignettes that convey succinct and moving truths about the extraordinarily complex relation of humans to nature. A story from his book *The Firmament of Time* will serve as a departure point for discussing the role of world religions and interreligious dialogue in responding to the environmental crisis. Eiseley writes:

> There is a story about one of our great atomic physicists . . . [that] illustrates well what I mean by a growing self-awareness, a sense of responsibility about the universe.
>
> This man, one of the chief architects of the atomic bomb, so the story runs, was out wandering in the woods one day with a friend when he came upon a small tortoise. Overcome with pleasurable excitement, he took up the tortoise and started home, thinking to surprise his children with it. After a few steps he paused and surveyed the tortoise doubtfully.
>
> "What's the matter?" asked his friend.
>
> Without responding, the great scientist slowly retraced his steps as precisely as possible and gently set the turtle down upon the exact spot from which he had taken him up.
>
> Then he turned solemnly to his friend. "It just struck me," he said, "that perhaps, for one man, I have tampered enough with the universe." He turned, and left the turtle to wander on its way.
>
> The man who made that remark was one of the best of the modern men, and what he had devised had gone down into the whirlpool. "I have tampered enough," he said. It was not a denial of science. It was a final recognition that science is not enough for humans. It is not the road back to

the waiting Garden, for that road lies through the human heart. Only when humans have recognized this fact will science become what it was for Bacon, something to speak of as "touching upon Hope." Only then will we be truly human.

Eiseley's story calls us to a new way of relating to nature, one that is more humble and less manipulative; more reciprocal and less hierarchical. As his story suggests and as Holmes Rolston has noted, it is becoming increasingly clear that we are in grave need of both *reverence for* and *responsibility to* nature. But from where will this emerge?

Ethics have emerged traditionally from particular religious or philosophical worldviews. For the most part, the worldviews associated with the Western Abrahamic traditions have created a dominantly human focused or anthropocentric morality. Within these anthropocentric worldviews, nature's well-being has had only secondary importance. Thus our present difficulty is that we in the West have developed ethical systems for homicide and suicide, but not for biocide or geocide. We are in need of a comprehensive ecological ethics as the most compelling context for motivating change. For what is at stake in the environmental crisis is not simply the future of sustainable development, but the viability of sustainable life itself.

Religion, Ethics, and the Environment

How does religion relate to this crisis of ethics and the environment? Some people may simply dismiss the question. However, for many others who are concerned about the rapid rate of destruction of our global environment, nothing less than a major change in our religious attitudes toward nature will suffice to reverse a potential environmental catastrophe. Those interested in issues of sustainable development, population control, social justice, and equitable distribution of resources realize that without a healthy natural environment and the religious and ethical principles to maintain such an environment, life on the planet will be difficult at best.

This environmental crisis, then, requires a major rethinking of the relationship of humans to the earth. While certainly economic, social, and political programs will be instrumental in creating long-term policies for global survival, clearly religious and philosophical attitudes will also be crucial to rethinking the future of human-earth relationships. As Eiseley suggests, even science cannot provide all the answers. It must be accompanied by new "self-awareness, a sense of responsibility about the universe." Our challenge is to approach the environmental crisis with both appropriate urgency and sufficient hope. How can we maintain our balance between paralyzing predictions of ecological collapse and naive notions of unlimited growth and consumption? A sober realism combined with a long-term perspective of evolution may be our best hope. For without reverential awe, wonder, and care for the integrity of nature and its intrinsic value all may be lost. We are, as Thomas Berry emphasizes, part of a larger universe story; and that realization, in all its scientific and revelatory capacity may create the appropriate reverence and responsibility which will be indispensable to reverse our destructive course. But will the world's religions play their needed role in this process?

Origins of the Debate on the Role of Religion

Historian Lynn White, upon examining "The Historical Roots of Our Ecologic Crisis" (White 1967), presented the controversial thesis that the Judeo-Christian tradition is, in large part, responsible for the apparent indifference of Western civilization toward care for nature. He pointed to the rise of monotheism as the beginning of the removal of the divine from nature. Salvation theology concentrated on the relation of humans to a God which transcended nature. Thus, White maintained, the transcendence of God in Western religions led to a devaluing, objectification, and exploitation of nature as something separate from humans. In other words, the Genesis mandate to have "dominion" over nature has caused an anthropocentric arrogance and, indeed, an indifference toward nature. White called for a radical reevaluation of the Judeo-Christian tradition in light of our present ecological crisis and invoked St. Francis of Assisi as a potential patron saint of ecology.

White's article set off a major debate in academic and religious circles. Some questioned the validity of the thesis, seeing the connection between religion and ecology as having a wide spectrum of possibilities. Yet it sent many scrambling to explore the resources for developing some form of environmental ethics based on particular religious or philosophical positions.

Biologist Rene Dubos, for example, disagreed with White's Franciscan model of the passive conservation of nature. Dubos advocated a Benedictine model of active stewardship of the land. He claimed that humans will inevitably interfere with natural environments, but if they do so with a sense of proper management, such as the Benedictine monasteries demonstrated, they will be able to use and distribute resources properly. Others claim, however, that the stewardship model puts humans in a framework of controlling nature, which can become manipulative or exploitative rather than reciprocal or protecting. The whole issue of the ecological role of humans in religions is an enormously complex one. While it has put many within the Western traditions on the defensive, it has opened up the possibility of exploring worldviews from indigenous traditions and Asian religions which are more anthropocosmic, namely, seeing humans as part of a larger cosmos and derivative from that cosmos.

Monotheistic Traditions and Approaches to Nature

Within monotheistic traditions of the West the debate has sent some scholars pouring over biblical and Quranic texts to determine whether or not an environmental ethics can be found in these sources. The works of various Jewish, Christian, and Islamic theologians have also been analyzed for guidelines on current environmental discussions. Some twenty years ago several prominent Christian theologians including John Cobb, Paul Santmire, and Joseph Sittler began writing on the relationship of religion, ethics, and the environment. Similarly, Seyyed

Hossein Nasr wrote extensively on the role of nature in Islam. The topic is currently being revived in the creation-centered spirituality of Matthew Fox, in the ecofeminist theology of Rosemary Ruether and Sallie McFague, and in the stewardship theology of Richard Cartwright Austin and others. Potential sources for environmental ethics in monotheistic traditions include sacred texts (Bible and Quran), traditional and contemporary theological developments (including various liberation theologies), historical movements (such as the Benedictines), and cosmological perspectives (for example, *The Universe Story* by Thomas Berry and Brian Swimme).

Interreligious Dialogue and Ecology: Methods and Process

Interreligious dialogue may well play an important part in formulating needed responses to the environmental crisis. This in turn will inevitably have significant consequences for Christian theology. As the Harvard Confucian scholar, Tu Wei-ming, has noted, the Enlightenment project of the last two hundred years has begun to reveal its limitations. Rationality, science, and technology have produced enormous benefits as well as uncalculated costs. As these make themselves felt in terms of diminishing resources, increasing pollution, burgeoning population, and deteriorating health effects, the human community is beginning to reevaluate the meaning of unlimited growth.

It is both in the critique of unrestrained progress and in the reconstruction of new moral attitudes toward nature that the world religions have a unique role to play. As Tu Wei-ming has suggested, calling on the spiritual resources of the world's community at this time is an unavoidable imperative. Already members of the scientific community, as well as the United Nations Environment Programme, have called for such reflection and leadership from theologians of the world's religions. This newly emerging field has enormous potential and promise.

In response to the critique of our present situation of impending environmental crisis, the world's religions have begun to enter into dialogue that will no doubt have important consequences. This dialogue has various dimensions and employs multiple methodologies resulting, inevitably, in livelier theologies.

1) It is necessary to have *critical appraisal of individual traditions* in relation to attitudes toward nature and toward human-earth relations. This will draw on both scripture and tradition and will result in phenomenological descriptions of possible resources for addressing the ecological crisis.

2) *Openness to other traditions* as presenting alternative perspectives on nature and on human interaction with nature is critical. This will require a history of religions approach to develop a clear understanding of the texts and commentaries, myths and rituals, and the historical and doctrinal development of other religions.

3) *Vulnerable dialogue* can then take place within a more fruitful context for mutual understanding and appraisal. This will demand not only informed openness and mutual tolerance, but the genuine willingness to be trans-

formed by the dialogue. Such vulnerability may be a key element for both dialogue and for the constructive reevaluation of traditions.

4) With constructive reevaluation comes an essential theological task, namely, the *constructive reappropriation* of tradition in response to contemporary need. This may be one of the most challenging tasks of our time. Just as the early Church Fathers and medieval theologians drew on the resources of the Greco-Roman Mediterranean world, so too in our period there have been important efforts to construct various theologies of liberation emerging from the dialogue of Christianity in Latin America, Asia, and Africa. A formidable challenge for contemporary theologians will be the construction of eco-justice theologies in dialogue with other religions and in response to the call of the earth community.

The challenge, then, is to move from medieval theologies primarily centered on God and contemporary theologies focused on the human condition, to twenty-first-century theologies of the earth. In doing this the other two forms of theologies need not be abandoned. Instead, *the time is ripe for anthropocosmic theologies* where the divine, human, and earth are more fully integrated. These theologies inevitably range from those focusing on new cosmological understandings to those concerned with economic and environmental justice. Social justice is increasingly being understood as impossible apart from a sustainable earth and vice versa (see Boff 1995). As the quest for personal salvation and communal liberation continues in the context of a diminished earth, new integrative theologies should receive more attention. These theologies will develop in dialogue with other religions just as earlier Christian theologies emerged from dialogue with philosophies in the Mediterranean world. Key to these theologies is a rethinking of the role of the human in relation to both care for the earth and care for other humans.

Reconceptualizing the Role of the Human: A Prismatic View

The search for conceptual and symbolic resources in other religious traditions (and in newly emerging eco-philosophies) moves toward revisioning the role of the human as part of, not apart from, nature. Such theologies take a *prismatic view*, which is

- multiperspectival; honoring difference
- globally oriented; responsive to wider horizons
- locally grounded; attentive to individuals and community
- cosmologically embedded; sensitive to the context of connectedness.

Such a prismatic view illumines a *transformative ethics* aimed not at sustainable growth and development but at *sustainable life* on the planet. It invites us to embody a functional ethics which embraces nature, social-economic structures, individual rights and the well-being of communities. Several key elements are needed for formulating this functional ethics: openness, entering, listening, receiving, and transforming.

What *is* openness and tolerance to "other religions" and what can it be? Vatican Council II some thirty years ago acknowledged that there was "truth" in religions outside of Christianity. The difficulty of exclusive claims to truth and the reality of pluralism is still an enormous challenge to theology today. What does mission mean in an era of inculturation and dialogue?

What does it mean to enter another tradition with empathy and authenticity? John Donne's book *The Way of All the World* may be helpful in this process. Donne suggests that in studying another tradition one "passes over" into that tradition with openness and understanding and then returns to one's own tradition inevitably changed.

What does it mean to hear the voices of other traditions? What role does ethnicity play and what role does scholarship play? Can we be attentive to the inner and outer understandings of traditions? Being able to honor and critically appraise both involves attention to inclusivity of perspectives and voices.

What is receiving and what is appropriation? Who decides what is appropriate and what is inappropriate? Certainly we want to avoid exploitation of other traditions—indiscriminate taking, grasping, using, and abusing. Instead, we need both appreciative understanding and critical evaluation of concepts and practices. We need to "stand under," recognizing the limits of our knowledge.

Finally, we need to ask ourselves what Christian eco-theologies will look like. How will Christian thought help to shape an ethics of eco-justice in varied forms? Insights will be gained from the presence of ecological cosmologies and environmental ethics in other traditions, such as indigenous religions, and Asian traditions, such as Buddhism, Taoism, and Confucianism.

World Religions and Environmental Ethics

While recognizing the sometimes inevitable disjuncture between theory and practice, the exploration of the world's religions as resources for environmental ethics is an enormously important project. No tradition to date has faced such an environmental crisis, so none has been forced specifically to develop an environmental ethics. Yet the potential for real attitudinal change toward nature as something merely to exploit may lie in the ethical power of religions. Some of the richest resources for such efforts lie within the indigenous traditions and within the traditions of Asia.

In surveying world religions it is clear that indigenous religions are frequently cited as having developed a high degree of sensitivity to the rhythms of nature and an ability to live lightly on the land. Asian religions such as Buddhism, Confucianism, Taoism, and Shinto have also been invoked by historians of religions as containing an ecological cosmology of greater reciprocity with nature, rather than dominion over it. A comprehensive series of papers on this subject was published as *Nature in Asian Traditions* (Callicott and Ames 1989). Moreover, the journals of *Environmental Ethics* and *Environmental Review* have had articles exploring various religious and philosophical traditions as sources for evoking a heightened awareness of the sacredness of nature. Ronald and Joan Engel published an important edited volume in 1990 titled *Ethics of Environment and Development: Global Challenge, International Response*, which has selected chapters reflecting the religious perspectives of Western, non-Western, and indigenous traditions.

In 1992 the World Wide Fund for Nature published a series of books on World Religions and Ecology. It includes volumes on Judaism, Christianity, Islam, Buddhism, and Hinduism. An edited volume on *Worldviews and Ecology* (Tucker and Grim 1993/1994) has tried to provide an overview of attitudes toward nature in the world's religions and in contemporary ecological thought as a means of helping to formulate a more global environmental ethics. Recently, Baird Callicott completed a comprehensive book called *Earth's Insights* (1994), which is subtitled "A Survey of Ecological Ethics from the Mediterranean Basin to the Australian Outback" (Berkeley: University of California Press, 1994). It includes discussions of the Western traditions of religion, philosophy, and myth as well the traditions of South Asia and East Asia. It also surveys selected indigenous traditions of Asia, Africa, and North and South America.

Ethics and Agenda 21 (Brown and Quiblier 1994) attempts to bring various world religions and ethical orientations to bear in implementing the Earth Summit proposals agreed upon in Rio de Janeiro in June 1992.

Case Studies: The Ecological Resources in Taoism and Confucianism

As an example of the resources available in other traditions for rethinking ecological cosmologies and environmental ethics we will briefly explore the two great Chinese traditions of Confucianism and Taoism.[1] In many respects these traditions can be seen as having complementary perspectives, somewhat like the yin and yang of coexisting opposites. Taoism celebrates primary causality as residing in the Tao, while Confucianism emphasizes the importance of secondary causality in the action of humans. For Taoists, it is crucial to foster an unmediated, spontaneous harmony with the Tao, the ineffable source of all existence. For Confucians, human effort and energy needs to be cultivated to create harmonious societies and benevolent governments. Naturalness is highlighted by the Taoists while humaneness is encouraged by the Confucians. Intuitive knowledge is fostered by the Taoists while the cultivation of learning is promoted by the Confucians.

For both Taoists and Confucians harmony with nature is very important. The Taoists developed techniques of meditation so as to evoke an unmediated closeness to nature and a simplicity of action that could be spontaneous. This is seen particularly in the notion of *wu wei* or non-purposeful action that arises from the wellsprings of naturalness. The Confucians, especially the later Neo-Confucians, suggest that harmonizing with the changing patterns in nature is essential for creating balanced human relations and for establishing an appropriate government. The whole Confucian triad of heaven, earth, and humans rests on a seamless yet dynamic intersection between each of these realms. Without harmony with nature and its myriad changes, human society and government are threatened. The *Book of Changes* was a key text for maintaining such a harmonious balance.

For the Taoists—to be in relation to the Tao—persons needed to withdraw from social and political affairs so as to preserve nature and prolong human life. The ideal figure in this respect was the Taoist hermit, often in mountain retreat. For the Confucians, moral and spiritual cultivation of the individual was essential so as to participate in the betterment of the social and political order. Thus the Confucian sage, teacher, or scholar-official was admired as the ideal person.

The implications of these two traditions for an ecological cosmology and environmental ethics are clear. Indeed, it may be some combination of these two traditions which can be fruitful in rethinking our own interactions with nature in the West. The Taoists help us to be conscious of the need to attune ourselves to the deep rhythms and processes of nature. This is not unlike the call of the deep ecologists who harken back to such rhythms and processes of nature. On the other hand, the Confucians remind us that appropriate interaction with nature and humane institutional constructs of society, education, and government can be a means of fostering a sensitive ecological ethic.

Cosmology and Ecology

A significant spokesperson for a cosmologically based ethics is the cultural historian Thomas Berry, who describes himself as a geologian. His book *The Dream of the Earth* is the first in a Sierra Club series on nature and natural philosophy. Using the thought of the French paleontologist Pierre Teilhard de Chardin, Berry develops his own understanding of reexamining the role of the human in relation to the story of evolution. Science, he maintains, is revealing a new sense of our place in the universe by its explorations of cosmology and evolution. How we are energized by this dynamic, unfolding universe may determine our survival as one species within a vast community of life, as Berry explains in the introduction to *Theology for Earth Community*. Working with cosmologist Brian Swimme, Berry has also published *The Universe Story* (1992), which is a comprehensive synthesis of a functional cosmology like earlier creation stories. Berry suggests there is a need for a "new story" of the universe, which will empower us to act on our knowledge of the profound interconnection of ourselves with nature.

Examples of Multireligious Perspectives on the Environment

Movements and conferences across the country reflect the growing awareness that more comprehensive ethical attitudes derived from various religious and philosophical perspectives must be a factor in implementing long-range environmental policies. On an international level, the United Nations Environment Programme (UNEP), under the leadership of Noel Brown, has launched a major effort to involve the world's religions in caring for the environment. Since 1986 UNEP has encouraged communities to observe an "Environmental Sabbath" on the first weekend in June, and to include its themes in services at other times of the year.

Efforts to incorporate a reverence for nature in rituals and liturgies have culminated in the Earth Mass (Missa Gaia) of Paul Winter. Since 1980 the Cathedral of St. John the Divine in New York City has celebrated the Earth Mass each October on the Feast of St. Francis of Assisi. Paul Winter's music draws on the sounds of birds, animals, and whales, and the celebration includes a procession and blessing of animals in the cathedral. Other significant environmental efforts at the cathedral include the Gaia Institute and the Lindisfarne Association. In addition, the National Religious Partnership for the Environment directed by Paul Gorman has organized the distribution of over fifty thousand packets of materials for use in Jewish and Christian congregations across the United States. Gorman also helped to issue the "Joint Statement of Scientists and Religious Leaders," urging cooperative and interreligious efforts in response to the environmental crisis. The Union of Concerned Scientists in their 1992 "Warning to Humanity" similarly called for the leadership of the world's religious communities to speak out in behalf of the environment.

Across the United States, various conferences have been held focusing on ecological and religious issues. In 1987 the first North American Conference on Christianity and Ecology was convened in Indiana. Two major national organizations have continued since then, the North American Conference on Christianity and Ecology, and the North American Conference on Religion and Ecology. In addition, a conference titled "Spirit and Nature" was held at Middlebury College in 1991, organized by Steven Rockefeller and later broadcast on public television. In 1993 the Parliament of World's Religions in Chicago sponsored several key plenary speeches and workshops on religions and ecology. Earlier in the same year the Center for Respect for Life and Environment, a division of the U.S. Humane Society, joined with the Program on Ecology, Justice, and Faith funded by the MacArthur Foundation to launch a national program titled, "Theological Education to Meet the Environmental Challenge."

With regard to interreligious dialogue, the Fourth International Buddhist-Christian Dialogue held at Boston University in August 1992 had as its central theme the healing of the earth. In August 1994 another interreligious dialogue conference was held at Boston University between Confucians and Christians, again focusing on the environment. There will be future conferences on Buddhism and ecology and Confucianism and ecology.

Several international multireligious meetings have taken place with a focus on global survival through environmental protection. These include conferences of spiritual leaders and parliamentarians sponsored by the Global Forum and held in Oxford (1988), Moscow (1990), Rio (1992), and Kyoto (1993). Former Soviet President Gorbachev addressed the Moscow and Kyoto conferences, calling for a new ecology of spirit and announcing the formation of an International Green Cross for environmental emergencies.

Ecology was a major theme of the 1993 Parliament of World's Religions (Beversluis 1995), marking the 100th anniversary of the first such parliament. The keynote address by Gerald Barney (1993) focused on the urgency of the global ecological crisis and the need for world religions to respond to this crisis with an adequate environmental ethics. Thomas Berry and other leading spokespersons also addressed the Parliament on this issue. In addition, German theologian Hans Küng (1993) proposed a statement on global ethics to be adopted by the conference.[2]

Conclusion

The interest in religion and the environment is wide-ranging and diverse. We are, in many respects, on the brink of a new understanding of the fragility of human-earth relations and of the need to establish an ethics of ecological integrity and intergenerational responsibility. Indeed, the renewed sense of reverence for nature, and the environmental ethics this evokes, may shift significantly the direction and focus of all the world's religions in the next century. This is already taking place among those who have come to recognize that the earth is primary and humans are derivative. As Loren Eiseley noted, it is crucial that we begin to foster this growing awareness.

Notes

1. In drawing on other religious traditions it is important to keep in mind the distinction between the ideal of the tradition and the historical realities in which it existed. In other words, while the Chinese had ecologically oriented religious traditions, this did not prevent them from destroying their environment at certain times.

2. While the Parliament can be critiqued from various perspectives, especially the lack of strong representation from the academic community and from the major denominations, the fact that the environment was a major focus is in itself noteworthy. Certain controversies which surrounded some of the New Age groups at the Parliament reflected ongoing tensions between the "established religions" and newer movements and cults which are also interested in participating in interreligious dialogue on the environment.

PART 4

ENVIRONMENTAL JUSTICE

A society that accepts environmental degradation tends also to tolerate human degradation. The Environmental Justice Movement is a "wing" or "branch" of environmentalism that responds by demanding equity in the distribution of environmental risk and benefit. This movement emerged in North America and on other continents, with help from the ecumenical churches, as Manning Marable indicates.

This focus is especially salient in poor and minority communities that face inordinate pollution hazards. Contemporary justice-oriented environmentalism has roots in a century of social analysis and action, led by outstanding individuals deeply concerned with the effect of urban and industrial forces on daily life in the city. One of these was Alice Hamilton, a pioneer of occupational medicine. Decades ago she was at the forefront of struggles over hazardous workplaces, environmental racism, gender discrimination, access to information or a community's right to know, and strategies to organize powerless constituencies.

In recent decades Environmental Action and the Citizen's Clearinghouse for Hazardous Wastes have led the way toward local environmental justice for low-income communities. Several member communions of the National Council of Churches have helped to sharpen the focus on environmental justice for people of color.

Some economists and politicians who are enthusiasts for unregulated markets still insist that income, not gender or race, is the only relevant factor in environmental inequity—and they manipulate statistics to "prove" it. Obviously, there *is* a correlation between having economic-political clout and not getting dumped on as recipients of toxic wastes and depositions. But gender and race matter, also. Often, women and people of color, and sometimes whole nations, are treated as disposable or are "raped for profit." As was discussed in chapters on ecofeminist theology (see Part 2), women and nature must have equity with men and "their" institutions, for the sake of earth community.

Part 4 focuses on racial justice as an aspect of eco-justice. People of color in North America experience much more toxic exposure, as blacks, hispanics, Asians, and Native Americans in cities or on farms and reservations know firsthand. In recent years, the Congressional Black Caucus has shown its recognition of this fact by having the best group voting record in the eyes of the League of Conservation Voters.

Environmental justice involves "redress for the structures and situations arising from environmental discrimination and, particularly, environmental racism,"

153

explained Michael Gelobter in a recent issue of the *Fordham Urban Law Journal.* The segment of his article incorporated at the end of chapter 12 details the ways in which communities of color have significantly less access to *high-quality* environments. He concludes that this environmental challenge requires better community organizing. Picking up this theme, Manning Marable underscores the importance of coalitional activity to meet the threat.

George Tinker comes at the subject in light of American Indian experience with environmental despoliation. After reporting some of the unique impacts on indigenous peoples of the Western hemisphere, Tinker discusses the philosophical underpinning of colonization and degradation in the idolization of individualism and lack of interest in the appropriate place of indigenous nations in relation to modern states. He concludes that American Indian cultures and values are crucial to sustainability of the earth as we know it.

Thomas Hoyt, bishop of a CME district that includes some of the continent's most chemically polluted communities, puts these concerns in the context of a black theology of liberating community. He interprets biblical revelation post-individualistically, in light of the black community's experience with survival issues. His essay focuses on theological and ethical meanings of the land, exodus and creation, dominance and sin, the Sinai covenant, incarnation, redemption and reconciliation, eschatology, and the church.

The eco-justice crisis requires that we reexamine our assumptions in light of critical social analysis, and that we rethink and restate basic theological affirmations accordingly. Attention to issues of environmental justice, and ways to respond to them, should be part and parcel of theological education or religious studies.

12

Environmental Justice

The Power of Making Connections

MANNING MARABLE

The greatest power of any oppressed people is in the realization that they share common interests with others. The forces which perpetuate their exploitation and inequality are not usually isolated to their own group, however their identity is defined. To address the basic problems or concerns within a particular community or group, one must transcend the narrow boundaries of parochialism and self-awareness, to draw parallels and cite common conditions that exist with other groups.

One of the best examples of the power generated by making theoretical, political and conceptual connections is between people who experience social problems illustrated by the dynamics of the environmentalist movement. In the 1960s concerns about the general quality of life, the condition of our air, water, and physical environment, usually were expressed by middle- to upper-class whites, who had the leisure to be worried about such matters. Members of organizations like the Sierra Club and the Audubon Society were drawn from the privileged elite, who seemed to care more about maintaining wetlands off the coast than about saving the lives of Latino, black and poor white children from hunger, toxic wastes in their communities, and poverty. With the initiation of Earth Day in 1970, interest in environmental issues soared. As a college student that year, I recall spending most of Earth Day picking up trash and non-biodegradable items from the periphery of a state highway in Richmond, Indiana. Despite feeling good about my meager contribution to the environment that day, I perceived some degree of alienation and isolation from my fellow white students, who had busily picked up garbage and refuse all day long without a single word of complaint.

In my own mind I wondered at the time, "What does any of this have to do with *racism*?" The whole issue of the survival of the human species and the planet appealed to my holistic sense of politics, the necessity to create a vision of society which was non-antagonistic and non-threatening to societies of divergent cultures and conditions. But I was also aware that, at least for most African-Americans, the issue of environmentalism would appear to be, at best, abstract, and at worst, irrelevant, to the practical conditions of daily life.

Somehow, the issue of the environment had to make the conceptual and political leap from demands to purchase biodegradable paper products in the local supermarket, to a passionate commitment to improve the quality of the air, water and physical environment of cities, where the vast majority of people of color in the United States lived. For environmentalism to make a difference, it had to incorporate the four critical issues that comprised the background to the protest politics of people of color: the problems of racism, class exploitation, sexism or women's inequality, and the crises of the central cities. Somehow, the struggles for social justice in the ghettoes and barrios of our country had to link up with the problems articulated by what were admittedly "elitist" and affluent whites from the suburbs and fashionable urban townhouses of America.

The odds for this kind of political dialogue, much less an effective, permanent coalition, seemed less than hopeful, at least at first. Back in 1970, at the Earth Day mobilization at San Jose City College in California, white environmentalists purchased a new Cadillac and then buried it, symbolizing their opposition to the culture of conspicuous consumption and the rampant materialism of the Nixon years. African-American students, by contrast, were outraged by this display of white, middle-class protest. They argued that the thousands of dollars used to pay for the posh automobile should have been put to better use. In the aftermath of Three Mile Island in 1979, when the East Coast nearly experienced a nuclear meltdown, and the nuclear tragedy of Chernobyl, in which tens of thousands of Russian people were nearly destroyed, it appeared that environmentalism would continue to be perceived as a "white issue."

Two political activists were largely responsible for transforming the environmentalist issue into a dynamic context in which people of color could become engaged: the Reverend Jesse L. Jackson, head of the Rainbow Coalition, and the Reverend Benjamin Chavis, director of the United Church of Christ Commission for Racial Justice. In his presidential campaign of 1984, Jackson repeatedly raised environmentally related issues, from the toxic wastes dumped in working class and minority neighborhoods, to the connections among poverty, institutional violence and the overall physical quality of life which minorities and the poor experience. After the departure of George McGovern from the 1984 Democratic primaries, Jackson was the sole presidential candidate left who represented environmental issues. After listening to Jackson speak out against acid rain in New Hampshire, for example, David Brower, founder of the environmental lobby Friends of the Earth, characterized the candidate's remarks as "the best environmental statement that any presidential candidate has ever made." White environmentalists who shared Jackson's progressive political views were active in the campaign at many levels. As Sheila Collins, a national officer in the Rainbow Coalition campaign later observed, white environmentalists learned that their concerns could "be translated into language and campaign strategies that will speak to constituencies not traditionally associated with the predominantly white middle-class environmental movement," and that "minority communities are the strongest base" for the construction of progressive environmentalist movements "that can win power."

Three years later, under Chavis's leadership, the Commission on Racial Justice produced a major report entitled *Toxic Wastes and Race in the United States*. This crucial study deepened the awareness of the links among institutional racism, corporate greed and the environmental problems of the poor. The study found that three out of five African-Americans lived in communities with abandoned toxic-waste sites, and that blacks comprised higher percentages of the populations of urban areas with the highest number of toxic waste sites. Although African-Americans comprise less than 12.5 percent of the total United States population, they account for 43.3 percent of Memphis, which has 173 uncontrolled toxic waste sites; 27.5 percent of St. Louis, with 160 sites; 23.6 percent of Houston, with 152 sites; and 37.2 percent of Chicago, with 103 sites. Heavily black Sumter County, Alabama, alone accounts for nearly one quarter of the nation's total capacity for commercial hazardous waste disposal. About 50 percent of the petrochemical and hazardous waste companies that operate across the South, for example, locate their facilities in largely black communities.

United States industries are responsible for pumping 2.4 billion pounds of toxic chemicals into the air each year (as of 1990). But all too often, the people most tragically affected by toxic pollution are people of color and the poor. In Houston, for example, until the 1990s, all of the city's landfills and six of the eight garbage incinerators were located inside the black community. As sociologist Robert Bullard has noted, the result was "lower property values, accelerated physical deterioration, and disinvestment." The neighborhoods in effect became "dumping grounds." The consequences of environmental racism were most clearly manifested in health care statistics. In Chicano farm communities, where pesticides are abundantly used, childhood cancer rates are several times the national average. Because of urban air pollution, African-American young men are dying of asthma at three times the rate of white young men.

Charles Lee, the principal author of the 1987 study *Toxic Wastes and Race in the United States*, highlighted these devastating statistics:

- That the predominantly African-American and Latino South Side of Chicago had the greatest single concentration of hazardous waste sites in the nation.
- That African-American children of a West Dallas neighborhood had suffered irreversible brain damage from exposure to lead.
- That Puerto Rico is one of the world's most heavily polluted sites, poisoned for decades by massive wastes from pharmaceutical companies, oil refineries and petrochemical plants.

The movement for multicultural environmentalism moved forward again in January 1990, when the University of Michigan sponsored a major conference on "Racism and the Incidence of Environmental Hazards," bringing together over twenty of the nation's major authorities on the subject. The Reverend Jesse

Jackson's Rainbow Coalition mobilized a national tour of minority communities with environmental problems in conjunction with the Earth Day 1990 Organizing Committee and other grassroots activists. All of these activities culminated into a movement for a more "inclusive environmental movement."

This was the impetus for the National People of Color Environmental Leadership Summit, held in Washington, D.C., in October 1991, which attracted over three hundred delegates from all fifty states, plus representatives from Canada, Puerto Rico and Latin America. People came together to share the many examples of resistance and struggle against environmental racism—from the mobilization of American Indians in Arizona, who were fighting against uranium mining in the Grand Canyon, to African-American activists from Louisiana, who were mobilizing the Gulf Coast Tenants Organization. Most importantly, the delegates learned that the historical divisions that have tended to separate people of color from each other, and the barriers of language, culture, ethnicity, gender and class, are all secondary to the fundamental processes which should bring us together for the preservation of our environment and for the saving of future generations. Corporate power and racist disregard for our lives and our bodies had culminated in a pattern of environmental disaster, and only our collective strength and resistance would overcome this process.

Where do we go from here? The environmental movement within white middle-class America must confront the reality that the state of the environment is inextricably connected with the existence of social justice, the possibility for all members of society to gain a share of the decision-making, the resources and the power within the social order. Environmental racism is a symptom of the inequality of power relations between people of color, working people, the poor and those with power, resources and privilege. So unless we are prepared to discuss the next logical extension of democracy, moving from narrowly defined political relations to the more substantive socioeconomic relations, we will never resolve the roots of the problem. Upper-class whites who lament the endangered status of the spotted owls of the Pacific Northwest, for instance, or who are deeply concerned with the plight of the whales, but who show little awareness or interest in the reality of poverty, death and disease in our own ghettoes, barrios and Indian reservations, are prisoners of a limited vision of democracy.

We will succeed in challenging the power of the corporations to destroy the environment only when we mobilize in concert those among us whose children and families are the greatest victims of these policies. Our approach must be to listen to the actual voices of the people, to link questions of the environment to the pressing daily concerns of poverty, unemployment, homelessness, disease, and the destructive power of the criminal justice system. We must make the connections politically, theoretically and morally, if we are to redefine what American democracy has become, and what it may become if all are truly empowered.

(The following Afterword by Michael Gelobter makes concrete many of the problems discussed in my own essay.)

Afterword:
*Key Urban Environmental Justice Problems**

MICHAEL GELOBTER

The roots of urban environmental injustice can be traced much further back in time than the start of the formal environmental movement of the 1960s. Environmental problems faced by urban low-income communities and urban communities of color around the world stem instead from the institutionalized webs of class and race that have been, and continue to be, central to the city's functions. Although the outcomes of environmental injustice are obvious, the embedded nature of power relations in the city sometimes obscures the causes.

Thus, I distinguish between three different types of urban environmental justice problems: health-based problems, space-based problems, and structural/economic problems. These three categories are not separable in reality. Problems in each area contribute to and compound difficulties in other areas. But these categories provide a framework in which to organize and to understand the different components of urban environmental oppression.

Health-Related Environmental Injustices

There are innumerable proximal causes of the urban environmental disease. Cancer, respiratory illness, and heart disease abound in urban areas[1] and it is a wonder that more do not succumb to the chemicals and smells, the heat, the crowding, the stress, the time pressures, and the crime. Given such universally low background levels of environmental quality, people of color and low-income groups have strikingly higher incidences of environmental disease than their white, richer urban counterparts.[2]

The most important study to date on the environmental basis for the differences in overall morbidity and mortality was conducted by researchers from the

---

*Excerpted from the *Fordham Urban Law Journal* 21:3 (1994), 849ff. Used by permission.

[1]See generally L. W. Pickle et al., Public Health Services, United States Department of Health and Human Services, *Atlas of Cancer Mortality Among Nonwhites: 1950-1980* (1980); U.S. Dept. of Health and Human Services, *Report of the Secretary's Task Force on Black and Minority Health, Executive Summary* (1985); W. Carr et al., *Variations in Asthma Hospitalizations and Deaths in New York City,* 82 AM, J. Pub. Health 54 (1992).

[2]See generally Commission for Racial Justice, United Church of Christ, *Toxic Wastes and Race in the United States* (1987) [hereinafter UCC Report].

Human Population Laboratory in Alamedia, California. In that study, they compared health levels of Oakland residents that lived in the city's federally-designated poverty area to those that lived in the balance of the city.[3] Even after adjusting for important risk factors (i.e., baseline health—including blood pressure and heart disease—employment status, access to medical care, health insurance coverage, smoking, alcohol consumption, physical activity, body fat, and marital and social status), the study found an average, age-adjusted difference in mortality of over fifty percent.[4] Since it controlled for nearly all known risk factors—except for environmental factors—the study offers very strong evidence that disparity of environmental quality is the source of disparity in morbidity and mortality between communities.

This study also must be interpreted in light of a continuing decline in the life expectancy of people of color in the United States, particularly African-Americans.[5] This trend is precisely opposite of that faced by whites and is quite telling in the case of urban asthma. Over the last ten years, asthma has become a leading killer of inner-city youth of color, age fourteen to twenty-four.[6] In New York City, asthma is the number one cause of child hospital admissions, accounting for over ten percent of child admissions year-round and over forty percent of child admissions at peak periods in winter months. The causes of such disease prevalence are numerous, but poorly understood. Contributing factors may include poor outdoor air quality (specifically particulate matter, ozone, and nitrogen oxides), poor indoor air quality (stemming from indoor/kerosene space heaters, poorly tuned gas stoves, and household pesticides and toxics), the disproportionate presence of allergens (cockroach eggs, dust, and fumes from nearby industrial operations and/or dry cleaners), and poor overall environmental conditions in dwelling units (inadequate/sporadic heat, breeziness, the infiltration of secondary smoke from other rooms/dwelling units). Perhaps more than any other environmental disease, the prevalence of asthma reflects the diversity and magnitude of environmental risks faced by people of color and low-income communities.[7]

Lead poisoning is another major urban environmental disease that disproportionately affects people of color. Again, in New York City alone, over 600,000

---

[3] Mary Haan et al., *Poverty and Health: Prospective Analysis from the Alamedia County Study*, 125 *AM. J. of Epidemiology* 989, 994 (1987).

[4] *Id*. The 95% confidence interval, the range of numbers within which it is 95% likely that the difference between whites and blacks falls, is approximately 1.05-2.20.

[5] Interview with Phillip J. Landrigan, Director, Occupational and Environmental Health Clinic, in New York, N.Y. (Mar. 19, 1994).

[6] Id.

[7] See generally M. L. Penna & M. P. Duchiade, *Air Pollution and Infant Mortality from Pneumonia in the Rio de Janeiro Metropolitan Area*, 25 *Bull. Pan Am. Health Organization* 47 (1991). This problem is clearly international in scope. Penna and Duchiade analyzed the relationship between asthma and air pollution in Rio de Janeiro, Brazil, and were unable to detect an effect until they controlled for income levels. Those familiar with Brazilian social structure, particularly in the vicinity of Rio de Janeiro, also will recognize that most of the poor facing this disease were Afro-Brazilians. See Shepard, *supra* note 22, at 744-49.

children are estimated to be at risk for lead poisoning.[8] 200,000 of this estimate are anticipated to be actually poisoned. Of the 200,000, over 84% are likely to be Latino or African-Americans. This immediate health-related injustice is compounded by state structural and regulatory neglect and degraded property status in communities of color. Lead poisoning is a result of widespread use of lead paint and leaded gasoline in the postwar period. Despite the fact that the hazards of environmental lead have been known for thousands of years,[9] most states and cities in the United States have not adopted regulations for the prevention, abatement, and removal of lead contamination. This lack of regulation leaves the door open for developers and land owners to sue to stop lead abatement under federal law.[10] Thus, the legality of most attempts at removing lead paint is open to serious challenge.

Even interim measures for lead poisoning prevention must skate along the shadow of the law. For example, a useful technique for reducing exposure to lead paint is to wet vacuum exposed areas of apartments and houses. In most jurisdictions, however, the water in such vacuums must still be treated as a hazardous waste[11] and, therefore, must be disposed of at expensive hazardous waste treatment, storage, and disposal facilities to stay within the bounds of law. This is in contrast to well established asbestos contamination procedures, for which there are specially designated asbestos dumps equipped to dispose of the substances properly without imposing an undue burden.[12] Such regulatory neglect can be attributed only to the fact that property owners in communities of color have no incentive to assure that their properties are safe for the residents and that the health and safety concerns of such communities are subordinate to concerns of the urban property market.

Spatial Environmental Injustice

Inner-city communities of color have lesser access to high-quality environments. The clearest urban manifestation of this is the organization and design of the spaces in which people of color and low-income people live.

Most immediately, people of color are forced to live nearer to environmentally hazardous facilities. A number of studies have shown that urban communities of color contain a disproportionate number of hazardous and solid waste facilities.[13] Moreover, recent attention has focused on the overall burden of municipal infra-

---

[8]See School of International and Public Affairs, Columbia University et al., Proposal for a Youth Lead Poisoning Prevention Project 3 (1993) (unpublished proposal on file with author).

[9]See e.g., Agency for Toxic Substances and Disease Registry, *The Nature and Extent of Lead Poisoning in Children in the United States: A Report to Congress II-3* (1988); "Toxic Lead from the Ancients," *N.Y. Times*, Apr. 19, 1994, at C6.

[10]Resource Conservation and Recovery Act, 42 U.S.C. §§ 6901-92 (1988).

[11]42, U.S.C. §6901 (1988).

[12]20 U.S.C. §4014 (1988).

[13]See generally Robert D. Bullard, *Solid-Waste and the Black Houston Community*, 53 *Soc. Inquiry* 273 (1983).

structure facilities faced by such communities. Although communities of color have long struggled against the location of an unfair share of social service and penal institutions in their neighborhoods,[14] the environmental justice movement has helped them to mobilize against facilities that more directly threaten their environmental health, such as municipal sewage treatment plants, incinerators, and large transportation facilities (including diesel bus depots and garbage transfer stations).

Low-income communities and communities of color have an even longer history of struggle over the *kinds* of space to which they are relegated by the urban system.[15] Many inner-city ghettos are among the most inhuman living environments ever designed and built. In city after city, the most densely populated neighborhoods are those occupied by people of color and the poor. These neighborhoods are not only unpleasant to live in, they actively serve to enforce the oppression and psychological imprisonment of their residents. They trap people of color, and particularly youth, in the confines of brick alleyways, litter-strewn lots, flooded back streets and corners. For generations, the spatial arrangement of the city has cut off effectively the social aspirations and economic options of the most oppressed populations.

Within the often horrific configurations of urban spaces, people of color historically have been denied access to those public amenities designed to ease urban tension and provide outlets for physical activity, recreation, and relaxation. Parks and open spaces in the city traditionally have been developed in white, well-to-do neighborhoods. For example, in New York City from 1930 to 1939, Robert Moses—then New York City's Parks Commissioner—built 255 neighborhood parks, yet only two of these were in African-American communities.[16] Moreover, he designed the expressways leading to public beaches specifically with stone bridges too low to allow the passage of buses and other public transportation. Public parks and beaches across the nation also historically have been the site of outright racial struggle. In Detroit, a bitter history of racial harassment kept African-Americans out of lakeshore parks until well after the election of the city's first black Mayor in 1968.[17]

Finally, race and class segregation—and the resulting governmental fragmentation within metropolitan areas across the United States—increase the disparity in air pollution exposure by race and income through two distinct mechanisms. First, metropolitan areas are organized to preserve the relative privilege of differ-

---

[14]Luke W. Cole, *Environmental Justice Litigation: Another Stone in David's Sling*, 21 *Fordham Urb. L.J.* (1994) (citing Yale Rabin, *Expulsive Zoning: the Inequitable Legacy of Euclid in Zoning and the American Dream* 101 [Charles Haas & Jerrold Kayden, eds., 1990]).

[15]See generally Keith Aoki, *Race, Space, and Place: The Relation between Architectural Modernism, Post-Modernism, Urban Planning, and Gentrification*, 20 *Fordham Urb. L.J.* 699, 757-73 (1993) (discussing land use controls and urban renewal in the context of urban migrations).

[16]Robert A. Caro, *The Power Broker* 510 (1974).

[17]Andrew Hurley, "Environmental and Social Change in Gary, Indiana, 1945-1980" (1990) (unpublished Ph.D. dissertation, Northwestern University, on file with author).

ent groups.[18] Suburbs and other sub-jurisdictions reflect lines of class and race, and serve to enforce differential access to education, safety, health, and environmental quality. Second, within the metropolitan system, lower status communities are forced to raise more money to keep up with the greater demands for police, health, welfare and social support services necessitated by the conditions within those communities. To raise this money, those communities must turn much more frequently to industrial and polluting sources of tax revenue. In effect they must run faster than their wealthy and middle-class counterparts to stay in place.

Structural/Economic Environmental Injustice

Finally, environmental injustice in the city has a structural and economic dimension. Cities, as the economic engines of the global economy, continue to have a voracious appetite for labor and create a constant draw, across national boundaries, of populations from rural areas to urban areas. In most economies, this phenomenon does not improve quality of life, but rather serves to continue the devaluation of labor internationally. Although this problem is discussed generally in the context of urbanization of less developed countries, urban migration has radical international environmental effects. The specific environmental effects differ based on the country or origin and destination of migrants.

Some common effects are accelerated land abandonment and the loss of local land use traditions. Moreover, this phenomenon often results in increasingly abusive land management practices in rural and urban areas. Rural abuses increase due to the loss of local tradition, the need to raise capital for the urban move, and the consolidation of properties under agro-industrial conglomerates with unsustainable practices. Because of massive immigrant influxes, urban abuses increase due to the increased need for housing and educational and sanitary facilities.

One longer-term impact is the loss of specific cultures as peoples are uprooted from their traditional homes and go into hostile urban areas. Another is increased gender oppression as women either are left behind to deal with depleted environments or are driven to the city by poor economics to serve as an even cheaper, fallback labor pool.

Urban Environmental Justice Solutions

This essay has shown the embeddedness and the depth of environmental problems faced by people of color and low-income communities. To understand the soaring asthma rate in Rio de Janeiro or in *El Barrio* of New York City, scholars, activists, and students must analyze urban environmental injustice in the context of urban health, struggles over spatial organization, and the global economic and structural context within which urban residents operate. The three must be addressed individually and together in the struggle for urban environmental justice.

---

[18]Norton E. Long, *Political Science and the City*, in *Urban Research and Policy Planning* 243, 254 (Leo F. Schnore & Henry Fagin, eds., 1967). "The Suburb is the Northern

How are we to mobilize the necessary resources, both financial and social, to redress such problems? Most importantly, how are we to do so in the face of competing needs and perspectives on inner-city problems?

It is clear to communities of color that there are no massive urban environmental rehabilitation programs that will be underway any time soon. In the absence of outside assistance—and despite rhetoric to the contrary—the first level of action has been the family unit. Asthma, lead poisoning, and lack of access to recreation and/or nature—these are all problems which arise long before an inner-city child enters "the system"—whether the system consists of government sponsored day care, day school, or day camp. Parents, siblings, grandparents, uncles, aunts, and cousins in most inner-city neighborhoods are, thus, already at the forefront of dealing with the urban environmental crisis. This must be recognized, and interventions must be designed to buttress and to magnify this critical network of environmental workers.

This is, in fact, the primary level of environmental justice organizing. But movements for urban environmental justice also recognize the broader context within which they are operating and are adapting distinct approaches to achieving their goals. In Los Angeles, for example, the Labor/Community Watchdog is building a coalition of neighborhood based activists that directly target the city's corporate underpinnings. In New York, West Harlem Environmental Action (WHE ACT) struck back by winning compensation for the loss in property values and in quality of life incurred by the city's newest and most experimental sewage treatment facility. The South Bronx Clean Air Coalition (SBCAC) is advocating for alternatives to incineration for medical wastes.

SBCAC is also working with the Rheedlen Center for Families and Children. Their joint goal is to take charge of the lead poisoning problem in the city. Through their Youth Lead Poisoning Prevention Program they seek youth involvement in early intervention at the family level. Furthermore, they plan to train older youth in safe lead abatement so that the children identified by youth outreach workers can get immediate relief from the toxic conditions in their own homes.

All of these movements share a recognition that environmental justice must be linked to increased economic and political control over the life of the city. Sustainability cannot be achieved by existing urban power structures. Environmental justice activists are working not only for immediate justice, but also for new models of economic and environmental activity that will form the foundation of true justice and sustainability for cities around the world.

13

Environmental Justice and Black Theology of Liberating Community

THOMAS L. HOYT, JR.

It is my goal here to give a brief theological basis for what we are calling environmental justice. Charles Lee of the UCC Commission for Racial Justice has challenged us to recognize three overlapping subsystems of the ecosystem of the city: the natural or biophysical environment, the manufactured or built environment, and the social environment. Elements of the biophysical wasteland which need to be addressed include polluted rivers and water supplies, air in constant violation of federal health standards, toxic emissions from nearby factories and waste incinerators, and so on. Elements of the built wasteland include a mounting trash problem; antiquated water, sewage, and mass transit systems; and bridges, roads, and an infrastructure that are old and in disrepair. Elements of the social environment include crime, less than minimal education, drugs, violence, residential apartheid, racism in housing and health-care delivery.

What is the theological basis for habits of life and politics that can address these subsystems of the ecosystem? I want to suggest briefly the following theological themes to illumine environmental justice, with the black theological agenda undergirding our discussion (see Nash 1991).

Black Theology and James Cone

James Cone has rightly stated that an authentic black theology makes sense of the black experience; recognizes the religious character of the black community; relates the biblical experience to the black experience; reveals God in black culture, and depicts God as actively involved in black liberation (Cone 1970, 53-81). Cone's criterion of theology guides us in our thinking about environmental justice. He says of the liberation theologies in general:

> We do not begin our theology with a reflection on divine revelation as if the God of our faith is separate from the suffering of our people. We do not

believe that revelation is a deposit of fixed doctrines or an objective word of God that is then applied to the human situation. On the contrary, we contend that there is no truth outside or beyond the concrete historical events in which persons are engaged as agents. Truth is found in the histories, cultures, and religions of our peoples. Our focus of social and religio-cultural analyses separates our theological enterprise form the progressive and abstract theologies of Europe and North America. It also illuminates the reason why orthopraxies in contrast to orthodoxy has become for many of us the criterion of theology (Cone 1984, 148).

Scripture and Experience

Among the many questions that black theologians ask which impinge upon our topic of environmental justice is: What is scripture's relation to the present? For Cone, scripture is placed in juxtaposition with social context and the black tradition. The slave narratives, blues, gospel songs, sermons, and prayers are determinative for the black religious experience. He thinks that the theme of liberation from political oppression is the chief factor governing the biblical record. When Cone began to develop his theological agenda, the black struggle against white racism was, for him, the chief social context of the contemporary scene. He now feels that we have gone through two stages of black theology and presently are in the third stage, which began in The Black Theology Project conference meeting in Atlanta in August 1977. The third stage is "characterized by a return to the black church and community as the primary workshop of black theology, a focus on the Third World, and the identification of sexism and classism as evils along with racism" (Cone 1984, 110; see also Traynham 1973, 65).

While I would not dare suggest that Cone's analysis is invalid for our time, I suggest that a nuance of racism presently coming clearly into our view is environmental racism.

Experiences of Environmental Racism

The 1987 United Church of Christ's study "Toxic Waste and Race" clearly "shows that there is a functional relationship between poverty, racism and powerlessness and the chemical industry's assault on the environment," says Dr. Barry Commoner, noted environmentalist and activist. This seems to say that communities that are poorer, less informed, less organized, and less politically influential become likely targets for the dumping of toxic wastes and other abuse from polluters. As the just peace movement had to be linked so must the just environment movement be linked.

It is no secret that black theology was born out of a people's response to deliberate, oppressive, anthropological, rational schemes of color domination that became inculcated in economic, political, social, educational, and religious systems. Exploitation of peoples of color seems endemic to the American system. We need only specifically designate African-Americans, Hispanic Americans,

Asian Americans, Pacific Islanders, and Native Americans. Oppressive schemes and actions against these groups of people have been in the form of genocide, chattel slavery, indentured servitude, and racial discrimination in employment, housing, and nearly all aspects of life in the United States.

Little wonder, therefore, that when we begin to examine the environmental issues so prominent in the news today, African-Americans, other people of color, and the poor are an adversely affected population group. Part of the reason for this disproportionate effect is that we as a nation are in a social, economic, cultural, and political decline. When that happens in the larger culture, those who have traditionally been oppressed suffer even more of a scapegoating within the culture. Thus when we read statistics like the following, the public outcry is muted or ignored. Listen to some of the stories:

1. The nation's largest hazardous waste fill, receiving toxic materials from forty-five states and several foreign countries is located in predominantly African-American and poor Sumter County, in the heart of the Alabama "black belt."

2. The predominantly African-American and Hispanic South Side of Chicago has the greatest concentration of hazardous waste sites in the nation.

3. In Houston, Texas, six of the eight municipal incinerators and all five of the municipal landfills are located in predominantly African-American neighborhoods.

4. In my own state of Louisiana, between Baton Rouge and New Orleans, we confront what is known as "cancer corridor," a place where toxic waste is doing harm to the land and its inhabitants.

These are just a few of the environmental injustices which typify treatment of African-American, poor, and marginalized groups.

The Task of Theology

Theology must deal not only with what the text of scripture meant but must understand what it means. Scripture, social sciences, and epistemology greatly influence a theological agenda.

Experience and Interpretation of Events

Because of the sociological grid that conditions each person, there are certain antennas which pick up nuances of scripture conducive to his or her own condition. The oppressor picks up one meaning and the oppressed another, but the fact that interpretations are shaped by our biases does not lead to a hopeless relativism which nullifies the possibility of any knowledge. People can transcend their cultural history. Juan Luis Segundo (1976, 9) contends that the fact of biases means that the interpretation of scripture needs to be as systematically critical in its understanding of itself and its own present as it is in its approach to the ancient documents of the faith. For Segundo, this is the only way to grow in perception of the significance of scripture.

One determines which impressions are true and which are counterfeit by looking seriously at the biblical revelation. We can find the truth about God, the universe, and humankind by listening to the truth of God's Word as revealed by God in Jesus Christ, appropriated by the Holy Spirit, and attested to in the Holy Scriptures.

When survival issues like the lack of jobs, housing, food, clothing, and health are daily experiences, important issues of tomorrow don't seem so important. This is true even when those so called issues of tomorrow are shown to impinge negatively upon today. We would do well to look at the basic and simple factors of life in order to get the attention of those for whom environmental justice must become a priority. Nothing is more basic than land.

The Land

We begin where the biblical writers began: "In the beginning God created the heavens and the earth" (Gen. 1:1). This affirmation stresses the importance of the land and the universe. We have been reminded by biblical scholars that land is a central—if not the central—theme of biblical faith. This land emphasis is a prominent theme of Deuteronomic history.

Deuteronomic Tradition and the Land

The land is above all regarded as a gift. It does not belong to Israel, but to Yahweh. "The land is mine and you are but aliens who have become my tenants" (Lev. 25:23). This is a fertility God, who, as Brueggemann has stated, "grants his people enduring, wholesome continuities, enjoying the span of planting and harvest, participating in the full cycle with the earth—and all under Yahweh's attentive protective eyes" (Brueggemann 1977, 51).

The theme of God's gift of the land is striking because it is first done in the northern context of the worship of Baal, "the god of nature," where fertility would have been a major theme. The difference is that Baal is the deity of natural cycles, while Yahweh is the Lord of nature and history. That is why this fertility God is coupled with the idea of divine blessing. The land which is fertile also blesses. Claus Westermann suggests that when God's deliverance of human beings is set forth in the biblical text such deliverance is always accompanied with divine blessing. This theme of blessing and deliverance is seen most fully in Deuteronomy. Thus, in Westermann's view, "No concept of history that excludes or ignores God's activity in the world of nature can adequately reflect what occurs in the Old Testament between God and his people" (Westermann 1978, 6).

This stress on the fertility of the land and the continuity of divine blessings flowing from the land has significance for Israel's valuation of the whole earth. This is seen in the affirmation of creation in Genesis 1—"and God saw that it was good" (Gen. 1:31)—coupled with a celebration of its rich diversity, as in some of the psalms—"The earth is the Lord's and the fullness thereof" (Ps. 24:1). God takes delight in the results of the creative process (Ps. 104:31), because they correspond with God's intentions and expectations. Thus the ecosphere is valued by the Source of Value even in all its ambiguity—including the predation, parasitism, and wastefulness which are inherent parts of the dynamics of evolution and ecology. The creation and its creatures are declared to be good, according to Genesis 1, before the emergence of human beings. In other words, they have value independent of human interests, and this value exists even in a wild, virginal state, prior to the taming, technological transformations of human managers. The world was created as a habitat not only for humanity but also for all created beings. Since fidelity to God implies respect for the divine purposes, we are called to love what God loves, and that includes the whole good creation.

Just as Israel could not think of itself apart from the land, neither could it think of human creatures in general apart from the earth: Adam is of the earth (*adamah*). Behind this lies the idea that the very self, the *nephesh*, permeates the land (Pedersen 1953, 170, 458-59, 474). We belong to Nature and nature belongs to us.

Year of Jubilee

Leviticus 25 is part of the Holiness Code (Lev. 17-26), which reflects a distinctly priestly point of view. This chapter presents the proposal that a year of Jubilee be celebrated every fifty years in which all land would be restored to its original family. This would prevent the permanent building up of large estates with the corresponding result of driving small farmers from their inheritance. Furthermore, physical handicaps, death of a breadwinner, or less natural ability might cause some people to become poorer than others. But God did not want such disadvantages to lead to greater and greater extremes of wealth and poverty among the people. Jubilee was prescribed to equalize ownership every fifty years. Since the land belongs to Yahweh, as do the people, neither could be sold permanently. Obedience to this statute would result, according to the code, in productive land, plentiful food, and security (Lev. 24:18-19). Whether or not the institution was ever any more than theory is a matter of speculation. Nevertheless, Leviticus 25 challenges us as a part of canonical truth. The people are to be taken care of by means of the productivity of the land; no one is entitled to hold on to the land forever; and the land is to rest based on the shorter mandate entailed in the Sabbath year.

The Exodus and Creation

The Exodus and creation themes are crucial in any theology concerned with environmental justice. Recognizing that the land is central to Israel's faith, the question naturally arises, What is the relationship of the God of creation and the God of human redemption? First, we must contend that the election faith is first and foremost an encounter with the Lord of heaven and earth, who graciously delivers the people and calls them to obedience. Israel's knowledge of God came not from a general belief in creation but from a concrete happening in history: deliverance from the land of Egypt, where they were held in slavery.

Who is this God who calls Israel from among the nations, who delivered the people from bondage in Egypt, and revealed God's will to them at Sinai? God is clearly the God who has power, who can work God's way in the waters of the Reed Sea and feed God's people in the wilderness. Maybe early on this God was not reflectively thought of as "Creator," but this God was surely known as "Lord of heaven and earth." This Lord of heaven and earth delivers by using historical actors and political events but also uses forces and elements of nature. This is seen in the plagues against the Egyptian oppressors; in the parting of the waters of the Reed Sea; in the sending of the manna, quails, and water; in separating the waters of the Jordan; in making the sun and moon stand still for Joshua. Whether we call this God Creator or Lord of heaven and earth, only such a God, the One who made the sea, the animals, the heavenly bodies, and all of nature, could employ these elements in God's redemptive work.

Israel praises God not only for what God does in redemptive history but for the majestic power that God exercises throughout the world of nature (Ps. 29). For the ancient people, what happened in nature displayed the purposes of God. Those purposes are, however, aborted by sin. A word is therefore needed about the image of God, dominion, and sin.

Dominance and Sin

Humans are created to be in the image of God and to exercise dominion (Gen. 1:26). The two concepts are closely related. Often, however, both have been interpreted as the divine grant of a special status making humanity the sole bearer of intrinsic value in creation, or as a special mandate to pollute, plunder, and prey on creation to the point of exhausting its potential. The Bible actually places emphasis on humanity's God-given assignment to exercise dominion in accord with God's values. The image is of a special role or calling in recognition of humanity's peculiar creative powers and moral capacities. Humans act in the image of God when they are responsible representatives, reflecting, like ambassadors of antiquity, the interests of their Sovereign. They exercise dominion properly when they are faithful stewards, who care for God's good creation in accordance with the will of the ultimate Owner. In fact, when interpreted in the context of Christ, the realization of the image and the expression of dominion are representations of nurturing and serving love.

None of this denies, however, that humans must subdue or overcome the earth's resistance in order to survive and maintain civilization. Genesis 1:28, chose the right word, *dominion*. The ecosphere is potentially hospitable to human interests, but that hospitality must be coerced by overcoming the earth's manifestations of seeming hostility or neutrality, for example, predators and parasites, floods and flames. From the beginning, the survival of the human species has been a struggle for food, shelter, fuel, health, and other basics. And human ingenuity—manifested in plows, shovels, axes, weapons, medicines, and their modern, sophisticated equivalents—has been essential for both primitive and civilized survival. The ecological crisis, however, is a result of imperialistic overextension; it reflects the abuse of what was divinely intended for use, subduing far beyond the point of necessity, failing to nurture benevolently nature's potential hospitality. That is sin.

Sin is a declaration of autonomy from the sovereign source of our being. It is the refusal to act in the image of God as responsible representatives. It is the distortion of dominion into despotic domination. Ecologically, sin is expressed as the arrogant denial of the creaturely limitations on human ingenuity and technology, a defiant disrespect for the interdependent relationships of all creatures and their environments established in the covenant of creation, and an anthropocentric abuse of what God has made and values. Seeing the ecological crisis in the context of sin alerts us to the power behind the plundering and the intimidating obstacles to reform.

God of Redemption and Reconciliation

The world now has an interim goodness; it overflows with wonders and sustains diverse forms of life, for a time. But it is also a world of systemic alienation: racism, sexism, classism, naturism, ageism, and more, in which all life is distorted and is destructive of other life. The creation needs liberation and reconciliation. Thus, the Christian church has always combined creation with redemption. Christ is the mediator of creation (Jn. 1:1-3; 1 Cor. 8:6; Col. 1:15-17; Heb. 1:2-3). To say with the Nicene Creed that "all things were made" through Christ is to affirm that creation had a redemptive purpose from the beginning. The creation is very good because it is in the process of being brought to fulfillment by a good God—an expectation which enhances Christian responsibility for environmental protection.

Incarnation

The Word became flesh and dwelled among us (Jn. 1:14). In the life and ministry, humiliation and glorification, of the fully human Jesus of Nazareth, the Christian church experienced its definitive encounter with the saving Christ. The fullness of divine grace entered the human condition, becoming immanent in the material identifying with the finite, in this representative Human. God thus united with the whole biophysical universe, which is micro-embodied in humans and on which their existence depends.

We are products of photosynthesis and every other earthly process. Through the flora, fauna, minerals, chemicals, and radiation we imbibe by eating, drinking, breathing, and simply being, humans embody a representative sampling of all the elements of the ecosphere. Humans are of the earth, interdependent parts of nature—and this totality is what God associated with in the incarnation.

The ecological implications of the incarnation are significant. The doctrine confers dignity not only on humanity but on biophysical materiality, everything earthly and heavenly. It sanctifies creation, making all things meaningful and worthy in the divine scheme. It sanctions human humility, reminding us of our common roots and connections with otherkind. It justifies "biophilia," the affiliation with and affection for the diversity of life forms. When we destroy life, as predatory creatures must to survive in this unredeemed world, we should do so sparingly and reverently, in recognition of the incarnation and in respect for our co-evolving kin. Wanton pollution, unnecessary consumption, and extinctions are sins from the perspective of the incarnation.

Creation and Apocalypticism

Some in the black church have made a mockery of the idea of a good creation and the relevance of the incarnation by substituting a doctrine of eschatology and apocalypticism. Let me give one example:

William L. Banks, a black minister whom no one would question for his sincerity, raises questions with "social gospelers" who emphasize abundant life in this world. Feeling that sin is pervasive and impossible to eradicate by human effort, he uses the Bible to show how "social gospelers" are wasting their time in the arena of socio-political endeavors. Such passages as Mark 16:15, Acts 6:4, Acts 26:18, 1 Corinthians 1:17, Ephesians 4:11-12, and 2 Timothy 4:2 are used to downplay the mundane and emphasize the spiritual. The following opinion represents the view of one who has spiritualized the scripture to the extent that creation is viewed as evil and consequently the fight for justice seems irreligious and futile. Banks says:

> The Evangelical recognizes that the world system is in the lap of the devil, and that injustice, war, poverty, and prejudice are all parts of the system. But the social gospeler appears to be deluded. He thinks God has left it up to man to make the world a better place in which to live. Surely there is little evidence today that man is succeeding. Indeed, the idea of man's improving the world is not biblical. It is a poor concept, certainly not based upon the truths of scriptures, and it has caused some men to assume roles God never intended or called them to have. God's plan is to let things get worse and worse (2 Tim. 3:13), and only the return of Jesus Christ will alter world condition for the better. The social gospeler's failure at this point finds him seeking an imaginary pot of gold at the end of the rainbow of humanism (Banks 1972, 87).

William Banks and others like him have stressed world-negating eschatology and have not taken seriously the incarnation or the Hebraic-Christian concept of creation which declares the work of God to be "very good" (Gen. 1:31). This view has been detrimental to blacks and the poor because of the concern expressed for the "souls" of human beings to the exclusion of the environment and structures which dehumanize.

In spite of the differences of opinion among some black interpreters of scripture who stress spiritualized eschatology as opposed to a good creation or here-and-now liberation, it is apparent that fundamental to any black biblical hermeneutic is the universal parenthood of God and the concomitant universal kinship of humankind. Consequently, blacks have been able to (1) allow the Bible to speak both constructively and critically to each new situation; (2) strive for political and social justice, confident of the presence of the God spoken of in the Bible; (3) solidify theological grounds for opposing racism; and (4) establish the authority of the Bible on grounds they can understand. This latter point relates to the fact that the Bible is not the only source of the norm; experience and culture play a very significant role in the discriminating manner in which the text is evaluated.

The biblical stories have inspired blacks with a retrospective view of their own history and have given them a confession which tells of what God has done in the history of another people, evoked a telling of what God has done in their own history, and provided a perspective of faith and hope in regard to what God will do for their freedom. In this respect, the Bible is one of the chief components of the black experience, which presents and enables functional mythologies out of which one may live.

The Covenant with Noah and Sinai

The covenant with Noah or the rainbow covenant (Gen. 8:9-17) is a powerful biblical symbol for ecological responsibility. God is portrayed in this story of the flood as making an unconditional pledge in perpetuity to all humanity, to all other creatures, and to the earth itself, to preserve all species and their environments so that all can "increase and multiply." This "ecological covenant" along with the story of the Ark itself, implicitly recognizes the interdependent relationships of all creatures in their ecosystems, and suggests that the Creator's purpose is to provide living space for all. It is a symbol of the unbreakable bonds among all creatures and with their Creator.

The story provides a symbolic mandate for responsive loyalty to God's ecological fidelity. Environmental contempt, manifested, for example, in pollution, dehabitation, and extinctions, is a violation of the rainbow covenant and, therefore, an attack on the created order. It is disloyalty to God, other creatures, other humans, and ourselves, for we are all bound together with common interests in saving the integrity of our home, the earth.

The Sinai Covenant

Again and again the prophets—Nathan, Elijah, Amos, Hosea, Isaiah, Micah, Jeremiah, and Ezekiel—rise up and remind the nation of their corruption of the Sinai covenant, the disobedience of the family of God. They pronounce judgment, but in a larger context of hope. The covenant qualities of justice and righteousness are to guide the community of faith away from self-interested action. The prophetic preaching calls hearers to repentance and restoration of covenant obedience, so that Israel can become a light to the nations. The family of God in the narrow ethnic sense was always seeking expansion in the imagination of the people of Israel.

God's covenantal purposes in the context of an ethnic people were never taken as the final goal. In the book of Isaiah a deep hope begins to be articulated that someday the faith will be extended to the nations of the earth. We are all familiar with the passage in Isaiah 2:2-4.

In Isaiah 19:23 there is a rather shocking prophecy that someday the Lord will build a highway between Egypt and Assyria. In Old Testament times there was great enmity between the Hebrews and the Assyrians, and between the Hebrews and the Egyptians. And yet, the prophecy goes on to say: "In that day Israel will be the third with Egypt and Assyria, a blessing in the midst of the earth, whom the Lord of hosts has blessed, saying, 'Blessed be Egypt my people, and Assyria the work of my hands, and Israel my heritage'" (Isa. 19:24). Someday God will make a new kind of nation that is no longer defined in ethnocentric or anthropocentric terms. The community will be diverse but co-existent.

Isaiah foresees all nations coming to worship on God's holy mountain. God promises to select some Gentiles to be priests and Levites (Isa. 66:21). The Jews desperately wanted a restoration of the legitimate priesthood; yet, the vision here is that non-Jews will be part of the religious leadership as God's glory is proclaimed among the nations. Practicing stewardship of the earth and justice in relationships among the peoples are the demands of a righteous, redemptive, providing and caring God.

The Church

The church must show involvement at the level of values and as an advocate for the poor. The church can help. The church is a value guardian. Values such as survival, social justice, and an equitable sharing of resources are easily being forgotten during negotiations. Churches can constantly highlight their crucial significance. Churches are people's movements which can challenge power, act as vanguards and as advocates for change. That is essential, because people, and in particular the poor, are easily forgotten during environmental policy negotiations (Banks 1972, 6).

The church in relation to the poor possesses a fourfold function: (1) *kerygmatic*, or the proclamation of the good news of grace; (2) *diakonic*, or the healing of wounds between the rich and poor; (3) *koinoniac*, which includes the visible and genuine acceptance of the indigent, being a caring community so that actions of a political nature can be initiated with integrity; and (4) *exorcistic*, which concentrates on the expulsion of demonic structures which perpetuate poverty. These functions characterized the ministry of Jesus as well as the life of the primitive church. To ignore them now would amount to apostasy.

Concluding Postscript

Beyond Individualism. The dominant mindset of oppressed people, to which their leaders readily appeal, is one of group solidarity or corporate personality rather than individual freedom. This message has not always been welcomed among upwardly mobile persons within the American ethos, whether persons of the majority or minority group.

While individualism, which stresses opportunity available to anyone who will take it, has had good and bad effects, minorities have had to stress corporateness in order to effect those things the majority culture takes for granted as prerequisites for practicing individualism. Because opportunities have long been denied blacks, for example, blacks have had to become inventive, creative, and competitive in ways which fostered some of the same attitudes as the majority culture but aimed at different ends. Blacks had to advocate "sticking together" so that as a body freedoms could be gained. They had to stress corporate efforts and act in creative ways so that human necessities and rights taken for granted by others could be secured and ensured.

Blacks in too many instances became competitive among each other so that their own social grouping would not get worse or lead to a loss of those freedoms and the upward mobility they had achieved. Just as Euro-American culture's individualism led to success without community values, so has the practice of blacks and others witnessed their corporate orientation degenerate into an individualism which has become destructive of community and which affects how the faith is expressed. Upwardly mobile blacks today have begun to reassess their community goals and the theme of unity that portends.

Minorities who feel oppressed as a group may have a closeness to the communitarian quality of Christianity, but their faith confession must carefully avoid the victim motif while seeking to stress the victor motif in light of the confessed resurrection faith that empowers. Stressing corporateness derived from suffering becomes selfishly victim-oriented without this confession of faith in the resurrection of Jesus.

Beyond materialism. The fruit of individualism divorced from God is materialism just as the fruit of corporateness divorced from God is despair and consumerism. There are upwardly mobile, black intellectuals or those on the way to middle-class status who are experiencing a creeping materialism. The majority of African-Americans, however, have had to escape a mere survival status. Confession of faith among most black Christians today is still done in the context of a hand-to-mouth economic existence which cannot be equated with the so-called materialism of the dominant affluent majority culture.

Materialism in a positive sense refers to humans who creatively use resources to build up human community and promote human dignity. Caring, conserving, and sharing are presupposed as the proper use of goods. When rugged individualism is combined with glorification of the capitalist system, stressing success measured by the pursuit of status and the acquisition of wealth and use of power to protect that wealth, this is materialism gone wrong.

Many poor people, as they confess faith, ask how they can go beyond being mere consumers to begin to take control of their own destiny through economic, political, and social power, which hopefully will be used for sharing and caring. Their faith is confessed in this real-life context. After all, Jesus came to bring "abundant life," which includes the total person. We must be diligent for the abundant life, without doing injury to the environment, by seeking justice for human beings and being stewards of God's good creation.

14

EcoJustice and Justice

An American Indian Perspective

GEORGE E. TINKER

From an American Indian perspective, the linking of ecological and social injustice is an absolute necessity if there is to be significant transformation from the current global crisis to a healthy and sustainable future. It needs to be said at the outset that ecological devastation, while it eventually affects the well-being of everyone, initially and most particularly affects peoples of color on this continent and Two-Thirds World peoples in general.[1] As Ward Churchill implies, genocide seems all too often to accompany ecocide.[2] Hence, it becomes empty quixotism to think of treating ecological devastation apart from treating issues of racism and on-going colonialism, including especially those new forms of colonialism which some have called neo-colonialism.

While I am unsure whether I am a post-structuralist or an anti-post-structuralist and perhaps a little unclear as to what postmodernism is, Gerald Vizenor (1994),

---

[1]See Benjamin F. Chavis, Jr., and Charles Lee, eds., *Toxic Wastes and Race in the United States: A National Report on the Racial and Socio-Economic Characteristics of Communities with Hazardous Waste Sites* (New York: Commission for Racial Justice, United Church of Christ, 1987); and Benjamin A. Goldman and Laura Fitton, *Toxic Wastes and Race Revisited: An Update of the 1987 Report on the Racial and Socioeconomic Characteristics of Communities with Hazardous Waste Sites* (Washington, DC: Center for Policy Alternatives, 1994). I find Gregg Easterbrook's essay on Two-Thirds World pollution problematic, especially in what I see as his short-sighted proposal for resolving Two-Thirds World eco-justice concerns: Easterbrook, "Forget PCB's. Radon. Alar: The World's Greatest Environmental Dangers Are Dung Smoke and Dirty Water," *The New York Times Magazine* (September 11, 1995): 60-63.

[2]Ward Churchill, *Struggle for the Land: Indigenous Resistance to Genocide, Ecocide and Expropriation in contemporary North America* (Monroe, ME: Common Courage Press, 1993); Mark Zannis, *The Genocide Machine in Canada: The Pacification of the North* (Montreal: Black Rose Books, 1973).

an Anishinabe novelist and essayist at the University of California Berkeley, has nearly convinced me that I must be a "postindian simulation of survivance," a "postindian warrior of resistance" against the discourse of "manifest manners," whether structuralist or postmodernist. Actually, to paraphrase American Indian author Betty Louise Bell, I rather like to think of myself as the academic's worst nightmare: a premodernist with a word processor.[3] In any case, I want to speak from a Native American, or American Indian, or postindian, perspective.

In particular, I want to argue that the two-fold problem of Ecological and Social Justice is systemic in nature, a point I can already begin to illustrate with a simple example. Over the past ten to twenty years many of us have been converted to the vocation of *recycling*, a calling that has piqued our consciences as individual consumers to an extent that our kitchens and garages have become dangerous labyrinths of plastic, aluminum and glass repositories as we have committed ourselves to a new lifeway behavior. Yet our national situation with respect to garbage disposal and landfill capacity has gotten consistently worse. Despite our committed new behavior, the United States generated more landfill garbage during the decade of the 1980s (the decade we began actively and broadly recycling) than all the garbage generated during the first two hundred years of the existence of the U.S. Changing individual patterns of behavior has failed us as a strategy. We will need more holistic and systemic solutions, and systemic solutions call for theological and philosophical foundations.

It needs to be said here that by a theological response to the systemic I do not have in mind just another individualistic intellectual exercise of the sort that have plagued our seminaries too much, but rather a theological reflection that is far more communal. Theology must become an exercise in expressing the self-identity of whole communities. For this sort of theology, we need stories rather than treatises, rather than essentialist discourse, problem-resolution or structuralist puzzle solving. Not even some post-structuralist deconstruction that never seems to emerge from the text will finally be able to touch the hearts and minds of whole communities. For theology of this magnitude, we must have stories.

The West has stories, of course, but they tend to be stories of conquest. For instance, Columbus is the quintessential all-American culture hero, the perfect exemplar for the righteous empire, the "discoverer" and conqueror who knew no sin. Even Jesus, the most important culture hero of America, has become a conqueror in Western storytelling. The cross has become a symbol of conquest that seems to encourage more conquest.[4]

My response to the concerns of ethno-eco-justice must move beyond the mere naming of ecological devastations that are affecting Indian peoples today. But the myth of Columbus and the stories of conquest continue to play themselves out with disastrous consequences in the lives of modern Indian peoples. For instance, it should not go unmentioned that Exxon is once again pressing forward with the attempt to build its zinc mine in Crandon, Wisconsin, threatening the health and

---

[3]Bell, an Indian fiction writer, names the nightmare (i.e., herself) "an Indian with a pen." *Faces in the Moon* (Norman, OK: Univ. of Oklahoma Press, 1994).

[4]See Tinker, "Columbus and Coyote: A Comparison of Culture Heroes in Paradox," *Apuntes* (1992): 78-88.

well-being, the traditional sustainability, of neighboring Indian nations.[5] The resistance has brought together unlikely allies: indigenous national communities like Lac Court Oreilles Ojibwa Nation; along with environmental activists; and sports activists who are better known for their violent responses over the past ten years to Wisconsin Indian treaty rights with regard to traditional hunting and fishing but who suddenly see a much greater threat to their sports economy. In part, I want to say that creating a sustainable future will mandate these kinds of cross-interest coalitions. Yet the coming together must be facilitated by someone or some community of people who can name the history of violence in North America that is racism and colonialism.[6]

Likewise, we should also give notice to the eco-social devastation being wrought on Cree peoples and other Native national communities in northern Quebec by the state-owned corporation Hydro Quebec and its James Bay hydroelectric damnation projects (see Churchill 1993, 329-74; McCutcheon 1991). This is a multi-billion dollar project aimed as insuring the economic sustainability of French Quebecois if and when they are able to claim sovereign national status. That freedom, however, is now to be won at the genocidal cost of the existing sustainable Native communities to the north.[7] Already, many people who have sustainable traditional economies predicated on the consumption of fish have had to give up a significant part of their cultural existence because of radically increased levels of mercury in the fish, caused by the ecological changes generated by huge new reservoirs backed up by the first dams constructed.[8]

---

[5]Zoltan Grossman and Al Gedick, "Exxon Returns to Wisconsin: The Threat of the Crandon/Mole Lake Mine," *Dark Night Field Notes* 1 (Summer, 1994): 15-18. See also, Al Gedick, *The New Resource Wars: Native and Environmental Struggles Against Multinational Corporations* (Boston: South End Press, 1993), 57-82.

My use of the term "nation" for Indian communities is preferable to the more usual referent to "tribe." See Ward Churchill, "Naming Our Destiny: Towards a Language of Indian Liberation," *Global Justice* 3 (1992):22-33. It could be added that the first European official language about the native inhabitants of the Americas in the late sixteenth century referred to native peoples as "nations." See, for instance, the Alexandrian Bull, *Inter cetera*, in Paul Gottschalk, *Earliest Diplomatic Documents of America* (New York: 1978), 21.

[6]See Al Gedicks, *The New Resource Wars*, for a description of a working Native-environmentalist-sports activist coalition working against multinational corporate profiteering.

[7]This was the judgment of an independent team of fifteen ecological scientists with respect to the James Bay project as early as 1972 when it was in the early stages of implementation. Their findings are published: John and Gillian Spence, eds., *Ecological Considerations of the James Bay Project* (Montreal: 1972). Also, James Penn, "Development of James Bay: The Role of Environmental Assessment in Determining the Legal Rights to an Interlocutory Injunction," *Journal of Fisheries Research Board of Canada* 32 (1975): 136-160; and McCutcheon, *Electric Rivers*, 48f.

[8]Boyce Richardson, *Strangers Devour the Land: the Cree Hunters of the James Bay Area Vs. Premier Bourassa and the James Bay Development Corporation* (Post Mills, VT: Chelsea Green, 1991); Robert Hecky, "Methylmercury Contamination in Northern Canada," *Northern Perspective* (October, 1978): 8-9; and Peter Gorrie, "The James Bay Power Project," *Canadian Geographic* (Feb.-March, 1990): 21-31. That these devastations are characterized as genocide is fully in keeping with the broad understanding of the meaning of the term. See Ward Churchill, "Genocide: Toward a Functional Definition," *Alterna-*

Nor can I allow this opportunity to slip by without reminding us all of the long history of uranium mining and its devastating consequences on Indian lands, devastation severe enough to cause U.S. government policy thinkers to write off certain Indian nations as "national sacrifice areas."[9] Two-thirds of the uranium resources on this continent are on Indian lands, and virtually all of the active mining. As Winona LaDuke reminds us, all U.S. nuclear testing has occurred on the lands of indigenous peoples, with some six hundred detonations on Western Shoshone land alone. Add to this the emerging reality of the attempt to locate uranium and other toxic waste facilities on Indian lands. Indian nations are currently hosts for fifteen of eighteen monitored, retrievable nuclear storage facilities (LaDuke 1993, xiii). The clear racism here is that we are too poor and too demoralized and dysfunctional from generations of colonization to be able to say no to the offer of what seems like a sizable income from these waste storage projects.

Likewise, an Indian analysis of eco-justice must include Indian peoples in the southern hemisphere, where ecological devastation is equally pervasive and destructive to Native cultures, lands, economic sustainability and the health and lives of peoples. The reports of destruction caused by oil exploration and extraction in Bolivia, Brazil, Ecuador, Colombia and Peru are astounding. Yet central (state) governments there seem bent on increased oil and gas development at whatever ecological cost to the lives of peoples as the only possible solution to the state's increasing economic problems.[10] In Ecuador, for instance, oil extraction has made its way into the previously impenetrable lands of the Huaorani. Texaco and Petro Ecuador have transected Huaorani lands with miles of one-hundred-yard cleared swaths spaced at one mile intervals. The resulting pollution caused by land erosion makes jungle waterways uninhabitable for many species that have long been a sustainable part of the Huaorani economy. Compounding erosion pollution is the constantly recurring problem of oil leaks from wells and pipelines, hundreds or thousands of gallons at a time, which again devastate both land and waterways.[11]

---

tives 11 (1986): 403-430; and Raphael Lemkin, *Axis Rule in Occupied Europe* (Concord: Rumford Press and Carnegie Endowment for International Peace, 1944), 79. Lemkin is the person responsible for coining the word in response to Nazi atrocities during World War II.

[9]This terms seems to have been coined in a study commissioned by the National Academy of Science on resource development on Indian lands. It was submitted to the Nixon administration in 1972 as input toward a national Indian policy. See Thadis Box, et al, *Rehabilitation Potential for Western Coal Lands* (Cambridge: Ballanger, 1974), for the published version of the study. Churchill, *Struggle for the Land*, 54, 333, 367. Also, Russell Means, "The Same Old Song," in Churchill, ed., *Marxism and Native Americans* (Boston: South End Press, 1983), 25; and Churchill and Winona LaDuke, "Native America: The Political Economy of Radioactive Colonialism," in *State of Native America*, 241-266.

[10]See "Increased Oil Development Rejected in the Amazon," *Abya Yala News: Journal of the South and Meso American Indian Information Center* 8 (Summer, 1994): 31-33.

[11]Two very enlightening articles on the struggle of resistance being waged in Ecuador's Oriente region by the Huaorani against the combined forces of state government and multinational petroleum corporations, particularly Texaco: Joe Kane, "With Spears From All Sides," *New Yorker* (September 27, 1993):54-79; and "Moi Goes to Washington," *New Yorker* (May 2, 1994): 74-81.

These examples represent only the tip of the iceberg, as it were, yet they are significant enough to press us toward the natural response of "What can we do?" What can theological educators do? What can the church, or the churches, or your church do to impact creatively and positively this course of destruction? At one level, the easy (non)solution is what is called, in alcohol and drug addictions therapy, denial. It seems to me that too many churches and too many theological educators have lived out such a denial, like ostriches with our heads in the sand, as if such eco-devastation and national injustice and immorality cannot possibly affect us, living as we do in protected comfort zones of American society. Easy answers are too often given that reflect some level of denial: It is too late to rectify injustices perpetrated against Indian nations; too much water has gone under the bridge. Or it is sometimes insisted that Indians are too small a percentage of the population to merit attention. We are forced, they claim, to concentrate on the vast majority of Americans, to maximize the good (and wealth) for the most people.

In any case, we go about our business in theological education of parsing verbs as if the world depended on our critical solution to knotty problems of syntax in some ancient text or offering our heady interpretation of some finer point of liturgical aesthetic. Even issues of direct pastoral care seem so rooted in concern for the individual that the larger encompassing issues of communal well-being are given only the most generalized and non-specific attention. I would, however, carry my own analysis further. Even in those cases where we have begun to address specific cases of community well-being and eco-justice, we seem to do so with isolated strategies and a much too narrow focus. Especially at the level of theological education we have not yet begun to deal with eco-justice, let alone ethno-eco-justice and racism, as a systemic whole, as a system of oppression rooted in structures of power that touch every part of our lives. That is to say, not even our solutions are systemic enough to genuinely address the problem.

I want to move beyond the mere reporting on how eco-justice issues uniquely impact the indigenous peoples of the western hemisphere. Rather, I want to suggest that these examples are indicative of a systemic problem that is pervasively political and intellectual. If we in theological education do not pay particular attention to the philosophical and theological foundations, then the political realities of interethnic and international injustice and ecological devastation have little chance of changing for the better.

In this analysis, I want to argue two correlative points addressing the systemic level, focusing on the rise of western individualism and the systematic destruction of indigenous communities worldwide. Further, I will insist that the dismantling of indigenous communities has happened at a philosophical as well as political level. To put it another way, I am arguing that modern ecological devastation is in no small part generated by the western, European shift devaluing corporate (communal) interests in favor of the increasing prominence of the individual; and that this shift can be measured in the lack of political and economic respect and the lack of theoretical recognition given to the legitimacy of self-governing, autonomous, long-lived indigenous communities. Let me state the argument as provocatively as possible.

First, the western commitment to individualism colors all of the academy's intellectual and theoretical posturing, whether theology, philosophy, political theory, politics or law. The Euramerican, corporate level of denial is rooted in a cultural flaw that emerges from a trajectory that has its beginning in the later Greek philosophies of the Hellenistic period. From the Stoics in particular, but no less so the Epicureans and Skeptics of the third century B.C.E. the shift to the philosophical prominence of the individual can be traced through philosophy and through religious movements beginning with the mystery religions of the first century B.C.E. on into the modern period.

The resulting modern theologies of all of our churches continue this over-weening concern for the individual and the individual's need for, and impediments to, salvation and well-being. Thus, our systemic interpretations tend likewise to emphasize individualist analyses: The problem is original sin or, in its secularized version, the individual failings of human beings. Even our interpretations of sacred text—themselves far less invested in our own individualism—are regularly interpreted from the individualist perspective. For instance, the Synoptic Gospels' metaphoric paradigm for the good, the goal of all life, the *basileia tou theou* (the so-translated "kingdom of God") is consistently interpreted in individualistic terms (Tinker 1994). The *basileia*, we are told, has to do with the individual's relationship with God or with the individual's call to decision. Any notion of it being many people together, or all peoples, or all of creation, is little mentioned (Tinker 1989).

Moreover, this problematic is not exclusive to theological education but extends to all important academic disciplines like political theory, international law, economics, and the like. The culture of the west (European and Euramerican) is a culture of the individual, and, through modern colonial institutions (neo-colonial, some would say) like the World Bank and the International Monetary Fund, the imposition of this culture of individualism is quickly being extended throughout the colonized (Two-Thirds) world in terms of economic and political development. In the ongoing disciplinary discourse about human rights, for instance, most proponents would argue for understanding human rights in terms of individual rights while vehemently denying extension of the category to groups. Human rights are rights held inherently by individuals, by definition, and not rights of culturally discrete, indigenous national communities. Hence, the cultures of these communities can be destroyed with impunity.[12]

Secondly, I want to argue that the very emergence and eventual dominance of the modern state and the concomitant degradation of indigenous national entities

---

[12]See Richard Falk, "The Rights of Peoples (In Particular Indigenous Peoples): A Non-Statist Perspective," 17-37; and Ted Robert Gurr and James R. Scarritt, "Minorities Rights at Risk: A Global Survey," *Human Rights Quarterly* 11 (1989): 375-405.

contributes significantly to our situation of eco-justice and ethno-eco-justice dev-astation.[13] It should not be surprising that indigenous cultural groups, being fundamentally defined by their communitarian values and communal coherence, have been consistently attacked and destroyed by colonial intruders and usurpers of their lands and resources. Yet it needs to be said that the conquest of indig-enous peoples has not been merely a military, political or economic colonization but that the conquest has been equally engaged at an academic, intellectual level. In my own analysis, I would argue that quintessentially natural national entities of self-governance have given way to new larger and more centralized but artifi-cial government structures identified in common parlance as the modern state.

It is symptomatic that modern political theory has little interest in defining the appropriate place of indigenous nations in relationship to states. To the contrary it is assumed that the states have some natural sovereignty over their defined terri-tories even if their territory claims wholly include ancient indigenous nations that have never relinquished their own sovereignty to that state. In general in our critical analyses and in our imagination of solutions, we tend to concede too much to modern state systems and institutions. We assume too readily the au-thenticity and validity of the state and the broad bureaucratic institutions formally and informally associated with it—including our modern denominational struc-tures.

The systemic nature of the problem as it relates to American Indians becomes apparent in the systematic erosion of Indian national sovereignty and self-deter-mination over the past five hundred years. The erosion began the moment that Columbus first claimed Indian land as property of his Spanish monarchs. It was unabated as the liberal Las Casas insisted on the peaceful conquest of Indian peoples as the rightful subjects of those same monarchs. And it continued in nine-teenth-century U.S. jurisprudence and legislation with the legal canonization of the "domestic" and "dependent" nature of Indian sovereignty, wholly dependent on and accountable to the plenary power of the U.S. Congress.[14] Today, Indian sovereignty has become a shadow of its former self that invariably fades dimmer

---

[13]Many identify the eighteenth century with the emergence of the modern state. See Cornelia Narari, "The Origins of the Nation-State," in Leonard Tivey, ed., *The Nation State: The Formation of Modern Politics* (New York: St. Martins, 1981), 13-38. It seems more useful and accurate to date the emergence to the sixteenth century with the strong move toward centralization and bureaucratization during the reign of Henry VIII in En-gland; or even the late fifteenth century with the formation of a "modern" Spanish state in the merging of Castile and Aragon with the marriage of Ferdinand and Isabela. See Robert Williams, *American Indians and Western Legal Thought* (Oxford: Oxford University Press, 1990); and Stephen L. Collins, *From Divine Cosmos to Sovereign State: An Intellectual History of Consciousness and the Idea of Order in Renaissance England* (New York: Oxford University Press, 1989).

[14]See Chief Justice John Marshall's decision, "The Cherokee Nation vs. The State of Georgia." Ward Churchill, *Struggle for the Land*, 42-45; Howard R. Berman, "The Con-cept of Aboriginal Rights in the Early Legal History of the United States," *Buffalo Law Review* 28 (1978): 637-667; and Felix S. Cohen, "Original Indian Title," *Minnesota Law Review* 32 (1947): 28-59. On the "plenary power" of the U.S. Congress over Indian "sov-

with each new incursion of the U.S. Government and multi-national corporate power brokers interested in wresting natural resources away from one Indian nation or another at unreasonably cheap prices to themselves and equally unreasonably high long-term costs to those nations in terms of their environmental well-being.[15]

To carry the systemic nature of the problem a step further, the poverty that has consistently plagued Indian peoples since the onslaught of colonization and conquest is a natural result experienced by the colonized throughout the modern world. And post-modernist deconstruction seems to have little creative effect on the colonizer or on the colonized—except that we, the colonized, continue to experience the deconstruction of our cultures, our ecospheres, whatever is left of our Native economies and our internal sustainability.

With a poverty level that puts American Indians chronically at the bottom of nearly every social indicator, we suffer a resulting level of community dysfunctionality that increases our lack of sustainability and makes us all the more susceptible to forces of external political and economic power. Indian unemployment is stuck chronically at more than fifty percent across the continent.[16] Per capita income is the lowest of any ethnic community in the U.S. Indian longevity figures are more than twenty years less than the American average. The infant mortality rate is the highest of any group in the U.S. And diseases like tuberculosis (nearly eradicated for most of the U.S. population) and diabetes occur at seven and six times the average U.S. rates.[17] In some states (like Montana or South Dakota) Indian inmates number more than half of the state's prison population even though the general Indian population in the state is under ten percent.

Given poverty statistics such as these, we have precious few political, legal or even intellectual resources for capitalizing on or controlling our immense natural

---

ereignty" and the Congress' resulting fiduciary or trust responsibilities, see: C. Harvey, "Constitutional Law: Congressional Plenary Power over Indian Affairs—A Doctrine Rooted in Prejudice," *American Indian Law Review* 5 (1977): 117-150.

[15]Obviously, I have distinguished between nation and state in this essay. For the scholarly critique of statist doctrines, see: Bernard Nietchmann, "Militarization and Indigenous Peoples: The Third World War," *Cultural Survival Quarterly* 11 (1987): 1-16; Russell L. Barsh, "The Ethnocidal Character of the State and International Law," *Journal of Ethnic Studies* 16 (1989): 1-30; Scarritt and Gurr, "Minority Rights at Risk;" and Falk, "The Rights of Peoples."

[16]Tinker and Loring Bush, "Native American Unemployment: Statistical Games and Cover-ups," in *Racism and the Underclass in America*, edited by George W. Shepherd, Jr., and David Penna (Greenwood Press, 1991).

[17]U.S. Bureau of the Census, Population Division, Racial Statistics Branch, *A Statistical Portrait of the American Indian Population* (Washington, DC: U.S. Government Printing Office, 1984); U.S. Department of Health and Human Services, *Chart Series Book* (Washington, DC: Public Health Service HE20.9409.988, 1988). We know enough about the 1990 census at this time to say that these statistical horrors will not shift dramatically in any category for Native Americans. See Glenn T. Morris, "International Law and Politics: Toward a Right to Self-Determination for Indigenous Peoples," in *State of Native America*, 71, 84n; Ward Churchill, *Struggle for the Land*, 54f., 79.

resources.[18] Of course, the cultural-economic question for Indian nations may be not only how we develop natural resources but whether we feel that they can be "respectfully" developed and exploited at all. The continuing reality of our oppression, however, would leave this as a moot point, because our poverty leaves us with few defenses against the pressures brought to bear on our national indigenous communities from the outside. Hence, the prior question is one of Indian sovereignty, for the sake of reclaiming Indian community sustainability, first of all; but, so I shall argue, for the sake perhaps even for the healthy sustainability of the world community as well.

First, Indians want life. But the truth is, we do not just want existence, that is, life in the sense of mere biological survivability. What we want is life in the sense of self-sufficient, cultural, spiritual, political and economic sustainability—on our own terms. At this late date, the question is not whether Indian peoples should have the right to self-determining autonomy, but how our communities can regain this rightful heritage without the continuing colonial imposition and pressure to feed the consumptive habits of White America. We believe that the systemic justice issue involved is one of both political hegemony and ecological survivability. The answer to this systemic question may contain something of the answer of sustainability for all people on this earth.

Secondly, American Indian cultures and values have much to contribute in the systemic reimagining of the West and the value system that has resulted in our contemporary crisis of eco-justice. The main point that must be made is there were and are cultures that take their natural world environment seriously and attempted to live in balance with the created whole around them in ways that helped them not overstep environmental limits. Unlike the West's consistent experience of alienation from the natural world, these cultures of indigenous peoples consistently have experienced themselves as part of that created whole, in relationship with everything else in the world. They saw and see themselves as having responsibilities, just as every other creature has particular responsibilities, for maintaining the balance of creation in an on-going process. This is ultimately the spiritual rational for annual ceremonies like the sun dance or green corn dance. Lakota peoples planted cottonwoods and willows in their tipi rings and campfire sites as they broke camp to move on, thus beginning the process of reclaiming the land which humans had necessarily trampled through habitation and encampment.

Brazilian rainforest peoples, we now know more and more, had a unique relationship to the forest in which they moved away from a cleared area after farming

---

[18]For an official U.S. Government indication of the vast mineral resources of American Indian tribes, see U.S. Department of the Interior, *Indian Lands Map: Oil, Gas and Minerals on Indian Reservations* (Washington DC: U.S. Government Printing Office, 1978). Churchill comments with a bitter irony: "With such holdings, it would seem logical that the two million indigenous people of North America . . . would be among the continent's wealthiest residents. As even the government's own figures reveal, however, they receive the lowest per capita income of any population group and evidence every standard indicator of dire poverty: highest rates of malnutrition, plague disease, death by exposure, infant mortality, teen suicide, and so on." *Struggle for the Land*, 262.

it to a point of reduced return, allowing the clearing to be reclaimed as jungle. The group would then move to clear a new area for a new cycle of production. The whole process was and is relatively sophisticated and functioned in harmony with the integrity of the jungle itself. So extensive was their movement that some scholars are now suggesting that there is actually very little of what might rightly be called "virgin forest" in what had been considered the "untamed" wilds of the jungle.

What I have described here is more than just a coincidence or, worse, some romanticized falsification of Native memory. Rather, I am insisting that there are peoples in the world who live with an acute and cultivated awareness of their intimate participation in the natural world as part of an intricate whole. For indigenous peoples, this means that when they are presented with the concept of development, it is sense-less. Most significantly, it is important to realize that this worldview is the result of self-conscious effort on the part of traditional American Indian national communities and is rooted first of all in the mythology and theology of the people. At its simplest, the worldview of American Indians can be expressed as Churchill (1993, 17) so aptly describes it:

Human beings are free (indeed, encouraged) to develop their innate capabilities, but only in ways that do not infringe upon other elements—called "relations," in the fullest dialectical sense of the word—of nature. Any activity going beyond this is considered as "imbalance," a transgression, and is strictly prohibited. For example, engineering was and is permissible, but only insofar as it does not permanently alter the earth itself. Similarly, agriculture was widespread, but only within norms that did not supplant natural vegetation.

Like the varieties of species in the world, each culture has a contribution to make for the sustainability of the whole. Given the reality of eco-devastation threatening all of life today, the survival of American Indian cultures and cultural values may make the difference for the survival and sustainability for all the earth as we know it. What I have suggested in this essay implicitly is that American Indian peoples may have something of value, something corrective to western values and the modern world system, to offer to the world. The loss of these gifts, the loss of the particularity of these peoples, today threatens the survivability of us all. What I am most passionately arguing is that we must commit to the struggle for the just and moral survival of Indian peoples as the peoples of the Earth, and that this struggle is for the sake of the Earth and for the sustaining of all of life.

PART 5

PRACTICAL DISCIPLINES

Adequate intellectual reflection is reciprocally related to a praxis of sustainability and justice, informing and being informed by it. Praxis involves doing while thinking. Eco-theological reflection and eco-justice activity are spiritually linked as inner and outer aspects of thoughtful praxis.

In this volume's introduction, Rosemary Ruether calls for theological education to pursue "both critique and construction in a praxis-based context. Ecologically attuned theology is not just a way of absorbing a series of new and interesting ideas; it has to be embodied in praxis. That approach to learning means paying more attention to the 'field' settings of education, and it means examining the institutions of our daily lives as case studies of how to, and how not to, deal with the whole eco-community around us."

In this section, Dan Spencer's chapter, "Pedagogical Issues and Teaching Models for Eco-Justice," identifies relevant factors in, and offers specific examples of, praxis-based teaching and learning about ecology, justice and faith. He organizes his discussion of transformative, engaged pedagogy according to the "Spiral of Praxis," a four-step educational model.

In tandem with Spencer's *educational* praxis, Rick Clugston discusses *institutional* praxis, concerned with fostering habits of just and sustainable community throughout an institution of higher education. Cultivating eco-justice habits in and outside the classrooms of a theological school entails "greening" course work in various ways, making institutional operations (including maintenance and grounds-keeping) sustainable; shifting toward locally grown, humane, organic food; reducing energy consumption and doing comprehensive recycling; making purchases that are "green" and equality-oriented; revising investment policies in light of the environmental challenge; and participating in the wider movement toward eco-just community. Clugston's chapter refers to initiatives being taken by several "lead institutions" of theological education, and it concludes with John B. Cobb, Jr.'s "Critical Questions for Evaluating Theological Education," which pulls together many aspects of institutional greening.

Pedagogical and institutional reforms to meet the environmental challenge cross political boundaries and can draw the support of both conservatives and liberals. Nonetheless, Bob Edgar, president of the School of Theology at Claremont, cautions that to achieve such an effect requires involvement by persons in all three levels of institutional governance that occur in a theological school: the administration, concerned primarily with finding money; the faculty, most worried about work load and academic rewards; and students, who have seasonal interests and

187

immediate goals. All three levels of institutional life must be engaged, with the encouragement of small groups concerned about greening in depth.

What comes into view in those two chapters, as well as the practical theology chapter by Robert Kispert, is a shift of emphasis from the classically liberal project of "defending religious belief in the face of a crisis of cognitive claims, to reflecting critically on structures of oppression, alienation, and participating in the development of redemptive, liberating praxis." With an eco-justice criterion, Kispert provides a stimulating critical overview of writings in the practical theology disciplines of pastoral care, homiletics, catechetics, liturgics, and church law (polity). He especially likes Howard Clinebell's ecological-systems model for pastoral care and counseling.

Kispert begins to assess the existing environmental practices and witness of the churches, a subject that is picked up in more detail in Hessel's chapter on the churches and environmentalism in the United States. In those two chapters taken together, an important ambiguity surfaces regarding the significance of the churches' current praxis, which is rather "decadent" vis-à-vis the eco-justice crisis. Churches in North America are captive to deregulated market and consumerist logic, and generally have shown little deep commitment to a green future. So, it is important to reflect on the potential direction and better examples of praxis, rather than to assume that the churches are already doing a lot for eco-justice worthy of reflection. Segments of the laity and particular congregations, however, may be readier to move toward a just and sustainable way of life than are many entrepreneurial clergy.

Kispert also opens up an inquiry into the shape of the civil religion. He does this by noting the serious witness of non-Christian faith communities in addressing the eco-justice problematic. He contends that "especially important are projects which engage contemporary environmental traditions, those for instance that correlate Christian witness and practices with [non-Christian communities of conviction]."

15

Practical Theology Focused on Eco-Justice

ROBERT C. N. KISPERT

Three questions organize these reflections on practical theology and eco-justice: What currently occupies writers in the field of practical theology? What is the leading edge of research, reflection and writing by practical theologians in response to the environmental challenge? And what is the contribution made by that work in practical theology to further understanding and response to the challenges of environmental degradation and social injustice in theological education and in religious communities?

1. What Currently Occupies Writers in Practical Theology?

A comedy routine from a decade or so ago featured a plain-looking little man who stepped out on stage and introduced himself as Ray Johnson. He would pause, and then with increasing speed, proceed to offer alternatives. You can call me Ray Johnson, or you can call me Mr. Johnson, or you can call me Mr. J., or you can call me Ray, or you can call me Ray J. . . . Similarly, practical theologians in the United States and Europe have been engaged for the last several years in trying on a number of alternative identities and offering them up to the ecclesia and the academy. Practical theologians today are engaged in revisioning the foundations of their discipline, even to the extent of offering a challenge to the foundations of theology itself. To give some sense of this discussion, I will trace three shifts which have taken place in how the field—by which I mean both the discipline and the field of action which it addresses—of practical theology is defined.

The first shift in the definition of practical theology in recent years changes the discipline's focus from equipping clergy to perform the duties of ministry to reflection on the life and witness of faith communities. In the early 1980s Edward Farley challenged theologians to move theology and practice in the church "beyond the clerical paradigm." Farley argued that as ministry has become professionalized over the last three centuries, theological studies have become organized around preparing clergy for their professional responsibilities. At least as far back as Schleiermacher's *Brief Outline of the Study of Theology* (1963), practical theology has been defined as the application to ministerial practices of the gleanings of the theological sciences: biblical studies, systematics (or in Schleiermacher's schema, dogmatics), theological ethics, and church history. Farley called for retrieval of a definition of theology which antedates theology as a science or discipline: theology as *habitus*, a disposition or habit of wisdom born from knowledge of God. Theology, in the view of Farley and others, is primarily reflection on the redemptive activity of God as it is manifest in the tradition and ongoing life of Christian faith communities, and only secondarily concerned with the activities of the clergy (Farley 1983, 21-41; see also Farley 1983b, 27-110).

A second shift in the self-understanding of practical theology redefines the entire theological endeavor as being fundamentally practical. In this view, Christian theology needs now to shift its emphasis from the liberal project of defending religious belief in the face of a crisis of cognitive claims to reflecting critically on structures of oppression, and alienation, and to participating in the development of redemptive, liberating praxis. This amounts to a redirection of theology from one audience, the academy, to what Farley and others argue should always have been the primary audience as well as the locus of theological reflection: the churches. This shift also establishes a new foundation for theology. Fundamental theology now aims to ground the theological undertaking, not according to criteria of cognitive adequacy and coherence alone, but in relation to criteria of authenticity and transformative praxis. The plight of the poor, the oppressed, the unredeemed—even the depleted, polluted, defiled earth and its natural communities—becomes theology's first project. Furthermore, theological reflection begins with awareness of itself as already embedded in practice and shaped by interests and by sin, and commits itself to redemption and renewal, to let itself be shaped into more authentic and transformative, liberating praxis. This is what it means to say that theology is fundamentally practical.[1]

A third shift in the self-understanding of at least some practical theologians carries forward the second shift's project of relocating theology in faith communities but redefines the scope of such communities. Ostensibly secular social groups committed to transformation of public or private praxis—ranging from Earth First! to La Leche League—are interpreted as faith communities where God's redemptive activity occurs alongside the practices and witnesses of the churches. These groups are made the objects of a theology-of-culture hermeneutic, which discloses their religious horizons, ontological presuppositions, and ethical imperatives. In turn, these findings are brought into dialogue with the practices and witnesses of the churches, subjecting both social group and church to critique in hopes that each will be transformed into a more fully redemptive community. Models of practical theology born from this third shift in the self-definition of the field can be important vehicles for the creative transformation of churches, environmental groups and social justice movements by subjecting our praxis in these communities to the critical reflection of all three.[2]

2. What Is the Leading Edge of Practical Theology in Regard to Eco-justice Issues?

In this section I first will review writings in one of the classic disciplines of practical theology in order to illustrate three different kinds of response to the eco-justice agenda. Next, I will review writings that critically examine existing and pre-existent practices and witnesses of Christian faith communities and can serve as guides or counterexamples in our present responses to the environmental challenge. Finally, writings which engage in mutually critical dialogue with non-Christian faith communities about their and our environmental practices and witnesses will be reviewed.[3]

The Classic Disciplines of Practical Theology

The classic disciplines organized by practical theology in the clerical para-digm are homiletics, catechetics, church law (polity), pastoral care, and liturgics. Surveying current literature in these disciplines, it soon becomes obvious how little has been published which directly responds to the eco-justice problematic. Also a pattern emerges. Writings in the classic disciplines can be catalogued in three groups. First are those which are prophetic calls for action, setting forth general visions and principles for praxis in a particular discipline. A second category is comprised of works which incorporate ecological images, concepts, and styles of thinking into reflection about the technical practice of their discipline. Third are writings that could be described as being fully practical. These writings are practical in the classic sense—concerned with moral or spiritual practice (Farley's *habitus*) and also in that they address a range of questions from the abstract and foundational to the concretely strategic. I will illustrate these categories by reference to the discipline I know best, pastoral care.

Robert Fuller's *Ecology of Care: An Interdisciplinary Analysis of the Self and Moral Obligation* (1992) argues both from socio-biology and psycho-social theories of development that altruism, caring for others, is genuinely possible for the human species, and furthermore that it is essential to human fulfillment. Socio-biologists claim that, as social animals, human beings have evolved tendencies not only to care for their young but to act in solidarity with their kin group. Psychologists since Erik Erikson have claimed that human persons seem to have a biological need to create and to "take care of" others for their fulfillment. *Ecology of Care* goes beyond these claims. It argues that an individual's survival and thriving are only possible in a network of relations that begins with our parents and extends to the natural world and to God as the ultimate horizon of our existence. What is true at the level of ontogeny is true for phylogeny as well: our species has evolved, and it survives and thrives in this same ecology of relatedness—natural, human, and divine.

The problem is that human evolution, which is cultural more than biological, has produced technologies which threaten to destroy the sustaining ecology of human existence. Already it is destroying the creatures of God, robbing the life of species and robbing us of the joy and meaning they give us. In response, Fuller proposes an ethic of care guided by the principle that "while it is good to meet any need, the 'moral' action is one that is sensitive to the larger ecosystem (inclusive of the interconnecting of generations both present and future)" (Fuller 1992, 64). While the socio-biological foundation for this environmental ethic is human care for humans, Fuller insists that "moral rationality translates human care into a hierarchy of commitments or obligations that establishes a clear priority to those . . . needs, desires, interests . . . that contribute to the long-term benefit of individuals and the ecosystems they inhabit" (ibid.). *Ecology of Care* ends with the following reflections on the implications of Fuller's ethic for "care, commitment and the cure of souls":

> The ecology of care makes it clear that those entrusted with the cure of souls are entrusted with more than simply alleviating emotional or motivational difficulties. They are also entrusted with helping to establish, maintain, and disseminate a cultural vision that will enable people to make meaningful commitments. . . . Practitioners of the cure of souls must also project a cultural vision that deepens each person's perceptions of the divine life, which ultimately empowers and bestows meaning upon the whole web of life (ibid., 104).

Whatever difficulties attend the project of grounding ethics in biology, Fuller's ecological ethic of care is significant for its advocating an ethic and spirituality of active care for God's creation. It is an important and inspiring response to the need for a new vision of pastoral care which responds to the eco-justice problematic. Yet, it leaves questions unanswered: How might practitioners of the cure of souls best establish, maintain, and disseminate a vision of eco-justice so that the media does not violate the message? What exactly is this cultural vision, and what would it look like in practice? How would my actual practice of pastoral care be transformed by this vision? Writings in this category are found in the other classic disciplines of practical theology as well. In homiletics, for example, there are sermons and recommendations for sermons which preach ecology and justice, which articulate new visions and general principles, yet do not critically engage questions about, for instance, what it would mean to preach ecologically or justly, or on the contribution of preaching to creating a community which would practice as well as witness to eco-justice. Two works exemplify my second category, the incorporation of ecological images, concepts, and styles of thinking into the technical repertoire of a classical discipline of practical theology. First is an essay by Belden Lane entitled "The Tree as Giver of Life: A Metaphor in Pastoral Care (1991)." Lane's article contrasts two classic tree stories, Shel Silverstein's *Giving Tree* (written in 1964) and Chuang Tzu's "Useless Tree," of Taoist tradition, as two models of life and love. Lane writes:

> The first is a compassion grounded most deeply in the renunciation of the self. It grows by denial. It risks anything for the sake of love. The second is

less given to frantic action than quiet acceptance. It knows that sometimes presence can be better than sacrifice. It heals by doing nothing (p. 21).

Lane concludes his article by reminding his readers of other tree stories, metaphors which "point us back, at last, to the deciduous turning of our own relentless need to grow and to love" (p. 22).

Writings like this one remind us of a totemic relationship our distant ancestors may have enjoyed with the creation. We are invited to re-engage with the lives of trees or cells, with the creation and the Creator, and also with our ancestral past. This is important, learning how to think like a tree, a mountain, an endangered species, or an oppressed people. Yet, thinking like a tree may help us better understand our roles as pastoral caregivers without necessarily inspiring or informing eco-justice praxis. Re-engaging us in these manifold relations may prepare the ground for such praxis, but also can substitute for it, becoming yet another form of cheap grace.

The same ambiguity attends works which borrow ecological concepts and apply them to a field in practical theology. For instance, in pastoral care there are those writings which develop relational, systemic models of human personhood in community. Like Belden Lane's meditation on trees, these writings can produce mixed effects. They do tend to redirect us from self-contained, market-consumer individualism toward a recognition of the often suppressed and denied relationality of our existence. They help us to think differently, to have a more ecological ontology of the self, to take a new look at trinitarian doctrines, Sophia, and other ways to rethink God, and perhaps even to re-envision our relationship with nature and with the unseen poor and oppressed on our planet. But again, whether in pastoral care or another practical-theological discipline, writings in this category seem less to produce an eco-justice praxis than to prepare the ground for one.

The third category of writings I found in the classic disciplines of practical theology go the furthest toward outlining the contours of a redemptive, liberating praxis which answers to the eco-justice problematic. Illustrating this category is an article by Howard Clinebell (1992) entitled "Looking Back, Looking Ahead: Toward an Ecological-Systems Model for Pastoral Care and Counseling." Clinebell's article invites pastors and pastoral psychotherapists to rethink the parameters of their practice in several dimensions, insisting that "healing and enhancing relationships with the natural as well as the human environment is one essential focus of therapeutic concern in our counseling, supervision, and teaching." He continues: "Wholistic planet-caring is now and will be an increasingly essential dimension of our pastoral care ministries in the decades ahead" (p. 267). Clinebell offers specific methodological suggestions, "ten ways in which pastoral counselors and pastoral care administrators may implement an ecological-systems model" (p. 268). For example, he recommends that "ecological components" be included in pastoral diagnostics.

Our diagnostic methods should include discovering how people relate to the internalized and external natural environment. Exploring gently for possible ecological *Angst*, grief, and despair, is appropriate (p. 269).

Clinebell also lists a number of "spiritual pathologies that feed our short-sighted, exploitative treatment of the planet." The list includes

> our species-centered narcissism . . . alienation from the feminine aspects of the Divine Spirit and . . . our personality . . . our paranoid demonizing of wild animals and wilderness places, and our projection onto them of our rejected shadow side . . . our idolatrous tribal theologies and value systems . . . and magical rescue fantasies of being saved from the brink of the abyss by a heavenly quick fix or the powerful omniscience of political or religious figures (pp. 271-72).

This article offers suggestions for treatment, ranging from "nature-izing" the setting where we do pastoral care to "ecotherapy"—encouraging "clients/students/parishioners to open themselves up regularly to the healing energies of nature"—to "involving people in planet-caring action." Clinebell relates an account of an alienated adolescent boy who refused to do his schoolwork and declared in a counseling session: "Why bother when the world's going to hell in a handbasket!" The family was encouraged to get involved in a peace and justice group in their congregation, successfully combining therapy for the boy with therapy for the planet, and joining the pastoral and prophetic sides of the pastoral therapist's ministry "as two sides of one redemptive process" (pp. 270-71, 268).

Reflection on Practice and Witness of the Churches

Several types of literature are included in this category. First are the official statements of Christian denominations and associations, including the National Council and World Council of Churches. Next are reflections on those statements like Martti Lindqvist's *Economic Growth and the Quality of Life: An Analysis of the Debate within the World Council of Churches 1966-1974* (1975) and Donal Dorr's *The Social Justice Agenda: Justice. Ecology, Power and the Church* (1991), a review of recent social teachings and agendas of the Roman Catholic Church and the W.C.C. A third type is made up of scholarly treatises on the resources of major theological and denominational traditions in Christianity. Examples include an article by Gordon and Jane Douglas (1989) entitled "Creation, Reformed Faith, and Sustainable Food Systems" and Alexander Schmemann's *For the Life of the World* (1963), which advances an Eastern Orthodox vision of the power of liturgy and sacraments to usher in cosmic redemption. A fourth type is comprised of critiques of existing practices. These are typified by *The Predicament of the Prosperous*, by Bruce Birch and Larry Rasmussen (1978), which amends the familiar image of the suburban captivity of American churches to show their failure to address the eco-justice problematic, and Yong Bock Kim's ideology critique of the notion of a sustainable economy from the point of view of an Asian liberation theology.

Representatives of the four types of literature just described tended to address the eco-justice at the level of vision or general principles, and also to move deductively from theory (or vision) to practice. Few of them are fully practical, beginning with description of the concrete practices of the churches, then moving to critical reflection on those practices, developing vision and general principles, and finally prescribing specific structures or practices that more adequately address the eco-justice problematic. There are works which do initiate descriptive retrievals of the witness, and sometimes the practices of church fathers, saints, and monastic orders. Among these are Rene Dubos, "Franciscan Conservation Versus Benedictine Stewardship" (1972, chap. 8); Matthew Fox, "Creation-Centered Spirituality from Hildegard of Bingen to Julian of Norwich" (Joranson and Butigan 1984); Bernard Przewozny, "Elements of a Catholic Doctrine of Humankind's Relation to the Environment" (based on early Christian writers) (1987, 233-55); and Richard Woods, "Environment as Spiritual Horizon: The Legacy of Celtic Monasticism" (Joranson and Butigan 1984). These retrievals, however, are often less critical of the past than the present and need further development if the practices of exceptional saints and communities are to be successfully translated into the ordinary lives of citizens and communities in our time.

Reflection on Practices and Witness of Non-Christian Faith Communities

Corresponding to the third shift in the self-definition of practical theology outlined above are writings which take non-Christian faith groups as their subject, bringing these groups and their traditions of praxis into correlation with the practices and witnesses of the churches. Within this category are works which focus on the practices of three different kinds of faith communities: self-defined religious communities in differentiated modern societies, civil-religious and other ostensibly secular traditions in modern societies, and indigenous traditions from so-called premodern societies.

Three different foci dominate the literature which analyzes self-defined traditions. First, and most plentiful, are writings which explore and at the same time create the new religious movement of ecofeminism. Three works published between 1991 and 1993 seem destined to be classics: Anne Primavesi's *From Apocalypse to Genesis: Ecology, Feminism and Christianity* (1991); Rosemary Radford Ruether's *Gaia and God: An Ecofeminist Theology of Earth Healing* (1992); and an anthology edited by Carol Adams entitled *Ecofeminism and the Sacred* (1993). The second focus is represented by two works that explore the implications for eco-justice of the emerging cultural movement known as postmodernism: *Shaping the Future: Resources for the Post-Modern World* by Frederick Ferré (1976), and *States of Grace: The Recovery of Meaning in the Postmodern Age* by Charlene Spretnak (1991). Representing the third focus is a critical correlation of Christian tradition and Buddhism aimed at creating a biocentric spirituality advanced by Jay McDaniel in *Of God and Pelicans: A Theology of Reverence for Life* (1989).

The witnesses and sometimes the practices of civil religions and other ostensibly secular traditions are explored in a number of books and articles. Ron Engel has written *Sacred Sands: The Struggle for Community in the Indiana Dunes* (1983) and an article entitled "Ecology and Social Justice: The Search for a Public Environmental Ethic" (Engel 1988, 225-42). Both of these recommend the American civil religion of democracy as a basis for a "humanitarian and environmental ethic." Shannon Jung treats two value-traditions in American agriculture—agrarian and business—that at least can be said to comprise public, if not civil, religion, in "The Recovery of the Land: Agribusiness and Creation-Centered Spirituality." Similarly, in *Brother Earth: Nature, God and Ecology in Time of Crisis* (1970) Paul Santmire discusses two American public traditions, one which advocates exploitation, the other adoration of nature, and how these have shaped the political witness and internal life of the churches.

If the concept of civil religion is broadened to include the international tradition centered around the United Nations, Wesley Granberg-Michaelson's *Redeeming the Creation: The Rio Summit, Challenges for the Churches* (1992) is of interest. Related are studies of dominant world ideologies, social, cultural, and economic. Among these are Rosemary Radford Ruether's article, "Ecology and Human Liberation: A Conflict Between the Theology of History and the Theology of Nature?" (1981); Charles West's "God—Woman/Man—Creation: Some Comments on the Ethics of the Relationship" (1981, 13-28); and Philip Wogaman's *The Great Economic Debate: An Ethical Analysis* (1977).

Particularly relevant to the theological endeavor to address the eco-justice problematic are studies of the religious dimension of ostensibly secular environmental movements and traditions. Significant in this regard is Barbara Ward's *A New Creation?: Reflections on the Environmental Issue* (1973), which claims that the most radical perceptions of what she calls the "environmental revolution" have a Christian basis. Though this study is dated (it was published in 1973), its thesis is startling after Lynn White's indictment of Christianity for causing the environmental crisis, and it offers the hope that the churches have more say in response to the eco-justice problematic than is apparent in their existing witnesses and practices. Similarly my own dissertation, entitled "Alienation and Nature: A Practical Theological Analysis of the Resource Conservation and Wilderness Preservation Pieties in American Civil Religion," brings environmental traditions and Christian witness into mutually critical dialogue.

Reflection on the Practices and Witness of Indigenous Traditions

A number of works lift up the vision or practices of Native American, African, and Amazonian indigenous cultures. These writings are significant for having initiated a dialogue with indigenous traditions and for calling us out of our nationalistic and materialistic narcissisms. However, like retrievals of monastic traditions and the lives of Christian saints, these treatments often need further development. A fully practical and mutually critical exploration would ask: What are the environmental weaknesses as well as the strengths in the indigenous tradition? What is the society's treatment of its neighbors and of difference in its midst? What breakdowns in the indigenous people's relationship to the land and its neighbors can we predict as it comes in greater contact with the modern, industrialized cultures? What realistically can a culture or faith community like ours appropriate from this premodern culture? And finally, a question raised by Andy Smith in an article entitled "For All Those Who Were Indian in a Former Life" (1993b, 168-71), how do we appropriate indigenous ways so that we are not engaging in yet another oppressive form of colonialism?

3. What Kind of Studies Remain to Be Done?

Thanks to the pioneering work of the writers whose work I have reviewed here, and others, eco-justice seems finally to have arrived as a legitimate topic for theological discourse. However, we have just begun to address an urgent situation.

Many different perspectives and methods are needed if the churches are to respond adequately and authentically to the eco-justice problematic. Writings that retrieve forgotten witnesses of the churches or which construct new visions and general principles for living with creation are important. Writings which incorporate ecological images, concepts, and styles of thinking into our public or private roles and disciplines have a place. So also do works which retrieve the practical ecological wisdom of lost or suppressed traditions.

Especially important are projects which engage contemporary environmental traditions, those, for instance, that correlate Christian witness and practices with the visions of ecofeminism, postmodernism, world religions, civil religion, and dominant ideologies of the industrialized world. These writings may hold the greatest promise for transforming the practices of the churches and the civil order without sacrificing the integrity and coherence or the practical wisdom of our Christian inheritance. This promise will be fulfilled to the extent that their method is a mutually critical dialogue and their focus is on the concrete practices of the churches and our conversation partners. In Jesus's parable about the two sons sent by their father to work in the vineyard, the first said, "I go sir," but did not go, while the second said, "I will not," but went. We are challenged to conform our praxis to the eco-justice we preach.

Notes

1. An important articulation of the vision of theology as fundamentally practical is found in Don S. Browning, *A Fundamental Practical Theology: Descriptive and Strategic Proposals* (Minneapolis: Fortress Press, 1991). The theological method portrayed here is Browning's, moving from descriptive theology (which elaborates the present situation which gives rise to the praxis concern prompting theological reflection), to historical theology (incorporating biblical studies), to systematic theology (incorporating theological ethics), to strategic practical theology (which adapts praxis proposals to the situation).

Several theologians have written about the need to rethink the classic theory-to-practice methodology. Among these are David Tracy, "The Foundations of Practical Theology," in Browning 1983, 61-82; and Charles Wood, *Vision and Discernment* (Atlanta: Scholars Press, 1985).

The observation about the shift in theology from defending religious belief to shaping praxis comes from Rebecca Chopp, "Practical Theology and Liberation," in *Formation and Reflection*, ed. Lewis Mudge and James Poling (Philadelphia: Fortress Press, 1987), 120-38.

2. James N. Poling and Donald Eugene Miller have identified six types of practical theology. Their Type IIIA, "critical confession with a primary emphasis upon the church's vision for the larger society," captures part of this third shift in practical theology (*Foundations for a Practical Theology of Ministry* [Nashville: Abingdon Press, 1985], 50-57).

The basis for this model, however, is the definition advanced by David Tracy: "*Practical theology* is the mutually critical correlation of the interpreted theology and praxis of the Christian fact and the interpreted theory and praxis of the contemporary situation" ("The Foundations of Practical Theology," in Browning 1983, 76). Tracy's call for theology of culture analyses of non-Christian social groups is more explicit in a later statement: "*Practical* theologies are related primarily to the public of society, more exactly to the concerns of some particular social, political, cultural, or pastoral movement or problematic which is argued or assumed to possess major religious import" (*The Analogical Imagination: Christian Theology and the Culture of Pluralism* [New York: Crossroad, 1986], 57).

3. The rationale for these criteria is that praxis always begins somewhere, is an evolution or revolution from existing practices and witnesses. Critical reflection on existing practices and witnesses is a vehicle for uncovering both valid reasons and inauthentic rationalizations, a hermeneutic both of retrieval and suspicion. Furthermore, reflection on existing practices fosters ethical realism about what is possible, both in general and for this particular community, helping us to avoid the difficulties of utopianism. Finally, thick description of the practices of a faith community teaches us about the complex interrelations of what Don Browning has called the "five dimensions of practical moral thinking," fostering a fuller vision and set of prescriptions for redemptive praxis" ("Practical Theology and Religious Education," in Mudge and Poling, 79-102).

16

Where Were/Are the U.S. Churches in the Environmental Movement?

DIETER T. HESSEL

Asking where the churches were and are in relation to environmentalism opens up a large, previously hidden, topic. Not only does the environmental movement have multiple facets, but the term "church" has no simple meaning. Church refers to the ecumenical movement worldwide and nationally, to communions and denominations across a wide spectrum, to agencies and conferences, to parachurch networks and organizations, to congregations gathered and members dispersed (some as exploiters of nature and people, others as environmental stewards and leaders, many doing both, still others as scholars and consumers, the whole bunch being citizens for better or worse). Church means all of this, with varied accents depending on context.

Communions with a hierarchy of bishops or strong governing bodies tend to think of the Church beyond as well as in each local community. But most folks just think of a local congregation when someone says church. And few have experienced their church as environmentally engaged beyond showing vague concern or doing a little recycling.

What have the churches been doing, and what do they intend to do to meet the environmental crisis. The record, of course, is ambiguous, and the prospect unclear. On the one hand, the National Council of Churches—comprised of mainline communions, both white and black—for three decades administered an extensive summer ministry in the national parks. In the 1980s, the NCC became an important early supporter of community organization to fight toxics by meeting with, and helping to co-fund, organizers in poor and minority communities. But the

The occasion for this overview was an Institute for Ecology, Justice and Faith held in Chicago, March 15-18, 1995. The essay is a first, limited effort to fill a religious void in recent histories of environmentalism. A longer version, including some material on international ecumenical awakening to the environmental crisis, appeared in *Theology and Public Policy* VII,1 (Summer 1995). Used and shortened by permission of The Churches' Center for Theology and Public Policy, 4500 Massachusetts Ave., NW. Washington, D.C. 20016.

ecclesial base of environmentalism remains narrow. Few in the churches have been asking: Now that we're getting organized against toxic injustice, who shall speak for the Sun (that's S*un*)? And what is the churches' role in seeking sustainable community?

On the other hand, parachurch organizations of the Religious Right speak very assertively for the S*on*, but organize against environmental preservation, regulation or real movement toward a solar future. They even oppose environmental education in public schools as an aspect of moral education that is too controversial—ecology activism is deemed to be "pagan" liberalism; besides, it upsets industrialists. Here we have radical "conservatives" in league with profiteering business to fight basic education in ecology and conservation. Thus many conservative churches are neutralized, though a good number of their members want to conserve.

North American churches across the spectrum have remained reluctant to commit to environmental ethics and action, partly because of other preoccupations, and also because the ecological-integrity agenda first gained public prominence at a time (around the first Earth Day) and in a manner (when some whites quit the struggle for racial justice) that seemed to make environmentalism competitive with working for justice and peace. A growing commitment to multifaceted environmental action is still not integrated with engagement in struggles for social justice. Even so, there have been some important contributions by the church.

Five Phases of Ecumenical Environmental Response

In the untold story of ecumenical environmentalism since the 1960s, there are five overlapping phases of U.S. church involvement:

1. Awakening to Ecotheology and Ecoethics

This phase featured "forerunner" theologians such as Joseph Sittler, Paul Santmire and John Cobb, along with other participants in a "Faith-Man-Nature" Working Group formed in 1965 by the National Council of Churches. This early period is summarized in Roderick Nash (Nash 1989, chap. 4). But Nash doesn't discern the beginnings of a theological bent toward eco-justice ethics, and his overview completely misses the next two phases of the story. Nor does he illumine what the churches, not just the theologians, actually said and did in proximity to Earth Day. In fact, many denominations were quite articulate, in a reinforcing way.

Still, Nash's account shows that a set of ecumenical theologians encouraged the churches to recycle their message while beginning to think through a new ethic for a new earth (see Stone 1971). This phase of theological awakening occurred from 1965 through 1974, influenced by *Silent Spring*, the Port Huron Statement, Sittler's sermon, "The Care of the Earth," passage of the National Environmental Policy Act, organizing around Earth Day, and United Nations conferences on development (at Stockholm) and population (at Bucharest). Church statements and quality educational resources on environment and faith issued during the early 1970s were not matched again until the early 1990s, as can be seen in the annotated bibliography *Ecology, Justice and Christian Faith* (Engel, et al. 1995). This time, there are diverse voices representing both genders and people of color as well as whites from various Christian streams—Catholic sacramentalist, mainline Protestant, and conservative evangelical.[1]

2. Sustainable Food Systems

Because hunger is the number one biblical social concern, churches typically work to feed the hungry. Especially during the 1970s, churches in the NCC became quite expert about government food and farm programs, as well as international aid and trade, and the churches invested considerable energy in leadership development for hunger education and action. Denominational agencies and advocacy organizations like Bread for the World helped to put domestic feeding programs in place and to establish special cooperative mechanisms—for example, through Church World Service and CODEL (Coordination in Development)—to support grassroots development of sustainable food systems on several continents. The Canadians did even better through their mechanisms of ecumenical cooperation and in partnership with their government in the educational program "Ten Days for Development." Development education programs in North America also attended to ethical questions of population policy as an important response to global limits. Some of the mainline Protestant churches did solid thinking about appropriate ways to reduce population growth, offering an analysis that anticipated by two decades the emphases of the International Conference on Population and Development in Cairo.[2]

The environmental dimensions of sustainable food systems—for example, decreasing monoculture, pesticide use, export cropping, and grain-fed meat consumption while protecting the health and organizing rights of farm workers and shifting toward appropriate technology for local food sufficiency—got some attention and project funding within the hunger programs that the churches institutionalized in the late 1970s. Church participation in grape and lettuce boycotts, spearheaded by the United Church of Christ, lent support to the United Farm Workers from the late 1960s through the 1970s (see Hoffman 1987). And in the deepening farm crisis of the 1980s, when U.S. agricultural policy took center stage, church groups, influenced by Wendell Berry and Dean Freudenberger, began to show concern for sustainable agriculture. That carried over into current modest efforts to foster church- and community-based agriculture, or "food security." But most of the solid analysis, education and advocacy has occurred through parachurch centers for land stewardship and "rural life," most notably in the upper Plains states.

In 1980, all of the seventy-two active and retired Roman Catholic bishops of a twelve-state Midwestern area issued *Strangers and Guests: Toward Community in the Heartland*, a substantive pastoral letter, largely drafted by social ethicist John Hart, addressing the loss of owner-operated farms and land misuse and devastation (Hart 1984 and 1994). But, beyond that vigorous regional expression of concern for rural community life, little else happened among Roman Catholics to express environmentalism during the 1980s hiatus—just when a potential "Catholic moment" in the U.S. came and went. As the decade came to a close, one could see a stirring of interest in creation spirituality here and there among Catholic religious and laity. But not until 1991 did Roman Catholic bishops nationwide address the ecological crisis, in the pastoral letter *Renewing the Earth.*

U.S. churches and ecumenical structures never quite put together their intentions and expertise regarding sustainable food systems, lifestyle change, environmental-economic justice, and community redevelopment.[3] Reduced consumption, voluntary conservation and appropriate patterns of eating were also themes of educational programs during this era (see Gibson 1979 and 1977), foreshadowing a return to these same life-integrity concerns in the mid-1990s. Evangelicals for Social Action actively participated, as evidenced in writings by Jim Wallis and Ron Sider.

3. Responsible Energy Production and Use

Prior to the first oil price shock, U.S. churches and the NCC were uninvolved in energy policy debates, viewing them as too technical or merely "political." But in 1974, the Division of Church and Society of the NCC launched a committee of inquiry, chaired by Margaret Mead and Rene Dubos, on the use of plutonium as a commercial nuclear fuel. When, in October 1975, the committee proposed a policy statement condemning such use of plutonium, the nuclear industry and utility executives attacked the NCC for being irresponsible. A resolution calling for a moratorium was substituted for the policy statement and in the same action the Council mandated a broad study on the ethical implications of energy production and use, directed by the late Chris Cowap, who was NCC Director of Economic Justice. She wrote a concise, instructive overview of that highly conflicted study for the book I edited on energy ethics (Cowap 1979). Her description of the outcome of the three-year process, involving a panel of 120 knowledgeable persons, shows how intellectually demanding and politically sophisticated was this timely ecumenical endeavor. The energy policy study also shows that in reality the church can be powerfully present among competing interests with contradictory answers to the environmental challenge. The energy policy study process coincided with the movement to stop nuclear power plant building and to take a "soft energy path" (Amory Lovins); it helped to delegitimize nuclear power from an eco-justice perspective, focusing on ecological *and* social effects of energy production and use.

The energy policy study was followed by inter-church programs to foster local energy responsibility, by several denominations adopting substantive energy policy statements, and in ecumenical efforts to demand corporate accountability to communities on the part of utilities building unwanted, unneeded power plants. The churches and a set of religious orders had formed the Interfaith Center on Corporate Responsibility (ICCR) several years before to grapple with weapons making and both racial and gender justice requirements. Now the environmental dimensions of ICCR work, and that of a comparable Canadian task force, developed around energy issues, culminating a decade later in adoption of the CERES principles for voluntary corporate environmental responsibility.[4] Local congregations, however, tended to limit their participation to energy-efficient retrofitting of their own buildings, to the exclusion of significant education and advocacy focused on reforming energy policies—still deemed by many to be too technical for the churches to engage effectively.

In retrospect, this period of intensive ecumenical attention to energy production and use gave the churches confidence to enter into the next period of energy-related concerns over acid rain and global warming, thanks also to helpful leadership on these concerns by the United Church of Canada, collaborating with other Canadian churches. For example, a 1994 WCC study paper entitled "Accelerated Climate Change: Sign of Peril, Test of Faith," drafted primarily by Protestant ethicists from the U.S. and Canada, offers a well-thought-out response to "the distinctively contemporary global crisis, of which accelerated climate change [global warming and ozone depletion] is a prime symbol." It proposes that participants in economic life must meet the ethical claims of *ecological sustainability, sufficiency of sustenance, community through work, participation by all, and respect for diversity*. The study paper on climate change became the subject-matter of a leadership development event held at the Church Center for the U.N. in December 1994. Thus, agencies of the ecumenical churches have enabled the minority of interested congregations and community groups to comprehend and embody this environmentally responsible posture.

4. Community Organizing for Environmental Justice

The most distinctive involvement of U.S. churches with environmentalism has been to foster the Environmental Justice Movement. A church agency—the UCC Commission on Racial Justice—first published and circulated widely the documentation of severe inequity in locating toxic facilities. Since then, a lot of other documentation has appeared. The churches also took the initiative to contact struggling community organizations, to bring some of their leaders together and to find funding that would enable them to challenge unjust waste creation and management. The churches did not start the movement to combat the placement of hazardous wastes in poor and minority communities. The Citizens' Clearing House on Hazardous Wastes deserves more credit. But the churches helped to make more environmental justice possible for communities of color, parts of Appalachia and some Indian nations.

By late 1987, these initiatives were being coordinated through an Eco-Justice Working Group (EJWG) newly formed in 1986 by the National Council of Churches, again with Chris Cowap as staff director; I was an initial co-chair. Church journals and environmental periodicals have recently told aspects of that community-organizing story. But those accounts have not highlighted other parts of the EJWG story, particularly its early leadership development activity and the creation of ecumenical mechanisms for church members to participate in public policy advocacy focusing on environmental stewardship.

The dominant style, which was to support community organization for environmental justice, carried over to church participation—mostly incognito—in the National People of Color Environmental Leadership Summit, where community groups challenged establishment environmental organizations to give this aspect of environmentalism much more attention. This was soon followed by the Black Church Environmental Summit (late 1993), which brought together pastors and community organizers. Since 1992, there has also been significant collaboration between parachurch groups and people's NGOs at U.N. meetings such as the Rio Earth Summit and the Cairo Conference on Population and Development.

The U.S. churches' focus on environmental justice has been, and will continue to be, quite significant. But a preoccupation with grassroots community organizing to combat toxics tended to preempt other styles of engagement and to narrow eco-justice work of churches in the U.S. into becoming a subset of economic-justice advocacy. Now it needs to be broadened again to encompass the full range of environmentalism—including ecocentric concerns for preservation and biodiversity—utilizing a variety of involvement styles and linkages.

5. Leadership Development for Enviro-Integrity and Eco-Justice

There are both denominational and parachurch aspects to this latest phase of church involvement with environmentalism, launched in the late 1980s by the North American Conference on Christianity and Ecology, from which the North American Coalition on Religion and Ecology split off. Such organizations incorporated quite a spectrum of religiously motivated individuals, and encouraged the denominations to give at least some ecclesial prominence to environmental responsibility.

At this point, the churches (and synagogues) remembered that it is not enough to support grassroots groups of activists on the side of the most powerless. There is a continuous task of developing leaders and nurturing members, of gaining a voice in the media and a hearing with public officials, and of trying to engage indifferent or hostile institutions to think harder about respecting the web of creation, about otherkind in relation to humankind, about patterning a good life, and about entering into personal and organized ministry long-term for the sake of earth community. Without more pedagogy of the privileged, and better structuring of church involvement, will there be significant implementation of a preferential option for the poor and the earth?

As on any other major transgenerational concern, it is essential to "map" the dimensions of worship-education-witness and to clarify a model of congregational ministry that has public and coalitional expression, as well as in-church features. This has begun to happen extensively through some denominational programs of environmental stewardship and justice, and through production and dissemination of congregational packets financed by a grant from The Pew Charitable Trusts to an interfaith mechanism called the National Religious Partnership for the Environment (NRPE). Each of the four streams in that consortium—NCC Mainline, Conservative Evangelical, Roman Catholic and Reform Jewish—has autonomy, but together they have agreed to the priority of eco-justice, and each presents a multidimensional model for congregational involvement with staying power. In February 1995, NRPE executive director Paul Gorman sent magazine editors a memorandum that said, in part:

> The broad consensus and range of activities among diverse mainstream faith groups—rooted in "orthodox" theology, supported at the highest levels of governance, alive at the grass roots—testifies to something far more funda-

mental than "environmentalism" conventionally understood and reported. Environmental protection is a fundamental part of who we are. . . . [We] hold care of the natural world and human well-being within it as an essential, irreversible, moral responsibility of individuals, the private sector, and government.

Meanwhile, there is also the collaborative effort with which I am associated—distinct from, though complementary to, the above—to organize occasional graduate-level professional development opportunities for theological scholars and to assist schools of theology and university departments of religious studies to reform course work, community life and institutional practice in order to better prepare religious leaders and other professionals for faithful and effective response to the environmental challenge. Though the churches themselves have not been all that interested in intellectual inquiry, Theological Education to Meet the Environmental Challenge (TEMEC) has become an effective way to foster the in-depth theological reflection and cross-disciplinary study that are needed for sustained engagement with environmentalism on the part of scholars, ministers and members.

It remains to be seen whether the initiatives being taken in this new phase of religious thought and action to renew creation and seek eco-justice will help bring scholars, church leaders, institutions and members to a new level of seriousness, revitalize ecumenical engagement and encourage tired environmentalists, including religious participants, to challenge a systematic dismantling of environmental protection or the ungreening of social and economic policy.

Conclusion: How Much Was Accomplished, and What's Next?

There is much more to the recent story of church participation in the environmental movement than this chapter covers (for example, details of involvement by particular denominations and organizations, patterns of activity in undiscussed areas such as relief work with environmental refugees and special efforts to support Native Americans in preserving their habitats). But this overview exposes some basic contours. To summarize: the churches have been environmentally engaged in part, with particular concerns, usually communicated sotto voce. Engaged work groups, church agencies, and congregations have done substantive things that made some public or ecclesial difference. But the churches themselves have too often forgotten their environmental ministry, and church involvement has been unrecognized in published histories of environmentalism.

On the whole, church engagement with environmentalism has remained quite anthropocentric—that is, ecological problems are still viewed in instrumental terms through the lens of God-human relations. There is some irony in the heavy anthropocentrism characteristic of churches and theologians throughout this "second social gospel" era. The humane movement to protect against cruel treatment of animals was actually of more concern to religious educators and church groups engaged in public action during the first Social Gospel Movement of the late nineteenth and early twentieth centuries. One can see a similar pattern of declining church interest in land ethics as the century "progresses," except perhaps among

Mennonites and Lutherans in mid-America. Belatedly, concern for these sustainable community requirements, long dormant in the churches, is resurfacing.

Still, it must be said that churches in the U.S. have *not* been as engaged with environmentalism as one would reasonably expect. It is quite sobering to ask: What environmental mission and ministry—with depth and breadth—was institutionalized by and in the churches during these five phases of involvement? While the United Methodist Church Board of Church and Society is perhaps an exception that proves the rule, my answer would have to be: Not much was institutionalized, compared to a restructuring of community ministry, social service and peace education/action by the churches during the same period. And there was little greening of the latter. Why? Was and is it the culture, the theology, the social location of most members, the press of other concerns, narrow vision, poor leadership, dysfunctional organization, episodic activism or shallowness within environmentalism? Apparently, some of each and more. The question deserves careful pondering but not quick answering.

I have alluded to some missed opportunities to think and act more integrally and to raise the sights of those involved. One crucial missed opportunity among theologians themselves was their failure—for at least a decade and a half—to carry on a meaningful dialogue between liberation theologies and ecotheology. In the ecumenical movement, liberation theologies and eco-justice ethics have finally begun to interact constructively, though not yet extensively.

The really big missed opportunity was and is the absence of a strategy to bring ecumenical and environmental energy together in order to achieve just and sustainable community life. In other words, there has been no serious counterbalance to a well-organized Hard Right; mainstream churches have yet to collaborate with secular groups for the good of the commons. Both church groups and environmental organizations remained very "columnized"—separate social sectors, indifferent to each other—and each sector is splintered into relatively weak denominations. (Environmental organizations also function as voluntary "religious" associations, denominationally and internally fractured, often inept.)

Another failure, now very obvious to someone who entered into professional ministry in 1960—just as ecumenism rediscovered the laity—is the lack of church and seminary programs of continuing education for lay ministry with an environmental focus. The crisis of earth community raises vocational dilemmas for aware people in many occupations. Environmental engagement is a common point of contact. Why aren't the churches equipping members for this?

We cannot grapple with the eco-crisis, or do eco-justice, by staying in our religious, philosophical, disciplinary and occupational compartments, or by just adding some praxis. A meaningful response requires deep reflection, purposeful repentance, concerted action. The churches share an obligation to enter ecumenically and coalitionally into a new kind of education-embodiment for earth and people.

Notes

1. Especially prominent among eco-feminists is Rosemary Radford Ruether. American theologians and church leaders of color George Tinker, Thomas J. Hoyt, Jr. and Vernice

Miller have contributed articles to various symposia. Among conservative evangelical voices, see Calvin DeWitt (1991) and Loren Wilkinson (1991).

2. A Report on "Population Policy and the Church" (General Assembly of the United Presbyterian Church in the U.S.A., 1972) emphasized interacting "causes" of population growth, and the reinforcing relationships between liberty, equity, empowerment, health care and food security (especially for women and children) in efforts to stabilize population.

3. Some integrative possibilities that could have been pursued are indicated in essays drafted by regional work teams involving interested theologians and church leaders published in Hessel (1977). One Christian social ethicist, Ian Barbour, did put it together effectively (see Barbour 1980).

4. The Interfaith Center on Corporate Responsibility is located at 475 Riverside Dr., New York, NY 10115. For the Principles announced by the Coalition for Environmentally Responsible Economies (CERES), see Smith 1993. Regarding Canadian activity, see the *1993-94 Annual Report* issued by the Taskforce on the Churches and Corporate Responsibility, 129 St. Clair Ave. West, Toronto, Ontario, CANADA M4V 1N5.

17

Pedagogical Issues and Teaching Models for Eco-Justice

DANIEL T. SPENCER

The litany of shared histories among theological educators gathered to discuss teaching eco-justice subject matter in a theological context soon took on a familiar pattern: while each had benefitted from some of the finest theological instruction available during student days in the '50s, '60s, '70s, and '80s, virtually every person had first discovered or been introduced to the critical ecological issues now facing our planet *outside* the context of theological studies. Ecological concerns simply had not been addressed as theological issues for most of us. Yet now we gathered out of a shared conviction that not only can our ecological context be understood theologically, but it must be if students of theology and religion are going to play a constructive role in confronting the environmental challenge and its related social justice issues. The question, therefore, became not if, but *how:* how do we address complex and interconnected eco-justice questions in a theological framework?

The purpose of this essay is to explore pedagogical questions that need to be addressed in incorporating eco-justice in the heart of the curriculum and courses of theological and religious education. The first section briefly surveys what occupies teachers and writers currently in this area. The second section uses the Spiral of Praxis (or Hermeneutical Circle) to raise critical questions and areas that need to be addressed in teaching eco-justice in a theological/religious context. It suggests several components of experiential and praxis-based pedagogies that can contribute to effective teaching and to learning that is transformative of students and institutions over the long haul. A final section examines factors distinctive to teaching eco-justice and considers some models, highlighting examples currently being used by educators that can assist in designing effective eco-justice curricula and courses.

Along with growing awareness of the ecological crisis, theological and religious education in the past three decades has undergone radical challenge and change as a result of being confronted by the demands and insights of people of color, women, and lesbian, gay, and bisexual persons. This questions not only the content of theological and religious education, but, equally important, the pedagogy as well. Transformative or praxis-based models that teach about justice, faith, and ethical issues through active involvement and experiential learning challenge more traditional, passive, content-oriented pedagogies. They pay attention to both cognitive and affective learning processes and draw from diverse sources, such as the work of Brazilian literacy expert Paulo Freire and the insights of feminist and black liberation theologies.

Related, but distinctive challenges to teaching styles emerge from taking seriously the ecological crisis—most broadly defined—as the starting point and grounding for theological and religious education. It is less obvious how many of the primary constituents of eco-justice—especially the nonhuman members—can be present and reshape our approaches. Yet attention to the praxis-based pedagogies of other justice movements may suggest several possibilities and factors to take into consideration in designing pedagogies for eco-justice. In each section of the Spiral of Praxis, I begin by describing what function it plays in praxis-based approaches and use this to raise questions and make suggestions for what needs to be considered in eco-justice approaches. The essay thus serves primarily as an exploration rather than exposition of relevant factors and examples of "Pedagogical Issues and Teaching Models for Eco-Justice."

The Current Context: Where We Are

In May 1993 over one hundred theological and religious educators interested in eco-justice issues gathered at Stony Point, New York, for a working conference entitled "Theological Education to Meet the Environmental Challenge: Toward Just and Sustainable Communities." Directors of the Program on Ecology, Justice, and Faith and of the Center for Respect of Life and Environment collected course syllabi from many of the conference participants and analyzed them to gain a better understanding of the current status of teaching eco-justice in a theological context in at least some sectors.[1] This analysis provides a helpful overview of the current context of pedagogical issues related to eco-justice.

The overview revealed that while most respondents shared certain assumptions, the wide variety of approaches, use of texts, and emphases indicates "that there is not yet much agreement as to what must be learned in studying theology/religion to meet the environmental challenge" (p. 4). The syllabi cluster into four primary groups dealing with:

- Biblical faith and environmental reality or ethics.
- Ethics (religion) and problems of technology or economics.
- Religion and the search for appropriate eco-social paradigms.
- Comparative views of nature and human responsibility.

From the submitted syllabi the overview synthesizes nine emphases and theses that must be incorporated into teaching eco-justice theology and ethics:

1. Examination of *foundational assumptions* about basic reality, divine purpose, the good life, community, the human vocation and social tasks—and especially calling into question modern-era Christian theology's anthropocentric theo-anthropology.

2. The *challenge of ecology and biology* to Christianity to be clearer about *common human duty* to plants, species, ecosystems, and the earth as a whole.

3. The need for *holistic responses* to the environmental challenge that encompass both created reality and human subjectivity.

4. The need for Christianity to recover, reform, and apply both the *covenantal and sacramental traditions* as complementary approaches to ethical spirituality.

5. A commitment to *reexamine the matrix and content* of firmly held beliefs and doctrines in light of contemporary understandings of planetary history and the ecological matrix in order to *meet the eco-justice crisis*, realizing that *both social and religious integrity* are at stake.

6. Recognition that *economically and environmentally marginalized communities* have important insights to teach, and a *priority justice claim on the wider community.*

7. Theological education and religious studies contribute to *cultural transformation* by focusing on the center of value and embodiment of a new social paradigm, as well as spiritually formed, practical ethics.

8. The *practice of justice and sustainability* must go hand in hand with intellectual reflection in teaching eco-justice. In other words, teaching must incorporate praxis-based approaches that integrate action and reflection inside and outside of the classroom.

9. The importance of incorporating *natural and social science understandings of ecology* into theological education.

The analysis concludes that "significant tensions, conflicts and issues are apparent in teaching theology and religion to meet the environmental challenge" such as the amount of attention to give to biblical materials, the appropriate method of interpretation, how much to utilize the mainstream theological heritage, and the appropriate balance between human and ecosystem interests (p. 3). Yet this variety of approaches and subject matters may also be a strength in teaching eco-justice, theology, and religion in the current context, as it provides flexibility in adapting strategies, materials, and approaches best suited for a diversity of different settings, including denominational and nondenominational seminaries, colleges, universities, and graduate schools.

The nine emphases and theses of the 1993 overview provide a helpful starting point for further exploration of the issues and questions that must be addressed in developing a pedagogically transformative course/curriculum. Yet with the exception of point 8 (and perhaps point 6—where primary focus must lie), their emphasis is primarily on the *content* of eco-justice education rather than the *pedagogy* or teaching style. In the following section, the question of how to integrate these important content concerns into transformative teaching styles is addressed.

The Spiral of Praxis as a Heuristic Device in Developing Transformative Pedagogical Models for Eco-Justice in Theological and Religions Education

An important observation that needs to be mentioned before entering into discussion of the different components of the Spiral of Praxis is the role of less tangible or quantifiable elements that are critical to effective, transformative education. One of these is the spirit or style of eco-justice education, and in particular the role of the teacher. Many of those surveyed recalled that their initial "conversion" to an eco-justice perspective came about because of contact with a teacher or individual imbued with a deeply ecological spirit or perspective that proved contagious to students and others. Effective teaching, therefore, nearly always stems from the teacher's enthusiasm, passion, and commitment to the subject matter. Once this spirit is recognized as a critical grounding, what then, are other elements that can contribute to constructing effective pedagogical models?

The Spiral of Praxis is one model that helps address several essential components of praxis-based approaches to transformative learning, namely: critical examination of the context and starting point, social analysis, theological and ethical reflection, and [planning for] engagement.[2] It assumes an active engagement in social and/or ecological issues and provides a framework for analysis and reflection that is comprehensive and ongoing. While there is a certain logic to the order of the steps as described here, it should be emphasized that they actually all occur simultaneously and each influences the others in an ongoing process of deepening insight and involvement. Using the Spiral as a means to explore pedagogies can help people in widely divergent contexts (geographical as well as socio-historical) think about what pedagogical approaches may be most appropriate in their time and place.

Pre-Step: Points of Entry

Educators using the Spiral of Praxis long have noted that there are varieties of experience that provide people with points of entry into deepened commitment to, and reflection on, issues of human and natural well-being. In the conference at Union Theological Seminary, people mentioned such things as a love of trees threatened with removal, exposure to Joseph Campbell and how other cultures think about nature, talking to young people about vegetarianism and recycling, making connections on water issues in the city, a felt kinship with animals, the stories of Foxfire and the generational passing on of cultural and natural skills, the St. Francis Blessing of the Animals Liturgy each October, trips as a child to the botanical garden . . . the list goes on and on. Here the diverse possibilities work to the advantage of eco-justice educators, especially as we recognize the experiential-relational element common to most of these. Good eco-justice education will build where possible experiential opportunities invite deeper reflection, investigation, relation, and analysis. How one enters this process and by which path are not nearly so important as the entering itself—without this, moving on to the following steps of the Spiral becomes a detached, distanced, intellectual exercise rather than an existential journey with possibilities for change and transformation.

Step 1: Context and Starting Point

Critical to any transformative learning is understanding the context and starting point, as well as one's primary community of accountability. These combine to shape what individuals and communities experience as the *primary* ecological and social *contradictions* that must be addressed in theo-ethical analysis and reflection. They in turn shape the kinds of analysis chosen in Step 2 of the spiral. Some factors/questions to be addressed in designing transformative pedagogies that keep issues of power dynamics visible and central include:

- What is the nature of the contemporary *ecological* context/crisis we face and what is the minimum understanding of it needed to begin to address it theologically and ethically?
- How much understanding of ecology as a science (as well as other relevant sciences such as biology, geology, meteorology, etc.) do students of religion need to engage eco-justice issues?
- *Which* context does one use as the *primary* point of departure for analysis and praxis, and why: the educational institution (such as in courses built around greening the institution)? The local community? The bioregion where one lives? The primary political unit where one is located, such as a state or nation? The global ecological crisis that must be addressed through international cooperation? While all of these are interrelated, the one chosen as the primary focus will in turn shape much of the praxis and analysis/materials chosen in the course.
- How is contact with nonhuman nature integrated into the pedagogy of the course? Experiential education is premised on the conviction that actual contact and interaction with the subjects of study leads to the most effective and long-term learning. What opportunities and constraints are there to building in contact with diverse parts of nonhuman nature?
- What is the social-ecological context of the community and institution where learning is taking place? The student's own context (which may be different from both the institution and the community where it is located)? How does teaching rooted in eco-justice address these contexts, and how do these contexts in turn shape our understanding of the *primary contradictions* that need to be addressed and the appropriate point of departure?
- What is the primary *community of accountability*, and how is this decided? What does it mean and what would it look like to have an ecological community of accountability, and how do human power dynamics (such as environmental racism) affect this? How do the concerns and interests of socially and environmentally-marginalized human communities relate to these?
- What are the primary *sources* for learning about and addressing eco-justice issues, how are these chosen, and who decides? What are left out and why? How will this affect the resulting analysis and praxis?

- What are the primary questions/areas of eco-justice to be addressed, and why? How will choice of these affect the resulting analysis and praxis? Whose voices are primary and whose secondary in these choices, and why? How are the interests of nonhuman members of the eco-community represented? Who is involved in framing the issues?

- What role does experiential learning—through immersion experiences, through service-learning projects and internships, through opportunities to teach their learnings to others—play in the structure and expectations of the course? What is the format of these projects? Individual? Pairs? Small groups? What connections can students learn about issues of eco-justice with *how* we work together to respond?

Step 2: Scientific and Social Analysis

Once preliminary questions of context and starting point have been addressed (and attention paid to the power dynamics inherent in each decision), thought should be given to the kind of scientific and social-historical-cultural-political-economic analysis needed to deepen our understanding of the ecological crisis. Here it is important to pay attention to both *what kind* of analysis is needed, and *how* it is obtained.

- What is the best way for students to gain a *holistic understanding* and analysis of the context? Through immersion experiences? Library research? Work in teams? Focus on specific problems? Combinations of these?

- What is the best *scientific* understanding of the scope and nature of the ecological issues to be addressed? What are the *historical* roots of the crisis, and how are these dynamics still present and influential today? What *political* and *economic* factors have shaped the current context, and how do they influence the way the context—both social and ecological—is understood?

- How do these problems affect different communities—both human and nonhuman—in different ways, and why? What kinds of power issues are present, and how are they manifested?

- How does the analytical approach employed understand the relationship between ecological and social issues, that is, between "natural" historical processes and human historical processes, and how does this affect the resultant analysis? What is the relation of these assumptions to the theological and ethical values drawn on in Step 3 below?

- What *sources* are used to get at these questions, and who decides? Are students involved in researching and selecting some of the readings/sources for the class? Who are involved in doing the analysis, and how do they do it? Are students encouraged to develop a critical-appreciative stance toward the natural and social sciences as authoritative sources in eco-justice theology and ethics?

- How do our community's and family's past experience of the land and environment shape values, attitudes, and practices? How do our social histories and cultural values influence our understanding of these?

- How does social analysis help students to reflect critically on their own experience? Are students encouraged to do autobiographical reflection and analysis going back several generations in order to understand how their own experience has been shaped by social and ecological factors, and how this in turn influences the ways they see and analyze the problem? What does the mode of analysis communicate to students about the value of their own experience and insights?

Step 3: Theological and Ethical Reflection

Once (or as) a holistic and in-depth understanding of the social-ecological context is gained, it is time to ask what this means and what its implications are in light of relevant, shared theological and ethical values. In liberation theologies, this is the point at which one clarifies the primary *hermeneutic* or interpretive filter with which one approaches the resources of the tradition. Liberation theologies employ both a *hermeneutic of suspicion* to examine ways the religious tradition may have contributed to the problem (the deconstructive task), and a *hermeneutics of remembrance or recovery* to explore ways positive resources, which may have been lost or neglected, can help to address the problem in constructive ways (the constructive or reconstructive task). Here one's educational setting (for example, seminary *vs.* college, denominational *vs.* secular) may shape the nature of the religious/theological tradition focused upon.

Often this hermeneutic is shaped both by what has occurred in the first two steps, that is, naming the primary contradiction and context, and analysis of why this is so, and by the individual's and community's prior loyalties and faith commitments. For example, if (1) the primary contradiction of a given community is identified as sexism, and (2) the historical-social analysis reveals the roots and dynamics of sexism in the contemporary community, then (3) if sexism is seen as violating an important value and commitment—justice for women—an appropriate next step would be to explore the theological-ethical tradition to see in what ways it has contributed to sexism and to see if there are constructive resources that can be appropriated to combat sexism. Here also alternative theo-ethical sources from *outside the normative tradition may be explored*—a particularly important task in eco-justice issues where non-Christian and non-Western sources have made a critical contribution to rethinking ecological issues. Some questions include:

- What is the tradition's understanding of the relationship between human beings and the rest of nature, and of humanity's and nature's relations to the divine/sacred? How does the way the sacred/divine is imaged affect the interactions between human beings and other parts of nature?
- In what ways do these understandings contribute to confronting eco-justice crises, and in what ways do they present obstacles, and why?
- What part of the tradition is considered authoritative and why? What place is given to historically excluded or marginalized voices and beliefs? With what hermeneutic does one approach the tradition(s), and why? How is this shaped, and who is involved?

- What place do resources outside the normative tradition have in constructing theological and ethical resources grounded in and responsive to eco-justice concerns? How does one draw on resources from other traditions and communities without perpetuating historical dynamics of exploitation and misappropriation?
- As in the other steps, are students encouraged to reflect critically on their own theo-ethical perspectives, and to try to understand the sources of these?
- Are there participatory and interactive means of learning possible, such as designing and participating in an eco-justice liturgy, or observing/participating in and critically reflecting on worship experiences of other traditions?

Step 4: [Planning for] Engagement

Because this model assumes active engagement and participation in eco-justice issues and struggles, the final stage of planning for engagement is parallel to the initial stage of engaged participation. Pedagogically, therefore, thinking about the students' active engagement in experiential learning is an ongoing process, made more intelligible and explicit following reflection on the first three steps, but is an integral part of the process from the beginning. The ancient Chinese maxim "Tell me and I forget, show me and I remember, involve me and I understand," illustrates the central conviction of praxis-based learning; it is only as the student's own world and experience is involved and made integral to learning that true learning and the potential for ongoing development by—and transformation of—the student occurs. In this step many of the key pedagogical questions are addressed (although one can see how connected they are to the questions in the other sections). These include:

- What does the format of the class communicate about power dynamics in the student-teacher relation, and the value of the students' experiences and insights?
- How are the more abstract results of theoretical and research learning connected to concrete problems and conditions? Are students given skills to begin to change conditions where the results of their work suggest the need (such as in the greening of institutions or confronting a community problem)?
- What do students (and teachers) do with the *results* of their research—both in the classroom and outside? Is there outreach to the wider community built into course expectations, such as teaching a class in an elementary school, developing a biblical reflection and discussion series, or submitting an op-ed piece to a newspaper? How does the course give students the grounding and impetus to carry their learning and involvement beyond the course—to continue the Spiral of Praxis in other contexts and settings?
- What connections are made/encouraged between the learnings of this course and the students' other classes and coursework?

- Are there experiential ways to synthesize, recognize, and celebrate the learnings of the course, such as designing and participating in an eco-justice liturgy or a commissioning into the initial stages of ecological praxis?

Important Factors and Selective Examples for Using Transformative Pedagogies in Teaching Eco-Justice

In this final section, we will look at several examples of different approaches to teaching eco-justice issues and theology/ethics in different educational settings. Each example is selected not as the only—or even the best—example, but rather as a conversation starter that illustrate some of the features discussed above as well as institutional limitations that must be factored into designing courses.

1. Teaching Eco-Justice in the Seminary: The Environmental Ethics Course

Carol Robb has been teaching environmental ethics for several years at San Francisco Theological Seminary, a Presbyterian seminary in San Anselmo, California. The course is designed in two sections both to meet the curricular requirements of the seminary and the Graduate Theological Union, as well as to address urgent current issues in environmental ethics. Part I of the course therefore covers the basics of ethics: teleology, deontology, character, and response as modes of moral argument, and gives an overview of the different factors that go into doing ethics (value system, loyalties, data, starting point, analysis of the roots of oppression, etc.), but does so not in a vacuum, but rather by examining the writings of different environmental ethicists (in this case, William Baxter and Paul Taylor). Included in this section is the development of a critical perspective on the use of authorities. In Part II of the course Robb selects an "issue focus," such as, "Is Christianity an Unecological Religion?" (Other issues she has used include population, ecofeminism, and developmental ethics.) This in turn shapes much of the analysis and theological reflection of this portion of the course, such as the use of specifically Presbyterian materials relevant to the theme.

An important—and required—course component is a class project, chosen and developed by the students. The only stipulation is that "it must help us to learn to live at least an early stage ecological praxis" (letter to author, 5 August 1994). These have ranged from class members cooking for each other, using recipes from low on the food chain, and then compiling the recipes and making them available on campus, to starting an organic herb garden, to organizing toxic tours through a neighboring city dominated by petrochemical plants. In each case, part of the goal of project was to integrate experientially the more theoretical analytical and theological learnings from readings and class discussion into an early stage praxis of eco-theological living that in turn contained an element of outreach to the broader community.

Robb's course thus integrates elements of all four steps of the Spiral of Praxis. The context and starting point is shaped by a number of factors, including the institutional and curricular setting, the students' own experience and perspectives, and the social-ecological setting of the San Francisco area. While weighted more toward ethical writings, the texts incorporate both natural and social scientific analysis, as well as theo-ethical reflection and analysis. Students are encouraged to develop and defend their own ethical stance, and a critical part of this is developing some praxis in eco-theological living.

2. Teaching Eco-Justice in the Seminary: Communal Learning and Care of the Earth

In 1991 Frank Rogers, Jr., and Mary Elizabeth Moore taught a course at the School of Theology at Claremont entitled "Communal Learning and the Care of the Earth." It provides an excellent example of an experiential course that integrates several learning style with a praxis-based pedagogy.

The goal of the course was "to create a living and environmentally caring community of faith" among the course participants through an interactive rhythm of worship, reflection, and work around the central theme of the course: care of the earth. Thus both the community context and starting point were determined by structuring the class as the learning *and living* community, and making care of the earth the point of departure and reference point for life together in community. The course was structured so that the form was appropriate to a living community in order "to create a pattern in which a faith-filled community may be nurtured" (Rogers, letter to author, 21 June 1994).

Because they were not limited by the normally rigid academic structures of one- to two-hour class periods, the class could structure weekly a large block of time in which to move through a rhythm of work, reflection, and worship. Consistent with a praxis-based approach, the biblical study, reflection, and analysis emerged out of the group activities of prayer and work. The work projects emerged out of an analysis of the ecological needs of the seminary itself, thus structuring the bounds of their "eco-community." In addition, primary emphasis was put on student initiative in selecting and leading the worship, prayer, reflection, and work components of the course. This included designing an educational event that would take the learnings of the course beyond the classroom.

Space limitations preclude an in-depth discussion of the results of this course, but one of the unexpected outcomes was that the praxis of the course quickly moved beyond the confines of the class to involve a significant portion of the campus in moving toward a more ecologically sound praxis in the institutional life of the seminary. In addition, the holistic design of the course facilitated this praxis in integrating cognitive, affective, and spiritual dimensions of living, learning, and acting. For school settings with some degree of programming flexibility it offers elements that could be adapted to a local setting in order to design a holistic, praxis-based approach that uses the community itself as the community of accountability and ecological context.

3. Teaching Eco-Justice in the Seminary: The Bible and Eco-Justice

Central to most seminary curricula and church teaching is the Bible, so it is imperative to develop courses that examine eco-justice concerns from biblical perspectives (and also to examine critically biblical teachings about ecological issues). C. Dean Freudenberger at Luther Seminary in St. Paul, Minnesota, has for several years taught biblical courses (often teamed with biblical scholars) on eco-justice issues. Reflecting the approach of the Lutheran community, which always works from biblical texts, Freudenberger designs his courses to begin with the Bible and then move toward eco-justice questions. This process weaves back and forth between biblical texts and relevant contemporary issues throughout the course. Examples include examining themes of "representative royalty" in Genesis 1 as a means to look at global perspectives of the ecological crisis; or moving from consideration of the "carnival of animals" in Genesis 6-9 to exploring issues of animal welfare and environmental ethics.

Freudenberger cites two important pedagogical issues in biblical courses on eco-justice.

1. Because much of recent Western Christian thought is so highly anthropocentric, it is essential to deal with "first" testament literature (the Hebrew scriptures), particularly because the "second" (New) testament does not deal directly with many of the critical environmental/human relations issues. (Freudenberger notes that a continuing challenge in many seminaries is to help students who wonder how to make the connection between earth caring and the gospels.) This approach may challenge more traditional views that place primary emphasis on the gospels and Pauline literature divorced from their more "earthy" Jewish historical and theological context.

2. The need to confront the "Pollyanna and Paralysis Syndrome." Freudenberger finds that students typically respond in one of two ways to being confronted with the environmental crisis (other than simply denying its reality): either searching for a simple solution to a massively complex problem, or falling into paralysis because the crisis is too big and there is little an individual can do. Freudenberger's response is to challenge students to prepare themselves to address critical issues that are ambiguous in many ways and yet have few solutions: "Dealing courageously with the issues is a sign of maturity, particularly in a culture that wants immediate answers, or if none are in sight, responds 'why address the problem in the first place?'" This raises the questions of Christian spirituality: how do we develop the skills and attitudes and value systems that enable one to address "foolishly" the impossible? (letter to author, 9 August 1994).

Once Freudenberger has addressed these two pedagogical issues, the class is able to move on to address eco-justice issues from a biblical perspective. He combines social and scientific analysis of the social-ecological crisis with biblical and theological reflection to move students preparing for pastoral ministries to think about interpreting the eco-justice crisis in the congregation.

From the perspective of the pedagogical model outlined in Section II, this approach covers the first three steps well: it is tailored for the Lutheran congregational context and integrates biblical-theological reflection with social and scientific analysis. It is less clear from the course outline how much it follows a praxis-based learning style, although students are encouraged to address the question of how to interpret their learning in a congregational setting. It would be interesting to see such a course have as a requirement the actual development of more ecologically sensitive liturgies, biblical studies, sermons, and so on, perhaps coming out of the more experiential interaction that typifies the Rogers-Moore course in model 2 above.

4. Teaching Eco-Justice in Undergraduate Institutions: Religious Studies and Ecology

The undergraduate institution offers a different educational setting for teaching eco-justice issues related to theology and religion. Here much of the instruction takes place within departments of religion or religious studies not limited to Christianity or the Judeo-Christian tradition. Steven Rockefeller of Middlebury College has researched and written a chapter entitled "Religion and the Ecological Conscience" for a book about teaching ecological issues in college that addresses several of the issues raised here and offers a number of sample course syllabi for educators interested in incorporating these themes into their courses (Rockefeller 1994). Rockefeller cites a rapidly expanding body of new scholarship in the field of religious studies and the environment that makes possible a wide range of options for developing courses in religion with ecological themes. Such courses are of interest not just to religion majors, but also to students working in environmental studies, the humanities, and general liberal arts curricula.

Rockefeller notes:

> The major religious traditions are expressions of the worldviews and values that have emerged as different peoples throughout the world have struggled to respond creatively to the challenge of their unique environments and histories in the light of their awareness of the sacred. The study of religion and the environment provides, then, an excellent opportunity to explore past and present human ideas, attitudes, and values pertaining to non-human species, the land, and the universe (ibid., 2).

Courses such as those described by Rockefeller could be adapted in several ways to follow a praxis-based pedagogy, such as:

- student involvement in researching and presenting on an ecological issue that illustrates issues dealt with in the U.S. context;
- participation/observation of worship services in traditions different from one's own (as well as one's own) and critical reflection on them in light of ecological issues and the resources of the tradition.
- researching and writing a critical autobiographical reflection on how the student's own family and community religious traditions have shaped his or her attitudes toward nature and environmental issues.[3]

5. Teaching Eco-Justice in Undergraduate Institutions: Greening the Campus

One effective praxis-based model for teaching eco-justice within a theological/religious framework is to use the campus itself as a laboratory for creating an ecologically sustainable community. This can occur in several ways. The most ambitious, long-range, and effective efforts are those schools that have made a school-wide interdisciplinary commitment to "green" the campus, such as efforts underway at Bucknell College in Lewisburg, Pennsylvania, and Tufts University in Boston. By integrating campus-wide efforts to green the campus with the curriculum, students are constantly engaged in a praxis-based learning style with their own educational setting forming the ecological context. Such efforts, however, require the commitment of significant sectors of the administration, faculty, staff, and student body, and may follow earlier and less ambitious efforts.

One such example is a course taught by Jay McDaniel at Hendrix College in Arkansas: "Religion, Animals, and the Earth." McDaniel has students focus on eco-justice issues of sustainability, animal rights, and linking earth liberation to human liberation within a religious and spiritual framework by having the students study what it would take to convert Hendrix College into a model of humane, sustainable community that can advertise itself as an example of "liberal arts education in an ecological age" (letter to author, 22 June 1994). The reading and discussion students engage in around religious and ethical issues related to eco-justice are thus grounded in their analysis of their own campus community—the ways it is ecologically and spiritually healthy and unhealthy. Evaluation of their research results is based both on the visionary quality and feasibility of their proposal for the college.

Conclusion

In this chapter I have tried to highlight several pedagogical issues that need to be addressed in order to design transformative theological and religious courses on eco-justice that increase our commitment to and participation in the praxis of ecological living. It is written to be suggestive rather than conclusive, giving conference participants a place from which to engage in discussion based on their own experience, questions, and insights, and those of others. An important ongoing area that needs to be addressed is how to think and work strategically to get these concerns into the heart of the curriculum where each of us is located—but that is the topic of another essay!

Notes

Several people were enormously helpful in getting this essay off the ground and into the word processor. Lengthy conversations and materials from Dieter Hessel, Mary Evelyn Tucker, Rick Clugston, Will Kennedy, and Larry Rasmussen gave the initial impetus and direction to the project, as well as provided numerous contacts and sources. In addition, the following educators sent course syllabi and other materials related to the topic: John Cobb, Jr., Ron Engel, Dean Freudenberger, Jim Martin-Schramm, Jay McDaniel, Sallie McFague, Carol Robb, Steven Rockefeller,

Frank Rogers, Jr., Rosemary Radford Ruether, Mike Schut, and Bob Stivers. Will Kennedy provided helpful suggestions for revisions of the original state-of-the-art background paper after he discussed it with participants at the Theology for Earth Community Conference.

1. "Resources for Ecojustice Education in Theology and Education," from The Center for Respect of Life and Environment, 2100 L Street, NW, Washington, D.C., 20037; (202) 778-6133. It is important to recognize that this survey and overview makes no claims to be exhaustive or comprehensive, but rather looks at a particular slice of the current reality of theological and religious education on eco-justice issues which may or may not be representative of the broader context. Nevertheless, it provides a helpful starting point for initiating the conversation and inviting other contributors to participate in order to expand our understanding of the current status of the field and the critical questions that need to be addressed.

2. I use the term *praxis* here in its broadest sense: the ongoing interaction of action and critical reflection in learning. This model draws on elements of the work of the Brazilian literacy expert, Paulo Freire, liberation and feminist theologies, and the pedagogical work of Will Kennedy at Union Theological Seminary. Helpful sources include Freire 1970; Harrison 1985; Evans, et al. 1987. For one of the best explications of use of the Spiral of Praxis in local communities, see Holland and Henriot 1983. For an excellent compilation of essays and case studies on praxis-based approaches to theological education, see Evans, et al. 1993. Other helpful sources include Freire 1985 and Wren 1982. My own writings on this process include Spencer 1988 and 1989.

3. I have adapted an example of this from Carolyn Merchant (1992) in my own teaching by having students write an "Environmental Autobiography" and then analyze it to reveal social factors that have shaped their family's and community's relation to the land. I give them the following worksheet as a way to begin their analysis:

Environmental Autobiography: "How has my family's and community's relation to the land influenced the way I approach the land and environmental issues?" Consider your own family's and/or primary community's history and place in society going back three to five generations (and farther if you can). What have been some of the important historical, social, cultural, and economic factors that have shaped your family's and your attitudes toward the land and environmental issues. Why? How did your families and/or communities use the land and relate to nature?

Factors:

Economic:

Historical:

Race:

Geographic:

Cultural:

Religious:

Other:

- What large events—wars, depressions, revolutions, social movements—shaped their lives? Have these had any influence on their/your values, attitudes, behaviors?

- Which of your family's values have you retained? Which have you revised or rejected? Why?

- What insights do you gain from this exercise on how you have been shaped to view the land and environmental issues? Are there any implications from this for globalization and/or social change? (see Merchant 1992, 1-2).

18

The Praxis of Institutional Greening

RICHARD M. CLUGSTON

A theology of institutions is an examination, from a Christian point of view, of the basic values and assumptions underlying institutional life, and where these assumptions are found inadequate or inappropriate, it includes the proposal of alternatives.

—John B. Cobb, Jr., 1993

Competence in ecological design means incorporating intelligence about how nature works into the way we think, build and live. Design applies to the making of nearly everything that requires energy and materials or that governs their use. When houses, farms, neighborhoods, communities, cities, transportation systems, technologies, energy policies, and entire economies are well designed, they are in harmony with the ecological patterns in which they are embedded.

—David Orr, 1994

Institutional greening is a process through which social institutions—schools, churches, businesses, government—can embody an effective response to the eco-justice crisis. It asks us to restructure our curricula and practices to embody both ecological integrity and social justice. This agenda is not yet widely accepted as an essential aspect of the mission of higher education generally, or of theological schools in particular. But institutional greening is gaining more attention. It is a praxis that focuses on two interconnected dimensions of academic life, asking: 1) How should our theological study, with its assumptions concerning the nature of reality and the good life, be transformed in light of the global problematique? And, 2) How shall we embody justice and sustainability in the design and functioning of our learning community?

Greening requires that the academic mission (including scholarship, teaching, and professional socialization) emphasize not only a solid grounding in theological disciplines, but also an understanding of the environmental challenge and a commitment to change toward consistency with the emerging "ecological" paradigm. It also demands that faculty pay special attention to institutional practices such as investments, building design, food services, lawn care, waste management, and so on. In these mundane activities as well as the most stimulating courses, the learning community teaches by what it does. The embodied curriculum (praxis) of the institution as a whole shows the adequacy, or not, of that learning community's response to the environmental challenge.

Many of the papers in this volume emphasize the importance of praxis considerations in theological education. They critique the modern, liberal separation of theory and practice, and the fragmentation of theology into academic disciplines ("disciplinolatry") much more concerned with "cognitive adequacy and coherence" than with "authenticity and transformative praxis." That contrast is discussed by Bob Kispert, who then argues in chapter 15 that

> Christian theology needs now to shift its emphasis from the [classically] liberal project of defending religious belief in the face of a crisis of cognitive claims to reflecting critically on structures of oppression, and alienation, and to participating in the development of redemptive, liberating praxis.

Dan Spencer, in chapter 17, frames this praxis question as:

> How are the more abstract results of theoretical and research learning connected to concrete problems and conditions? Are students given skills to begin to change conditions where the results of their work suggest the need (such as in the greening of institutions or confronting a community problem)?

Praxis concerns are wide ranging, emphasizing transformation of ethical frameworks, personal lifestyles, and political structures.

A Growing Movement in Higher Education

One early research step to be taken by a group that would initiate seminary "greening" is to learn about the larger movement in colleges and universities toward an environmentally responsible campus and curriculum. *Education for the Earth* (Alliance for Environmental Education 1994) is a good place to begin. Tufts University has been a leader in requiring that all students deal with environmental issues and in sponsoring an environmental literacy institute for faculty from other institutions. A major greening initiative also occurred in February 1994 at Yale University, where 450 faculty, staff, and student delegates from twenty-one countries, six continents, and all fifty states of the U.S. met in a "Campus Earth Summit" to consult several environmental leaders and then to craft a *Campus Blueprint for a Sustainable Future*.[1] The *Blueprint* offers specific recommendations in ten areas:

- Integrate environmental knowledge into all relevant disciplines.
- Improve environmental studies course offerings.

- Provide opportunities for students to study campus and local environmental problems and impacts.
- Conduct a campus environmental audit.
- Reinvent campus purchasing policy (to serve sustainability).
- Decrease campus waste.
- Promote campus energy efficiency.
- Redesign campus land-use, transportation, and building plans.
- Establish a student ecology action center.
- Support careers in the environmental field.

The assumption behind this *Blueprint* is that higher education can influence society by turning out ecologically literate and active citizens and by demanding environmentally sound goods and services. Similarly, green seminaries can interact influentially with churches to encourage ecclesial and community action for sustainability and justice. But the point is not simply to replicate the secular movement toward green higher education. Seminaries and schools of theology have their own denominational-ecumenical context in which to pursue this concern, and should bring to bear a coherent faith-based ethical perspective, plus considerable experience in liberative cross-cultural learning.

Embodying Christian Ethics in Institutional Lifestyles

As noted in chapter 15, Edward Farley has retrieved a definition of theology that antedates theology as a science or discipline: theology as *habitus*, a disposition or habit of wisdom born from knowledge of God. Part of the cultivation of such wisdom is listening to the scriptural critique of unresponsive persons and institutions who disregard the divine will. Individuals, institutions, and whole societies are prophetically criticized for putting their own power, glory, and cravings to own and consume above compassion for others and humble responsiveness to the spirit. Idolatry, legalism, pride, and greed make us blind and deaf to God's presence; both personal and institutional lifestyles become excessively "worldly" in their imbalanced pursuit of wealth, power, and intellectual mastery or control. They (and we) must be transformed to embody authentic eco-social values—solidarity, sustainability, sufficiency, participation—that are expressive of deep spiritual reality.

It is critical to refashion both personal and institutional lifestyles to be congruent with this reality. Such a commitment should guide the operation of the institution as well as the teaching of subject matter. In fact, the practices of the institution—its investments, energy use, food and supply purchases, and its decision-making and conflict-resolution processes—are the embodied expression of its most treasured purposes.

David Orr, formerly of the Meadowcreek Center and now teaching at Oberlin College, describes these daily operations of an educational institution as its "crystallized pedagogy," which demonstrates to all what the organization *really* values. It is a question of practicing what we preach. To allow an institution's money to enrich tobacco companies, for example, when the college classrooms are smoke-free, is rank hypocrisy. It is critical to consider the ecological and social responsibility of the enterprises one purchases from or invests in, the sources and quality of the food served, the soundness of paper purchases, waste management and energy use, and so on.

Maximizing short-term profit without regard for the manner in which such profit is generated is morally bankrupt. Making the extra effort to direct one's money toward the good is a moral imperative arising from a genuine commitment to spiritual life in community.

Four Directions for Greening

The following agenda is suggestive for a seminary context. Each institution needs to find its own way of greening, congruent with its mission and history, faculty capabilities, student interests, and community concerns.

1. Greening Theological Disciplines

Academic work—scholarship, teaching and service—is organized in fields such as systematic theology, church history, and biblical studies. Thus, change in theological education depends significantly on the active engagement of disciplinary leaders in promoting ecologically sensitive theory and sustainable practices as central to the scope and mission of their fields (for example, in peer review criteria for journal articles and in the themes and organization of professional associations). Happily, more course work in these fields is becoming interdisciplinary. This in turn should enable more young scholars and persons acquiring a professional education to grasp the new paradigm which animates "theology for earth community." So each set or department of teachers in a field of theology/religious studies must become critically conscious of engaging the new eco-social situation, instead of being just another local, campus-based manifestation of its discipline. What is taught in a particular school must draw on an eco-justice oriented body of fact and theory accepted by the disciplines, while being responsive to the local setting.

Many of the papers published in this volume describe the current state of the art in the various theological disciplines and fields in light of the eco-justice crisis. They offer substantive leads for serious (shall we call it "deep"?) greening of course work in theological education.

2. Teaching and Learning in the Information Age

Much of the recent criticism of higher education attacks it for failing to prepare students to perform well in an era of information revolution intersecting with accelerating environmental and social change. This critique asserts that decent jobs in the twenty-first century will require people who are extremely adaptable, possessing higher order, symbolic skills. Less often noted is the need for holistic knowledge and enough wisdom to meet perplexing problems and moral dilemmas.

Colleges and universities, and theological schools, are faulted not so much for what they teach—since specific facts, theories, and some sets of skills soon become obsolete—but for how they teach. The lecture format and multiple-choice test, or other "regurgitative" measures of progress, promote the passive absorption of material, thus imparting the wrong skills. Students need to be engaged and actively learning, working in teams to solve problems, as well as producing quality products and services (since that is what real work entails).

Reform in this context emphasizes setting clear and high expectations for mastery of learning objectives, and then encouraging faculty and students, often in cooperation with real-world settings, to figure out the best way to accomplish these objectives. Active learning engages students constantly and consistently in discussing, processing, and applying information. Pursuing a range of learning paths (other than lecturing, reading, multiple choice testing) also allows those with different learning styles to thrive.

A variety of post-secondary institutions have implemented broad-based, active, and experimental learning programs—some, such as Prescott College and Goddard College, with coherent, comprehensive environmental focus. Teaching and learning is being reshaped by the introduction of computers (with CD-ROMs), interactive television, and other technologies, along with greater reliance on "field-based" learning and cross-cultural study. The School of Theology at Claremont and other "lead institutions" discussed later are experimenting with more holistic and experiential learning.

The promise these engaging pedagogical methods hold for eco-theological education has yet to be realized. But those exploring this subject-matter—interdisciplinary by nature, restless with consensus orthodoxies, organically focused on places, and quite interactive with movements for social justice—want to learn differently.

3. Embodying Just and Sustainable Communities on Campus and Supporting Their Emergence in the Wider Society

The central concern here is that institutional members become conscious of the extent to which their practices contribute to a sustainable future. Particularly important is the linkage of academic research and course work to the functioning of the institution. Two examples of institutions which have made strong commitments to model sustainable ways of living are the Center for Regenerative Studies at California State Polytech and Slippery Rock University Master of Science in Sustainable Systems.

At the Center for Regenerative Studies, the "idea is to create a community in which students and faculty members learn about and demonstrate sustainable and regenerative systems." The students are focused on energy efficiency, alternative sources of energy, sustainable food production, and, most important, changes in lifestyle habits which "don't destroy ourselves." All of the students living in the center must minor in regenerative studies and commit to doing the necessary chores.

Slippery Rock's programs in agroecology, built environment, and energy and resource management utilize an on-campus site demonstrating responsible renewable energy use, building design, and landscaping and sustainable agriculture. These systems mimic the diversity, stability, and resilience of natural systems demonstrating the sustainable provision of food, energy, and shelter.

What would be a parallel initiative in theological education? Some concrete examples are being developed in the "green zone" program of some Evangelical Lutheran seminaries, and now in the commitment of several United Methodist and Roman Catholic schools of theology to function as "lead institutions" for creation awareness and eco-justice.

4. Developing a "Postmodern" Theological Education Core

Constructive, postmodern theological education affirms a deeply ecological worldview, reintegrating spirit and matter and the disparate disciplines in a coherent, cosmological-ethical framework. Such education emphasizes core ecological concepts—for example, energy flow, interdependence, carrying capacity and cycles—grounded in a deeper sense of an unfolding, uncompleted universe. Here ecology is understood not only as the study of the relationships between organisms and their environment, but as the ultimate grounding of all beings in life-giving mystery and an unfolding universe. This general education core emphasizes the ultimate worth and diverse vitality of the beings and systems of the earth. Persons who are attuned to these sensibilities are more likely to practice sustainable lifestyles, and to develop and utilize appropriate technologies, ones more congruent with the processes of the natural world and contributory to the common good.

Examples of Institutional Greening

Various institutions of theological education and universities with eco-sensitive religion departments are taking leadership in efforts to meet the environmental challenge in one or more of the above four areas. The following five institutions have volunteered to be in the first set of "lead institutions" collaborating with the project on Theological Education to Meet the Environmental Challenge (TEMEC). They illustrate various paths toward institutional greening.

1. Appalachian Ministries Educational Resource Center (AMERC), Berea, Kentucky

AMERC is a consortium of forty-four Catholic, Orthodox, and Protestant theological seminaries that offers specialized training in Appalachian and rural ministries to theological students and other church leaders. AMERC is a pioneer in "contextual theological education" that helps students to experience regional culture, economy, ecology, and religious traditions with knowledgeable guidance and interpretation. AMERC has recently purchased an eighty-acre farm in Berea, Kentucky, where it is developing a residential campus. Farming activities will introduce students to rural life and culture while providing food for the residential community. Land-based experiences will contribute to pioneering curriculum innovations that seek to infuse theological education with ecological sensitivity.

AMERC's intention is to equip Appalachian and rural Christian leadership for the challenging tasks of healing the earth and restoring creation within the more traditional Christian missions of honoring God, restoring human wholeness, and repairing torn communities. The Appalachian setting provides distinctive opportunities to embrace Christian ministries of eco-justice, infusing them within traditional ministries of redemption and social justice.

Curriculum development is focused on incorporating nature and agriculture within a modern program of liberal, theological education. This task has Jeffersonian roots. It taps the rich tradition of Appalachian "mission farm schools" (including Berea College), which were the first—and in their time, the most creative—providers of an education that was at once liberal and practical. The liberal task is to grasp the value of all life and to understand the challenge to faith posed by the worldwide ecological crisis—and then to see the oppression and pollution that corrupt particular human and natural communities within which ministry must take place. The practical task is to train ministers and other Christian leaders who may help to heal broken persons, communities, and systems of life.

2. United Theological Seminary, Dayton, Ohio

United Theological Seminary was founded as a United Methodist seminary and now serves a range of denominations, including American and Southern Baptist, Presbyterian, UCC, and African-American churches (both AME and CME). It offers a full range of religious and clerical degrees, including the Master of Divinity, Master of Arts in Theological Studies, and the Doctorate of Divinity.

United Theological Seminary's Environmental Ministries Project was created in 1991. Its goals have been 1) to explore the theological and scientific underpinnings of environmental ministries; 2) to determine its implications for educating Christ-centered clergy for the twenty-first century; and 3) systemically to incorporate these into every phase of seminary life. To accomplish these goals the project has established a series of intensive seminars to educate UTS faculty and administrators and selected colleagues from regional seminaries and universities on the relationship among theology, ecology, and justice.

United has used major lecture series, campus Earth Day, student forums, and other means to raise the awareness of and interest in environmental ministry of all members of the United Community, including seminarians, faculty, and staff. Working with the physical resources staff, environmental ministries has improved the stewardship of the campus in a number of ways. These include elimination of lawn chemicals, increased recycling, composting, and improved heating, lighting, and water efficiency. They have also established student garden plots and have just begun to reach out to practicing clergy in the area.

3. Seattle University, Institute for Theological Studies, Seattle, Washington

Seattle University was founded in 1891 by Jesuit fathers. The Institute for Theological Studies (ITS) offers a Master of Arts in Pastoral Studies, a Master of Theological Studies, and a Master of Divinity through a partnership between Seattle University and the Seattle Archdiocese. Though mostly Roman Catholic, students and faculty represent several Christian denominations. Each degree integrates three major components: 1) solid academic foundation in scripture and theology; 2) development of pastoral skills; and 3) personal and pastoral spiritual formation.

In addition to standard theological offerings, ITS has initiated a Sacred Earth Program as a specialized track. This track emphasizes new cosmological understanding based on the integration of science and spirituality and experiential learning and liturgical forms emphasizing connection to nature and sustainability. ITS is also participating in a college-wide effort to integrate scientific and spiritual concerns with applied sustainable practices.

This ecologically oriented, field-based, integrative program emphasizes:

- A focus on ecology and its central concept of ecosystems.
- Linkage of the human with the natural, emphasizing the interactions between natural ecology and human ecology.
- An integrative understanding interweaving the natural sciences, social sciences, and humanities.
- Community involvement with citizens-based groups as well as mainline environmental groups, government agencies on the local, state, and federal levels, businesses, schools, the state environmental education community, and so forth.
- Service-based internships.
- The inclusion of a spiritual dimension. The recognition that our planetary ecological crisis is also, at root, a spiritual crisis, means that we shall draw deeply upon our Christian, Catholic, Jesuit traditions, as well as other values, to fashion a new vision and cultural approach to the epochal questions that face us.
- An emphasis on sustainability as a key value and goal. This program shall seek innovative ways to help sustain ecosystems and communities.

4. St. Thomas University, Miami, Florida

In a Catholic university, research necessarily includes a) the search for an integration of knowledge, b) a dialogue between faith and reason, c) an ethical concern, and d) a theological perspective. To realize the human vocation requires an education that is value laden rather than value free, and that places each human agent within a broader context of accountability to God and service to a wider community—a community that includes all of creation.

St. Thomas, a private, four-year Catholic University, is the only university in Florida sponsored by an archdiocese. It offers the bachelor degree in twenty-eight fields, from accounting to travel and tourism. It also has a law school and offers eleven graduate programs, including pastoral ministries, sports administration and business. About 38 percent of the university's twenty-five hundred students are Hispanic, 33 percent are non-Hispanic white, 15 percent are black, 7 percent are international students, and 7 percent are of other ethnic groups.

St. Thomas has begun to transform major aspects of its entire curriculum according to an ecological perspective. The philosophy department was dramatically reoriented from traditional human-centered courses to ones centered in the new ecological cosmology, where the sense of the sacred pervades all disciplines and is at the core of all experiences of learning. The science division and other faculty in the humanities division, especially history and religion, are adopting an ecological perspective as the foundation of their teaching.

The Miccosukee Indians built a chickee hut where many of St. Thomas's students come to learn from the earth first, and then from their teacher. They engage in farming and "put back into the system" twenty hours of themselves. They experience real, interdependent learning in a wider relationship with themselves, all creatures, and all life. These developments have led to many new experiments—the creation of a special "summer abroad for the earth" (SAFE) program in Italy, involving leading ecological thinkers as teachers; the founding of a student ecological organization which has led the university's recycling program, and so on.

The department of history has created a very popular course in Florida studies, in which students learn through field trips the significance of place, environment, and human impact on the bioregion. New cooperation between the division of humanities and religious studies and the division of science is breaking down the modern, mechanistic separation of matter and spirit. One practical result of this cooperation has been the development of an interdisciplinary environmental studies minor. Administration and faculty are taking steps to implement sustainable practice in energy, food services, and purchasing. An "EcoVillage" is being planned for the campus, in which students, faculty, and community members would live in a sustainable fashion. The Humus Project will provide campus and composting services.

5. The School of Theology at Claremont (STC), Claremont, California

The School of Theology offers a range of degrees, including the Master of Divinity, M.A. in Religion, M.A. in Theological Studies, Doctorate in Ministry, and the Ph.D. in Pastoral Counseling. Last year the school enrolled students from thirty-seven different denominations, including Methodist, Korean Methodist, Evangelical Lutheran, Roman Catholic, African Methodist, American Baptist, and Seventh Day Adventist.

Under the leadership of John B. Cobb, Jr., STC began experimenting with various ways of developing "ecojustice" course work, community life, policy advocacy, and institutional practices some twenty years ago. Efforts have ebbed and flowed depending on faculty and administrative interest, but under the current leadership of President Robert Edgar, STC is gearing up for more eco-justice innovation. Major efforts include a focus on black and minority theology, a theology of institutions, the development of courses integrating ritual, sustainable campus practices, and concerns for social justice.

An example of STC's innovative, praxis-oriented, eco-justice education is an experiential course in which the class functions as a community engaged in a common rhythm of worship, study, fellowship, and service in care of the earth. In addition to exploring issues of community life and environmental care, the class reflects on the dynamics of learning that arise from communal action and practice. Possibilities are pursued for envisioning the educational ministry of the church from within this paradigm.

This course, co-taught by Frank Rogers and Mary Elizabeth Moore, encourages all participants to create a living and environmentally caring community of faith. The teachers emphasize that a community *of faith* seeks to

> rest in and participate with the Spirit of God whom we worship and with whom we are called to serve. The community seeks a rhythm of worship, reflection and work which is empowered by this Spirit. As an *environmentally caring* community, we identify as the central theme of our community the care of the earth. This theme guides our worship, reflection and work. As a living community, we recognize that life is a synthesis of form and spirit. Though we seek to create a form appropriate to a *living* community, this community is dependent upon each of the members to give themselves and participate in its movement.

Summary

These five lead institution initiatives illustrate various paths to developing theological education to meet the environmental challenge. The wave of the future will be marked, no doubt, by how well the goals expressed in such initiatives are understood and pursued in many more theological schools. The changes needed to move toward just and sustainable society are extensive, but they can be approached in stages. The objective overall is for humans and nature to begin a new period of coexistence for the good of subsequent generations in earth community.

Process theologian John B. Cobb, Jr., pulls together many aspects of institutional greening in posing a set of questions to seminaries. First presented during a national ecumenical conference, "Theological Education to meet the Environmental Challenge," held at Stony Point Center, New York, in May 1993, these questions highlight the importance for authentic Christian ethical practice of many mundane aspects of institutional operations, and they provide a useful framework for assessing progress in embodying "green" practice comprehensively.

Some Critical Questions for Evaluating Theological Education in Response to the Environmental Challenge

JOHN B. COBB, JR.

A theology of institutions examines, from a Christian point of view, basic values and assumptions underlying institutional life; where these assumptions are found inadequate or inappropriate, it includes the proposal of alternatives.

Since I am emphasizing the process by which a just and sustainable community comes into being, and since that process is a participatory one, it would be inappropriate to say what the resulting community would look like. On the other hand, since leadership includes introducing proposals to be discussed rather than simply facilitating other people in expressing their concerns, it is appropriate to note some of the topics to consider. You, no doubt, can add others.

First, there is the content of the curriculum. To what extent is it shaped by awareness of the most pressing needs of the world? Does it offer a vision of a just and sustainable community. To what extent does it motivate students to lead in forming such communities and enable them to do so? To what extent does it help them to understand both how the existing church blocks appropriate response and also its resources for *metanoia*? To what extent should students participate in determining the curriculum? What role should the church play? If we cannot truly rethink the curriculum, so that the horizon of all of the teaching is the reality of the world in which ministry occurs, any other changes that are made will be unsustainable.

Second, there is the method of instruction. Is the content and style of instruction pertinent to equip leaders of just and sustainable community? In what ways is it sensitive to the ethnic diversity of the students? Does it meet their differing vocational needs and involve them in ways appropriate to their cultural differences?

Third, there is the matter of how we worship. How can worship perform its function of building community around a shared love of God and the world? Can it overcome the deepseated habits of associating God with the individual human soul and reestablish the self-evidence of God's primary relationship to the world? How does it manifest and internalize the unity of the concern for the oppressed and for the Earth?

John Cobb, a United Methodist minister and prominent philosophical theologian who has mentored a generation of ecotheologians, is director of the Center for Process Studies, Claremont, California, and author of numerous books (see bibliography).

Fourth, there are questions of hiring practices. What combination of competencies should be built into a seminary faculty that takes the environmental challenge seriously? Should special consideration be given to having a faculty and staff that in some way mirror the ethnic diversity within the student body? Should concern for the Earth—commitment to a preferential option for earth community—be a requirement of those to be appointed?

Fifth, there are questions of rank, tenure, and salary. Do salary differences between tenured and non-tenured faculty and the different ranks contribute to a just and sustainable community or inhibit its development? Is there significant opportunity for administrative and maintenance staff who "operate" the institution to have substantive dialogue with faculty and students regarding the common life of the school?

Sixth, there are questions about the relation of employment and finance to the students. Could or should students constitute a larger portion of the employees of the school, reducing their need to work elsewhere? Would that enhance community or hurt it? Could seminaries organize themselves so that financial pressures on students would be reduced and more of them could give primary attention to their participation in the life of the school? Can this participation become a central part of their preparation for ministry?

Seventh, there is the governance of the institution, the separation of powers among students, faculty, staff, and trustees. Can we find ways of governance that allow for greater participation of the whole community without making undue demands on participants or clouding the diversity of roles and responsibilities within the institution?

Eighth, there is the question of the funding of the institution and the investment of its resources. If funding is now dependent on sources that resist institutional change, can these sources participate in discussions that would reassure them about such change? Can other sources of funding be found which would be enthusiastic about a just and sustainable community? Can investments be withdrawn from companies whose role works against justice and sustainability? Or should the trustees use the institution's investments to work for change within such companies? How can money be invested in small, local businesses, especially minority ones or even in student-operated businesses meeting the needs of the community?

Ninth, there are buildings and grounds. When new buildings are constructed, can they be designed to make minimum use of scarce resources? Can they be built so as to encourage community among those who occupy them? How should old buildings be remodeled to such ends? Can the grounds be replanted in ways that reduce the pressure on resources—such as water in dry areas or the need for air conditioning where it is hot? Is maximum use being made of solar energy for heating and cooling as well as for hot water? Are there other ways that some of the energy needed on campus can be produced locally?

Tenth, there are purchasing policies. Can the school meet more of its requirements through purchase of locally produced goods? For example, can more of the food served on campus be grown on local farms? Can the school support those farmers who are growing food organically? Can places be found on campus to grow some food there? Can the school engage in affirmative action with regard to purchasing from small minority businesses? Can we avoid supporting unjust and unsustainable ways of producing food? Can faculty, students, and staff also arrange their purchases with similar considerations in mind?

Eleventh, there are other questions about the food served on campus. What role should meat play in the diet? Are there reasons to avoid meat altogether or at least to eat further down on the food chain? Can we avoid supporting those forms of factory farming that cause extreme suffering to animals? How can the school become a positive supporter of community-based agriculture and local marketing? Should there be an effort to introduce the whole community to the sustainable foods of different cultural groups represented within it?

Twelfth, there are still other questions about the use of resources in the functioning of the community. Should we not only recycle but also reduce the amount of paper and metals used in the academic and business life of the school? Can we avoid so much packaging? To take the use of paper as an example of our institutional consumptive habits, must papers be written on only one side of a page? Can they use the backs of used paper? Do we need as many copies of documents as we typically make? Can modern technology substitute for so much use of paper instead of increasing it? Can we dry our hands on less paper?

Thirteenth, there are other issues of lifestyle. Can or should life on the campus become more communal? Should this reflect cultural lines, or should there be more experiments in cross-cultural intentional community? Can changed lifestyles be a means of living more cheaply and reducing financial pressures on students and on the school budget? How can changes of this sort have an effect on faculty and staff also?

Fourteenth, there are questions about the nature of student life and organization. Should the community strive to integrate each student directly into its total life, or should it affirm instead a diversity of caucuses or groups within it? In short, should it aim to be a single community, or should it model itself as a community of communities? How can it best implement either goal? If caucuses continue to be needed in a just and sustainable community, how will the new context affect their self-understanding? Can their present focus on grievances shift to a more constructive one?

Fifteenth, there are questions about how a seminary relates to other schools of theology. Is this relation primarily competitive, costing each seminary money that could do more for the church and the world if it were spent cooperatively? Can just and sustainable communities develop just and sustainable relations with one another? For example, can course work and field engagement for eco-justice ministry become more cooperative and less competitive?

Sixteenth, there are questions about how faculty members relate to their guilds. If we learn to teach with different focus and emphasis, as the environmental challenge demands, perhaps we will become less isolated from one another and give more emphasis to the needs of the world, of students, and the church. How can the academic disciplines themselves be reformed? Or should ways of organizing inquiry and teaching other than through traditional disciplines actually replace the disciplinary and guild systems?

In conclusion, it is important to underscore the importance of designing courses for the study of the institution itself. This would activate both the process of working towards just and sustainable community and eventuate in ecologically-sensitive curriculum reform, also. A just and sustainable community must be one that is continuously reflective about its own nature. Yet, the one object of study most assiduously avoided in contemporary higher education is higher education itself, and especially the institutions that provide it. Many theological schools devote considerable attention to a critical study of the church, and of society. Thus far, few have given much time to a critical study of themselves. What could be more important than self-study as the central way to engage in a theology of institutions that would meet the environmental challenge?

Note

1. For more information about the *Campus Blueprint for a Sustainable Future*, contact Chris Fox, Heinz Family Foundation, 1201 Pennsylvania Ave., NW, Suite 619, Washington, D.C. 10004.

PART 6

Spiritual Formation and Liturgical Reform

"A now-globalizing culture *in* nature and wholly *of* nature runs full grain *against* nature," Larry Rasmussen warns in this book's epilogue. Similarly, David Rhoads began his 1989 inaugural lecture as Professor of New Testament, Lutheran School of Theology at Chicago, with the words:

> Every week we pray the offertory prayer to God: "We dedicate ourselves to the care and redemption of all that you have made." These words articulate an adequate vocation for humankind in our time, but they are bitter words to speak in light of massive betrayal of this vocation in our domination and exploitation of the earth. . . . Concern for the environment [must be brought] into the orbit of faith, because no technological fix will heal what we have done to creation. Healing will require a major change of lifestyle, a profound human transformation.

For churches to love one earth and many bodies—their own and those of otherkind—requires vital rituals of transformation, including prayers of confession, lamentation, intercession, and regeneration. The authors of the chapters in this concluding section heartily agree! Nancy Wright suggests ways to develop spiritual discipline and Beryl Ingram explores liturgical life to accompany theological-ethical reflection for earth community. This community of "earth and all stars" encompasses city streets and peopled buildings, production and marketing processes, as well as stormy hills and woods thriving with wildlife.

Metaphors of God in the world, and of humans exercising their vocation, play a powerful but paradoxical role in spiritual formation. So, what themes and images should we de-emphasize? And which ones emphasize? The answer has to be contextual, as is all pertinent eco-justice theologizing. Stewardship imagery should be used with increased caution, or more careful interpretation, in a culture that worships the techno-fix. Mending the web of life has possibilities but also some ambiguity about who does the weaving and whom the web catches. Among biblical images, we can consider varied uses of "tree": "Tree of . . . , " yes, and mustard seed, of course, but also "the leaves of the tree were for the healing of the nations" (Rev. 22:2).

There is plenty to be done in spiritual formation to cultivate patterns of post-anthropocentric consciousness without becoming overly romantic, the goal being to develop liturgies worthy of faith's depth as well as eco-justice need. Wright and Ingram call us to get started and point to some guiding principles, such as:

1. Identify with your particular geographical, ecological place, not only individually, but as a worshiping community.

2. Worship with nature in forms other than cut flowers. In liturgy, utilize symbols from your locale as well as your church's tradition, without neglecting either.

3. Be alert to appropriate liturgical boundaries in appropriating earth/nature symbols from other cultures and peoples. But also be daring; for example, think of earth as Christ's body, with a crown of thorns. Make more of the *elements* in baptism and eucharist.

4. Don't lose the distinctiveness between awesome, finite Earth and the imminently transcendent, while radically personal, God.

5. Foster gratitude, lamentation, repentance, and conversion.

6. In your spiritual discipline and worship, do something of transformative quality that may be worthy of recycling.

19

Christian Spirituality

Mending the Web

NANCY G. WRIGHT

If the soul could have known God without the world,
the world would never have been created.
—Meister Eckhart

We in North America live at a time when popular interest in spiritual growth and practice is on the rise. This reflects interest in personal health and happiness, as well as in self-transcendence. But a broad strain underlying this spiritual longing is for harmony with the Earth and within the human family. Can Christianity speak to this hunger for depth of spiritual life within broad parameters?

I approach the subject as a spiritual director and pastor who works with people of varying sophistication. Trained in Ignatian spirituality, I am concerned with harmonizing that rich legacy with the challenge of caring for our Earth community. In this general outlook of mine there is also an appreciation of Jung's intuition of the suppressed feminine, and I agree with the consensus that subordination of women has its counterpart in the abuse of the Earth. In less speculative terms, I also worked for CODEL, Inc. (Coordination in Development), a Christian consortium that supported environmentally sound projects in developing countries. To me, there is an obvious connection among spirituality, reverence for nature, and work for justice.

I have always felt God in natural settings. The contemporary church, however, has only rarely explored the connections between the natural world and spiritual growth. Yet I am heartened by the potential of the Bible and of certain Christian theological perspectives to become important sources of help for the great challenges we face. The church has much to learn and much to do now, if it is to answer helpfully such questions as these: How does the whole Earth community participate in God? Where is God in the natural world? Can we experience God in forests, rocks, and trees as well as in human community? If so, how do we bring this experience to bear on our Christian faith and spiritual nurture?[1]

Promising Beginnings

Biblical Heritage

Christians have not fully lived according to the biblical vision, and few in modern society have seen it clearly. Many have missed how the Creator in the Old Testament has a personal connection with all species of natural life. Without the eyes of faith some modern humans see predation, reproduction, and adaptation in an ecosystem of mutual support. Hebrew writers, on the other hand, saw the Lord feeding the lion and the raven, serving as midwife for the successful birth of the fawn, and freeing the ass for life in the wilderness (Job 38:39–39:8).

The biblical story includes a vision of justice for nature. Each species has its own place in creation, its own needs and purposes. The one God knows and respects all creatures, lovingly providing sustenance and time for rest for all the inhabitants of the Earth. The Sabbath Laws, recorded in Exodus 20:8-11, mandate a day of rest for all people and all livestock. In Exodus 23:10-12 these laws are expanded to govern nature as well: "For six years you shall sow your land and gather in its yield; but the seventh year you shall let it rest and lie fallow."

This new vision culminates in a covenant between the Creator and the created. The Creator's claim to the land prevails. "For the land is mine; with me you are but aliens and tenants" (Leviticus 25:23). Rights of tenancy become a sacred concern, with such rights shielded from political and economic manipulation. The promised land is thus drawn within the circle of ethical reflection at the very heart of Hebrew faith; it recognizes human obligations to the landscape and to other creatures who live there.

At the greatest breadth of their reflection, the Hebrews struggled to appreciate what it meant to serve a God who was not a tribal deity tied to a particular landscape: "Indeed the whole earth is mine" (Exodus 19:5). They tried to appreciate the claims of animals, domestic and wild, who shared the land with them:

> O LORD, how manifold are your works!
> In wisdom you have made them all;
> the earth is full of your creatures (Psalm 104:24).

In the biblical understanding of created relationships, the Earth participates in a mysterious way in the consequences of sin. God uses so-called natural or man-made calamities to punish sinfulness (see Amos 8:7-8, 11). For the prophets, the cleansing of pollution requires radical changes —repentance—and they call upon leaders and the people alike to confess their transgressions.

It has been said that the poor harm the Earth out of need and the rich out of greed. We may be sure there are many more connections between human sinfulness and environmental destruction that we have not yet analyzed. Accountability to a creator God, who covenants with all creation, is a basis for conversion and new recognition of human responsibility to the created order.

In the New Testament, opening his Gospel with a meditation on the Word of God, John identified Jesus Christ with the whole creative process. "In the beginning was the Word . . . without him, not one thing came into being." John sees Jesus Christ associated deeply with the creation of all things, including all species. Often, the popular concept of Christian tradition ignores this most important aspect of the reality of Jesus Christ, which imbues with a sacrality all that exists. Many Christians find themselves focusing only on the redemptive role of Jesus of Nazareth for human beings, failing to recognize that in Christ, the drama of creation unfolds. This is a major tenet of "creation spirituality" (see Fox 1983 and 1988).

Luke records that Jesus' concern for the creatures of the Earth went far beyond the value that human commerce placed on them: "Are not five sparrows sold for two pennies? Yet not one of them is forgotten in God's sight" (Luke 12:6). Paul, convinced that the new covenant was coming alive in Christian life, remembered nature's interest in liberation (Romans 8:19-21). The kingdom that Jesus announced embraced the life of this world—animal, vegetable, and human. And so we should, also (see Ruether 1992).

Monastic Spirituality

Monastic spirituality is particularly suggestive for those concerned with Christian spirituality to meet the environmental challenge. Saints Francis and Benedict, and Julian of Norwich, give promising affirmations. Francis knew that nature untiringly and endearingly revealed God's power, goodness, and love. Benedict fostered a sense of place. He required his monks to take the vow of stability to one place throughout their lives. The Benedictines' legendary husbandry of a landscape reminds us of a twentieth-century Christian farmer's evocation of what it might mean "to take a place seriously: to think it worthy, for its own sake, of life and study and careful work."

These are words of Wendell Berry, who continues with a thought that the Benedictines would understand, "The right scale of work gives power to affection. . . . An adequate local culture, among other things, keeps work within the scope of love" (Wendell Berry 1991, 62-63). The Benedictines were determined to keep work within the scope of love of the land; visitors to the all-too-frequently forgotten Benedictine monastery of Camaldoli in Tuscany will see a vast forested area kept green and sacred in the eyes of God for nine hundred years.

Julian of Norwich, the fourteenth-century anchorite, describes in her *Revelations of Divine Love* the vision of Christ holding the Earth in the palm of his hand "like a hazelnut." She was given to understand that "the firmament and the earth failed for sorrow, according to their nature, at the time of Christ's dying, for it belonged naturally to them as a property to know him" (Julian of Norwich 1977, 112).

The Ecumenical Patriarch Dimitrios of the Orthodox church recently lifted up the eucharistic and monastic traditions of Orthodoxy as a challenge to humanity's "endless and constantly increasing desires and lust, encouraged by the prevailing philosophy of the consumer society." Orthodox monastic spirituality teaches asceticism, or frugality, and a "celebratory use of resources" (Dimitrios 1990, 2,11).

Unravelling Web: The Enlightenment

The biblical writers, and many early and medieval Christian thinkers, did not answer questions about God and the Earth with the inner rift that we all feel. For we have been taught that the Earth is not sacred and that God is separate from the Earth community. The Enlightenment sundered the delicate web linking spirit and nature. No longer creditable was the medieval sense of the Earth, society, and realm of the sacred as participating in one reality. The Enlightenment period, which has fashioned so many Western values, posited polarities from which we and nature still suffer. We live with these false dichotomies, which include lower/ higher, public/private, mind/matter, spirit/body, individual/community, rich/poor, nature/God, and human/nature.

In terms of intellectual history, the great precursor is Rene Descartes, the mathematician and philosopher, with his mechanistic view of nature. His near contemporary Francis Bacon emphasized experimentation, followed by induction, followed by experimentation. Bacon's aim was to exert power and control over nature. Isaac Newton systematized with genius these intuitions. He stressed matter and nature as collections of machines or objects. Thomas Hobbes, turning to the political implications of this approach, concluded that humans are "self-moving systems of matter in motion" (Clarke 1989, 26), basically selfish and competitive, who maximize their self-interest economically. In economics, Adam Smith argued that the economic system, running on its own, with little government interference, would benefit the whole society.

Positive values of individualism and free markets helped establish Western democracy and science. But they had a dark side. Neither justice nor environmental awareness is a product of unbridled individualism or profit-driven economic systems. God, the Creator, is hopelessly distant in this system. Having set the world in motion, God watches as people, who are now the center of the universe, pursue only their own self-interest, regardless of its effect on the environment. The sacred disappears in the material world. Humans are reduced to competing individuals, not participants in a larger human or Earth community. Individual rights are more important than obligations to other humans or the created world. The function of nature is to be consumed or refashioned to create "wealth" used by humans. And many areas of life, previously interconnected as in the web, are no longer considered as complementary but contraries.

What, then, did the new worldview [of the] Enlightenment accomplish? To begin with, it totally changed people's image of their place in the universe. From being servants of God (whatever their worldly station) each contributing to the life of His Church on Earth, they became isolated, competing agents. Human nature, once made in the image of God and innately capable of brotherly love, became a self-centered consumer of pleasure, the sole purpose of whose Reason was to further its own existence. If an image of God still lurked in human nature, it was one of omnipotence rather than compassion (Clarke 1989, 269).

For the church, the Enlightenment legacy fostered a loss of appreciation of incarnation. Further, nurturing and compassion became qualities less important than belief and moral action. Nature fell out of the realm of important activity. We are beginning to acknowledge that here lie buried roots of profound spiritual hunger and grief.

Beginning to Mend the Web

Only a small number of recent publications on spirituality respond to the environmental crisis. In the New Catalogue of records (since 1976) in the Burke Library at Union Theological Seminary, a combined reference of "spiritu*" with "ecology" yielded eighteen entries out of 1,801 books in the area of spirituality as a whole. The Religious Index Data Base (produced by the American Theology Library Association), providing a list of journals and essays, uncovered seventeen entries under "spirituali*" or "spiritual growth*" and "ecology" out of seventy-two entries for "spirituality."[2]

The seed of awareness is taking root and slowly growing. Many denominations have produced statements on the environment. And, happily, the new Catholic catechism recently translated into English lifts up the environment as an area of moral responsibility and refers to environmental sins.

Three Basic Themes

The basic age-old themes of life in the spirit found throughout recent writings in spirituality are being recast in the environmental crisis. What follows is a personal summary of some of these.

Who Are We?

Christians who seek to discover again the connection between spirit and matter affirm that humans are interconnected to the Earth, with a special responsibility because of our power and number. We are interconnected with everything that exists on a living planet, the Earth community.

Further, say some of these proponents, Christians should find affirmation and challenge from the biblical tradition. Scripture teaches that we are to mirror God's relation to creation, which is that of life-giver and champion of justice. We are unique among living species in that we are capable of thinking morally about ourselves and the planet. This entails responsibility and stewardship (Brueggemann 1977; Wilkinson 1980; Hall 1986).

In addition to scripture, we have several other sources of wisdom to help us reclaim our identity as Christians who care about the Earth. The medieval monastic traditions were mentioned above. Further, the science of ecology uncompromisingly stresses interconnectedness, the web of life, and diversity. Humans are as much a part of the created world as trees, water, and soil.

Another source of wisdom is emerging feminist spirituality, which seeks a renewed vision to heal splits and hierarchies and affirm the organic tissue that is both spirit and matter linking all. Eco-feminism reveals Christianity's sometimes ambiguous response to matter, women, and interiority. We see more clearly that Christians have trouble affirming the worthiness and trustworthiness of interiority or essence of minds, souls, and bodies. And what is the connection between mother/Earth/matter and the God who has compassion as a mother hen for her chicks? Feminists may inquire whether the male-dominated drive for progress, defined in terms of what is bigger or faster, has been thrown askew by the lack of the feminine principle in culture and church (see Ruether 1992; McFague 1993; Merchant 1982; Diamond and Orenstein 1990; Plant 1989).

The spirituality of indigenous peoples, as a rule not separated from the Earth, also contributes to our emerging awareness (see Wright and Kill 1993). A helpful understanding of the change that indigenous peoples' visions make has been encapsulated by Fr. Vince Busch, a Columban who works with tribal peoples in the Philippines. Fr. Busch contrasts the "Prayer of the Earth Community" with the "Prayer of the Modern World" on the occasion of an imagined student's graduation from agricultural school.

Prayer of the Earth Community

We thank you God, our nurturing Mother on Earth, for the many opportunities we have to enhance the Earth community today. We are grateful for Inday's ability to listen to and to learn from all things that interact to nurture the fertility of the soil and community. We pray that she may continue to live in harmony with the natural world. Bless her family, whose concern for the soil has taught her the wisdom of living lightly on the Earth. Guide her to use that wisdom to promote the health, fertility, and diversity of all beings here and throughout the Philippine archipelago.

Prayer of the Modern World

We thank you God, our almighty Father in heaven, for the many things that satisfy our needs in the modern world today. We are grateful for the culmination of Inday's professional course of studies, enabling her to make the soil more productive and profitable. We pray that she may find gainful employment. Bless her family who, through hard work and self-denial, saved the money for her professional training. Guide her to use her technical expertise to help industry and commerce flourish and to increase salaried employment for the human beings of our place and of our nation.

Out of several strands of wisdom, Christians flesh out a new awareness of humanity in the context of creation. Our Christian faith will then imbue our self-recognition with capacity for newfound humility and caring.

Who Is God?

Another way of stating this question is: Where do we locate the holy? What is the deepest meaning, for example, of John 1:3 and Colossians 1:17? If without the Word not one thing would exist, and if in Jesus Christ all things hold together, then the loving mystery of Jesus Christ is embedded in creation (or creation is embedded in Jesus Christ) (see McDaniel 1989, chap. 1). Have we been missing much in the past four hundred years because of our inability to see and feel this mystery aright? Such texts seem to indicate that the holy is much more within the Earth community than we Western, Enlightenment-influenced Christians have thought. *This is a most important area for further Christian reflection and experience*, undertaken in joy, fear, and trembling.

The so-called common creation story is a scientifically and theologically informed attempt to face the environmental challenge. The Passionist priest and "cosmologian" Thomas Berry is one of its most eloquent proponents. A cultural historian, Berry draws upon his knowledge of both world religions and modern science. He pleads with contemporary scientists to go beyond the measurable realities of the Earth and universe so that they can hear and see the significance of their discoveries. Talking to an inquiring young person, Berry exclaimed:

> You scientists have this stupendous story of the universe. It breaks outside all previous cosmologies. But so long as you persist in understanding it solely from a quantitative mode you fail to appreciate its significance. You fail to hear its music. That's what the spiritual traditions can provide. Tell the story, but tell it with a feel for its music (in Swimme 1984, 19).

Berry writes of an Earth that begins with the story of the origin and development of the universe as a whole as discovered by Western science (this is the common creation story). Understanding human beginnings in terms of the universe, Berry maintains, empowers us to "reinvent" the human within the unfolding drama of creation. When we are once again in communion with the universe, freed from the narrow windows of sensitivity imposed on us by industrial society and narrow world-views, we can know what we are about as a species. Getting in touch with the Earth in this way will reawaken in us a sense of the sacredness of the natural world, of God present to us in and through the ongoing creative process.

The common universe story is a helpful and hopeful retelling of who we are and of God's earthy being and doing. Based in part on the work of Teilhard de Chardin, as Berry tells the story, it also draws into itself ambiguities and controversies that arise when Christianity confronts the environmental challenge. Perhaps most important, the common creation story helps us to affirm that when we have spiritual experiences in nature—experiences of power, mystery, order, creativity, love, awe—they reveal something of God. The Earth, to use the splendidly baroque phrase of Sallie McFague, is God's body. This metaphor speaks eloquently of a primary religious experience, which can be supported as part of Christian life. In this acceptance of nature there is no mistrust or hostility. Nature is revelatory, as are the Bible and the sacraments. This larger source of what is ultimately true immeasurably enriches our lives with joys, freedom, and responsibilities. It bridges the centuries-long split between religion and science.

When I was in training as a spiritual director, we learned that Ignatius of Loyola thought vertically—the soul and God. We were encouraged, however, to add the horizontal dimension, that is, an awareness of social justice and of community as another realm for God's revelation and our task of discernment. And so we interpreted Ignatius's rules for discernment and the biblical fruits of the spirit not only within individuals but in a communal setting as well. We were taught that sooner or later a spiritual directee will feel the Spirit's call to attend to social concerns, and that we should "midwife" this prompting. Now I am wondering whether we spiritual directors should wait expectantly for spiritual directees to see God in creation. I think we should. If God's spirit is activating the Earth, God's body, we affirm that the spirit groaning and growing in each person will reflect the Earth's spirit. Just as Ignatius's rules for discernment were enhanced by adding a concern for social justice, an eye that encompasses the common creation story, the whole cosmos, enhances and enlarges the frontiers for our discernment.

Although we may utilize a common creation story, we should expect individual experiences of the spirit of the Earth. Some, we all know, are moved to celebration, ecstasy, and joy. Others feel grief. They may be moved to pray for the suffering of the Earth, for extinct species, and moved to action. This experience will vary and be stamped by their own bodies and psyches. One retreatant, watching emerging shapes of the world come into dawn light, was moved to pray, "First light of the soul! Oh, Holy One, I have been blessed by thee as thou takes shape around me." Another parishioner, a psychotherapist influenced by creation spirituality, observed, "Whether I am conscious of it or not, the Trinity—the transcendent heart of the universe, the human beings, and the communion/conversation among them—is there whenever I sit with a client."

But a caveat must be stated: we cannot lose the distinctiveness between God and the Earth. If we do, we lose the Judeo-Christian heritage. God is not only Earth-bodied. The ways in which God is disclosed to many give intimations of a Person at the heart of the universe. Can the elements of the common creation story do justice to the awesome notion and experience of a transcendent and—at the same time—personal God? Does the common creation story adequately convey something of the personal love that Jews and Christians affirm God expresses for us? Certainly there is room for debate. Up to now, most of my spiritual directees, when asked their opinion of this matter, would answer that they feel loved by God while in nature. But it is not simply nature loving them; God is intrinsic in nature, even while transcending it.

Further, there can be an anonymity and immensity about the scientific story of the universe; a fearsome, sometimes crushing vastness that may leave the believer untouched. As Pascal said, "The eternal silence of the stars terrifies me." We sense some of the ancients' awe and fear at creation, which were gradually exorcised relating to a loving personal God. Will this spiritual progress be endangered by conflating the divine and natural?

"Scripture teaches us how to go to heaven, not how the heavens go." Obviously the dichotomy of that statement has long since, and rightly, been surpassed. Genesis makes three points—there is a creator God, the Earth community participates in that creation, and creation participates in the goodness of God. These truths are necessary elements of the common creation story, or so my spiritual directees would say, and I with them.

The common story of the universe may, like its theological cousin creation spirituality, also present other problems. The story has an open ending and focuses on becoming, emergence, and growing consciousness. In this view the Earth is always changing, leading to the growth of human consciousness and to human celebration of all in existence. But if this progressive energy cannot also somehow intermingle with the cyclical energy of the suffering, dying, and resurrection of Jesus Christ, it moves a distance from Christian spirituality. For a Christian spirituality to blossom, there must be some sense of the cruciform/resurrection existence within ourselves and God. The Christian spirit encompasses death and resurrection, taken materially and spiritually. By extension, Christian theology affirms that good overcomes evil in a mysterious way, something we know by faith and hope rather than evidence (see Rasmussen 1992). But we look to the next world for a final beatitude.

The common creation story can tell us much about life but little about death followed by the experience of a loving that cannot die. We may be in danger of losing the poetics of intuited or revealed truth, the paradoxes that Christianity formulates and holds for us about a world partly unseen. Granted, the world unseen has enabled Christians to overlook the devastation of this planet. But we give up a piece of our heritage when we are no longer moved by the words, "Eye has not seen, nor ear heard nor the heart conceived what God has prepared for those who love God." Again, the consolation of future beatitude in which one's longing for self, others, and creation are met in the presence of God has yet to be addressed through the new story of the universe and earth. The spiritual experiences of people who have seen these visions and hoped these hopes must be taken seriously.

A last question, Is the cosmic Christ manifest in creation spirituality the same Jesus Christ to whom a believer turns in prayer? This christological question must take account of the crucified Lord as a stumbling block or particular scandal that lies at the heart of Christian faith (see Rolston 1987).

An important convergence between the common creation story and Christian spirituality is possible, nevertheless, as we share the sense of the Earth as the home we share with God and all creatures. We should not tire of reaffirming this truth.

What Are We to Do?

However we reformulate the relation of spirituality, the Earth, and God, we must act, undergirded by a holistic view that includes matter and spirit. The common creation story (or any other method of expressing an understanding of themes of God/environment/humanity) must not lapse into a system of intellectual understanding necessary for salvation, a new Gnosticism. Salvation is a matter of open-hearted response to the love of God given in creation, wherein we repent, foster eco-justice, pray humbly, and leave something for God to do.

Repent. A Christian response to the devastation that humans cause on the Earth and to the unequal distribution of wealth, land, opportunity, and freedom requires repentance and change in lifestyle. Grief, repentance, and conversion follow one another. Rituals and liturgies focused on creation, and individual prayers of lamentation for the dying parts of our world foster repentance and conversion.

Foster Eco-Justice. Spiritual awareness leads to a critique of society from the point of view of the Kingdom of God. A spiritual grounding in the inner Source lays waste to assumptions, addictions, misuses of being—opening up a critique of self and culture. We ask leading questions: How can we all live on this planet together? What is sufficient for each and for all? How is God's will done on Earth?

Spiritual traditions provide some answers. Simplicity and frugality have always been part of the Earth's spiritual traditions and communities, a consciously loving response to God's graciousness, and so this must be part of our approach. Difficult as they may be, lifestyle changes on the part of the wealthy in the world's family are essential (see Gibson 1977; Nash 1994).

The Spirit of Jesus Christ leads to a new vision for the Earth community. Moved by this spirit, Christians will concern themselves with complex areas perhaps new to them: ecology, economics, sustainable development. Sustainable development involves meeting present human needs without undermining future generations' abilities to meet their needs. In developing sustainably we see that each person has what is needed while we protect nature. We hear the call of Gandhi's words, "Whenever you are in doubt . . . apply the following test. Recall the face of the poorest and the weakest man whom you may have seen, and ask yourself, if the step you contemplate is going to be of any use to him. Will he gain anything by it? Will it restore him to a control over his own life and destiny?" (in Durning 1989, 54).

Pray for and with creation. We can, in keeping with Paul's injunction, pray for the Earth and its groaning, while joyfully contemplating its manifold realities. To help people see "the earth charged with the grandeur of God" or "the world in a grain of sand" is the work of spiritual directors. Can we help people adopt a vision similar to Gerard Manley Hopkins's, who, we know, likened the felling of a grove of trees to the putting out of his eye and compared the Blessed Virgin Mary to the air we breathe?

Leave something for God to do. An awareness that Jesus Christ is revealed through the developing Earth, and human celebration of it means that, happily, the needed conversion is not all up to us; God's Spirit will be calling God's people to faithfulness. We are aware of Christ's call to continued conversion as the demands of the times change. The joy and sometimes burden of loving and knowing the holy in creation go hand-in-hand with an awareness that the seeds we plant, God waters.

Notes

1. The following sections of this paper on biblical heritage and the Enlightenment are based in part on the treatment given to them in *Ecological Healing* (Wright and Kill 1993). I want also to thank five readers of this paper for their helpful comments: Dieter Hessel, Mary Coehlo, Martha Robbins, Rose Zuzworsky, and Heather Elkins.

2. With thanks to Seth Kasten, Research Librarian, Burke Library.

20

Eco-Justice Liturgics

BERYL INGRAM

*Religion binds the whole cosmos starting from above; ecology binds the
whole cosmos starting from below. Together, they are the heaven and earth
of the understanding that we urgently need in this new millennium.*
                                                    —James Parks Morton
                                        Dean, Cathedral of St. John the Divine

Introduction

Despite the tremendous surge of energy toward environmental concerns since
the mid-1980s, there is astonishingly little being done to bring together the ecological and the liturgical. Although Jewish and Christian scriptures praise the
God of creation, and our hymnals and prayer books enjoy a wide variety of hymns
with creation themes, today's bent toward "peace, justice and the integrity of creation," is still remarkably absent from the corporate worship of Christian bodies.

The first section of this chapter tells us that very little is presently happening to
bring liturgics and ecology together. Section 2 depicts the smattering of hopeful
signs pointing the direction for a new field—that of eco-justice liturgics. Section
3 combines examples of these new models with proposals for implementing eco-
justice liturgics at congregational levels.

Congregational worship practices and liturgies do not yet reflect eco-theological themes, but as eco-spirituality gradually permeates the collective global
consciousness eco-justice liturgies should begin to flourish. Fortunately, this ger-
minating awareness of human and nonhuman interconnectedness grows rapidly
as ethicists and theologians struggle to clarify what this means for people of faith.

At the end of the article, the reader will find five appendices listing various
resources for celebrating nature, our environment, and ourselves as part of God's
creation.

Two vignettes set the stage for my personal hope that it will not be long before
eco-justice liturgies fill us with holistic yearning for God.

First, the words of Roman Catholic priest Ed Eschweiler of Wisconsin:

> The Earth I believe in is a word, it is the first self-revelation of our God. It is a kind of incarnation. It is a sign of the goodness, the beauty, the love, and the life-giving presence of God. It is sacramental (Eschweiler 1993, 109).

The second is a story told by P. L. Travers, creator of Mary Poppins. I retell it not to evoke sentimentality but to remind us that the Holy is indeed manifest in this world:

> I have special feeling for sunflowers. When I was a very young child coming from my kindergarten, one of the gardens I passed had a sunflower. It had put its head through the fence, and this great golden lovely face looked at me as though it were that miracle you asked me for, the best I ever saw. I thought, *It's God.* I plucked it and I took it home, and the owner of the garden reported its theft to my parents. And they said: "You have your own garden. You shouldn't take other people's flowers." I said, "But it's God." That altered the whole question. They saw there was something very deep in this experience and didn't at all vilify me. They just advised me tenderly not to do it again (Witchel 1994, C-10).

If we who are theologians, ethicists and educators can prepare the way for the *sacramental moments* when persons see God in sunflowers—just as we may see God in other people—and rather than ignoring or picking the sunflowers are reminded to love God and otherkind all the more, we will have begun to make a way where before there was no way. It is hopeful thing to do.

I

For the most part, liturgical theologians have not yet engaged eco-theology as a liturgical issue. What currently occupies the highest priorities in the field of worship and liturgics? Not surprisingly, the issues that have absorbed liturgical theologians for centuries: baptismal and eucharistic practices, the seasons of the church year, preaching, church architecture, vestments, language, signs and symbols, and so on. Recent years have seen a renaissance of hymn writings, with major denominations producing new hymnals and in those processes struggling to articulate who God is and how God shall be addressed and known in metaphorical language. These processes have in turn engaged liturgical theologians in controversy and dialogue.

Creative forms of worship, which include movement, dance, visual arts, space awareness, liturgical furniture, architecture designed for multi-purpose usage, and what the "mega-churches" are doing right in worship to attract the "baby boomers" tend to dominate the trade magazines.

II

Where it is considered at all, the environmental challenge is still regarded by many liturgical theologians as theological but not necessarily liturgical. In preparation for writing this essay I contacted twenty North American professors of liturgy and worship to discover what they were doing to combine eco-theology and worship in their teaching. I asked them to respond to the following:

1. What issues come to mind that *must* be lifted up?
2. Are you aware of particularly fine liturgies or rituals that deal with eco-theology in any way?
3. How are you addressing environmental issues (however you define them) in courses you are teaching on liturgy/ritual/worship?

The results of my survey were not heartening. The reality is that the deliberate connection of ecology and liturgy is simply not yet happening in most of our seminaries. The majority of professors are not addressing these issues at all, although some teachers are aware of the need to do so and plan to integrate eco-theology into their courses eventually. Others are not convinced of its importance, given other things that must be taught.

Conversely, there is leadership from the few who are developing eco-community liturgy, and from other good friends of the Earth. The Very Reverend James Park Morton, dean of the "green Cathedral," St. John the Divine in New York City, believes that "ecology is the way to understand life in our time. It is the way to do theology" (Morton 1992, 3) To this end, the Cathedral is one sign of hope in the evolution of eco-justice liturgies (see section III for practical ideas that can be adapted from the Cathedral's practices.)

The Chinese poet Lu Xon, said, "Hope can be neither affirmed nor denied. Hope is like a path in the countryside; originally there was no path, yet *as people walk all the time in the same spot, a way appears*" (in MAPS 1994).

The way appears, for example, as serious consideration is given by faith communities to radical ideas like those articulated by theologian Sallie McFague in imaging the universe as "God's body, a body enlivened and empowered by the divine spirit." Such a notion advances the perception of mutual inner-connectedness between human and nonhuman creation and abrogates the stilted, hierarchial images of God as king, father and master. Although applauded by eco-theologians and other progressives, this image is not enthusiastically received by people who honor the exclusively male metaphors that are over-represented in the Bible, hymnals, prayer books and creeds, and who treat these metaphors as revelation. "Body of God" is a fresh and needed corrective, but it will be some time before hymns, prayers and other liturgical formulations adopt such an image in anything more than a marginal way because the entire patriarchal system is represented in singable images that convey God as male and thereby privilege the place given to males in both society and church. Early eco-feminists (see Gray 1981 and Ruether 1974) articulated the connections between male domination of women and human domination of Nature. The traditional dualistic identification of female with Nature and male with Spirit, and a higher valuing of what is male, led and leads still, to domination, violation and exploitation.

Most worship resources continue to image God as a transcendent, male Being "a-way-out-there," and presume human life to be the highest evidence of God's creative powers, descending hierarchically in the "great chain of being": God, angels, humans (male first, then female), animals, creatures and inanimate objects, over all of which "man" has dominion, power to use at will.

While the doctrine of dominion is increasingly criticized by eco-theologians, and while many Christians would now support a theology for ecology and creation that sees human beings as co-carers with God of creation, human life is still separated from the rest of creation and more highly valued, as evidenced by the 1990 address given by Cardinal John O'Connor, who said that "the earth exists for the human person—and not vice-versa." Rather than worrying about "snails and whales," O'Connor said that Christians must help the poor, the sick and "unborn babies" (O'Connor 1994, 11).

Only slowly does the awareness seem to grow that we are all interconnected and interdependent. Gradually the *web* of life replaces the *chain* of being. Every now and then a new hymn appears in which mutuality replaces domination, as in the lovely 1983 piece "God of the Sparrow" by Jaroslav J. Vajda, music by Carl F. Schalk.

> God of the sparrow God of the whale God of the swirling stars
> How does the creature say Awe How does the creature say Praise
> God of the earthquake God of the storm God of the trumpet blast
> How does the creature cry Woe How does the creature cry Save
> God of the neighbor God of the foe God of the pruning hook
> How does the creature say Love How does the creature say Peace
> God of the ages God near at hand God of the loving heart
> How do your children say Joy How do your children say Home.
> *(United Methodist Hymnal* 1989, 122[*])

New hymns are one means for new concepts and theologies to take root, because we retain much more readily what we sing than what we only read or hear. Unless eco-logians can come up with eco-theological metaphors that rhyme as well as "king—-bring, sing, ring," "man—-plan, can," we will not be able to capture the poetic imagination of worshipers. It may seem a quirky point to the general public, but church musicians will quickly recognize that there is such a thing as "lyrical theology," and it must be taken seriously.

Liturgists must ask whether or not images in worship services preserve the language of dominion and subordination. Do hymns, prayers and sermons reinforce the idea that God created with the intention that some would be "users" and others "used," some sacred and others profane, some valued and others expendable? If so, these images work against a holistic theology and must be challenged, again. I say "again," because feminist theologians in the 1970s and 1980s insisted on challenging images of subordination in theology and liturgy.[1] Their insights,

---

however, have only been integrated in some liturgical leadership and resources. Thus we encounter many clergy and lay liturgists who still use the language of "dominion and subordination" and some who defiantly challenge inclusive language as "idolatrous" (without seeing that they idolize patriarchal English)! Liturgists today should communicate a posture of being "with," *not* "over" other people and otherkind, taking shared responsibility within God's creation.

III

Where do we go from here? As indicated in sections I and II, the fields are dark and rich for sowing! Whereas spirituality, theology and ethics are bursting with ecological concerns, worship and liturgy are only now considering the possibilities. This section, therefore, offers concrete examples of eco-liturgical practices and suggests ways for implementation at congregational levels. It is followed by an extended series of appendices that call attention to an exceedingly rich treasury of ideas.

Before proceeding, however, a word of caution about the eco-spiritual movement in general. One problem with much of the New Age fascination with spirituality is its theft of rituals, ceremonies, words and symbols from other cultures, primarily, but not exclusively, Native American cultures.

I strongly caution against incorporation of bits and pieces of Native American rituals into otherwise Christian services. While non-Native peoples may gain some new appreciation of the richness and diversity of Native American spiritualities through participation in rituals or by using Native American symbolism, taking tribal rituals as though we have a right to them is a continuation of the exploitation of Native peoples. As Dr. Marjorie Procter-Smith, Professor of Worship at Perkins School of Theology, states, "Given the history of white domination of Native Americans, it looks a lot like just another example of cultural theft, religious grave-robbing" (letter to author, 23 August 1994).

On the other hand, there are others who would argue that since Native Americans are not all of like mind on this issue, if a Native American chooses to educate non-Indians about certain rituals and then leads these non-Indians in these rituals, that is acceptable. Where would any of us be if we could not benefit from each other's wisdom and ritual practices, borrowers ask. Don't we already incorporate traditions and rituals from many cultures into our North American worship contexts? Be that as it may, even as I articulate that thought, it is with the strongest caution that non-Natives must not simply appropriate ceremonies, rites and symbols from the Native Americans. Where does this caution end?, the reader might well ask. It doesn't. Cross-cultural borrowing in order to enrich our own particular community must recognize and honor the borrowed-from group.

There are many ways religious people can honor God, honor the Earth and honor our inner-connectedness. We can use our own God-given creativity to create our own eco-justice liturgies and eco-justice rituals. The following are some ideas:

1. Following the lead of the "green" Cathedral Church of St. John the Divine, congregations could commission poets, hymn writers or composers to create musical expressions with ecological themes.

The Cathedral recently commissioned the "Mass for the 21st Century," which will be performed around the globe by peoples of many cultures prior to returning to the Cathedral in 1999 for its debut. Likewise, it was the Cathedral that gave the world the *Missa Gaia* (1987), a Mass in celebration of the Earth, recorded live in the Cathedral of St. John the Divine and the Grand Canyon. The *Missa Gaia* is performed each October as part of the Cathedral's Feast of St. Francis of Assisi celebration.

2. Recapture the old English tradition of *Rogation Day*. According to Rev. Jeff Golliher, "green priest" at St. John the Divine, "It used to be a time of renewal of our relationships in an ecological sense. The entire congregation would walk the boundaries of the parish. It was taking care of the land in a ritual way, to remind the community that this is also part of what it means to be spiritual" (Golliher 1994, 11).

Our hymnals at one time contained more hymns suitable to an agrarian society than they do today. Use current hymnal indices to find hymns with Nature or Creation themes, or search under the heading "Seasonal Hymns" for hymns like "We Plow the Fields."

> We plow the fields and scatter The good seed on the land,
> But it is fed and watered By God's almighty hand;
> Who sends the snow in winter, The warmth to swell the grain,
> The breezes and the sunshine, And soft, refreshing rain.
> All good gifts around us Are sent from heaven above;
> Then thank the Lord, O thank the Lord For all this love.
> —Matthias Claudius, 1740-1815, adapted
> *(The Book of Hymns* 1966, 513)

3. Purchase and use the excellent resource *God's Earth Our Home* Partnership Packet produced by the Environmental and Economic Justice/Hunger Concerns Working Group of the National Council of Churches of Christ in the USA (see Appendix A). The sixteen-page worship section includes "The Earth Is the Lord's: A Liturgy of Celebration, Confession, Thanksgiving, and Commitment."

4. Develop *Earth Day* (April 22) liturgies that transform this day of ecological awareness into a theological celebration. School children participate in projects that honor the Earth—recycling, trash pick-up, reclamation of untended plots of land, and so on. As people of faith, the religious community can bear witness that "the earth *is* the LORD'S and the fullness thereof." Resources are available from Earth Day USA, Box 470, Peterborough, NH 03458. (603) 924-7720. Fax: (603) 924-7855.

5. Develop worship experiences for the *Environmental Sabbath*, Friday through Sunday in the first week of June. For resources contact: UN Environment Programme, Room DC2-0803, United Nations, New York, NY 10017.

6. Use organic images in preaching and prayers. For example, develop the photosynthetic process of light becoming chlorophyll, or waste becoming compost becoming viable soil, or the exchange of carbon dioxide for oxygen as illustrations of God's power of transformation. God is the original re-cycler.

7. Bring plants and trees into the sanctuary. Work with a local nursery, botanical garden or arboretum to utilize plants, trees and flowers in worship. These could be changed seasonally. For example, a vine maple in autumn, a fir in winter, a blossoming cherry in spring or an elm in summer would remind worshipers of God's bounty and beauty. This would be particularly effective in the inner city where many folks just don't see trees. In addition to the beauty of living trees in the worship space, the symbolism is radically different from that of the standard bouquet of cut flowers that often adorn altars. Flowers are lovely, but they do not speak to the same connected, ongoing reality that a living plant or tree does. A natural ally in tree planting would be the National Arbor Day Foundation. Though now secularized, this endeavor has roots in nineteenth-century Protestant concern for land preservation.

Why not plant a tree each time someone is baptized? If planted on church grounds, a marker could commemorate the person's name and the baptismal date. If you are fortunate enough to have a gardener in your midst, perhaps he or she would provide seedlings to be presented to each new Christian to be planted and tended by the newly baptized or their family.

Flowers, too, have a message in their life cycles. A congregation in Tacoma, Washington, combined its pastor's love of flowers with the need to change the image of its weary-looking building. The members planted daffodils and tulips all around the church one Sunday in September. Everyone got in on it, young and old alike, spades and trowels in hand, people still humming the closing "Hymn of Promise" by poet Natalie Sleeth.

> In the bulb there is a flower; in the seed, an apple tree;
> in cocoons, a hidden promise: butterflies will soon be free!
> In the cold and snow of winter there's a spring that waits to be,
> unrevealed until its season, something God alone can see.
> (*United Methodist Hymnal*, 707*)

In localities where milkweed grows, allow the swallowtail caterpillars to spin their cocoons in late summer and then bring some of the stalks into the sanctuary and wait until spring to marvel at the emergence of the butterflies. Make provisions for them to be set free immediately. This could be an occasion for designing an eco-ritual.

Dr. Miriam Therese Winter, Professor of Liturgy at Hartford Seminary, relates a ritual where women gathered to plant an apple seedling, symbolic of the fruit of the original garden. Each woman contributed to the planting process and also committed life experiences in symbolic form into the hole around the tiny stem. Instead of the usual four years to fruit bearing, this tree produced a bumper crop in two! Similarly, Dr. Winter suggested that people consider planting trees and designing their own rituals (telephone conversation with author, 6 September 1994). For example, a weeping willow or weeping cherry could commemorate Showa or the collective sorrowing of a people.

---

*Natalie Sleeth, author. Copyright © 1986 by Hope Publishing Co., Carol Stream, IL 60188.

8. Examine worship material for images that subordinate Earth and/or women and replace the blighted language with sustainable metaphors. For examples of creative linguistic nuances, see the Pilgrim Press *Sampler of New Church Hymns*, published in 1993.

9. Engage an artist to create banners for the worship space that celebrate the seasons or particular components of creation—earth, air, fire, water—as God's gift, as God's Self.

10. If eco-theology is to be grasped by other than scientists, academics and eco-theologians, then it must capture the popular imagination. St. John the Divine has led the way in New York City, creating a way, where before there was no way. Nowhere is this more dramatic than in the annual Feast of St. Francis and the Blessing of the Animals, including personal pets. The extraordinary procession enters the great nave through the monumental bronze doors flung wide to welcome an elephant, camel, python, llama, primate, birds, tortoise, and so on, down to the terrarium of ants and bowl of algae.

The animals are blessed. Surely pets provide the most tactile relationships for millions of housebound persons in this country, and care units have discovered that children or animals quicken the hearts of otherwise languishing residents. Blessing the animal companions of our daily lives reminds us that all creation is beloved of God.

11. Where space permits, create prayer gardens or labyrinths to encourage contact with the natural world as well as to provide sanctuary for pray-ers.

12. Birds can be encouraged to build nests, feed, bathe and sing their stories in the shrubbery around church buildings if someone will plant berries and trees that attract them.

13. Dr. Lawrence H. Stookey, Professor of Worship at Wesley Seminary in Washington, D.C., incorporates eco-theology into his liturgy classes in highly integrated ways. For example, in dealing with ecclesiology he stresses the difference between individualist and corporate approaches to life and illustrates this with examples of use of resources, food distribution, and so on.

Regarding weddings, he addresses confetti/rice/bird seed as ecological concerns and, similarly, plastic versus fabric aisle runners for the bridal party. He also encourages students to bring their in-class coffee in their own ceramic mugs instead of disposable paper cups, and he does the same.

Funerals provide conversations about cremation and donation of body parts or the entire body for use as a cadaver—all as ways of doing eco-theology. Stookey says, "Cremation no longer connotes trash; and why should millions of acres be used for cemeteries instead of for farms, forests, playgrounds, and other purposes consonant with a theology of creation as God's revelation?" (letter to author, 18 August 1994).

14. Liturgical theologian Hoyt Hickman believes that the way to teach eco-theology in liturgy is to re-educate worshipers about the meaning of the sacraments of baptism and eucharist. "Baptism is everything that water is. Enough means life, too much means death. Water sustains life on earth." However, water around the world today is usually polluted or scarce. Rare on this planet is "the water of life bright as crystal," envisioned in the Apocalypse of John (Rev. 22:1). What a

marvelous reciprocity it would be if Christians could grasp the significance of being cleansed in the water of baptism to go forth and cleanse the waters of the earth.

"Whatever the Lord's Supper is, it is everything that eating is," says Hickman (telephone conversation with author, August 1994). When we consider what we eat and what we drink, we recognize that it is past time for many of us to appraise what we feed ourselves—not just cutting back on fat and cholesterol—but assessing our responsibility in the ongoing destruction of creation. Consider, for example, the grassland it takes to feed beef cattle; the forests being destroyed to create grassland; the devastating connections between cattle and water pollution; the opposition fearful cattle ranchers have mounted over the reintroduction of wolves in Yellowstone National Park. What we take into our bodies has both political and theological ramifications. Eco-justice liturgies force us to rethink the meaning of our rituals from holy eucharist to daily meals!

15.   Consider developing rituals that bring healing to Earth and Earth's community. At one time I considered commissioning a musical piece that I called "Requiem for the Planet Earth." A friend reminded me, however, that a requiem is written for what is already dead. Was I without hope? No. Perhaps, then, a "Healing Service for Planet Earth" or "A Service of Anointing for This Fragile Earth, Our Island Home," might be more appropriate.

Consider developing a service for endangered species or a healing service for people forced to live with toxic waste, nuclear fallout, impure water, and so forth. Talk to people living in unsafe situations. How can conversation, prayer and liturgy be combined to contribute to social action for justice?

Consider designing an exorcism to call upon the powers of God to re-claim lands and peoples scarred by greed, racism and other disasters.

Bring theological perspectives to embattled ecological issues. For example, conduct a service in the forest and make clear-cut the fragmentation of the web of life there because of logging; or go to an area ravaged by environmental racism and in an eco-justice liturgy covenant to make justice where no justice exists.

If there is a park or green space accessible, plan an experiential worship service there. Remember that you may need to seek permission or even get a permit to do this. Consider the natural elements—trees, water, shrubs, grass, animals. The sermon might come from the participants as they consider a topic in small groups. For example, if it is a sunny day, ask people to tell each other in groups of three or four what sun means to them or to share their earliest memories of what sunshine has meant in their lives. Or if it is damp, ask what experiences they have had with water or lack of it in their lives. If animals are around, let people talk about how they were taught to think about "wildlife" and whether or not these learnings have changed through the course of their lifetimes. Ask people to make connections between these insights and how God is working in their lives.

16.   Learn about Judaism's High Holy Days as the birthday of the world. Every Sabbath celebrates creation. A Reconstructionist rabbinical student reminds me that Judaism has kept more nature in its liturgies than has much of modern Christianity.

17. Make the eco-justice connections in analysis and liturgy. Dr. Tom Driver, after a period of residence in Haiti, tells of the military junta uprooting trees across the island in 1994 just because they were planted during another regime. He proposes that citizens in other lands plant more trees in their own countries to ritualize their solidarity with Haitians and with Haiti.

18. Practice a discipline of eco-stewardship. My own evolving practice, developed because I walk my Bernese Mountain Dog several times a day, is to pick up trash from sidewalks and lawns in the area of New York City where I live. On the early morning walk I carry a garbage sack (re-cycled) and my mop handle with the spike in one end, and as I walk, I pray and pick up trash. This eco-justice ritual has become a spiritual discipline, leading me to view myself as a *practical*, not merely *theoretical* sacramental theologian.

Conclusion

This chapter is a call to the churches to *do* the urgently needed, and enjoyable, work of eco-justice liturgics. It is an exciting prospect because it involves our whole lives, and indeed, the life of this planet. It is a call to use the *language* of eco-theology in worship, to create *eco*-justice liturgies and rituals, and to reclaim from the secular sphere the conversations about landfills and leaching pits, environmental racism and ecosystems, solvents and sustainable societies. It will be a stellar day for God when a high school student is asked for the definition of economics and responds, "The management (*oikonomia*) of the household of God."[2]

It is no meager vision. It is, in fact, transcendent, for Creation's demise or survival may well depend on people of faith "taking the whole world in our hands" and loving it back to health and wholeness, and in the process, discovering not only God working in our midst, but ourselves at work in the midst of God.

> *Hope is like a path in the countryside;*
> *originally there was no path,*
> *yet as people walk all the time in the same spot,*
> *a way appears.*

The following five appendices give information on materials that worship leaders will find helpful in preparing liturgical celebrations centered on our life in and as a part of nature.

Appendix A
Resources for Worship

Canticles of Creation. Worship resource/bulletin inserts celebrating a different spiritual and environmental theme each month. Arranged according to the seasons of the year. Yearly subscription 16 cents per insert with a minimum of 25 copies. Order from the Center for the Celebration of Creation, 8812 Germantown Avenue, Philadelphia, PA 19119. (215) 242-9321.

Celebrating Earth Holy Days: A Resource Guide for Faith Communities. Susan J. Clark. New York: Crossroads, 1992.

Celebrating God's Good Earth in Prayer, Discussion, and Action. Father Ed Eschweiler. Milwaukee: HI-TIME Publishing Corp., 1991. Box 13337, Milwaukee, WI 53213-0337. Booklet. Complete eco-liturgies and suggestions for things to do and things to read in each section.

Celtic Prayers: The Passionate Religious Vision of Ancient Britain and Ireland. Robert Van de Weyer, ed. New York: Doubleday, 1990.

Earth Prayers from Around the World. San Francisco: Harper Collins, 1991.

Environment and Development Resource Packet. Worship and educational materials plus organizing tools. $5. United Church of Christ Board for World Ministries, Global Education, 700 Prospect Ave., Cleveland, OH 4415-1100. (216) 736-2174.

God's Earth Our Home. Partnership Packet prepared by The National Religious Partnership for the Environment (NCC), Shantilal P. Bhagat, editor. This is a superb collection designed to be used as a twelve part study/action course. Excellent 16-page section of Worship Resources including an eco-liturgy, "The Earth is the Lord's." $13. FaithQuest, 1451 Dundee Ave., Elgin, IL 60120. (800) 441-3712.

Jesus Christ—The Life of the World: A Worship Book for the Sixth Assembly of the World Council of Churches. Geneva: World Council of Churches, 1983. 150 route de Ferney, 1211 Geneva 20, Switzerland. Like *In Spirit and Truth*, it is available in English, French, Spanish and German.

Only One Earth. An "Environmental Sabbath" resource booklet with prayers, litanies, sermon topics, and personal action guide. $5 from UN Environment Programme, 2 UN Plaza, Room DC-0803, UN, New York, NY 10017. (212) 963-8210.

Peace with Justice Covenant Congregations. Guide including a worship service of covenant. Useful to churches joining the Peace with Justice program. CS1026. $1; 10-99 copies $.85 each; 100 or more $.75 each. United Methodist General Board of Church and Society, 100 Maryland Ave. NE, Washington, DC 20002. (800) 967-0880. Add $2 shipping for orders of $10 or more.

In Spirit and In Truth: A Worship Book. Geneva: World Council of Churches, 1991. 150 route de Ferney, 1211 Geneva 20, Switzerland. Produced for the Seventh Assembly in Canberra, Australia, this compilation of hymns and prayers is an invaluable collection available in four languages: English, German, Spanish and French. The theme of the Assembly was "Come Holy Spirit—Renew the Whole Creation." The accent on eco-justice is more pronounced in this resource than in the book for Sixth Assembly.

Whose Birthday Is It, Anyway? Booklet for enhancing and simplifying the celebration of Advent and Christmas. Contents include weekly meditations, services, and activities. Available in versions for various denominations and in a generic version. $3 plus shipping; discounts for larger orders. Alternatives, PO Box 429, Ellenwood, GA 30049. (404) 961-0102.

Women and Worship: A Guide to Nonsexist Hymns, Prayers and Liturgies, Revised Edition. By Sharon Neufer Emswiler and Thomas Neufer Emswiler. San Francisco: Harper & Row, 1984. A practical resource designed for local church study and worship-planning groups.

Appendix B
Music Resources for Worship, Rituals or Meditation

EarthSong. Miriam Therese Winter. Cassette tape and songbook of eco-theological, creation-centered music. Medical Mission Sisters, 77 Sherman St., Hartford, CT 06105. (203) 233-0875.

Earth Songs: Twelve Original Songs Honoring the Earth. The Narada Collection Series. 1993. 1845 N. Farwell Ave. Milwaukee, WI 53202. (414) 272-6700.

Symphony of the Universe. Wendy Mae Chambers. The four sections are, "Big Bang/ Organisms/Cosmos/Evolution." 1993. Newport Classic. CD $16.

By Paul Winter and/or the Paul Winter Consort. Living Music, Box 72, Litchfield, CT. 06759. Available on cassette ($12) and CD ($17):

Anthems. Ten years of Living Music.

Callings. 1980. A celebration of the voices of the sea. Living songs inspired by calls of fifteen different sea mammals and the actual voices of the creatures are woven into the fabric of the music.

Canyon. Music inspired by the Grand Canyon.

Concert for the Earth Live at the United Nations.

Icarus.

Missa Gaia. A Mass in celebration of Mother Earth recorded live in the Cathedral of St. John the Divine and the Grand Canyon.

Prayer for the Wild Things. An Earth Music Celebration of the Northern Rockies, inspired by the wilderness art of Bev Doolittle. Voices of twenty-seven mammals and birds. Native American musicians Arlie Neskahi and White Eagle Singers.

Solstice Live—A Celebration of the Winter Solstice. Special guests from Russia, Ireland, Ecuador, Spain, the Netherlands and the United States, recorded at St. John the Divine.

Sun Singer. 1983.

Whales Alive. Paul Winter and Paul Halley.

Appendix C
A Few Good Books for Children in Worship

Be a Friend To Trees. Patricia Lauber. Illustrated by Holly Keller. Harper Collins, 1994. Ages 5-9. $4.95. About trees. Tips for conservation, from refusing an unnecessary paper bag to planting a tree.

Earthwise at Play. Linda Lowery and Marybeth Lorbiecki. Illustrated by David Mayaya. Minneapolis: Carolrhoda Books, 1993. $7.95. Information about various animals and plants and their interdependence. Activities that can help and preserve them.

A Gift of a Tree. Greg Henry Quinn. Illustrated by Ronda Krum. New York: Scholastic Books, 1994. $5.95. Clear information. About third-grade reading level. Contains a Tree Starter Earth Kit by EarthPlan.

I Love You, Sun I Love You, Moon. Karen Pandell. Illustrated by Tomie dePaola. New York: J.P. Putnam & Sons, 1994. $5.95. Stiff pages, big words, delightful pictures.

SOS Planet Earth: Nature in Danger. Mary O'Neill. Illustrated by John Bindon. Mahwah, New Jersey: Troll Associates, 1991. $3.95. Discusses how the natural resources of the earth and the living things on it are all linked together and how the natural order of things is being continually threatened by our modern way of life. Juvenile literature.

Song for the Ancient Forest. Nancy Luenn. Illustrated by Jill Kastner. New York: Atheneum, 1993. $14.95. Beautifully illustrated, poetic, sensitive to fragility of ecosystems and livelihood of Pacific Northwest loggers.

Where Does the Garbage Go? Paul Showers. Illustrated by Randy Chewning. Harper Collins, 1972, 1994. $4.95. Explains how people create too much waste and how waste is now recycled and put into landfills.

Consider subscribing to one of the Nature magazines like *Ranger Rick, Big Back Yard*, or *World*. You'll find all kinds of ideas and projects that you can creatively tailor for eco-justice liturgies and rituals.

Appendix D
Resources for a Library on Eco-Justice Liturgy

The Body of God: An Ecological Theology. Sallie McFague. Minneapolis: Fortress Press, 1993. The body of God exists in the entire creation. This is an organic, ecological model of God. Forces the rethinking of all traditional metaphors for God.

To Care for the Earth: A Call to a New Theology. Sean McDonagh. London: Geoffrey Chapman, 1986. Includes examples of celebrations developed among the T'boli tribes of the Philippines where McDonagh was a missionary.

Caring for Creation. Anne Rowthorn. Wilton, CT: Morehouse Publishing, 1989. A personal reflection, from a biblical, eco-theological perspective, on the human destruction of creation.

Celebrating the Earth: An Earth-Centered Theology of Worship with Blessings, Prayers, and Rituals. Scott McCarthy. San Jose: Resource Publications, 1991. Many liturgies and rituals that can be used and/or adapted.

The Coming of the Cosmic Christ: The Healing of Mother Earth and the Birth of a Global Renaissance. Matthew Fox. San Francisco: Harper and Row, 1988. Fox understands the Cosmic Christ to be the One who calls the world to compassion and to the doing of justice.

Eco-Church: An Action Manual. Albert J. Fritsch and Angela Ladavaia-Cox. Detailed manual to help a congregation grow in environmental awareness, evaluate its life, and make appropriate changes. Resource lists and directories. $14.95. Resource Publications, 160 E. Virginia St., Suite 290, San Jose, CA. 95112.

Ecofeminism and the Sacred. Carol J. Adams, ed. New York: Continuum, 1993. An extraordinary collection of essays by leading feminist theologians. I cannot recommend this book highly enough. Every essay is excellent! State-of-the-art bibliography.

The Ecological Challenge: Ethical, Liturgical, and Spiritual Responses. Richard N. Fragomeni and John T. Pawlikowski, eds. Collegeville, MN: The Liturgical Press, fall 1994. Ten essays toward defining and engendering creational responsibility in the Christian faith community. Four sections: Scripture, Ethics, Liturgy, Spirituality.

Family of the Earth and Sky: Indigenous Tales of Nature from Around the World. John Elder and Hertha D. Wong, eds. Boston: Beacon, 1994. Excellent resource for preaching or other story-telling situations. This collection gathers the first global array of vivid responses to nature from indigenous oral traditions of Africa, Asia, Europe, Australia and the Americas. In the "Animal Tales and Transformations" section the indigenous understanding of kinship and reciprocity between human and nonhuman worlds is made clearer. $30.

Gaia and God: An Ecofeminist Theology of Earth Healing. Rosemary Radford Ruether. San Francisco: Harper, 1992. The earth may be healed through sacrament and covenant, through new communities of celebration and resistance that create a new consciousness of the interdependence of all creation.

Of God and Pelicans: A Theology of Reverence for Life. Jay B. McDaniel. Louisville: Westminster/John Knox Press, 1989. A deceptively simple title for an intriguing and very helpful process theologian's perspective on eco-theology. Refreshingly eclectic!

Healing and Defending God's Creation: Hands on! Practical Ideas for Congregations. Resources for worship, education, individual and congregational lifestyle, and public policy and community involvement. Vol. 1 DMS #259-91-907, $4.95. Vol. II DMS #259-93-939, $4.95. Vol. I & II #259-93-947, $7. Presbyterian Distribution Service, 100 Witherspoon St., Louisville, KY 40202-1396. (800) 524-2612.

Original Blessing: A Primer in Creation Spirituality Presented in Four Paths, Twenty-Six Themes, and Two Questions. Matthew Fox. Santa Fe, New Mexico: Bear and Company, 1983. Creation-centered theology argues against fall/redemption theology. Creation is itself the original blessing. Incorporates biblical wisdom with the wisdom of mystics, feminist and liberation theologians.

Renew the Face of the Earth. Albert J. Fritsch. Chicago: Loyola University Press, 1987. Fritsch provides possibilities for liturgy by combining the themes of the liturgical year with specific seasons of the natural year.

Appendix E
Videos

Caring for the House of Worship. 7-minute video to motivate energy conservation in religious buildings. Rental $5. purchase $20. Interfaith Coalition on Energy. P.O. Box 26577, Philadelphia, PA 19141. (215) 635-1122.

The Earth Is the Lord's. 17-minute video challenging attitudes and practices that blur the line between dominion and destruction. Tells stories of several change activists. Brethren Press, 1415 Dundee Ave., Elgin, IL 60120-1694. $19.95.

The Greening of Faith: Why the Environment Is a Christian Concern Part I: Theology and Spirituality. Biblical foundations for ecology. Creation spirituality in the Christian tradition. Nature as sacramental. The reconnection of faith and science. 1993. 30 minutes. $29.95.

The Greening of Faith: Why the Environment Is a Christian Concern Part II: Ethics. Environment and justice. Extension of ethical obligation beyond the human species. The unique role the church can play in the formation of attitudes and enabling of change. 27 minutes. $29.95. "Stunning nature photographs and the haunting music of Peter Kater, R. Carlos Nakai and Chris White flavor this sumptuous feast of creation themes" in both videos. Cathedral Films & Videos. Box 4029, Westlake Village, CA 91359.

Available on loan from the Evangelical Lutheran Church in America (ELCA) Environmental Stewardship and Hunger Education Office, 8765 W. Higgins Rd., Chicago, IL 60631-4190. (800) 638-3522:

Christians for the Earth with Wendell Berry and Wes Jackson.

EPA's "Green Lights." Ways to reduce church lighting bill by about 50 percent.

Available through the Presbyterian Distribution Service, PCUSA, 100 Witherspoon St., Louisville, KY 40202-1396. (800) 524-2612:

Restoring Creation for Ecology and Justice. 15-minute video for adults and youth, introducing General Assembly Report.

Special Places—Taking Care of God's World. 11-minute video for children with supplemental material for educators. DMS #918-88-655. $19.95. PDS.

Acknowledgment: Many thanks to Shantilal P. Bhagat, of the Church of the Brethren, who edited NCC Packet, *God's Earth Our Home,* for permission to quote material from that project in this list of resources.

Notes

1. Nelle Morton, in *The Journey Is Home* (1985) emphasized the importance of metaphor in forming community, identifying ways in which "patriarchal patterns of dominance subvert" human community and "the earth as the common home for us all." Also see Halkes (1989) for an exploration of the connection between "images at the root of oppression of women" and human relationships with nature or environment.

2. The word from which *economics* comes is the Greek *oikoumene*, literally translated "the household of God."

Epilogue

LARRY RASMUSSEN

Dorothee Soelle once remarked that addressing the pressing, interrelated is-sues of the day requires "revolutionary patience." "Theology for Earth Community" is part of that enterprise and asks no less of us. The urgency arises from the conditions of life now, while the scale and dimensions of those condi-tions beckon a commitment to work this ground thoroughly, carefully, imaginatively, as long as we are able.

As a matter of mood, eco-apocalypse as steady fare will not suffice for this task, even though the very soul of responsibility on a saturated planet requires utterly clear-eyed realism about degraded conditions and the genuine threats to life that surround us. Whatever "gospel" may mean, it is not more bad news, or even no more bad news. Something drawing us to life and extending life from us toward others must be uncovered and embraced. It may be ethically earnest and demanding, to be sure, but it cannot lack joy. Absent the *joie de vivre* itself, our fate is surely sealed.

There is a chapter in *The Brothers Karamazov* titled "Cana of Galilee," which closes with a vivid though quiet scene that captures the kind of spirit (and the kind of earth ethic) we must all be in search of. The scene centers on Alyosha, "the little man of God," who goes late at night to the monastery cell where his spiritual mentor, the saintly old Zossima, lay in his coffin. The scene comes, of course, after the tumultuous tears and tortured relationships of love, betrayal, and loyalty that inhabit all thick Russian novels. In the dark candlelight Alyosha hears the account of Jesus's first miracle of water to wine at the wedding in Galilee being read over the coffin. Exhausted, he drifts from the words into prayer and his own running commentary on the familiar verses, all in the presence of old Zossima's body and spirit. In this dreamlike state, Alyosha suddenly hears the voice of Zossima, who extends his hand and raises him from his knees. "Let us make merry," the dried-up old man says, "Let's drink new wine, the wine of new gladness, of great gladness." And a little later: "Begin your work, my dear one, my gentle one." It is in this moment of tender invitation and new vocation that Alyosha, who had in truth fallen asleep on his knees in prayer, suddenly awakens, goes to the coffin briefly, then turns abruptly and exits the cell.

Dostoyevsky writes:

> Alyosha did not stop on the steps, but went down rapidly. His soul, over-flowing with rapture, was craving for freedom and unlimited space. The

vault of heaven, studded with softly shining stars, stretched wide and vast over him. From the zenith to the horizon the Milky Way stretched its two arms dimly across the sky. The fresh, motionless, still night enfolded the earth. The white towers and golden domes of the cathedral gleamed against the sapphire sky. . . . The silence of the earth seemed to merge into the silence of the heavens, the mystery of the earth came in contact with the mystery of the stars. . . . Alyosha stood, gazed, and suddenly he threw himself flat upon the earth.

He did not know why he was embracing it. He could not have explained to himself why he longed so irresistibly to kiss it, to kiss it all, but he kissed it, weeping, sobbing and drenching it with his tears, and vowed frenziedly to love it, to love it for ever and ever. Water the earth with the tears of your gladness and love those tears, it rang in his soul. What was he weeping over? Oh, he was weeping in his rapture even over those stars which were shining for him from the abyss of space and he was not ashamed of that ecstasy. It was as though the threads from all those innumerable worlds of God met all at once in his soul, and it was trembling all over as it came in contact with other worlds. He wanted to forgive everyone and for everything, and to beg forgiveness—oh! not for himself, but for all and for everything, and others are begging for me, it echoed in his soul again. But with every moment he felt clearly and almost palpably that something firm and immovable, like the firmament itself, was entering his soul. A sort of idea was gaining an ascendancy over his mind—and that for the rest of his life, for ever and ever. He had fallen upon the earth a weak youth, but he rose from it a resolute fighter for the rest of his life, and he realized and felt it suddenly, at the very moment of his rapture. And never, never for the rest of his life could Alyosha forget that moment.

"Someone visited my soul at that hour!" he used to say afterwards with firm faith in his words. . . . Three days later he left the monastery in accordance with the words of his late elder [Zossima] who had bidden him [now new-born to earth] to "sojourn in the world" (Dostoyevsky 1963, 2:426-27).

There the chapter ends.

Note that Alyosha threw himself upon the *earth* and arose from it, after the soul's visitation, a resolute fighter. He did not throw himself upon "the environment!" The difference is not slight, and is the reason this collection of papers is not a meditation on the environment and its distress but a meditation on earth. If the subject had been "theology for the environment," the eco-crisis would have be depicted as a crisis of nature in which nature is the sumptuous stage of the human drama and the stock of steady resources needed to service that grand tale. Nature in this instrumental environmentalist view is now threatened by human use and encroachment. The eco-crisis is thus understood as a crisis of natural habitat, and worry about "the environment" gets slotted in as an issue somewhere on the same list with racism, poverty, domestic violence, crime, and homelessness. (It also competes with them for attention and resources.) In the halls of academe itself, "the environment" becomes the subject of "greening" this or that discipline, and the newest occasion for urgent interdisciplinary work together. That is an important but insufficient development.

People who speak of the eco-crisis as a crisis of the environment are certainly correct about one matter: what is happening to earth *is* the great drama of our time. The crisis is not one of nature, however, at least not as nature is commonly conceived. Nature degraded and diminished will survive nevertheless in a million different forms and for a very long time. The eco-crisis is a crisis of culture. More precisely, the crisis is that a now-globalizing culture *in* nature and wholly *of* nature runs full grain *against* nature. A virile, comprehensive and attractive way of life that is destructive of nature, culture and human community alike, operating by means of the same interlocking dynamics, is the issue. Soils, peoples, air and water are depleted and degraded together. (Or, on our better days, sustained together.) It is not the environment that is unsustainable, then, but life as we have come to know it. At least that is the sometimes spoken, sometimes unspoken assumption and implication of the foregoing analyses from across the spectrum of theological and religious studies.

The whiff of apocalypse *is* sometimes strong in these pages, as it usually is in that awkward time when one age is passing and the next is only in the early stages of a painful birth. In that respect, theological and religious studies mirror the mood of many scholars in both the arts and sciences. The mood is captured at its extreme in two modern renditions of the opening line of the most famous of Chinese poems, "Spring View." Composed by Du Fu, "Spring View" was written at the time of the An Lushan rebellion in 755 C.E. Lamenting the rebellion and in search of some consolation, the poet opens with this line: "The State is destroyed, but the mountains and rivers survive."

Nanao Sakaki, a twentieth-century Japanese poet, turned Du Fu's thought on its head: "The mountains and rivers are destroyed, but the State survives" (in Snyder 1990, 175).

As though that reversal were not enough, Thomas Fraser Homer-Dixon's study of socio-environmental causes of acute conflict offers an extended rendition: "The mountains and rivers are destroyed, and the State survives—but society unravels" (Homer-Dixon 1994, 60).

Most people have to travel outside most of North America, and certainly off college and university campuses, to appreciate this—China, Papua New Guinea, the Philippines and communities in Latin America, West Africa and India, Haiti, tracts in Siberia and Eastern Europe, Egypt, or the traditional homelands of native and indigenous peoples most anywhere. And even when degradation is apparent, most people, Homer-Dixon says, do not recognize what is happening to the earth. "For too long," he says, quoting Daniel Deudney, "we've been prisoners of 'social-social' theory, which assumes there are only social causes for social and political changes, rather than natural causes, too" (ibid.). This very bad habit of mind has been regnant since the Industrial Revolution, a revolution that lifted us wholesale from the rest of nature as a species apart.

In both its practice and its metaphysics, industrial civilization assumed the universe was the human world plus props; that myopia remains the underlying view of most of the practices and much of the thought in our day-to-day lives. So it is only now, when nature shows both vengeance and vulnerability, and the grim interplay of demographic, environmental and social stress turns increasingly cruel, that children of industrialized civilizations finally discover what other civilizations sometimes knew (the very ones we study without engaging): the fate of mountains, rivers and societies is a single fate; nature is not what is around us or where we live, but the reason we are alive at all and the reason each and every society and culture that ever existed did so.

This internal, not external, linkage of the social and the environmental, of nature and culture, of society, history and nature all together at the end of the century, is what this volume has struggled to be about, as probed in the varied ways of our respective fields of scholarly work and ministerial practice. We did not speak, then, of "theology for the environment" or even "theology in light of the eco-crisis." Rather, the proper name was the one given: *Theology for Earth Community*. It might have been another, of course, but only some variant that would also understand the comprehensive threat to life (and promise of life) as it is now bundled together from the inside out.

In this light, the selection from Dostoyevsky probably does not serve us particularly well. Reconciled of soul with earth, falling to earth a weak being and rising a resolute fighter with a new vocation in the world—this *does* serve us well and is, in fact, one of the hopes for these pages. But it is not the individual Alyosha alone under the starry heavens, a trembling and ecstatic soul, that best pictures us now, even when earth and its distress and our place in it is also about Alyosha's weeping and watering the earth with the tears of gladness, and loving those tears. ("The capacity to weep and then do something is worth everything," Greta Gaard writes in *Ecofeminism* [1993, 3].) Not only is it not Alyosha but, truth to tell, there *is* no one best figure or picture that fits our reality, unless perhaps it is earth itself as *oikos* [home], as Habitat Earth, the only life form we know of thus far in the universe. Or unless it be, in different words, earth as community, earth as understood in light of what may eventually be recognized as the most important scientific discovery of the twentieth century, that *nature, indeed creation, is a community*.

Beyond this profound recognition, we need many pictures, voices and analyses, together with the realization we simply will not be in possession of sure, comprehensive understanding for a long while, if ever. Yet in the meantime the work of scholars, teachers and students must go on with revolutionary patience in the necessary search for language and categories and symbols capable of saying precisely what is happening to the planet and what it means for the way we live. We are, it seems, set somewhere in the awkward space between worlds we trusted and ones strangely new to us. It is a sometimes puzzling, even bizarre, place to be, much less comprehend. All these chapters assumed, as a starting point, is that the Hebrew prophets were right after all—it is mountains and rivers and society all together, or not at all. The "vines languish" and "the merry-hearted sigh" together or thrive together (Isaiah), caught up in some complicated fate laced both with a "dearest freshness deep down things" (Gerard Manley Hopkins) and new levels of vulnerability. There is indeed an integrity about creation, for better and for worse. Tracing the implications of that for earth community has been the beginning work of these pages. Its very modesty—as beginnings—calls for more.

Bibliography

Abrecht, Paul, ed. 1978. *Faith, Science and the Future*. Geneva: WCC Publications. Second edition 1979. Philadelphia: Fortress Press.

Adams, Carol J. 1990. *The Sexual Politics of Meat: A Feminist-Vegetarian Critical Theory*. New York: Continuum.

_____. 1993. *Ecofeminism and the Sacred*. New York: Continuum.

_____. 1994. *Neither Man Nor Beast: Feminism and the Defense of Animals*. New York: Continuum.

Adams, Douglas. 1984. "Sacramental Worship for Creation Consciousness." In Joranson and Butigan 1994, 436-40.

Albrektson, Bertil. 1967. *History and the Gods: An Essay on the Idea of Historical Events as Divine Manifestations in the Ancient Near East and in Israel*. Lund: GWK Gleerup.

Alliance for Environmental Education. 1994. *Education for the Earth: A Guide to Top Environmental Studies Programs*. Princeton: Peterson's Guides, 1994.

Alt, Albrecht. 1968a. "The God of the Fathers." Trans. R. A. Wilson. In *Essays on Old Testament History and Religion*. Garden City, NJ: Archer Books. 1-100.

_____. 1968b. "The Origins of Israelite Law." Trans. R. A. Wilson. In *Essays on Old Testament History and Religion*. Garden City, NJ: Archer Books. 101-71.

Altmann, A., ed. 1966. *Biblical Motifs: Origins and Transformations*. Cambridge: Harvard University Press.

Anderson, Bernhard W. 1955. "Earth Is the Lord's: An Essay on the Biblical Doctrine of Creation." *Interpretation* 9 (January):3-20.

_____. 1975. "Human Dominion Over Nature." In Ward 1975, 27-45.

_____. 1984a. <*American Journal of Theology and Philosophy* 4/1 1983, 14-30>. "Creation and Ecology." In Anderson 1984b, 152-71.

_____, ed. 1984b. *Creation in the Old Testament. Issues in Religion and Theology*. Philadelphia and London: Fortress Press; SPCK.

_____. 1986. "Cosmic Dimensions of the Genesis Creation Account." Carl Michalson Memorial Lecture, 1985. *Drew Gateway* 56 (Spring):1-13.

_____. 1987. *Creation Versus Chaos: The Reinterpretation of Mythical Symbolism in the Bible*. Philadelphia: Fortress Press.

_____. 1992. "'Subdue the Earth': What Does It Mean?" *BR* (October), 4, 10.

Angel, J. L. 1972. "Ecology and Population in the Eastern Mediterranean." *World Archeology* 4:88-105.

Artson, Bradley Shavit. 1991. "Our Covenant with Stones." *Conservative Judaism* 44:1.

Bahr, Ann Marie B. 1991. "God's Family and Flocks: Remarks on Ownership in the Fourth Gospel.'" In Robb and Casebolt 1991b, 91-104.

Bakken, Peter (with Engel). 1995. *Ecology, Justice and Christian Faith: A Critical Guide to the Literature*. Westport, CT: Greenwood Publishing Group.

Baly, Dennis. 1987. *Basic Biblical Geography*. Philadelphia: Fortress Press.

Balzar, John. 1994. "Doomsayers of Overpopulation Sound a New Jeremiad." *Los Angeles Times* (7 June):A5.

Banks, William. 1972. *The Black Church in the U.S.:Its Origin, Growth, Contributions and Outlook*. Chicago: Moody Press.

Barbour, Ian. 1980. *Technology, Environment, and Human Values*. New York: Praeger Publishers.

_____. 1990. *Religion in an Age of Science*. San Francisco: HarperSanFrancisco.

_____. 1993. *Ethics in an Age of Technology*. San Francisco: Harper Collins.

Barney, Gerald O. 1993. *Global 2000 Revisited: What Should We Do?* A report on the critical issues of the 21st century prepared for the 1993 Parliament of World's Religions. Arlington, VA: Public Interest Publications.

BarYosef, Ofer, and Anatoly Khazanov, eds. 1992. *Pastoralism in the Levant: Archaeological Materials in Anthropological Perspective*. Madison, WI: Prehistory.

Barr, J. 1963. "Revelation Through History in the Old Testament and in Modern Theology." *Interpretation* 17.

_____. 1974. *Bulletin of the John Rylands Library 55/1*. Autumn 1972. 9-32. "Man and Nature: The Ecological Controversy and the Old Testament." In Spring and Spring 1974, 48-75.

Batchelor, Martine, and Kerry Brown, eds. 1992. *Buddhism and Ecology*. London and New York: Cassell Publishers Limited/World Wide Fund for Nature.

Bayles, Michael D. 1980. *Morality and Population Policy*. Birmingham: University of Alabama Press.

Bayles, Michael D., ed. 1976. *Ethics and Population*. Cambridge: Schenkman Publishing Co.

Beavis, Mary Ann. 1991. "Stewardship, Planning, and Public Policy." *Plan Canada* 31:6, 75-82.

Beer, Gillian. 1985. "Darwin's Reading and the Fictions of Development." In Kohn 1985, 543-86.

Beker, J. Christiaan. 1980. *Paul the Apostle: The Triumph of God in Life and Thought*. Philadelphia: Fortress Press.

Bell, Betty Louise. 1994. *Faces in the Moon*. Norman, OK: Univ. of Oklahoma Press.

Bergant, Dianne. 1987. *The World is a Prayerful Place: Spirituality and Life*. Collegeville, MN: Liturgical Press.

Berry, Thomas. 1988. *The Dream of the Earth*. San Francisco: Sierra Club.

Berry, Thomas, and Thomas Clarke. 1991. *Befriending the Earth: A Theology of Reconciliation Between Humans and the Earth*. Mystic, CT: Twenty-Third Publications.

Berry, Wendell. 1977. *The Unsettling of America: Culture and Agriculture*. San Francisco: Sierra Club.

_____. 1981. "The Gift of Good Land." In his collection of essays *The Gift of Good Land*. San Francisco: North Point Press. 267–81.

_____. 1991. "Out of Your Car, Off Your Horse." *The Atlantic*. (February).

Beversluis, Joel D., ed. 1995<1993>. *A Sourcebook for Earth's Community of Religions*. New York: Global Education Associates.

Biehl, Janet. 1991. *Rethinking Ecofeminist Politics*. Boston: South End Press.

_____. 1991. *Finding Our Way: Rethinking Ecofeminist Politics*. Montreal: Black Rose Books.

Bigwood, Carol. 1993. *Earth Muse*. Philadelphia: Temple University Press.

Birch, Bruce, and Larry Rasmussen. 1978. *The Predicament of the Prosperous*. Philadelphia: Westminster Press.

Birch, Charles, and John B. Cobb, Jr. 1990 <1981>. *The Liberation of Life*. Denton, TX: Environmental Ethics Books.

Birch, Charles, William Eakin, and Jay McDaniel, eds. 1990. *Liberating Life: Contemporary Approaches to Ecological Theology*. Maryknoll, NY: Orbis Books.

Bird, P. A. 1981. "'Male and Female He Created Them': Gen 1:27b in the Context of the Priestly Account of Creation." *HTR* 74(2):129-59.

Bloom, Harold. 1990. *The Book of J*. New York: Grove Weidenfeld.

Board of National Ministries of the American Baptist Churches in the U.S.A. 1974. "Ecological Wholeness and Justice: The Imperative of God." *Foundations* 17 (April-June), 133-57.

Boff, Leonardo. 1995. *Ecology and Liberation*. Maryknoll, NY: Orbis Books.

Boff, Leonardo, and Clodovis Boff. 1987. *Introducing Liberation Theology*. Trans. Paul Burns. Maryknoll, NY: Orbis Books.

Book of Hymns, The. 1966. Nashville: The Board of Publications of the Methodist Church.

Bookchin, Murray. 1989. *Remaking Society*. Montreal: Black Rose Books.

Borowitz, Eugene. 1991. *Renewing the Covenant: A Theology for the Postmodern Jew*. Philadelphia: Jewish Publication Society.

Borowski, Oded. 1987. *Agriculture in Iron Age Israel*. Winona Lake, IN: Eisenbrauns.

Bowman, Douglas C. 1990. *Beyond the Modern Mind: The Spiritual and Ethical Challenge of the Environmental Crisis*. Cleveland: The Pilgrim Press.

Box, Thadis, et al. 1974. *Rehabilitation Potential for Western Coal Lands*. Cambridge: Ballanger.

Boyarin, Daniel. 1993. *Carnal Israel*. Berkeley: University of California Press.

Braidotti, Rosi, et al. 1994. *Women, the Environment and Sustainable Development: Towards a Theoretical Synthesis*. London: Zed Books.

Bratton, Susan Power. 1992. *Six Billion and More: Human Population Regulation and Christian Ethics*. Louisville: Westminster/John Knox Press.

Brown, Lester. 1984-96. *State of the World* (annual vo(s.). New York: W.W. Norton & Co.

Brown, Noel, and Pierre Quiblier, eds. 1994. *Ethics and Agenda 21: Moral Implications of a Global Concensus*. New York: United Nations Publication.

Brown, Robert McAfee. 1988. *Spirituality and Liberation: Overcoming the Great Fallacy*. Louisville: Westminster/John Knox Press.

Browning, Don S., ed. 1983. *Practical Theology*. San Francisco: Harper & Row.

Brueggemann, Walter. 1977. *The Land: Place as Gift, Promise and Challenge in Biblical Faith*. Overtures to Biblical Theology. Philadelphia: Fortress Press.

_____. 1987. "Land: Fertility and Justice." In Evans and Cusack 1987, 41-68. Collegeville, MN: Liturgical Press.

Breuilly, Elizabeth, and Martin Palmer, eds. 1992. *Christianity and Ecology*. London and New York: Cassell Publishers Limited/World Wide Fund for Nature.

Budde, K. 1895. "The Nomadic Ideal in the Old Testament." *New World* 4.

Burton-Christie, Douglas. 1993. "A Feeling for the Natural World: Spirituality and Contemporary Nature Writing." *Continuum* (Spring).

Butler, Judith. 1990. *Gender Trouble*. New York: Routledge.

Bynum, Caroline. 1982. *Jesus as Mother: Studies in the Spirituality of the High Middle Ages*. UCLA Publications No. 16.

Caldecott, Leonie, and Stephanie Leland. 1982. *Reclaim the Earth: Women Speak Out for Life on Earth*. London: Women's Press.

Callahan, Daniel. 1976. "Ethics and Population Limitation." *Ethics and Population*. In Bayles 1976.

Callicott, J. Baird. 1989. *In Defense of the Land Ethic: Essays in Environmental Philosophy*. Albany, NY: State University of New York Press.

_____. 1991. "Genesis and John Muir." In Robb and Casebolt 1991b, 107-40.

_____. 1994. *Earth's Insights: A Survey of Ecological Ehtics from the Mediterranean Basin to the Australian Outback*. Berkeley: University of California Press.

Callicott, Baird, and Roger Ames. 1989. *Nature in Asian Traditions of Thought: Essays in Environmental Philosophy*. Albany: State University of New York Press.

Camara, Helder. 1990. *Sister Earth: Ecology and the Spirit*. New City.

Canadian National Round Table. 1991-92. *The 1991-92 Annual Review*.

Cane, Bill. 1992. *Circles of Hope: Breathing Life and Spirit into a Wounded World*. Maryknoll, NY: Orbis Books.

Chavis, Benjamin F., Jr., and Charles Lee, eds. 1987. *Toxic Wastes and Race in the United States: A National Report on the Racial and Socio-Economic Characteristics of Communities with Hazardous Waste Sites*. New York: Commission for Racial Justice, United Church of Christ.

Chopp, Rebecca, and Gabriel Fackre. 1994. "Recent Works in Christian Systematic Theology." *Religious Studies Review* 20:1 (January).

Christ, Carol, and Judith Plaskow, eds. 1989. *Weaving the Vision: New Patterns in Feminist Spirituality*. San Francisco: Harper & Row.

Churchill, Ward. 1992. "Naming Our Destiny: Towards a Language of Indian Liberation." *Global Justice* 3:22-33.

_____. 1993. *Struggle for the Land: Indigenous Resistance to Genocide, Ecocide and Expropriation in contemporary North America*. Monroe, ME: Common Courage Press.

Clark, J. Michael. 1993. *Beyond Our Ghettos: Gay Theology in Ecological Perspective*. Cleveland: The Pilgrim Press.

Clarke, Mary E. 1989. *Ariadne's Thread: The Search for New Modes of Thinking*. New York: St. Martin's Press.

Clifford, Anne. 1992. "Perspectives on Science: Implications for an Ecological Theology of Creation," *Journal of Feminist Studies in Religion* 8:65-90.

Clifford, Richard J. 1972. *The Cosmic Mountain in Canaan and the Old Testament*. Cambridge: Harvard University Press.

_____. 1984. *Fair Spoken and Persuading: An Interpretation of Second Isaiah*. Theological Inquiries. New York: Paulist Press.

Clinebell, Howard. 1992. "Looking Back, Looking Ahead: Toward an Ecological-Systems Model for Pastoral Care and Counseling." *The Journal of Pastoral Care* 46, no. 3 (Fall), 263-72.

Cobb, John B., Jr. 1970. "Ecological Disaster and the Church." *The Christian Century* 87: 1185-87.

_____. 1982. "Process Theology and an Ecological Model." *Pacific Theological Review* 15:27.

_____. 1992. "Postmodern Christianity in Quest of Eco-Justice." In Hessel 1992, 25-27.

_____. 1992b. *Sustainability: Economics, Ecology and Justice*. Maryknoll, NY: Orbis Books.

_____. 1992c. "Sustainability and Community." *The Egg: An Eco-Justice Quarterly* 12:3.

Cobb, John B., Jr., and Herman E. Daly. 1989. *For the Common Good: Redirecting the Economy toward Community, the Environment, and a Sustainable Future*. Boston: Beacon Press.

Cohen, J. 1989. *"Be Fertile and Increase, Fill the Earth and Master It": The Ancient and Medieval Career of a Biblical Text*. Ithaca: Cornell University Press.

Cohen, Jeremy. 1990. "On Classical Judaism and Environmental Crisis." *Tikkun* 5:2:74-78.

Cohn, Robert L. 1981. *The Shape of Sacred Space: Four Biblical Studies*. Chico, CA: Scholars Press.

Collins, John Joseph. 1977. *The Apocalyptic Vision of the Book of Daniel*. Harvard Semitic Monographs, no. 16. Missoula, MT: Scholars Press (for Harvard Semitic Museum).

Commission on Jewish Education in North America. 1991. *A Time to Act: The Report of the Commission on Jewish Education in North America*. Lanham, MD: University Press of America.

Cone, James. 1970. *A Black Theology of Liberation*. Philadelphia: J. B. Lippincott Company.

_____. 1984. *For My People: Black Theology and the Black Church*. Maryknoll, NY: Orbis Books.

Copeland, Warren R., and Roger D. Hatch, eds. 1988. *Issues of Justice: Social and Religious Meaning*. Macon, GA: Mercer University Press.

Cousineau, Phil. 1993. *The Soul of the World: A Modern Book of Hours*. San Francisco: HarperSanFrancisco.

Cowap, Chris. 1979. "Ethical Implications of Energy Study and Use." In Hessel 1979, 108-31.

Coward, Harold, ed. 1995. *Population, Consumption, and the Environment: Religious and Secular Responses*. Albany: State University of New York Press.

Cowdin, Daniel M. 1994. "Toward an Environmental Ethic," in Irwin and Pelligrino 1994.

Crenshaw, James L. 1981. *Old Testament Wisdom: An Introduction*. Atlanta: John Knox Press.

_____. 1993. "Wisdom Literature." In *The Oxford Companion to the Bible*. Eds. Bruce M. Metzger and Michael D. Coogan. New York: Oxford University Press. 801-3.

Croatto, J. Severino. 1981. *Exodus: A Hermeneutics of Freedom*. Maryknoll, NY: Orbis Books.

Cross, Frank Moore, Jr. 1973. *Canaanite Myth and Hebrew Epic*. Cambridge: Harvard University Press.

_____. 1989. "The Redemption of Nature." *Princeton Seminary Bulletin* n.s. 10(2):94-104.

Cummings, Charles. 1991. *Eco-spirituality: Toward a Reverent Life*. Mahwah, NJ: Paulist Press.

Curran, Charles E. 1985. "Population Control: Methods and Morality." *Directions in Catholic Social Ethics*. Notre Dame, IN: University of Notre Dame Press.

_____. 1978. *Issues in Sexual and Medical Ethics*. Notre Dame, IN: University of Notre Dame Press.

Curtis, Edward M. 1992. "Idol, Idolatry." In Anchor Bible Dictionary 3. Eds. David Noel Freedman, et al. New York: Doubleday.

Daily, Gretchen C., and Paul R. Ehrlich. 1992. "Population, Sustainability, and Earth's Carrying Capacity." *BioScience* 42:10.

Daly, Hermann E. 1991. "A Biblical Economic Principle and the Steady-state Economy." In Robb and Casebolt 1991b, 47-60.

Daly, Herman E., and John B. Cobb, Jr. 1989. *For the Common Good: Redirecting the Economy Toward Community, the Environment, and a Sustainable Future*. Boston: Beacon Press.

_____. 1994. *For the Common Good: Redirecting the Economy Toward Community, the Environment, and a Sustainable Future*. 2d ed. Updated and Expanded. Boston: Beacon Press.

Daly, H., R. Goodland, and S. El Serafy, eds. 1992. *Population, Technology, and Lifestyle: The Transition to Sustainability*. Washington, D.C.: Island Press.

Daly, Lois. K. 1994. "Ecofeminisms and Ethics." *The Annual of the Society of Christian Ethics*.

Daly, Mary. 1978. *Gyn/Ecology: The Metaethics of Radical Feminism*. Boston: Beacon Press.

Dankelman, Irene, and Joan Davidson. 1988. *Women and Environment in the Third World: Alliance for the Future*. London: Earthscan Publishers.

Davies, W. D. 1974. *The Gospel and the Land: Early Christianity and Jewish Territorial Doctrine*. Berkeley: University of California Press.

Derr, Thomas Sieger. 1973. *Ecology and Human Liberation: A Theological Critique of the Use and Abuse of Our Birthright.* WSCF Book, vol. 3, no. 1, serial no. 7. Geneva: WCC Publications.

DeWitt, Calvin, ed. 1991. *The Environment and the Christian: What Can We Learn from the New Testament.* Grand Rapids, MI: Baker Book House.

DeWitt, Calvin, and Ghillean T. Prance, eds. 1992. *Missionary Earthkeeping.* Intro. J. Mark Thomas. Macon, GA: Mercer University Press.

Diamond, Irene, and Kuppler. 1993. "Frontiers of the Imagination." Quoted in Seager 1993, 251.

Diamond, Irene, and Gloria Feman Orenstein, eds. 1990. *Reweaving the World: The Emergence of Ecofeminism.* San Francisco: Sierra Club Books.

Dimitrios, The Ecumenical Patriarch. 1990. *Orthodoxy and the Ecological Crisis.* Gland, Switzerland: World Wildlife Fund.

Dorr, Donal. 1990. *Integral Spirituality: Resources for Community, Peace, Justice, and the Earth.* Maryknoll, NY: Orbis Books.

_____. 1991. *The Social Justice Agenda: Justice, Ecology, Power and the Church.* Maryknoll, NY: Orbis Books.

Dostoyevsky, Fyodor. 1963. *The Brothers Karamazov.* Trans. with intro. David Magarshack. Baltimore: Penguin Books.

Douglas, Gordon, and Jane Douglas. 1989. "Creation, Reformed Faith, and Sustainable Food Systems." In Stivers 1989.

D'Souza, Corrine Kumar. 1989. "A New Movement, A New Hope: East Wind, West Wind and the Wind from the South." In Plant 1989.

Dubos, Rene. 1972. *A God Within.* New York: Charles Scribner's Sons.

Durning, Alan B. 1989. "Poverty and the Environment: Reversing the Downward Spiral." Washington: Worldwatch Institute.

Dyson, Martha. 1990. "Ecological Metaphors in Feminist Eschatology." *Daughters of Sarah* 16 (May/June).

Easterbrook, Gregg. 1995. "Forget PCB's. Radon. Alar: The World's Greatest Environmental Dangers Are Dung Smoke and Dirty Water." *The New York Times Magazine* (September 11): 60-63.

Eberstadt, Nicholas. 1991. "Population Change and National Security." *Foreign Affairs* 70:3.

Eck, Diana, and Devaki Jain, eds. 1987. *Speaking of Faith: Global Perspectives on Women, Religion, and Social Change.* Philadelphia: New Society Publishers.

Ecologist, The. 1993. *Whose Common Future? Reclaiming the Commons.* Philadelphia: New Society Publishers.

Ehrenfeld, David. 1981. *The Arrogance of Humanism.* New York: Oxford University Press.

Ehrenfeld, David, and Philip J. Bentley. 1986. "Judaism and the Practice of Stewardship." *Judaism* 34:301–11.

Ehrlich, Paul R., and Anne H. Ehrlich. 1990. *The Population Explosion.* New York: Simon and Schuster.

Eichrodt, Walther. 1961-67. *Theology of the Old Testament.* Trans J. A. Baker. The Old Testament Library. Philadelphia: Westminster Press.

Eliade, Mircea. 1954. *The Myth of the Eternal Return or Cosmos and History.* Princeton: Princeton University Press.

_____. 1959. *Cosmos and History: The Myth of the Eternal Return.* New York: Harper Torchbooks.

_____. 1969. *The Eternal Return: Images and Symbols.* New York: Sheed and Ward.

Ellingson, Mark. 1993. *The Cutting Edge: How Churches Speak on Social Issues.* Geneva: WCC Publications.

Elwood, Douglas J. 1980. *Asian Christian Theology: Emerging Themes*. Philadelphia: Westminster Press.

Engel, J. Ronald. 1983. *Sacred Sands: The Struggle for Community in the Indiana Dunes*. Middletown, CT: Wesleyan University Press.

_____. 1987. "Teaching the Ecojustice Ethic: The Parable of Billerica Dam." *Christian Century* 104 (May 13), 466-69.

_____. 1988. "Ecology and Social Justice: The Search for a Public Environmental Ethic." In Copeland and Hatch 1988.

Engel, J. Ronald, and Joan Gibb Engel, eds. 1990. *Ethics of Environment and Development: Global Challenge, International Response*. Tucson, AZ: University of Arizona Press.

Engel, J. Ronald, Peter Bakken, and Joan Gibb Engel. 1995. *Ecology, Justice and Christian Faith: A Critical Guide to the Literature*. Westport, CT: Greenwood Publishing Group.

Eschweiler, Ed. 1993. *Opening the Gift*. Milwaukee: HI-TIME Publishing Corp.

Evans, Alice F., Robert A. Evans, and William B. Kennedy. 1987. *Pedagogies for the Non-Poor*. Maryknoll, NY: Orbis Books.

_____. 1993. *The Globalization of Theological Education*. Maryknoll, NY: Orbis Books.

Evans, Bernard, and Gregory D. Cusack, eds. 1987. *Theology of the Land*. Collegeville, MN: Liturgical Press.

Fackre, Gabriel. 1993. "The Recent Surge in Systematics: A Commentary on Current Works." *Journal of Religion* 3:3 (April).

Farley, Edward. 1983. "Theology and Practice outside the Clerical Paradigm." In Browning 1983, 21-41.

_____. 1983b. *Theologia: The Fragmentation and Unity of Theological Education*. Philadelphia. Fortress Press.

Ferguson, Olander, et al., eds. 1990. *Discourses: Conversations in Postmodern Art and Culture*. New York: Massachusetts Institute of Technology and the New Museum of Contemporary Art.

Ferré, Frederick. 1976. *Shaping the Future: Resources for the Post-Modern World*. New York: Harper & Row.

Filippi, Linda. 1991. "Place, Feminism, and Healing: An Ecology of Pastoral Counseling." *Journal of Pastoral Care* 45, no. 3 (Fall), 231-42.

Flight, John W. 1923. "The Nomadic Idea and Ideal in the Old Testament," *JBL* 42. 158-226.

Fowler, Robert Booth. 1995. *The Greening of Protestant Thought*. Chapel Hill: University of North Carolina Press.

Fox, Matthew. 1983. *Original Blessing: A Primer in Creation Spirituality Presented in Four Paths, Twenty-Six Themes, and Two Questions*. Santa Fe: Bear & Co.

_____. 1984. "Creation-Centered Spirituality from Hildegard of Bingen to Julian of Norwich: 300 Years of Ecological Spirituality in the West." In Joranson and Butigan 1984.

_____. 1988. *The Coming of the Cosmic Christ: The Healing of Mother Earth and the Birth of a Global Renaissance*. San Francisco: Harper & Row.

_____. 1994. *The Reinvention of Work: A New Vision of Livelihood for Our Time*. San Francisco: HarperCollins.

Frankfort, H., H.A. Frankfort, et al. 1949. *Before Philosophy: The Intellectual Adventure of Ancient Man*. New York: Penguin Books.

Frankfort, Henri, H. A. Frankfort, John A. Wilson, Thorkild Jacobsen, and William A. Irwin. 1977 <1946>. *The Intellectual Adventure of Ancient Man: An Essay on Speculative Thought in the Ancient Near East*. Chicago: University of Chicago Press.

Freire, Paulo. 1970. *Pedagogy of the Oppressed*. New York: Seabury.

_____. 1985. *The Politics of Education: Culture, Power, and Liberation*. South Hadley, MA: Bergin & Garvey.

Fretheim, Terence E. 1984. *The Suffering of God: An Old Testament Perspective*. Overtures to Biblical Theology. Philadelphia: Fortress Press.

_____. 1987. "Nature's Praise of God in the Psalms." *Ex Auditu* 3:16-30.

_____. 1991a. "The Plagues as Ecological Signs of Historical Disaster." *JBL* 110(3):385-96.

_____. 1991b. "The Reclamation of Creation: Redemption and Law in Exodus." *Int* 45 (October):354-65.

_____. 1992. "Creator, Creature, and Co-creation in Genesis 1-2." In Hultgren, Juel, and Kingsbury 1992, 11-20.

Freyne, Sean. 1980. *Galilee from Alexander the Great to Hadrian, 323 B.C.E. to 135 C.E.* University of Notre Dame Center for the Study of Judaism and Christianity in Antiquity, no. 5. Wilmington, DE; Notre Dame, IN: Michael Glazier; University of Notre Dame Press.

_____. 1988. *Galilee, Jesus and the Gospels: Literary Approaches and Historical Investigations*. Dublin: Gill & Macmillan.

Fritsch, Albert J. 1987. *Renew the Face of the Earth*. Chicago: Loyola University Press.

Frymer-Kensky, Tikva. 1992. *In the Wake of the Goddesses: Women, Culture, and the Biblical Transformation of Pagan Myth*. New York: Fawcett Columbine, Ballantine Books.

Fuller, Robert. 1992. *Ecology of Care*. Louisville: Westminster/John Knox Press.

Gaard, Greta. 1993. *Ecofeminism: Women, Animals, Nature*. Philadelphia: Temple University Press.

Gebara, Ivone. 1993. "The Face of Transcendence as a Challenge to the Reading of the Bible in Latin America." In Schüssler Fiorenza 1993.

Gedicks, Al. 1993. *The New Resource Wars: Native and Environmental Struggles Against Multinational Corporations*. Boston: South End Press.

Gendler, Everett. 1971. "On the Judaism of Nature." In Sleeper and Mintz 1971. For a restatement of his views, see also "The Earth's Covenant." *The Reconstructionist* (November–December 1989).

Gibson, William E. 1977. "The Lifestyle of Christian Faithfulness," in Hessel 1977, 111-40.

_____. 1990. "Call to Restore Creation." In *Restoring Creation for Ecology and Justice*. Adopted by the 202nd General Assembly of the Presbyterian Church, U.S.A. Louisville: Office of the General Assembly.

_____ 1994. "Restoring Creation—Interpreting the Presbyterian Eco-Justice Statement." Unpublished paper presented to "Down to Earth Theology" Conference, Dubuque, Iowa.

Gibson, William E., ed. 1979. *A Covenant Group for Lifestyle Assessment*. Ithaca: Eco-Justice Project.

Gilkey, Langdon. 1974. "The Theological Understanding of Humanity and Nature in a Technological Era." *Anticipation* 19 (November), 33-35.

_____. 1992. "Power, Order, Justice, and Redemption: Theological Reflections on Job." In Perdue and Gilpin 1992, 159-71.

_____. 1993. *Nature, Reality, and the Sacred: The Nexus of Science and Religion*. Minneapolis: Fortress Press.

Gnanadason, Aruna. 1994. "Women, Economy and Ecology." In Hallman 1994, 179-85.

Granberg-Michaelson, Wesley. 1992. *Redeeming the Creation*. Geneva: WCC Publications.

Goetz, Ronald. 1987. "Cosmic Groanings." *Christian Century* 104 (2 December):1083-87.

Goldman, Benjamin A., and Laura Fitton. 1994. *Toxic Wastes and Race Revisited: An Update of the 1987 Report on the Racial and Socioeconomic Characteristics of Communities with Hazardous Waste Sites.* Washington, D.C.: Center for Policy Alternatives.

Golliher, Jeff. 1994. *Religious News Service News Reports* (July 8).

Goodland, Robert. 1992. "The Case That the World Has Reached Limits." In Daly, Goodland, and Serafy 1992.

Gordis, Robert. 1965. *The Book of God and Man: A Study of Job.* Chicago: University of Chicago Press.

_____. 1985. "Job and Ecology (and the Significance of Job 40:15)." *HUCA* 9:189-202.

Gore, Albert. 1992. *Earth in the Balance: Ecology and the Human Spirit.* Boston: Houghton Mifflin.

Gorrie, Peter. 1990. "The James Bay Power Project." *Canadian Geographic* (February-March), 21-31.

Gottlieb, Robert. 1993. *Forcing the Spring: The Transformation of the American Environmental Movement.* Washington, D.C.: Island Press.

Gould, Stephen Jay. 1988. *Time's Arrow, Time's Cycle: Myth and Metaphor in the Discovery of Geological Time.* London: Penguin Books.

Graham, Larry Kent. 1991. "Care of Persons, Care of the World." *Pastoral Psychology* 40 (Spring), 15-28.

Granberg-Michaelson, Wesley. 1984. *A Worldly Spirituality: The Call to Redeem Life on Earth.* San Francisco: Harper & Row.

_____. 1992. *Redeeming the Creation.* Geneva: WCC Publications.

Granberg-Michaelson, Wesley, ed. 1987. *Tending the Garden: Essays on the Gospel and the Earth.* Grand Rapids, MI: Eerdmans Publishing Company.

Gray, Elizabeth Dodson. 1981. *Green Paradise Lost: Formerly Why the Green Nigger?* Wellesley, MA: Roundtable Press.

_____. 1984. *Patriarchy as a Conceptual Trap.* Wellesley, MA: Roundtable Press.

_____. 1985. "A Critique of Dominion Theology." In Hessel 1985, 71-83.

Gregorios, Paulos Mar. 1978. *The Human Presence: An Othodox View of Nature.* Geneva: WCC Publications.

_____. 1987. "New Testament Foundations for Understanding the Creation." In Granberg-Michaelson 1987, 83-92.

Green, Arthur. 1992. *Seek My Face, Speak My Name: A Contemporary Jewish Theology.* Northvale, NJ: J. Aronson Press.

Green, Elizabeth. 1993. "The Transmutation of Theology: Ecofeminist Alchemy and the Christian Tradition." Unpublished paper.

Green, Ronald Michael. 1976. *Population Growth and Justice: An Examination of Moral Issues Raised by Population Growth.* Missoula, MT: Scholars Press for Harvard Theological Review.

Griffin, David Ray, ed. 1988. *The Reenchantment of Science.* Albany: State University of New York Press.

Griffin, Susan. 1978. *Women and Nature: The Roaring Inside Her.* New York: Harper & Row.

Grossman, Zoltan, and Al Gedick. 1994. "Exxon Returns to Wisconsin: The Threat of the Crandon/Mole Lake Mine." *Dark Night Field Notes* 1 (Summer): 15-18.

Gurr, Ted Robert, and James R. Scarritt. 1989. "Minorities Rights at Risk: A Global Survey." *Human Rights Quarterly* 11: 375-405.

Gustafson, James. 1981. *Theology and Ethics.* Vol. 1 of *Ethics from a Theocentric Perspective.* Chicago: University of Chicago Press.

_____. 1983. "Ethical Issues in the Human Future." In Ortner 1983, 491-516.

_____. 1984. *Ethics and Theology*. Vol. 2 of *Ethics from a Theocentric Perspective*. Chicago: University of Chicago Press.

_____. 1984b. "Population and Nutrition." In Gustafson 1984.

Gutiérrez, Gustavo. 1988 <1973>. *A Theology of Liberation: History, Politics, and Salvation*. Rev. ed. Trans. Sister Caridad Inda and John Eagleson. Maryknoll, NY: Orbis Books.

Habel, Norman C. 1971. *Literary Criticism of the Old Testament*. Guides to Biblical Scholarship. Philadelphia: Fortress Press.

Halkes, Catharina J.M. 1989. *New Creation: Christian Feminism and the Renewal of the Earth*. Louisville: Westminster/John Knox Press.

Hall, Douglas John. 1986. *Imaging God: Dominion As Stewardship*. Grand Rapids: Eerdmans Publishing Company.

_____. 1990 <New York: Friendship Press, 1982>. *The Steward: A Biblical Symbol Come of Age*. Rev. ed. Grand Rapids, MI: Eerdmans Publishing Company.

Hallman, David, ed. 1994. *Ecotheology*. Geneva: WCC Publications; Maryknoll, NY: Orbis Books.

Haney, Eleanor Humes. 1989. *Vision and Struggle: Mediation on Feminist Spirituality and Politics*. Portland, ME: Astarte Shell Press.

Hanson, P. D. 1986. *The People Called: The Growth of Community in the Bible*. San Francisco: Harper & Row.

_____. 1987. *Old Testament Apocalyptic*. Nashville: Abingdon.

Harcourt, Wendy, ed. 1994. *Feminist Perspectives on Sustainable Development*. London: Zed Books.

Hardin, Garrett. 1989. "There Is No Global Population Problem." *The Humanist* 49 (July/August).

Hareuveni, Nogah. 1974. *Ecology in the Bible*. In association with Helen Frenkley. Kiryat Ono, Israel: Neot Kedumim.

_____. 1980. *Nature in Our Biblical Heritage*. Trans. Helen Frenkley. Kiryat Ono, Israel: Neot Kedumim.

_____. 1984. *Tree and Shrub in Our Biblical Heritage*. Trans. Helen Frenkley. Kiryat Ono, Israel: Neot Kedumim.

Harrelson, Walter J. 1969. *From Fertility Cult to Worship*. Garden City, NY: Doubleday.

Harrison, Beverly, ed., with Carol Robb. 1985. *Making the Connections*. "Theological Reflection in the Struggle for Liberation."

Harrison, Paul. 1992. *The Third Revolution: Environment, Population, and a Sustainable World*. London: I.B. Tauris & Co.

Hart, John. 1984. *The Spirit of the Earth: A Theology of the Land*. Mahwah, NJ: Paulist Press.

_____. 1987. "Land, Theology and the Future." In Evans and Cusack 1987.

_____. 1994. "Church Teachings on Environmental Responsibility." Unpublished paper presented to "Down to Earth Theology" Conference, Dubuque, Iowa.

Harvey, David. 1989. *The Condition of Postmodernity*. Oxford: Basil Blackworth.

Haught, John F. 1993. *The Promise of Nature: Ecology and Human Purpose*. Mahwah, NJ: Paulist Press.

Hecky, Robert. 1978. "Methylmercury Contamination in Northern Canada." *Northern Perspective*. (October)

Hedstrom, Ingemar. 1990. "Latin America and the Need for a Life-Liberating Theology." In Birch, et al. 1990.

Hefner, Philip. 1993. *The Human Factor: Evolution, Culture, and Religion*. Minneapolis: Fortress Press.

Hegel, G.W.F. 1962. *Lectures on the Philosophy of Religion*. Trans. E. B. Speirs and J. Burdon-Sanderson. 3 vols. London: Routledge and Kegan Paul.

Hermisson, Hans-Jergen. 1984. "Observations on the Creation Theology in Wisdom." In Anderson 1984b, 118-34.

Hessel, Dieter T. 1985. *For Creation's Sake: Preaching, Ecology and Justice*. Philadelphia: The Geneva Press.

_____. 1992. *After Nature's Revolt: Eco-justice and Theology*. Minneapolis: Fortress Press.

_____. 1995. "Christianity in the World Today." In Beversluis 1995, 25-28.

Hessel, Dieter T., ed. 1977. *Beyond Survival: Bread and Justice in Christian Perspective*. New York: Friendship Press.

_____. 1979. *Energy Ethics: A Christian Response*. New York: Friendship Press.

_____, ed. 1985. *For Creation's Sake: Preaching, Ecology, and Justice*. Philadelphia: Geneva Press.

Hiebert, Theodore. 1986. *God of My Victory: The Ancient Hymn in Habakkuk 3*. Harvard Semitic monographs, no. 38. Atlanta: Scholars Press.

_____. 1989. "Ecology and the Bible." Harvard Divinity Bulletin 19(3):2-4.

_____. 1990-1. "The Quest for the Historical J: The State of the Search." Harvard Divinity Bulletin 20(4):18-19.

_____. 1992. "Theophany in the OT." In The Anchor Bible Dictionary. D. N. Freedman, et al., eds. New York: Doubleday. 505-11.

_____. 1993. "Nature and Ecology." In The Oxford Companion to the Bible. Ed. B. Metzger and M. D. Coogan. New York: Oxford University Press.

_____. In press. *The Yahwist's Landscape: Nature and Religion in Early Israel*. New York: Oxford University Press.

Hiers, Richard H. 1984. "Ecology, Biblical Theology, and Methodology: Biblical Perspectives on the Environment." *Zygon* 19:43-59.

Hinsdale, Mary Ann. 1990. "Some Implications of Ecofeminism for Christian Anthropology and Spirituality." Paper delivered at the College Theology Teaching Workshop, New Orleans. May 30.

_____. 1991. "Ecology, Feminism and Theology." *Word and World* 11:2, 156-64.

Hoffman, Pat. 1987. *Ministry of the Dispossessed: Learning from the Farm Worker Movement*. Wallace Press.

Holland, Joe, and Peter Henriot. 1983. *Social Analysis: Linking Faith with Justice*. Maryknoll, NY: Orbis Books.

Homer-Dixon, Thomas Fraser. 1994. "On the Threshold: Environmental Changes as Causes of Acute Conflict." As reported by Kaplan 1994.

Hooks, Bell. 1989. *Talking Back: Thinking Feminist, Thinking Black*. Boston: South End Press.

Hopkins, D. C. 1985. *The Highlands of Canaan: Agricultural Life in the Early Iron Age*. The Social World of Biblical Antiquity. Sheffield, Eng.: JSOT Press <Almond>.

_____. 1987. "Life on the Land: The Subsistence Struggles of Early Israel." *BA* 50 (September):178-91.

Horrell, Dana K. 1993. *Reclaiming the Covenant: The Eco-Justice Movement as Practical Theology*. 2 vols. Dissertation. University of Chicago.

Howard, George S. 1993. "Impaled Upon the Horns of Faith and Reason." *America* (March 6):12-15.

Huber, Wolfgang. 1991. "Rights of Nature or Dignity of Nature?" *Annual of the Society of Christian Ethics*: 43-60.

Hughes, J. Donald. 1983. *American Indian Ecology*. El Paso: Texas Western Press.

Hull, Fritz, ed. 1993. *Earth and Spirit: The Spiritual Dimension of the Environmental Crisis*. New York: Continuum.

Hultgren, Arland J., Donald H. Juel, and Jack D. Kingsbury, eds. *All Things New: Essays in Honor of Roy A. Harrisville*. Word and World Supplement Series. St. Paul, MN: Word & World, Luther Northwestern Theological Seminary.

Huntington, Samuel P. 1993. "The Clash of Civilizations?" *Foreign Affairs* 72:3.

Hynes, H. Patricia. 1993. *Taking Population Out of the Equation: Reformulating I=PAT*. North Amherst, MA: Institute on Women and Technology.

Hyun, Kyung Chung. 1991. "Come Holy Spirit Come, Renew the Whole Creation." *The Woman's Pulpit* (July-September 4-7).

_____. 1994. "Ecology, Feminism and African and Asian Spirituality: Towards a Spirituality of Eco-Feminism." In Hallman 1994, 175-78.

Inter Press Service Third World News Agency. 1993. *Story Earth: Native Voices on the Environment*. Toronto: Mercury House.

Irwin, Kevin W., and Edmund D. Pelligrino, eds. 1994. *Preserving the Creation: Environmental Theology and Ethics*. Washington, D.C.: Georgetown University Press.

Israeli Ministry of Education: The Branch for Religious Culture. 1971. *Judaism in Our Modern Society* (Hebrew Publication).

Jackson, Wes. 1987. *Altars of Unhewn Stone: Science and the Earth*. San Francisco: North Point Press.

Jacobsen, Thorkild. 1976. *The Treasures of Darkness: A History of Mesopotamian Religion*. New Haven: Yale University Press.

Jantzen, Grace. 1984. *God's Body, God's World*. Philadelphia: Westminster Press.

Jegen, Mary Evelyn, and Bruno V. Manno, eds. 1978. *The Earth Is the Lord's: Essays on Stewardship*. New York: Paulist Press.

Jeremias, J. 1976. "Theophany in the OT." In The Interpreter's Dictionary of the Bible, Supplementary Volume. Ed. K. Crim. Nashville: Abingdon.

John Paul II. 1981. *Laborem excercens* ("On Human Labor").

_____. 1987. *Sollicitudo Rei Socialis* ("Concern for Social Matters"). *CNS Documentary Service* 17, no. 3 (March 3).

_____. 1989. *Peace with All Creation*. CNS Documentary Service 19, no. 20 (December 14).

Johnson, Elizabeth A. 1993. *She Who Is: The Mystery of God in Feminist Theological Discourse*. New York: Crossroad.

_____. 1993b. *Women, Earth and Creator Spirit*. New York: Paulist Press.

Joranson, Philip N., and Ken Butigan, eds. 1984. *Cry of the Environment: Rebuilding the Creation Tradition*. Santa Fe: Bear & Co.

Julian of Norwich. 1977. *Revelations of Divine Love*. Garden City, N.Y.: Image.

Jung, Shannon. 1990. "The Recovery of the Land: Agribusiness and Creation-Centered Spirituality." In Sherill 1990.

_____. 1993. *We Are Home: A Spirituality of the Environment*. Mahwah, NJ: Paulist Press.

Kane, Joe. 1993. "With Spears From All Sides." *New Yorker* (September 27):54-79.

Kaplan. Robert D. 1994. "The Coming Anarchy," *The Atlantic Monthly* (February 4).

Karakashian, Steven, and Jon Collett, eds. 1994. *Learning to Think About Conservation: A Multidisciplinary Guide for College Teachers*. Washington, D.C.: Island Press.

Kaufman, Gordon D. 1972. "A Problem for Theology: The Concept of Nature." *HTR* 65:337-66.

_____. 1993. *In Face of Mystery*. Cambridge: Harvard University Press.

Kaufman, Yehezkiel. 1960. *The Religion of Israel*. Chicago: University of Chicago Press.

Kay, Jeanne. 1988. "Concepts of Nature in the Hebrew Bible." *Environmental Ethics* 10 (Winter):309-27.

_____ . 1989. "Human Dominion Over Nature in the Hebrew Bible." *Annals of the Association of American Geographers* 79(2):214-32.

Keck, Leander E., et al., eds. 1994. *New Interpreter's Bible*. Nashville: Abingdon.

Keller, Catherine. 1990. "Women Against Wasting the World: Notes on Eschatology and Ecology." In Diamond and Orenstein 1990, 249-63.

_____ . 1993. "Talking About the Weather: The Greening of Eschatology." In Adams 1993.

_____ . Forthcoming. *Apocalypse Now and Then: A Feminist Approach to the End of the World*. Boston: Beacon Press.

Kennedy, Paul. 1993. *Preparing for the Twenty-First Century*. New York: Random House.

Khalid, Fazlun, and Joanne O'Brien, eds. 1992. *Islam and Ecology*. London and New York: Cassell Publishers Limited/World Wide Fund for Nature.

Khazanov, Anatoly. 1983. *Nomads and the Outside World*. Trans. Julia Crookenden. Cambridge: Cambridge University.

Kheel, Marti. 1991. "Ecofeminism and Deep Ecology: Reflections on Identity and Difference." In Robb and Casebolt 1991b.

Kim, Yong Bock. 1979. "The Sustainable Society: An Asian Perspective." *Ecumenical Review* 31 (April): 169-78.

King, Martin Luther, Jr. 1967. "A Time to Break Silence." *The Trumpet of Conscience*. New York: Harper & Row.

King, Ursula. 1987. *Women in the World's Religions*. New York: Paragon House.

_____ , ed. 1994. *Feminist Theology from the Third World: A Reader*. Maryknoll, NY: Orbis Books.

Kinsley, David. Forthcoming. *Ecology and Religion: Ecological Spirituality in Cross-Cultural Perspective*. Prentice Hall.

Kirschenmann, Frederick. 1991. "The Ecology-economy-ethic Connection in Land Use." In Robb and Casebolt 1991b, 78-90.

Kispert, Robert C.N. Forthcoming. "Alienation and Nature: A Practical-Theological Analysis of the Resource Conservation and Wilderness Preservation Pieties in American Civil Religion." Dissertation. University of Chicago.

Kissling, Frances. 1994. "Theo-Politics: The Roman Catholic Church and Population Policy." In Mazur 1994.

Knierim, Rolf. 1981. "Cosmos and History in Israel's Theology." *Horizons in Biblical Theology* 3:59-123.

Koch, Klaus. 1979. "The Old Testament View of Nature." *Anticipation* 25 (January):47-52.

Kohn, David, ed. 1985. *The Darwinian Heritage*. Princeton: Princeton University Press.

Kristeva, Julia. 1990. Interview with Alice Jardine. In Ferguson, et al. 1990.

Küng, Hans. 1993. *Global Responsibility: In Search of a New World Ethic*. New York: Continuum.

Kwok, Pui-lan. 1991. "Ecology and the Recycling of Christianity." *Ecumenical Review* 44:3 (July).

LaChance, Albert J., and John E. Carroll, eds. 1994. *Embracing Ecology: Catholic Approaches to Ecology*. Maryknoll, NY: Orbis Books.

LaDuke, Winona. 1993. "Foreword: A Society Based on Conquest Cannot Be Sustained." In Gedicks 1993.

Lamm, Norman. 1972a. "Ecology and Jewish Law and Theology." In Lamm 1972b.

Lamm, Norman, ed. 1972b. *Faith and Doubt*. New York: Ktav.

Lane, Belden C. 1991. "The Tree as Giver of Life: A Metaphor in Pastoral Care." *Journal of Pastoral Care* 45, no. 1, 15-22.

Lasch, Christopher. 1991. *The True and Only Heaven: Progress and Its Critics*. New York: W.W. Norton & Co.

Lauretis, de, Teresa. 1986. *Feminist Studies/Critical Studies*. Bloomington: Indiana University Press.

La Vergata, Antonello. 1985. "Images of Darwin: A Historiographic Overview." In Kohn 1985, 958–62.

Leonard, H. Jeffrey, et al. 1989. *Environment and the Poor: Development Strategies for a Common Agenda*. New Brunswick: Transaction Books.

Levenson, Jon D. 1985. *Sinai and Zion: An Entry Into the Jewish Bible*. San Francisco: Harper & Row.

Lichtenstein, Aharon. 1971. "Man and Nature: Social Aspects." In Israeli Ministry of Education 1971.

Lindqvist, Martti. 1975. *Economic Growth and the Quality of Life: An Analysis of the Debate within the World Coundil of Churches, 1966-1974*. Annals of the Finnish Society for Missiology and Ecumenics 27. Helsinki: The Finnish Society for Missiology and Ecumenics.

Linzey, Andrew. 1976. *Animal Rights: A Christian Assessment*. London: SCM Press.

_____. 1987. *Christianity and the Rights of Animals*. London: SPCK; New York: Crossroad.

_____. 1994. *Animal Theology*. London: SCM Press.

Linzey, Andrew, and Tom Regan, eds. 1990. *Animals and Christianity: A Book of Readings*. New York: Crossroad.

Lonergan, Anne, and Caroline Richards, eds. 1987. *Thomas Berry and the New Cosmology*. Mystic, CT: Twenty-Third Publications.

Long, Ed. 1985. *Academic Bonding and Social Concern: The Society of Christian Ethics, 1959-1983*. Religious Ethics Inc.

Lorde, Audre. 1984. "Age, Race, Class, and Sex: Women Redefining Difference." In Lorde 1984b.

_____. 1984b. *Sister Outsider*. Trumansburg: The Crossing Press.

Lovelock, James. 1990. *The Ages of Gaia: A Biography of Our Living Earth*. New York: Bantam Books.

Macy, Joanna. 1983. *Despair and Personal Power in the Nuclear Age*. Philadelphia: New Society Publishers.

MacNeill, Jim, et al. 1991. *Beyond Interdependence: The Meshing of the World's Economy and the Earth's Ecology*. New York: Oxford University Press.

Maguire, Daniel. 1993. *The Moral Core of Judaism and Christianity: Reclaiming the Revolution*. Minneapolis: Augsburg Fortress.

_____. 1993b. "Poverty, Population, and the Catholic Tradition." In the Religious Consultation on Population, Reproductive Health, and Ethics 1993.

MAPS (Multi-faith AIDS Project of Seattle) newsletter. 1994 (September).

Martin-Schramm, James B. Forthcoming. "Population, Consumption, and Ecojustice: Challenges for Christian Conceptions of Environmental Ethics." Dissertation. Union Theological Seminary.

Marty, Martin E. 1982. "America's Iconic Book." In Tucker and Knight 1982, 1-23.

Marx, Emmanuel. 1992. "Are There Pastoral Nomads in the Middle East." In BarYosef and Khazanov 1992.

Mathews, Jessica Tuchman. 1991. *Preserving the Global Environment: The Challenge of Shared Leadership*. New York: W.W. Norton & Co.

Mazur, Laurie, ed. 1994. *Beyond the Numbers: A Reader on Population, Consumption, and the Environment*. Washington, DC: Island Press.

McCutcheon, Sean. 1991. *Electric Rivers: The Story of the James Bay Project*. Montreal: Black Rose Books.

McDaniel, Jay B. 1989. *Of God and Pelicans: A Theology of Reverence for Life*. Louisville: Westminster/John Knox Press.

_____. 1990. *Earth, Sky, Gods and Mortals: Developing an Ecological Spirituality*. Mystic, CT: Twenty-Third Publications.

_____. 1992. "Green Grace." *Earth Ethics* (Summer).

_____. 1994. "Images of God and Earth." Unpublished paper given at Meadowcreek Center, Arkansas (January).

_____. 1995. *With Roots and Wings*. Maryknoll, NY: Orbis Books.

McDonagh, Sean. 1984. *Passion for the Earth*. Maryknoll, NY: Orbis Books.

_____. 1987. *To Care for the Earth: A Call to a New Theology*. Santa Fe: Bear & Co.

_____. 1990. *The Greening of the Church*. Maryknoll, NY: Orbis Books.

_____. 1994. *Passion for the Earth*. Maryknoll, NY: Orbis Books.

McFague, Sallie. 1987. *Models of God: Theology for an Ecological, Nuclear Age*. Minneapolis: Fortress Press.

_____. 1993. *The Body of God: An Ecological Theology*. Minneapolis: Fortress Press.

_____. 1993b. "An Earthly Theological Agenda." In Adams 1993.

McKibben, Bill. 1994. *The Comforting Whirlwind: God, Job, and the Scale of Creation*. Grand Rapids, MI: Eerdmans Publishing Company.

Meadows, Donella H. 1992. "Population, Poverty, and Planet Earth." *Earth Ethics* 4:1.

_____. 1994. "Herman Daly's World Bank 'For the Common(s) Good.'" *EarthLight* (SummerFall):4.

Meeks, M. Douglas. 1985. "God and Land." *Agriculture and Human Values* 2:16-27.

Mellor, Mary. 1992. *Breaking the Boundaries: Towards a Feminist Green Socialism*. London: Virago Press.

Merchant, Carolyn. 1982. *The Death of Nature: Women, Ecology and the Scientific Revolution*. New York: Harper & Row.

_____. 1992. *Radical Ecology: The Search for a Livable World*. New York: Routledge.

_____, ed. 1994. *Ecology: Key Concepts in Critical Theory*. New Jersey: Humanities Press.

Midgley, Mary. 1992. *Science as Salvation*. London: Routledge.

Mies, Maria, and Vandana Shiva. 1993. *Ecofeminism*. New Jersey: Zed Books.

Miller, Donald. 1979. "The Biblical Basis for Ecology." *Brethren Life and Thought* 24:12-17.

Mische, Partricia M. 1978. "Parenting in a Hungry World." In Jegen and Manno 1978, 169-83.

Moltmann, Jürgen. 1979. *The Future of Creation*. Trans. Margaret Kohl. Philadelphia: Fortress Press.

_____. 1985. *God in Creation: An Ecological Doctrine of Creation*. Gifford Lectures 1984-85. London: SCM.

_____. 1985b. *God in Creation: A New Theology of Creation and the Spirit of God*. San Francisco: Harper & Row.

Moody, Robert, ed. 1993. *The Indigenous Voice: Visions and Realities*. Utrecht: International Books.

Morton, James Park. 1992. *The Rene Dubos Consortium for Sacred Ecology*. New York: Cathedral of St. John the Divine.

Morton, Nelle. 1985. *The Journey Is Home*. Boston: Beacon Press.

Moyers, Bill. 1990. *Spirit and Nature*. Film. Middlebury Conference on Religion and the Environment.

Mugambi, J.N.K. 1987. *God, Humanity and Nature in Relation to Justice and Peace*. Church and Society Documents, no. 2 (September). Geneva: WCC Publications.

Murphy, Nordan, ed. 1985. *Teaching and Preaching Stewardship: An Anthology*. New York: National Council of Churches, U.S.A.

Murray, Robert. 1992. *The Cosmic Covenant: Biblical Themes of Justice, Peace and the Integrity of Creation*. Heythrop Monographs. London: Sheed & Ward <Heythrop Monograph>.

Nash, James A. 1991. *Loving Nature: Ecological Integrity and Christian Responsibility*. Nashville: Abingdon Press.

_____ . 1992. "Human Rights and the Environment: New Challenge for Ethics." *Theology and Public Policy* 4:2.

_____ . 1993. "Biotic Rights and Human Ecological Responsibilities." *Annual of the Society of Christian Ethics*.

_____ . 1994. "Ethics and the Economics-Ecology Dilemma: Toward a Just, Sustainable, and Frugal Future." *Theology and Public Policy* (Summer).

Nash, Roderick F. 1989. *The Rights of Nature: A History of Environmental Ethics*. Madison: University of Wisconsin Press.

National Conference of Catholic Bishops. 1986. *Economic Justice for All: Pastoral Letter on Catholic Social Teaching and the U.S. Economy*. Washington, DC: United States Catholic Conference.

Newsom, Carol A. 1994. "The Moral Sense of Nature: Ethics in the Light of God's Speech to Job." The Princeton Seminary Bulletin n.s. 15(1):9-27.

Nicholson, Linda J., ed. 1990. *Feminism/Postmodernism*. New York: Routledge.

Niebuhr, Richard R. 1993. "Cosmic Patriotism." *Religion and Values in Public Life* 2 (Fall):12.

Niles, Preman. 1987. "Covenanting for Justice, Peace, and the Integrity of Creation: An Ecumenical Survey." *The Ecumenical Review* 39:470-84.

_____ , ed. 1992a. *Between the Flood and the Rainbow: Interpreting the Conciliar Process of Mutual Commitment (Covenant) to Justice, Peace, and the Integrity of Creation*. Geneva: WCC Publications.

_____ . 1992b. *Resisting the Threats to Life*. Risk Book Series. Geneva: WCC Publications.

Nystrom, Samuel. 1946. *Beduinentum und Jahwismus: Eine soziologische-religionsgeschichtliche Unterzuchung zum Alten Testament*. Lund: C.W.K. Gleerup.

O'Connor, John. 1994. *Religious News Service News Reports* (July 8).

Oduyoye, Mercy Amba. 1986. *Hearing and Knowing: Theological Reflections on Christianity in Africa*. Maryknoll, NY: Orbis Books.

Oelschlaeger, Max. 1995. *Caring for Creation: An Ecumenical Approach to the Environmental Crisis*. New Haven: Yale University Press.

Ortner, Donald J., ed. 1983. *How Humans Adapt: A Biocultural Odyssey*. Smithsonian International Symposia Series. Washington: Smithsonian Institution Press.

Owens, Owen D. 1974. "Salvation and Ecology: Missionary Imperatives in Light of a New Cosmology." *Foundations* 17 (April-June), 106-23.

Pannenberg, Wolfhart. 1993. *Towards a Theology of Nature: Essays on Science and Faith*. Ed. Ted Peters. Louisville: Westminster/John Knox Press.

Pattison, John. 1993. *Pastoral Care and Liberation Theology*. New York: Cambridge University Press.

Patton, John. 1993. *Pastoral Care in Context*. Louisville: Westminster/John Knox Press.

Pedersen, J. 1953. *Israel: Its Life and Its Culture*. Vols. 1 and 2. London: Oxford University Press.

Peeters, Denise. 1993. "Towards an Ecologically Informed Theology." *Theology Digest* 40:2.

Penn, James. 1975. "Development of James Bay: The Role of Environmental Assessment in Determining the Legal Rights to an Interlocutory Injunction." *Journal of Fisheries Research Board of Canada* 32.

Perdue, Leo G. 1987. "Job's Assault on Creation." Bibliography. *Hebrew Annual Review* 10:295-315.

Perdue, Leo G., and Clark W. Gilpin, eds. 1992. *The Voice from the Whirlwind.* Nashville: Abingdon Press.

Pitcher, Alvin. 1979. "Energy as a Moral and Religious Issue." In Hessel 1979, 33-55.

_____. 1993. *Listen to the Crying of the Earth: Cultivating Creation Communities.* Cleveland: Pilgrim Press.

Plant, Judith. 1989. *Healing the Wounds: The Promise of Ecofeminism.* Philadelphia: New Society Publishers.

Plaskow, Judith. 1990. *Standing Again at Sinai: Judaism from a Feminist Perspective.* San Francisco: Harper & Row.

Plumewood, Val. 1993. *Feminism and the Mastery of Nature.* London: Routledge.

Pobee, John S. 1985. "Creation Faith and Responsibility for the World." *Journal for Theology for South Africa* 50:16-26.

Pois, Robert A. 1986. *National Socialism and the Religion of Nature.* London: Croon Helm.

Polkinghorne, John. 1989. *Science and Providence: God's Interaction with the World.* Boston: New Science Library.

Prance, Ghillean T. 1992. "The Ecological Awareness of the Amazonian Indians." In DeWitt and Prance 1992.

Presbyterian Eco-Justice Task Force, Committee on Social Witness Policy, Presbyterian Church (U.S.A.). 1989. *Keeping and Healing the Creation.* Louisville: Committee on Social Witness Policy, Presbyterian Church (U.S.A.).

Primavesi, Anne. 1991. *From Apocalypse to Genesis: Ecology, Feminism and Christianity.* Minneapolis: Fortress Press.

_____. 1993. "The Wisdom Tree." Unpublished manuscript.

_____. 1993b. "A Post-Rio Perspective on Militarism." *Theology in Green* 8:20-26.

_____. 1994. "A Tide in the Affairs of Women." In Hallman 1994.

Prime, Ranchor, ed. 1992. *Hinduism and Ecology.* London and New York: Cassell Publishers Limited/World Wide Fund for Nature.

Propp, William Henry. 1987. *Water in the Wilderness: A Biblical Motif and Its Mythological Background.* Atlanta: Scholars Press.

Przewozny, Bernard. 1987. "Elements of a Catholic Doctrine of Humankind's Relation to the Environment." *Miscellanea Francescana* 87.

_____. 1988. "Integrity of Creation: A Missionary Imperative." *Sedos Bulletin* 11 (December 15), 363-74.

Rad, Gerhard von. 1962. *Old Testament Theology.* Vol. 1. Trans D.M.G. Stalker. New York: Harper & Row.

_____. 1966a. "Some Aspects of the Old Testament World-view." In *The Problem of the Hexateuch and Other Essays.* Trans E.W.T. Dicken, 144-65. New York: McGraw-Hill Book Company.

_____. 1966b. "The Theological Problem of the Doctrine of Creation." Trans. E.W.T. Dicken. In *The Problem of the Hexateuch and Other Essays.* London: SCM.

_____. 1972. *Wisdom in Israel.* Nashville: Abingdon Press.

_____. 1973. *Genesis: A Commentary.* Rev. Ed. Trans. J. H. Marks. The Old Testament Library. Philadelphia: Westminster Press.

Ramphal, Shridath. 1992. *Our Country, The Planet: Forging a Partnership for Survival.* Washington, D.C.: Island Press.

Rasmussen, Larry. 1992. "Returning to Our Senses: The Theology of the Cross as a Theology for Eco-Justice." In Hessel 1992.

_____. 1992b. "Ecocrisis and Theology's Quest." *Christianity and Crisis* (March 16):83-87.

_____. 1993. *Moral Fragments and Moral Community: A Proposal for Church in Society.* Minneapolis: Augsburg Fortress.

Reese, W. L. 1980. *Dictionary of Philosophy and Religion.* Atlantic Highlands, NJ: Humanities Press.

Religious Consultation on Population, Reproductive Health, and Ethics, The. 1993. *Religious and Ethical Perspectives of Population Issues.* Washington, D.C.

Ress, Mary. 1993. "Cosmic Theology: Ecofeminism and Panentheism: Interview of Ivone Gebara." *Creation Spirituality* (November/December):9-11.

Richardson, Boyce. 1991. *Strangers Devour the Land: The Cree Hunters of the James Bay Area Vs. Premier Bourassa and the James Bay Development Corporation.* Post Mills, VT: Chelsea Green.

Riley, Shamara Shantu. "Ecology is a Sistah's Issue Too: The Politics of Emergent Afrocentric Ecowomanism." In Adams 1993, 191-204.

Robb, Carol, ed., with Beverly W. Harrison. 1985. *Making the Connections: Essays in Feminist Social Ethics.* Boston: Beacon Press.

Robb, Carol S., and C. J. Casebolt. 1991a. "Introduction." In Robb and Casebolt 1991b, 1-23.

Robb, Carol S., and C. J. Casebolt, eds. 1991b. *Covenant for a New Creation: Ethics, Religion, and Public Policy.* Studies in Ethics. Maryknoll, NY, and Berkeley, CA: Orbis Books; GTU.

Rockefeller, Steven. 1994. "Religion and the Ecological Conscience." In Karakashian and Collett 1994.

Rockefeller, Steven, and John Elder, eds. 1992. *Spirit and Nature: Why the Environment Is a Religious Issue: An Interfaith Dialogue.* Boston: Beacon Press.

Rolston, Holmes, III. 1987. *Science and Religion: A Critical Survey.* Philadelphia: Temple University Press.

_____. 1992. "Does Nature Need to Be Redeemed?" *Horizons in Biblical Theology* 14:143-72.

Rose, Aubrey, ed. 1992. *Judaism and Ecology.* London & New York: Cassell Publishers Limited/World Wide Fund for Nature.

Rosenak, Michael. 1992. "On Ways and Visions: The Theological and Educational Thought of Irving Greenberg." *The Melton Journal.* Spring.

Rubenstein, Richard L. 1966. *After Auschwitz: Radical Theology and Contemporary Judaism.* Indianapolis: Bobbs-Merrill.

Ruether, Rosemary Radford. 1972. *Liberation Theology.* New York: Paulist Press.

_____. 1973. "Governmental Coercion and One-Dimensional Thinking." In Wogaman 1973.

_____. 1974. *New Woman, New Earth: Sexist Ideologies and Human Liberation.* New York: Seabury Press.

_____. 1981. "Ecology and Human Liberation: A Conflict Between the Theology of History and the Theology of Nature." In Ruether 1981b, 57-70.

_____. 1981b. *To Change the World: Christology and Cultural Criticism.* New York: Crossroad.

_____. 1983. "Woman, Body, and Nature: Sexism and the Theology of Creation." In Ruether 1983b, 72-92.

_____. 1983b. *Sexism and Godtalk: Toward a Feminist Theology*. Boston: Beacon Press.

_____. 1985. "The Biblical Vision of the Ecological Crisis." In Murphy 1985, 206.

_____. 1991. "Women as Subjects, not Objects." *Conscience* 12:5.

_____. 1992. *Gaia and God: An Ecofeminist Theology of Earth Healing*. San Francisco: HarperCollins.

_____. 1993. "Ecofeminism: Symbolic and Social Connections Between the Oppression of Women and the Domination of Nature." In Adams 1993.

Ryan, Maura Ann. "Reflections on Population Policy from the Roman Catholic Tradition." In Mazur 1994.

Sadik, Nafis. 1993. *The State of the World Population 1993*. New York: United Nations Population Fund.

_____. 1993b. *Population Issues Briefing Kit 1993*. New York: United Nations Population Fund.

Sanchez, Carol Lee. 1993. "Animal, Vegetable, Mineral: The Sacred Connection." In Adams 1993, 207-28.

Sanders, James A. 1984. *Canon and Community: A Guide to Canonical Criticism*. Guides to Biblical Scholarship. Philadelphia: Fortress Press.

Santmire, H. Paul. 1970. *Brother Earth: Nature, God, and Ecology in a Time of Crisis*. New York: Thomas Nelson.

_____. 1976. "Ecology, Justice and Theology: Beyond the Preliminary Skirmishes." *Christian Century* 93 (12 May):460-64.

_____. 1985a. "The Liberation of Nature: Lynn White's Challenge Anew." *Christian Century* 102 (22 May):530-33.

_____. 1985b. *The Travail of Nature: The Ambiguous Ecological Promise of Christian Theology*. Philadelphia: Fortress Press.

_____. 1986. "Toward a New Theology of Nature." *Dialog* 25 (Winter):43-50.

_____. 1991. "The Genesis Creation Narratives Revisited: Themes for a Global Age." *Interpretation* 45 (October):366-79.

_____. 1992. "Healing the Protestant Mind: Beyond the Theology of Human Dominion." In Hessel 1992, 57-78.

Sarna, Nahum M. 1989. *Genesis*. The JPS Torah Commentary. Philadelphia: Jewish Publication Society.

Schaeffer, Francis A. 1970. *Pollution and the Death of Man: The Christian View of Ecology*. Wheaton, IL: Tyndale House Publisher.

Schillebeeckx, Edward. 1980. "'All is Grace': Creation and Grace in the Old and New Testaments." In *Christ: The Experience of Jesus as Lord*. Trans. John Bowden. New York: Seabury Press. 515-30.

Schleiermacher, Friedrich. 1963. *Brief Outline of the Study of Theology*. Lexington, KY: American Theological Library Association.

Schmemann, Alexander. 1963. *For the Life of the World*. New York: National Student Christian Federation.

Schmid, H. H. 1984. "Creation, Righteousness, and Salvation: 'Creation Theology' as the Broad Horizon of Biblical Theology." In Anderson 1984b, 102-17.

Schneidau, Herbert N. 1976. *Sacred Discontent: The Bible and Western Tradition*. Berkeley: University of California.

Schorsch, Ismar. 1991. "Tending to our Cosmic Oasis." *The Melton Journal*. Spring. Taken from his "The Limits of History." *Proceedings of the 1989 Rabbinical Assembly Convention*.

Schumacher, E. F. 1973. *Small Is Beautiful*. New York: Harper & Row.

Schüssler Fiorenza, Elisabeth, ed. 1993. *Searching the Scriptures: A Feminist Introduction.* Vol. 1. New York: Crossroad.

Schwab, Jim. 1994. *Deeper Shades of Green: The Rise of Blue-Collar and Minority Environmentalism in America.* San Francisco: Sierra Club Books.

Schwartzchild, Steven S. 1984. "The Unnatural Jew." *Environmental Ethics* 6:347–62.

Seager, Joni. 1993. *Earth Follies.* New York: Routledge.

Seale, Morris S. 1979. *The Desert Bible: Nomadic Tribal Culture and Old Testament Interpretation.* London: Weidenfeld and Nicolson.

Segundo, Juan Luis. 1976. *The Liberation of Theology.* Maryknoll, NY: Orbis Books.

Shabecoff, Philip. 1993. *A Fierce Green Fire: The American Environmental Movement.* New York: Hill and Wang.

Sheldon, Joseph. 1972. *Rediscovery of Creation: A Bibliographical Study of the Church's Response to the Environmental Crisis.* Metuchen, NJ: Scarecrow Press and the American Library Association.

Shepherd, George W., and David Penna, eds. 1991. *Racism and the Underclass in America.* Westport, CT: Greenwood Press.

Sherill, Rowland A. 1990. *Religion in the Life of the Nation: American Recoveries.* Urbana: University of Illinois Press.

Sherwood, Diane E., and Kristin Franklin. 1987. "Ecology and the Church: Theology and Action." *Christian Century* 104 (May 13).

Shinn, Roger Lincoln. 1982. *Forced Options: Social Decisions for the 21st Century.* San Francisco: Harper & Row.

Shinn, Roger, and Paul Abrecht, eds. 1980. *Fatih and Science in an Unjust World: Report of the World Council of Churches Conference on Faith, Science, and the Future; Massachusetts Institute of Technology, Cambridge, U.S.A., 12-24 July 1979.* Geneva: WCC Publications.

Shiva, Vandana. 1988. *Staying Alive: Women, Ecology and Development.* London: Zed Books.

Shuman, Michael. 1994. "Gattzilla vs Communities." *EarthLight* (SummerFall):5.

Silverstein, Shel. 1964. *The Giving Tree.* New York: Harper & Row.

Sittler, Joseph. 1961. *The Ecology of Faith.* Philadelphia: Muhlenberg Press.

_____. 1962. "Called to Unity." *Ecumenical Review* 14 (January):177-87.

_____. 1964. *The Care of the Earth and Other University Sermons.* Philadelphia: Fortress Press.

_____. 1970. "Ecological Commitment as Theological Responsibility." Unpublished Paper. Geneva: World Council of Churches, Conference on Technology and the Future of Man and Society.

_____. 1972. *Essays on Nature and Grace.* Philadelphia: Fortress Press.

Sleeper, James A., and Alan L. Mintz, eds. 1971. *The New Jews.* New York: Random House.

Smith, J. Andy. 1993. "Corporate Public Accountability and the Environment: Approaches and Guidelines." *Theology and Public Policy* 1 (Spring).

_____. 1993b. "For All Those Who Were Indian in a Former Life." In Adams 1993.

Smith, J. Z. 1969. "Earth and Gods." *Journal of Religion* 49:103-27.

_____. 1970. "The Influence of Symbols Upon Social Change: A Place on Which to Stand." *Worship* 44 (October):457-74.

Smith, Susan. 1992. "Mother Earth: The Absorber, The Redeemer, A Personal Exploration in Moral Theology." *Sisters Today* 64:4(July):259-66.

Snyder, Gary. 1990. "Survival and Sacrament." *The Practice of the Wild.* San Francisco: North Point Press.

Snyder, Howard. 1983. *Liberating the Church: The Ecology of Church and Kingdom.* Downers Grove, IL: InterVarsity Press.

Soelle, Dorothy. 1984. *To Work and to Love: A Theology of Creation.* Philadelphia: Fortress Press.

_____ . 1990. *The Window of Vulnerability: A Political Spirituality.* Minneapolis: Fortress Press.

Song, C. S. 1980. "The Divine Mission of Creation." In Elwood 1980.

Spence, John and Gillian, eds. 1972. *Ecological Considerations of the James Bay Project.* Montreal.

Spencer, Daniel T. 1988. "Models of Learning in Building a Transformative Education," *Global Perspectives: A Quarterly Newsletter of the Center for Global Education at Augsburg College* (Winter).

_____ . 1989. "Experiential Education: A Method for Transformation and Liberation." *Global Perspectives: A Quarterly Newsletter of the Center for Global Education at Augsburg College* (Spring).

_____ . 1994. *Gay and Gaia: A Liberationist Contribution to Christian Ecological Ethics.* Dissertation. Union Theological Seminary.

Spretnak, Charlene. 1986. *The Spiritual Dimensions of Green Politics.* Santa Fe: Bear & Co.

_____ . 1991. *States of Grace: The Recovery of Meaning in the Postmodern Age.* San Francisco: Harper & Row.

_____ . 1991b. "Gaian Spirituality." *Woman of Power* 20(Spring):101-18.

_____ . 1993. "Critical and Constructive Contributions of Ecofeminism." In Tucker and Grim 1993, 181-89.

Spring, D., and E. Spring, ed. 1974. *Ecology and Religion in History.* New York: Harper & Row.

Stager, Lawrence E. 1985. "The Archaeology of the Family in Ancient Israel." *BASOR* 260: 1-35.

_____ . 1988. "Archaeology, Ecology, and Social History: Background Themes to the Song of Deborah." *VTSup* 40: 221-34.

Starhawk. 1990. "Power, Authority, and Mystery: Ecofeminism and Earth-based Spirituality." In Diamond and Orenstein 1990.

Stearns, Peter N., ed. 1994. *Encyclopedia of Social History.* New York: Garland Publishing.

Steinberg, Theodore. 1994. "Environment." *Encyclopedia of Social History.* New York: Garland Publishing.

Stivers, Robert. 1976. *The Sustainable Society: Ethics and Economic Growth.* Philadelphia: Westminster Press.

_____ . 1984. *Hunger, Technology, and Limits to Growth.* Minneapolis: Augsburg Press.

Stivers, Robert, ed. 1989. *Reformed Faith and Economics.* Lanham, MD: University Press of America.

Stoianovich, Traian. 1994. "Annales School." In *Encyclopedia of Social History.* New York: Garland Publishing.

_____ . "Theology for a Small Planet." Special Section on the Environment and Theology.

_____ . 1989. *Harvard Divinity Bulletin* 29 (Fall):7-14.

Stone, Glen C., ed. 1971. *A New Ethic for a New Earth.* New York: Friendship Press.

Suzuki, David, and Peter Knudtson. 1992. *Wisdom of the Elders: Honoring Sacred Native Visions of Nature.* New York: Bantam Books.

Swetlitz, Marc, ed. 1990. *Judaism and Ecology 1970–1986: A Sourcebook of Readings.* Wyncote, PA: Shomrei Adamah.

Swimme, Brian. 1984. *The Universe Is a Green Dragon.* Santa Fe, NM: Bear & Co.

Swimme, Brian, and Thomas Berry. 1992. *The Universe Story.* San Francisco: HarperSanFrancisco.

Talmon, Shemaryahu. 1966. "The Desert Motif: In the Bible and in Qumran Literature." In Altmann 1966, 31-63.

Thistlethwaite, Susan Brooks, and Mary Potter Engel, eds. 1990. *Life Every Voice: Constructing Christian Theologies from the Underside.* San Francisco: Harper & Row.

Tinker, George, 1989. "The Integrity of Creation: Restoring Trinitarian Balance." *The Ecumenical Review* 41:4.

_____. 1990. "Native Americans and the Land." In Thistlethwaite and Engel 1990.

_____. 1992. "Creation as Kin." In Hessel 1992.

_____. 1992b. "Spirituality, Native American Personhood, Sovereignty and Solidarity." *Ecumenical Review* 44:3 (July).

_____. 1992c. "Columbus and Coyote: A Comparison of Culture Heroes in Paradox." *Apuntes* (1992): 78-88.

_____. 1993. *Missionary Conquest.* Minneapolis. Fortress Press.

_____. 1994. "A Native American Reading of the Bible." In Keck, et al. 1994, 174-80.

Tinker, George, and Loring Bush. 1991. "Native American Unemployment: Statistical Games and Cover-ups." In Shepherd and Penna 1991.

Traynham, Warner. 1973. *Christian Faith in Black and White: A Primer in Theology from the Black Perspective.* Wakefield, MA: Parameter.

Troeltsch, Ernst. 1960 <1931>. *The Social Teaching of the Christian Churches.* Vol. 2. New York: Harper & Row.

Tschernichovsky, Saul. 1968. "Before a Statue of Apollo." In *Saul Tschernichovsky.* Ithaca: Cornell University Press. 97–98.

Tucker, Gene M., and Douglas A. Knight, eds. *Humanizing America's Iconic Book.* Biblical Scholarship in North America / Society of Biblical Literature / Centennial Publications / Society of Biblical Literature, no. 6. Chico. CA: Scholars Press.

Tucker, Mary Evelyn. 1985. *The Ecological Spirituality of Teilhard.* Chambersberg, PA:Anima Books.

Tucker, Mary Evelyn, and John Grim, eds. 1993/1994. *Worldviews and Ecology.* Lewisburg: Bucknell University Press; Maryknoll, NY: Orbis Books.

Turner, Frederick. 1983/92. *Beyond Geography: The Western Spirit Against the Wilderness.* New Brunswick: Rutgers University Press.

United Methodist Hymnal, The. 1989. Nashville: The United Methodist Publishing House.

USCC. 1991. "Renewing the Earth: An Invitation to Reflection and Action on Environment in Light of Catholic Social Teaching" (November 14):7.

Vanderkam, James C. 1992. "Weeks, Festival Of." In Anchor Bible Dictionary 6. Ed. David Noel Freedman, et al. New York: Doubleday.

Vatja, Vilmos, ed. 1971. *The Gospel and Human Destiny.* Minneapolis: Augsburg.

Vaux, Kenneth. 1989. *Birth Ethics: Religious and Cultural Values in the Genesis of Life.* New York: Crossroad.

Vaux, Roland de. 1961. *Ancient Israel: Its Life and Institutions.* New York: McGraw Hill.

Vescey, Christopher, and Robert Venables. 1983. *American Indian Environments: Ecological Issues in Native American History.* Syracuse: Syracuse University Press.

Vitousek, Peter M., et al. 1986. "Human Appropriation of the Products of Photosynthesis." *BioScience* 34:6.

Vizenor, Gerald. 1994. *Manifest Manners: Postindian Warriors of Survivance.* Hanover, NH: Wesleyan University Press.

Wallace, Howard N. 1985. *The Eden Narrative*. Dissertation, Harvard University; Atlanta: Scholars Press.

Ward, Barbara. 1973. *A New Creation?: Reflections on the Environmental Issues*. Vatican City: Pontifical Commission Justice and Peace.

Ward, Charlotte. 1990. "A Story for Our Times." *Daughters of Sarah* 16.

Ward, Miriam, ed. 1975. *Biblical Studies in Contemporary Thought*, Somerville, MA: Greeno, Hadden & Co.

Warren, Karen J. 1990. "The Power and Promise of Ecological Feminism." *Environmental Ethics* 12:142-43.

_____. 1994. *Ecological Feminism*. Colorado: Westview Press.

Waskow, Arthur, and Ari Elon, eds. 1995. *The Tu B'Shevat Anthology*. Philadelphia: Jewish Publication Society.

Wattenberg, Benjamin J. 1987. *The Birth Dearth*. New York: Pharos Books.

WCC Canberra Assembly. 1991. *The Report of the Seventh Assembly.*

Weigand, Paul. 1984. "Escape from the Birdbath: A Reinterpretation of St. Francis as a Model for the Ecological Movement." In Joranson and Butigan 1984.

Weil, Zoe. 1993. "Ecofeminist Education: Adolescence, Activism, and Spirituality." In Adams 1993, 311-19.

Weinfeld, Moshe. 1972. *Deuteronomy and the Deuteronomic School*. Oxford: Clarendon Press.

Weiskel, Timothy C. 1990. "The Need for Miracles in the Age of Science." *Harvard Divinity Bulletin* 20 (Summer):6, 11, 17.

_____. 1992a. "In Dust and Ashes: The Environmental Crisis in Religious Perspective." *Harvard Divinity Bulletin* 21(3).

_____. 1992b. "Religion, Belief, and Survival on a Small Planet." *Harvard Divinity Bulletin* 21(4):11,17.

_____. 1992c. "The Secular City and the Sacred Earth." *Harvard Divinity Bulletin* 22(1 <suppl.>):4.

_____. 1993. "God, the Environment and the Good Life: Some Notes from Belshaz'zar's Feast." Lecture. University of New Hampshire.

Wellhausen, J. 1957. *Prolegomena to the History of Ancient Israel*. Trans. Black and Menzies. New York: Meridian Books.

West, Charles C. 1981. "God—Woman/Man—Creation: Some Comments on the Ethics of the Relationship." *Ecumenical Review* 33 (January).

Westermann, Claus. 1963. "God and His Creation." *Union Seminary Quarterly Review* 18 (March):197-209.

_____. 1964. *The Genesis Accounts of Creation*. Trans. and intro. Norman E. Wagner. Philadelphia: Fortress Press.

_____. 1971a. "Creation and History in the Old Testament." In Vatja 1971, 11-38.

_____. 1971b. *Creation*. Trans John J. Scullion, S.J. Philadelphia: Fortress Press.

_____. 1972. *Beginning and End in the Bible*. Trans Keith Crim. Facet books, biblical series. Philadelphia: Fortress Press.

_____. 1978. *Blessing in the Bible and the Life of the Church*. Trans. Keith Crim. Philadelphia: Fortress Press.

White, Jr., Lynn. 1967. "The Historical Roots of Our Ecologic Crisis." *Science* 155 (10 March):1203-7.

Whitehead, Alfred North. 1925. *Science and the Modern World*. New York: MacMillan Free Press.

Whitney, Elspeth. 1993. "Lynn White, Ecotheology, and History." *Environmental Ethics* 15 (Summer):151-69.

Wilkinson, Loren. 1980. *Earthkeeping: Christian Stewardship of Natural Resources*. Grand Rapids: Eerdmans Publishing Company.

_____, ed. 1991. *Earthkeeping in the '90s*. Grand Rapids, MI: Eerdmans Publishing Company.

Williams, Delores. 1993. "Sin, Nature, and Black Women's Bodies." In Adams 1993, 24-29.

Winter, Gibson. 1981. *Liberating Creation: Foundations of Religious Social Ethics*. New York: Crossroad.

Witchel, Alex. 1994. "Where Starlings Greet the Stars." *New York Times* (22 September).

Wogaman, Philip. 1977. *The Great Economics Debate: An Ethical Analysis*. Philadelphia: Westminster Press.

_____. 1986. *Economics and Ethics: A Christian Inquiry*. Philadelphia: Fortress Press.

Wogaman, Philip, ed. 1973. *The Population Crisis and Moral Responsibility*. Washington, DC: Public Affairs Press.

Woods, Richard J. 1984. "Environment as Spiritual Horizon: The Legacy of Celtic Monasticism." In Joranson and Butigan 1984, 62-84.

World Bank, The. 1990. *World Development Report 1990*. New York: Oxford University Press.

World Commission on Environment and Development. 1987. *Our Common Future*. New York: Oxford University Press.

World Resources Institute. 1991. *World Resources 1990-91*. New York: Oxford University Press.

Wren, Brian. 1982. *Education for Justice: Pedagogical Principles*. Maryknoll, NY: Orbis Books.

Wright, G. Ernest. 1950. *The Old Testament Against Its Environment*. Studies in Biblical Theology, no. 2. London: SCM Press.

_____. 1952. *God Who Acts: Biblical Theology as Recital*. Studies in Biblical Theology. London: SCM Press.

Wright, Nancy, and Donald Kill. 1993. *Ecological Healing: A Christian Vision*. Maryknoll, NY: Orbis Books.

Wyshogrod, Michael. 1992. "Judaism and the Sanctification of Nature." *The Melton Journal* (Spring):6-7.

Young, Iris Marion. 1990. *Justice and the Politics of Difference*. Princeton: Princeton University Press.

Young, Robert M. 1985. "Darwinism Is Social." In Kohn 1985.

Zannis, Mark. 1973. *The Genocide Machine in Canada: The Pacification of the North*. Montreal: Black Rose Books.

Zerbe, Gordon. 1992. "Ecology According to the New Testament." *Direction* 21 (Fall):15-26.

Zimmerman, Michael E. 1993. "Rethinking the Heidegger-Deep Ecology Relationship." *Environmental Ethics* 13:205.

Zohary, Michael. 1982. *Plants of the Bible*. Handbook with 200 full-color pcitures. London; New York: Cambridge University Press.